Praise for *Attention Spans*

"A critic of Garrett Stewart's brilliance and scope deserves a 'Reader,' but this fascinating book is far more than a collection of an author's most salient publications. A 'writing journal' of a teaching career that incorporates brief extracts of important books in the inspiring narrative of an immensely wide-ranging critical practice, *Attention Spans* engages the major developments of recent criticism. A *tour de force*."
—Jonathan Culler, Class of 1916 Professor Emeritus, Department of Literatures in English, Cornell University

"Garrett Stewart is a multi-media close reader extraordinaire whose answerable style rewards close reading in turn. This selection of excerpts from each of his twenty books is interspersed with his own running commentary, stitching it all together and making his whole career's research and thinking-through seem as though it were all taking place in present time, while remaining full of scrupulous attention to the ways in which his work has evolved. After a dialogue with the editor, full of yet newer directions, this astonishing volume concludes with a glossary of Stewart's coinages."
—Paul Fry, William Lampson Professor Emeritus, Department of English, Yale University

"As David LaRocca tells us early in this volume, J. Hillis Miller described Garrett Stewart, on the jacket of his second book, as 'more or less *sui generis*.' This turned out to be a prophetic description of the most wide-ranging and least doctrinaire critic of his generation. It also aptly describes *Attention Spans*, a book like no other, and one that does not belong to any recognizable genre. In staging a critical rereading of his own work, Stewart offers us an exhilarating history of aesthetic theory since New Criticism, which is also a virtuosic display of fine readerly attention. Continually unsettled, continually restless, it is written in what Stewart himself calls a 'language not quite gelled into the print that transmits it.' To read it is to feel, again and again, the lifted joy of shared thinking."
—Peter Boxall, Goldsmiths' Professor of English Literature, New College, University of Oxford

Past Praise for Garrett Stewart's Varied Critical Attentions

"A characteristically dazzling, intellectually inventive, almost preternaturally informed *tour d'horizon* and analysis of the interplay between spaces of exhibition and recent (and not so recent) developments in video, film, medial manifestations of all sorts."
—Michael Fried, on *Cinesthesia* (2021)

"Garrett Stewart's unique sensibility—which combines textual perception with a vigilant receptivity for changes in technology—here affords us rich insights [...]. This is wonderful reading and thinking."
—Fredric Jameson, on *Framed Time* (2007)

"[... A] consummate study by (that rare thing) a scholar of genius. It gives us new ears and eyes for what we read and a new conceptual armature for thinking about how."
—Herbert F. Tucker, on *The Deed of Reading* (2015)

"[... A] continuously responsive, marvelously informed mind inspired by as surprising a range of films and as ample a range of serious writing about film as you will find in one place."
—Stanley Cavell, on *Between Film and Screen* (1999)

"With his most unusual gift for subtle stylistic interpretation, Garrett Stewart is more or less *sui generis*, belonging to no particular school of criticism."
—J. Hillis Miller, on *Death Sentences* (1984)

"In this remarkable book, [...] Stewart's innovative and imaginative concept of 'narratography' draws attention to those points at which both narrative and technological uncertainty erupt symptomatically into both image and idea on the screen."
—Laura Mulvey, on *Framed Time* (2007)

"At last, a scrupulous and sustained—'earsighted'—study of that shadowy yet vital intersection of sound and sense [...]."
—Geoffrey H. Hartman, on *Reading Voices* (1990)

"[… A] dazzling, transformative book. Garrett Stewart's supple, lambent, witty prose is itself a laboratory of the effects to which he pays attention."
—Susan J. Wolfson, on *The Deed of Reading* (2015)

"Stunningly articulate. […] Stewart offers new and dazzling interpretations of the 'poetics of prose. […] The book is a *tour de force*, no doubt about it. [… It] will have not only a wide but a lasting reception.'"
—Hayden White, on *Reading Voices* (1990)

"That peerless verbal acrobat/analyst Garrett Stewart has given us a new feast of words and images."
—Ross Posnock, on *The Metanarrative Hall of Mirrors* (2022)

"Stewart's style has a quality that most critical styles utterly lack: it's thoroughly vocalizable. To appreciate its rhythms and sonorities, you practically have to speak it aloud."
—D. A. Miller, on *Streisand: The Mirror of Difference* (2023)

Also by Garrett Stewart

Dickens and the Trials of Imagination
Death Sentences: Styles of Dying in British Fiction
Reading Voices: Literature and the Phonotext
Dear Reader: The Conscripted Audience in Nineteenth-Century British Fiction
Between Film and Screen: Modernism's Photo Synthesis
The Look of Reading: Book, Painting, Text
Framed Time: Toward a Postfilmic Cinema
Novel Violence: A Narratography of Victorian Fiction
Bookwork: Medium to Object to Concept to Art
Closed Circuits: Screening Narrative Surveillance
*The Deed of Reading: Literature * Writing * Language * Philosophy*
Transmedium: Conceptualism 2.0 and the New Object Art
The Value of Style in Prose Fiction
The One, Other, and Only Dickens
Book, Text, Medium: Cross-Sectional Reading for a Digital Age
Cinemachines: An Essay on Media and Method
Cinesthesia: Museum Cinema and the Curated Screen
The Ways of the Word: Episodes in Verbal Attention
The Metanarrative Hall of Mirrors: Reflex Action in Fiction and Film
Streisand: The Mirror of Difference

Authored, Edited, or Coedited Books by David LaRocca

On Emerson
Emerson's Transcendental Etudes by Stanley Cavell
The Philosophy of Charlie Kaufman
Estimating Emerson: An Anthology of Criticism from Carlyle to Cavell
Emerson's English Traits and the Natural History of Metaphor
The Philosophy of War Films
A Power to Translate the World: New Essays on Emerson and International Culture
The Bloomsbury Anthology of Transcendental Thought: From Antiquity to the Anthropocene
The Philosophy of Documentary Film: Image, Sound, Fiction, Truth
The Thought of Stanley Cavell and Cinema: Turning Anew to the Ontology of Film a Half-Century after The World Viewed
Inheriting Stanley Cavell: Memories, Dreams, Reflections
Movies with Stanley Cavell in Mind
Metacinema: The Form and Content of Filmic Reference and Reflexivity
The Geschlecht Complex: Addressing Untranslatable Aspects of Gender, Genre, and Ontology
Television with Stanley Cavell in Mind

Guest Edited by David LaRocca
Conversations: The Journal of Cavellian Studies, no. 7, "Acknowledging Stanley Cavell"

ATTENTION SPANS

Garrett Stewart, a Reader

Edited by
David LaRocca

BLOOMSBURY ACADEMIC
NEW YORK • LONDON • OXFORD • NEW DELHI • SYDNEY

BLOOMSBURY ACADEMIC
Bloomsbury Publishing Inc
1385 Broadway, New York, NY 10018, USA
50 Bedford Square, London, WC1B 3DP, UK
29 Earlsfort Terrace, Dublin 2, Ireland

BLOOMSBURY, BLOOMSBURY ACADEMIC and the Diana logo are trademarks of Bloomsbury Publishing Plc

First published in the United States of America 2024

Copyright © 2024 David LaRocca

Each chapter copyright © 2024 Garrett Stewart

All previously published material has been used by permission of the publishers. For legal purposes the Acknowledgments on pp. 355–358 constitute an extension of this copyright page.

Cover design by David LaRocca and Eleanor Rose
Cover image: "Radial Composition (Yellow)" © 2015 John Opera

All rights reserved. No part of this publication may be reproduced or transmitted in any form or by any means, electronic or mechanical, including photocopying, recording, or any information storage or retrieval system, without prior permission in writing from the publishers.

Bloomsbury Publishing Inc does not have any control over, or responsibility for, any third-party websites referred to or in this book. All internet addresses given in this book were correct at the time of going to press. The author and publisher regret any inconvenience caused if addresses have changed or sites have ceased to exist, but can accept no responsibility for any such changes.

A catalog record for this book is available from the Library of Congress.

Library of Congress Cataloguing-in-Publication Data

ISBN:	HB:	979-8-7651-0223-7
	PB:	979-8-7651-0222-0
	ePDF:	979-8-7651-0225-1
	eBook:	979-8-7651-0224-4

Typeset by Integra Software Services Pvt. Ltd.
Printed and bound in Great Britain

To find out more about our authors and books visit www.bloomsbury.com and sign up for our newsletters.

For ready readers
and
For those eager to get reading already

CONTENTS

An Introduction in Retrospect / David LaRocca   1
Inventory as Itinerary / Garrett Stewart   27
TexTcerpts / Garrett Stewart   49

I. DICKENS AS PROMPT TEXT
    1 / Trials—and Test Sites   53
       Dickens and the Trials of Imagination (1974)
    2 / Death Sentencing and Narrative *Parole*   61
       Death Sentences: Styles of Dying in British Fiction (1984)

II. READING IN, READING OUT
    3 / Literary Graphonics   69
       Reading Voices: Literature and the Phonotext (1990)
    4 / Re: Reading Under Address   77
       Dear Reader: The Conscripted Audience in Nineteenth-Century British Fiction (1996)

III. DISCIPLINE BRIDGING
    5 / From Imprint to Motion Picture   89
       Between Film and Screen: Modernism's Photo Synthesis (1999)
    6 / Pages Painted, Writing Withdrawn   99
       The Look of Reading: Book, Painting, Text (2006)
    7 / From Celluloid to Digitime   108
       Framed Time: Toward a Postfilmic Cinema (2007)

IV. CONVERGENCES: MEDIATION REVISITED
    8 / Mapping the Narrative Substrate   117
       Novel Violence: A Narratography of Victorian Fiction (2009)
    9 / Reading Foreclosed/Text Reinvented   130
       Bookwork: Medium to Object to Concept to Art (2011)
    10 / The Narrative Optics of Surveillancinema   139
       Closed Circuits: Screening Narrative Surveillance (2015)

Contents

V. MEDIUM, PHILOSOPHY, CONCEPT
    11 / Textual Act as Contract   145
        *The Deed of Reading: Literature * Writing * Language * Philosophy* (2015)
    12 / Material Transference and Medial Merger   153
        Transmedium: Conceptualism 2.0 and the New Object Art (2017)

VI. READING STYLE / STYLES OF READING
    13 / Verbal Expenditures, Narrative Dividends   159
        The Value of Style in Fiction (2018)
    14 / The Dickens Page, In and Out Loud   163
        The One, Other, and Only Dickens (2018)
    15 / Bookhood in Evolution   171
        Book, Text, Medium: Cross-Sectional Reading for a Digital Age (2020)

VII. KINETIC TEXTUALITY
    16 / Cinemachination and the Legible Apparatus   191
        Cinemachines: An Essay on Media and Method (2020)
    17 / Museum Screens   211
        Cinesthesia: Museum Cinema and the Curated Screen (2021)
    18 / Toward a Cinematographic Sentence   222
        The Ways of the Word: Episodes in Verbal Attention (2022)

VIII. AUDIOVISUAL MIRRORS: SCREENING TEXT AND VOICE
    19 / Reflex Reading   242
        The Metanarrative Hall of Mirrors: Reflex Action in Fiction and Film (2022)
    20 / The Legible Voice   261
        Streisand: The Mirror of Difference (2023)

IX. AUDIOPTICS   271

X. COVERAGE   283

A Dialogue on Critical Conversation   293
Terms of Use: Coinages Cashed Out—A Selective Glossary   340
Timelines: A Topographical Bibliography   348
Acknowledgments   355
Contributors   359

AN INTRODUCTION IN RETROSPECT
READING STEWART READING STEWART

David LaRocca

We don't need to keep our distance from formalism, merely to take our ease (comfort, on the order of desire, is more subversive than distance, on the order of censure). The formalism I have in mind does not consist in "forgetting," "neglecting," "reducing" content ("man"), but only in *not stopping* at the threshold of content (let's keep the word, provisionally); content is *precisely* what interests formalism, because its endless task is each time to push content back (until the notion of origin ceases to be pertinent), to displace it according to a play of successive forms.
—Roland Barthes, *The Grain of the Voice*[1]

Literary ethics or verbal ethic? There is of course no reason to choose. But many a distinction to be made [...]. And the more ethicist, in one sense, the critical instinct becomes (the more expressly committed, for instance, to a political barometer in taking the measure of character and event in narrative evidence), the more likely is "actual reading," with its ethic of verbal attention, to be sidelined—as implicitly irrelevant if not downright indulgent [...]. Philosophy recommends itself in this sense not because it has something new to say (which it may) about literature or writing separately, but because it can help find in literary writing a tacit philosophy of language in its own right that would otherwise fall beneath the bandwidths of prevailing reconnaissance in the contextual and political—and even the formalist—study of texts.
—Garrett Stewart, *The Deed of Reading*[2]

Technologies evolve quickly enough that DVD audio commentary is becoming a relic of a certain bygone era. What a unique thrill it was, and remains, to have an admired director, cinematographer, screenwriter, editor, or actor comment on a new or familiar cinematic scene—providing a sense of context, craft, the off-screen, with tidbits of both personal and professional significance. Intimate and informed commentary of this sort finds its way into the present volume, where a peerless literary critic and media theorist, Garrett Stewart, is drawn into conversation, debate even, with his own work written across the last five decades. Starting with his 1974 book, *Dickens and the Trials of the Imagination*, Stewart here artfully extracts portions from each of his twenty monographs—choices in themselves daunting—and then draws energy from his retrospective position not just to explain but to re-engage the selections. Given his skills at reading the work of others, we shouldn't be surprised that this unique resaturation in his own writing would yield still further depths and expanses.

And so, while a DVD commentary functions as a direct line to artistic genius, bypassing the film-school intermediary, so too does the explicit pedagogical focus of the book in hand serve to supercharge any encounter with Stewart's library of texts—whether you are just coming to his work for the first time or have been reading it since the 1970s. Stewart has mentioned that the whole reason for writing in the first place, way back when, just starting out, was to create a "ballast for the next course, the next term-length classroom experiment—getting something down so that I could refer to ground covered without having to till it all over again from scratch each time out." We might begin, then, by noting Stewart's twenty titles as twenty such pedagogical experiments—and across as many or more fields and subfields (among them Victorian literature, narratology, stylistics, film theory, media studies, metatextuality, visual studies, conceptual art, and recorded song).

What comes through in this serial grouping of excerpts is an intellectual timeline, first gestational, then gradually matured and cross-referenced, of a distinctive critical vision—as theoretical as it is intuitive. When we follow Stewart "across" media, among and between its various forms and genres, we probe beneath them as well for an ever more comprehensive grasp of mediation. It is at all such comparative transit points that reading becomes, for Stewart, an act of *surfacing* the material basis of any textual materialization, up from the depths: whether the internal airwaves of syllabic language, the plastic substrate of celluloid or pigment, the decommissioned paper of illegible (but ironically "readable") book sculpture, or the meshed pixel interlace of the digital image in Hollywood special effects. When reading happens at this pitch of intensity—as Stewart puts it in *Transmedium* (2017), varying Marshall McLuhan—the message delivers the medium. Such formulations about form—including inversions and doublings—resonate throughout Stewart's career, as in *The Deed of Reading* (2015), with its quintessential double-edged title ("deed" as invested act and interpretive contract at once).

Surfacing certainly deserves those italics in the last paragraph. Regarding the epigraphs above, it may not be clear that a refused "distance from formalism," and hence from the texts it would study in any medium, makes for Stewart, in Barthes' sense, exactly a "comfort" zone (as Stewart might pun across words with an evocative transegmental drift: to each his *own*)—given the generative instability his restless attention detects, all the noise in the system it hastens to recirculate. In Barthes' parenthetical notation of content as "man," presumably the whole broad berth of thematics in the "humanities," there remains its management in language, however at times discomfiting. But it certainly is clear that the ethic of reading in whose service Stewart enlists the philosophy of language depends on "not stopping at the threshold," not unduly respecting, as it were, the settled surface of things. He is busy instead lifting causes—Barthes' regress of "origins"—to the level of their legible manifestations: sources often (in Stewart's coinage) graphonic. That's why his own epigraph for *The Deed of Reading* seems slyly ironic, as if tagged with a Post-It in invisible ink to the effect of "to say the least": "The only real criterion for anybody's *reading* is the conscious act of reading, the act of reading the sounds off from the letters." Ludwig Wittgenstein, here in *Philosophical Investigations* (§159), is being flatly logical, foundational. But what Stewart hears when "reading off" the play of phonetics from given "letters" is a criterion of critical reading hardly so normative.

As connoted *and* evoked by the present book's title, the time and acts of attention spanned by this volume, and clocked by examples, retrace the very longevity of a "profession" in the double sense: a credentialed institutional practice and, within the cultural and historical transformations of a job description as "professor" of English amid the shifting fortunes of the humanities (the *pro* taking the lead against the *con*), one critic's singularly varied devotion to the declared principles of such a calling, including the calling out of its manifold vocables. Right there stands disclosed the structure of Stewart's methodological reading of his own work in this collection's "Inventory as Itinerary": the critic, all oars in, forging ahead upstream against those intellectual currents (currencies of value *and* of the present tense) that, even in literary study, have tended more and more to ignore the writing in the read, with English departments increasingly, in a given course offering, indifferent to the language that identifies them—if not openly hostile to its global hegemony. As Stewart quipped in *Novel Violence* (2009) about postcolonial accounts of Victorian prose fiction carried out without factoring in these novels' own prose, one should remember that the books were "written in English, not British." Then, too, his inventory—offering a manifest filled with rewarding entries—finds Stewart pushing with equal zeal against film studies programs inclined to forget that there are still films to be studied, and just as such, in their form as celluloid projection, and hence new parameters to be traced out in the shift to digital production. In sometimes embattled contrast to the latest "turn," Stewart's professed faith in the vitalizing power of medial interpretation is what leads this fiercely immersive critic into moments of radical invention: an inset feminist "backstory" novel for his study of the repressed maternal figure in Charles Dickens' *Little Dorrit* (*Novel Violence*), or a meticulously curated but imaginary Paris exhibit of conceptual artists' books (*Bookwork*, 2011), not to mention the frequent "mimetic form" of his monograph organization, from a filmic "pretitle sequence" in his first cinema study (*Between Film and Screen*, 1999) through the concert "Set List" structure of his latest book on Barbra Streisand's screen vocals.

J. Hillis Miller told us, in a commendation bestowed upon the young writer on his second book jacket, that Stewart is "more or less *sui generis*, belonging to no particular school of criticism." Part of our projects as readers of Stewart, here and elsewhere, is to decide which it is: more or less. *Attention Spans*—by way of the sheer display of Stewart's acumen across a range of texts and media—should apportion a clear, abiding, and generative answer. Yet, it's worth saying at the outset what "schools" of criticism are, and why Stewart might fall outside one of them, or all of them. Why he is, like few others, a genre unto himself—even while his work, first to last, has taken the pulse of the critical firmament, and ferment, of his changing times. In just this regard, Miller is, of course, tacitly alluding to a long cavalcade of critical trends in literary studies that have been tracking the humanities since at least the late nineteenth century, but picking up steam after the Second World War—a momentum that appears to continue into the present day despite troublesome signs that the humanities are languishing, or otherwise lost to the culture they emerge from and (attempt to) serve.

It is, in any case, against these shifting norms that Stewart's persistence stands out—his enduring commitment to exercise and epitomize a radical proximity to the nature of texts broadly construed. Starting with his first book, *Dickens and the Trials of the Imagination* (1974), and continuing through his most recent, *Streisand: The Mirror of Difference* (2023), Stewart has braved twin experiments, ones exemplified by both these titles: first in matters of content (Dickens and then … Streisand?); secondly in terms of form, or as we'll hear in these pages, style. One guesses that Stewart's roving curiosity is a function of his temperament, his version of the Emersonian sentiment that "what attracts my attention shall have it."[3] Sure, Stewart studies what he likes—not in the willful sense of whatever he wants to, but on account of what moves him, summons him to respond. What beckons him is a sustained perception that "style is language in action," as he notes in his exacting and eloquent analysis, *The Value of Style in Fiction* (2018); we too are hailed by Stewart, such that "style, once brought to the fore" can be recognized as "integral—even internal—to reading."[4]

Even so, his diversely drawn attunement to texts may sound like not much of a claim to fame, or praise. But in an academic environment that rewards specialization—and hyper-specialization at that—it is a marvel to find a scholar who not only *keeps* moving but also can operate capably, not just capaciously, across widely different terrains. For all his novelty—his "more or less *sui generis*" status—Stewart is not an eccentric but a writer at work near the very center of criticism's turbulent waters. If there is an outside or periphery, an inflection of the esoteric, a way in which he remains apart, it is in his own self-imposed—and thus, self-knowing—meta-method, which confirms his willing (and wily) intent to regard writing and reading from many levels simultaneously, and across any medium whose artifacts invite decoding into descriptive words. On screen and off, the audiovisual interplay of sound and scripted event is a recurrent crux for his analysis—including the rhythm of syllables in verse, the agitation of variable meaning in the seemingly fixed or stable prose of fiction, the syncopated action of cinematic frames, the fertile switch of foreground/background fields in painting, the mimetic dips, lifts, and prolongations of song delivery.

Then there is Stewart's style, its own verbal delivery: prodigious and unmistakable. In fact, anyone new to Stewart is in for the treat of encountering a talent one didn't know one needed, or until now, lamentably missed. For some writers—literary critics, philosophers, what have you—style is an afterthought, if it is thought about at all. Indeed, some theorists have imagined that style is not even part of one's thinking: as if whatever one writes, if written "clearly" enough, simply conveys the thought. As though language were either perfectly suitable for such transference or, in another trope, entirely transparent—where writers believe (pretend?) its behavior (across disparate languages and disciplines) is somehow mathematical. Quite to the contrary, Stewart's topics and *the way* he writes about them can make a claim in each syllable and grapheme, each etymology and phrase. Translation across media does more than serve to place varied texts in conversation, or confrontation, with one another; Stewart's interpretive flair also generously supplies unexpected supplements—salient affiliations, striking parallels, and the like (along with provocative disanalogies and discontinuities). As illustrated by "episodes in verbal attention," Stewart preoccupies himself with the literary in its etymological rather than canonical sense, an orientation that has him here, as in *The Ways of the Word* (2021), attending with "literary concentration" to the "lettered" text, in which "syllables and their words depend on an internal and serial structure analogous to the inclusive build of syntax in the temporality of reading."[5]

From the front row of the auditorium, listening intently to every syllable and word and taking notes all the while, *Attention Spans* provides a dramatic digest of Stewart's emblematic art and his inimitable craft. Readers will, for instance, learn not just about Dickens or Streisand, but how writing about them—the writing *itself*—enacts the interpretive potencies of prose, of voice, and of linguistic analysis; how the writing is already caught up in the reading, or as the reading. The novels and songs, in these cases, are "texts" for study, but they are also invitations for discovering how the critical work of a theorist and scholar-critic can be as intriguing, layered, and illuminating as the subjects under investigation. With such an interplay between Stewart's topics and Stewart's style, one is captivated by not only what he writes about but also how he does so. His style, in other words, should not alienate or confuse readers but introduce them to a deeper, more rewarding relationship with the text(s) under scrutiny.

As soon as one begins reading Stewart (and *Attention Spans* shares his company twice over—as editor of extracts and as commentator upon them), one returns to elemental questions: there is the book and there is the reader, but what is their relationship? Does the reader make the book (as Emerson thought) or does the book make the reader (as Plato thought)? It's worth letting the questions linger when reading Stewart, since there is reason to believe he cultivates a two-way creation. A book contains what it contains; its words do not change over time, and yet we do, and each time we return to a book, we are some further version of ourselves. In the interim, we have read and learned other things that inform what we think—and thus what we (can) think about our once-read source. *Attention Spans* uniquely exemplifies this tiered, multidirectional reciprocity, since in Stewart's "Inventory as Itinerary" (next up), he has retraversed a life's worth of pathways, chosen his own work to "return to" by way of new, present-day responses. And thus, as we read Stewart reading Stewart, the pleasures of metaphilosophy and beneficial effects of reflexivity are joined with the very real sense of being present for "a reading"—a critical séance in which Stewart himself is the medium—one among many such readings to be made, including by you, dear reader.

GARRETT STEWART WAS BORN IN DETROIT, Michigan, in the cold of January 1945, son of an elementary school-teacher mother and a car-salesman father, Rosemary and Gordon, and then raised more warmly, given his father's precarious health, in Southern Florida (Fort Lauderdale) and Southern California (Laguna Beach), where the then "Gary" divided his time between moviegoing and book reading, each of which formative interests figure, autobiographically, in the excerpts to come. He was in college by 1963, arriving in the midst of New Criticism's dominance, studying first at the University of Southern California, then for a doctorate at Yale University in the pre-dawn hours of its methodological heyday as "the Yale School" under the impact of scholars such as Harold Bloom, Geoffrey Hartman, Paul de Man, J. Hillis Miller, and later, Jacques Derrida. As befits his sensibility, Stewart appreciated the many isms on offer, but was more inclined to graft together elements carefully, selectively pruned from each—growing, in time, into his own distinctive hybrid. With a Ph.D. from Yale in 1971, he went on to teach, first, at Boston University (1971–6), then at the University of California, Santa Barbara (1976–93), and from there to his current home as the James O. Freedman Professor of Letters at the University of Iowa. Over the course of the decades, he also taught at Stanford University (1986), Princeton University (1987–8), University of Fribourg, Switzerland (1995–6), University of London (2012), University of Konstanz (2018), and again at Princeton (2019). He was awarded a Guggenheim Fellowship (1978–9), an NEH Senior Fellowship (1990–1), a Leverhulme Fellowship (2015), and was inducted into the American Academy of Arts and Sciences in 2010.

Such mobile teaching appointments can help chart the different senses of "itinerary" (intellectual and methodological) that his "inventory" unfurls in this book. Given the auspicious era for the evolution and proliferation of "criticism" in which Stewart came of age, and to which he then made substantive contributions of his own, it seems plausible that he could have become an adept at any number of methodologies—structuralist, existentialist, philological, phenomenological, linguistic, deconstructive, Marxian, Freudian, feminist, and so on—and yet, from an early and orienting engagement with Virginia Tufte at USC (with whom the precocious scholar published *Grammar as Style* in 1971), Stewart appeared launched on his own trajectory. As an undergraduate research assistant, he had been charged with finding, as he explains below, "telling examples of grammatical finesse" for a composition textbook she was developing. And here we are, in *Attention Spans*, more than fifty years later, turning our attention to Stewart's own telling examples of grammatical finesse—and pyrotechnics.

If forced to create a backlog of influences, one that would prove helpful to readers coming to his work for the first time, or veteran readers seeking new vantages by which to appreciate his more than five decades of writerly composition, one could do worse than to say that from structuralism, Stewart drew an understanding of an inbuilt patterning beneath the pace of wording; from deconstruction a sense of endemic differentials in writing more radical than the touted "ambiguity" of New Criticism; from film theory and its formal analysis, a feel for both the modularity and disruptive nodes of the narrative image; from the new semiotic paradigms of art history, a recognition of depicted space as signage as much as representation; from opera theory a way of accounting for the antithetical vernacular provisioning of pop recording's most intimate (even while mannered) voice; from the formal rigors of Marxian literary theory, Georg Lukács to Fredric Jameson, a way to enter the historicist and postcolonial phase of cultural studies with a "thick description" rooted in textual—that is, verbal rather than just contextual—tensions and contradictions.

On that last front, it's interesting to note that in one of Stewart's latest essays, for a special journal number on recent developments in the theoretical study of "form"—often at scales far beyond the literary—he recurs to this sticking point: "One does well to remember that Fredric Jameson's subtitle to *The Political Unconscious* influentially identified 'narrative' not as a 'social act' but a 'socially symbolic act'—its forms of symbolization laid bare as unique to literary genre and its discourse."[6] And yet, for all the ways in which Stewart's metaphoric ear was always kept to the ground in monitoring and commenting on these seismic disciplinary shifts, his actual ear, and its ocular correlate in an approach (up-close) to other than verbal media, tended to set him apart. Still does. The doubleness of "ear" (academically alert, textually perked) is more than playful, since the twinned companions mobilize Stewart's talent for hearing things others miss *and then* writing about them in ways that make art as well as sapience of such descriptions. In a temperament familiar to those familiar with Stanley Cavell, Stewart is not only attuned to varieties of voice as they inhabit the world (including those that have remained unheard or made unintelligible), but also to how an uncanny transference of such "sound" is possible on the page. And so, beyond Stewart's appreciation for the graphological and syntactical, his facility with the sonic efflorescence of text (pun, double entendre, phonetic word play, and the like), or likewise his sense of the cinematographic grain of film, the medium's potent display of montage, the graphic ironies of even realist painting, all of this has entailed (almost necessarily at times) a resistance to certain popular trends within or deriving from the abovementioned literary-critical, philosophical, and media studies agendas—as he hardly shies away from detailing in the coming pages.

But before any polemic comes Stewart's prose, where facets of textuality interpenetrate. There is the site of text—where to find it; the sight of text—reading it line by line; and the "cite" of it—noting its provenance. And then there is the *sound* of text. Most often the "voice" of a text is understood metaphorically (see again Cavell), and Stewart, adding to this evocative tradition, has noted the pleasing human peculiarity of subvocal literary enunciation, by which he means we "hear" a text we read (if only in our heads). There is, however, another, more literal sense of sound, and it is one that redounds to Stewart's craft as a prose-maker, which is to say that his writing often satisfies most, or at least *more*—and gives over further special potencies of form and stylistic inventiveness—when it is read aloud. In such cases, the enunciation is vocal, indeed, also conjuring along the way the incantatory, transfigurative powers of annunciation.

Readers need not take my word for it. Try it out—test it; essay the difference. Read a passage of Stewart's prose, say, this excerpt below, "silently" (if possible): that is, "to yourself." Under discussion here is the phonic contour of narrative writing by the "one and only" Dickens, in whose prose Stewart hears the linguistic third term suggested by his title, *The One, Other, and Only Dickens* (2018)—an effect, resurgent in each reading, sprung from the vital dynamics of his already inscribed but still self-performing "sentences":

> When taken up for reading, we may still sense their *being* written, rather than simply having been. The inventive pen is still evident in prose action. For if only in the right mode of attention, not mood of response, one reads in a way that deciphers something at the springs not so much of the writer's narrative oeuvre as of his immanent linguistic verve. The Other Dickens is simply a way of christening this disposition. One responds, when prompted, to exactly the upsurge and onrush, the catch and drag, the bends and rents of a language not quite gelled (yet, ever) into the print that transmits it.[7]

Hear how even the routine ellipsis of "having been" is shadowed by the over-and-done-with that the continued writtenness ascribed to these sentences resists—at a level mimed in its own turn by the assonance connecting "been" through "inventive pen" to "evident," to say nothing of a wordplay (a play of wording at least as effective on the ear as on the eye) between "oeuvre" and the almost anagrammatic "verve." Once our ears are geared (as Stewart might say) to this personified Otherness within narrative, it can thereby best be "christened" (nice shuffle of vowels and consonants with "disposition") rather than just designated. By an almost syllabic cause-and-effect nexus as well, which Stewart so often finds in the textual momentum he studies, "prompted" chimes lightly with "response" in the chain reaction of "up(surge)" and "on(rush)." This goes forward in sync with the light chiastic flip of "*urge*" into "*rush*," which "catches," one might say, its phonetic breath before the assonant twist of "bends" into "dents." And then there's the further short *e* stutter in that strategic time-lapse parenthesis (yet/ever), the effect of which seems syntactically as well as semantically to postpone any obvious closure.

Sometimes the very thread of the read in Stewart's own writing, as in the literature he audits, is all happy snags, forget-me-(k)nots. So that, yes, one is hardly above trying out some of these effects for oneself (ahem), as here again in saying that, when reading Stewart, what is *best rung out* (or in Wittgenstein's sense "read off") by way of internal echo is *first strung out* in deliberated syllabic increments. Notice, then, in Stewart's corpus, how close reading is *complemented* by vocalizing the matter on the page—how audible speech creates another kind of text (in the throat, through the mouth, on the tongue, against the teeth, along the lips, across the jaw, and into one's ears). By means of any such on-the-ground experiment with a book, you have experienced a semiotic surplus inherent in Stewart's writing; palpably, you have liberated it from its home in written language, given it voice, given it (another) life. The s(pan) of such attention—in lengthy duration, while panning from subvocal to vocal literary expression—supplies layers, sequences, and valences of meaning. Poets, writers of fiction, and filmmakers have known the truths of such "extras" for generations, but somehow the critics who read poems and novels and movies largely neglect the contribution of the sonic element in their own prose. They write for wooden ears and don't seem to mind if no one is listening. Not so Stewart.

Thus to "episodes of verbal attention," we add the quotient of vocal attention. For a taste of Stewart's own talents as an analyst of the sound of prose, join his conversation underway on Virginia Woolf's *Mrs. Dalloway*: "Clarissa was positive, a particular hush, or solemnity; an indescribable pause; a suspense (but that might be her heart, affected, they said, by influenza) before Big Ben strikes. There! Out it boomed. First a warning, musical; then the hour, irrevocable. The leaden circles dissolved in the air. Such fools, she thought, crossing Victoria Street." And here, by way of inscription, Stewart hears Woolf's prose in an expanded range of pitches:

> The passage is saturated almost beyond containment with the sonority it evokes. The actual linguistic term "vocable" broached in the phonic hint of "earrevocable" is followed by two cross-word (rather than cross-syllable) reverbs, first in the "susp*ense* before B*ig* B*en*

strikes," then in the muted echoic "din" of "lea*den* circles dissolve*d in* the air," where the last described attenuation also seems to offer its own vocalic thinning-out, in "the air," of the exclamatory "There!"[8]

Hear what I mean? Such lyrical playfulness—a ludic spirit of experiment, a restless inventiveness at work at the level of the syllable. When Stewart writes there of a "passage … saturated almost beyond containment with the sonority it evokes," he could almost be describing one of his own sentences elsewhere. Listen to his enacted sense of stylistic immanence for philosopher Giorgio Agamben's claims about literary "potentiality" and "the end of the poem" (from "After Wording," epilogue to *The Deed of Reading*—but still very much in the throes of such wording):

> So in the long run Agamben's central tenet, when further attuned to the auralteries of writing in particular, seems best understood this way: as showing how the receiving end of poetry is the re-sieving of its own potential through the filters of enunciation, where you never know in advance what may strike you, what sparks may be struck off, what linkages ignited by its signaling marks.[9]

Any writer might have liked the sound of "central" with "tenet" better than, say, with "proposition," and, if already having invented a portmanteau pun on alternate aurality, might have used it again in the self-performative plural. But few would have illustrated it with the slant rhyme between "receiving" and "re-sieving," and maybe fewer still would have exerted together, on the very subject of surprise, the gentle phonetic hammer taps that chip off the figurative "struck off" from the idiomatic "strike you" or, across the shift to passive grammar, the *ink/ign/ign* sequence, itself overlain by the echoic sibilant latch of "linkages <u>ign</u>ited"/"<u>sign</u>aling."

Though always unmistakable, the nature of Stewart's style has not stayed put. Increasingly in his prose—and not just as the themes become more metalingual, but also when similar scales of effect are probed in other media—his tendency toward a *writing out loud* becomes marked as just that: more and more *pronounced*. Neither strictly colloquial nor studiously eloquent, the stylistic ambition is what we might call locutional, an epiphenomenon of the "evocalization" he finds in literary description (see *Reading Voices*, Phase II / 3; see also "Terms of Use"). The very particles of wording, their bonds and borders, are often placed in the service of whatever evidence—whether visual, verbal, or directly acoustic—is being turned up, and over, in analysis. In such writing's micro-phonic texture, when reconstituting what it contemplates, prose's cellular fabric can sometimes appear more pixelated than syllabic, elsewhere montaged as much by cross-fade as by straight cut. And yet whenever we sense something of a mimetic characteristic in the prose, it is likely to take us straight back to the kinetic energy of word formation itself—and with it the dynamic dimensionality of phrase creation and concept generation. Given such gathered, elastic, experimental animation as a precondition of his own writing, it is just this nerve center of syllabic concatenation that Stewart's sentences often seem to be miming in the very process of mining its rich veins of lexical association.

In their further intermedial associations, such subliminal signals make for one signature effect of Stewart's own "secondary vocality" (a concept he extrapolates from the groundbreaking work of Walter Ong on "secondary orality"). And it is a vocality the critic puts to new work in describing—describing, yes, in words—the time-based "image strain" of celluloid film's inherent optic tensility in the frame-by-frame chain. From "Modernism's Flicker Effect," the closing chapter of *Between Film and Screen*:

> The linguistic equivalent of such rapid-fire filmic seriality is evinced repeatedly in that heightened, tightened linkage of subvocal filaments known as modernist *écriture*, where traditional literary diction, at loose ends with itself, forges new lateral ties in the disappearing flash of its own exposure time.[10]

In recognizing how "that heightened" can be heard to have "tightened" *itself* in the coils of its own repetition, we may also note again the elision of subvocal dental sounds on the next page, in evoking "that rapid treadmill of the read." Are we even keyed (up) to hear that "the read" has spun its own equivalent to the "thread" of images on the strip? Or to hear "filmic" elements spooled past again in syllabic "fil(a)m(ents)"? In any case, Stewart's cumulative and looped effects can be even more quietly mimetic, as in the last paragraph from this first of his film books, where three noun phrases in an emphatic sentence fragment turn verbal under differently accented repetition. It reads almost as if the frame grabs of formulaic categories—after the grammatic false lead of stasis, of mere listed ingredients—had suddenly been switched into cinematic gear with the activated force of their own conditions:

> Motion pictures, cinema screens, film frames, and I there, making up my mind both with and about their passing apparitions. Motion pictures a world. Cinema screens it. Film frames and advances it. This is why, finally, besides shutter, lens, and a certain distance, both nothing and everything must come between film and screen.[11]

In hearing these phrases accelerate to clauses under different—almost metrical—stress patterns, we are readied to appreciate further how that last phrase also incorporates, into a predicate of its own, the mere adverbial locus of the book's title. Stewart's writing, like his attention to cinema's address at the limit of its world (and the beginning of ours), frames experience reflexively: first, for our closer inspection of what draws his notice, then, for how the spur to his insight doubles back as stimulant to our own, spanning linked yields of attention.

After my suggesting above—as more than a thought experiment, rather an actual vocal exercise—the reading aloud of a Stewart sentence or paragraph, I see since that I am not alone in this pointed response to his writing. Where the jacket blurb from one famous Miller, J. Hillis, was early in spotting the uniqueness of Stewart's stylistic criticism, another renowned Miller, D. A., blurbs Stewart's latest book in terms that suggest an invigorating interplay between topic and treatment in what amounts to the "reading voice" of the critic's analysis:

> Stewart's style has a quality that most critical styles utterly lack: it's thoroughly vocalizable. To appreciate its rhythms and sonorities, you practically have to speak it aloud. That is why his voice has just the right pitch for writers, such as Dickens and Poe, whose prose has a likewise audible relation to language. One uncanny surprise in *Streisand: The Mirror of Difference* is that Stewart's voice proves so rich an instrument for rendering the voice of a singer. He listens to the great voice of Barbra Streisand like no one else.

Stewart, alas, is neither a poet nor a novelist, still less a maker of movies or a singer, but he charges his pages with the rhythms and dynamism of such varied work—the palpable shifts in mood and meaning from line to line, frame to frame, measure to measure. If only we have ears for it. With expanded and enhanced sense delivered—on par with the high expectations usually assigned to, or reserved for, live performances of drama and major cinematic projections—we may call to mind one of Stewart's own examples, *Gatz*, in which the entire text of *The Great Gatsby*, "word by (and for) word," is vocalized over the course of six hours.[12] A "completist" mindset is joined with one devoted to the pleasures of the vocalized text in "reading-en-scène"—as found in various group efforts to read *Moby-Dick* or *Ulysses* or Proust aloud. One can imagine a similar service for the sweep of Stewart's page stylistics—a speech-in for which we all gather to announce, and benefit from, the aforementioned annunciations.

IN AN ERA WHEN EYES AND MINDS ARE DRIVEN TO DISTRACTION, what can be said for the cultivation of the mental posture of attention? Enter Garrett Stewart, whose seemingly extreme swerves of critical focus have always been just that, focused—not at all, as might seem at first look, too easily diverted by one medium after another. Since the late 1960s, his vigilance has been indefatigable. But how to convey it in (re)print? That was the challenge. So let me explain the composition of *Attention Spans*—where "composition" is fittingly fractal. The book is divided into ten "phases"—each phase signaled by a Roman numeral (I through X); subsidiary chapters that illustrate and embody the phases by a chronological listing of Stewart's books are marked by Arabic numbers

(1 through 20). After these introductory remarks, Stewart makes not one, but two preliminary and proprietary comments: first, "Inventory as Itinerary" (in which he shares at one point a "Methodological Timeline," a visual display of evolving critical methods in the ever-evolving profession—a representation of the frenzy of textolatry across time—along with some illuminating auto/biographical remarks), then gives full-bodied exemplification to a neologism cultivated expressly for this collection, TexTcerpts. At a glance, the contents of the latter adduce the titles of Stewart's twenty books (published between 1974 and 2023). Above each monograph's title a new title is placed, a title given to frame, or reframe, selections Stewart has made from these books.

As part of the paratexts in this volume, readers will encounter handy **headnotes** placed before the excerpts from successive monographs, functioning largely as critical précis of each of Stewart's books. Turning to the back of the book, there is a one-of-a-kind **glossary**, which aims to gather and define a number of words, concepts, and portmanteaus Stewart has invented, repurposed, or otherwise transformed in (not counting this volume) his score of studies. Before this, a new and never-before-published interview takes shape as a **dialogue**, between Stewart and me, about the previous "critical conversations" into which his work has entered over the years—*and* about the fate and future of criticism as an artful practice for understanding ourselves, our world, and the texts that give sense to experience. Thus, after moving chronologically through Stewart's excerpts (again, TexTcerpts), we arrive at the most recent moment of engagement with our critic—a very present-tense dialogue illuminating where we stand—even as we look backwards, scan immanent circumstances, and make forecasts. In time, readers should find themselves (to give a further flip to the coinage) TexTperts in relation to Stewart's prose and points of reference. Still more, a **bibliography** of essential Stewart publications makes its debut, helping in its "topographic" demarcations to give both a chronological and a thematic cast to this overview of his multidecade endeavors. Lastly, newly added **endnotes** accompany the full sweep of the volume, aiming to provide essential—and at times novel—information for readers of *Attention Spans*.

Unlike "specialist" books that address a single work of literary fiction, have one literary movement or period in mind, or focus on one figure or theoretical question, this book contains, well, multitudes: it is a book of books, a catalogue of "commonplacing," a self-commented variorum with midrashic sensibilities, a dictionary and a reading list, an author's conversation with himself (and his sequence of former selves, as authors of those prior monographs), and a conversation with an editor about the stakes of the book itself—what it sets about in setting out to capture the energy of more than a half-century's worth of work. Stewart offers a veritable library of interests—in addition to commentary on them: Dickens as narrative maestro and wordsmith equally, or inseparably, his magnetic prose so indissociable from his storylines; Victorian fiction in its treatment of death, its hailing of the reader, and the violence of its social irony; cinema in archeological relation to photography; digital cinema its successor, and the transfiguration of the "documentary" qualities of lens-based movies in the wake of anti-indexical visual effects; the declension in painting from figures with open-page books to conceptual text art filling the nonrepresentation frame; then the inversion of this latter instance in the sculpting of codex objects unavailable for reading (in a vernacular sense) but densely rich in semiotic solicitations for "reading"; museum installations, including film as time-based art that carries different implications and impact when projected beyond the cinema; the nature of style in the execution of fiction; the meanings of reflexivity in cross-media comparison; and, of course, Barbra, as long-take screen auteur as well as "actress-who-sings." And for extra measure, Stewart even comments on the hard-won emblematics of his book covers (see Phase X, "Coverage"), which, of course, you can read without purchase, internal text sight unseen—covers that speak volumes, or just as ably for the single one in question.

Yet for those readers seeking a tutorial in *ekphrasis*—the artful description of art—the just-mentioned dispatch, "Coverage," is a new locus for Stewart's penetrating, synoptic attention. The cover images of Stewart's many books are, to our benefit, easily retrieved via an online image search, but the covers there don't arrive with the pedagogical affordances of this newly conceived chapter. Herewith, "Coverage" amounts to a sustained and self-contained linguistically elaborated laboratory of *ekphrasis*. Description in action—with the art at the margin, or on the screen, or elsewhere beyond the printed page of words. Notice how reading Stewart (as he deciphers anew his many cover designs) activates an awareness of attributes not immediately claimed by the art itself but rather found in his bespoke *description* of the art. By such worded measures, we are helped to fathom the features—and significance—of what otherwise would, quite minimally, simply "be there" in the form of photographic reproduction, typographical flourish, film frame, sound allusion, and so on (and despite such overtness may go unseen, unheeded). Like Cavell's "readings" of films, Stewart doesn't offer primary texts reproduced, of course, or merely secondary texts of commentary, but, better, critical *performances* of the works of art as verbal scores, interpretation made manifest.

Through it all, we read *Attention Spans* as if positioned on a fulcrum or at a crossroads, since the orientation of a present tense looking back is coupled here with a present tense looking forward. In this liminal spot, we readers of Stewart—of whatever age or "level" of training—seek to know what to do with his work now and into our receding futures. Hence the decidedly pedagogical ambitions of this volume, which only serve to activate and apply those same pursuits found in Stewart's twenty previous ones. Far from a vanity project where we are captivated by the distant talents of a rare and gifted lector, in *Attention Spans* we are pulled in close for an intimate look at the mechanics of Stewart's prose, the ideas that span his attention from early to late, and the teaching from which each has arisen—and to which these experiments have been continually returned. But how, more specifically, to read this subtitled "reader"? If you are a "general reader" (a term Stewart would no doubt want to interrogate for the hinted lack of specificity), *Attention Spans* will provide a topographic guide to the terrains you may wish to explore in more detail—at more leisure or, as the case may be, with more vigor. If you are a youth—excelling in high school or as an undergraduate—*Attention Spans* will deliver a ticket to access and explore Stewart's multifaceted contributions at an accelerated rate. As a college student, you can hunker down, as Stewart did once with his teacher, and revel as an initiate into the literary rather than just the technical mysteries of grammar. And if you are "advanced"—a postgraduate in the humanities or media studies, a professor of some rank, or an unaffiliated scholar with ambitions to read the best of contemporary literary/philosophical/media study, then *Attention Spans* will meet you too, where you are.

Contact with the lambencies of literary discernment happen, in part, by carrying you, any and all of you, back to basics. I was not surprised to learn, for instance, that Stewart begins his undergraduate writing course on "Prose Style," which he trades off with his colleague Brooks Landon, with partisan briefs from two novelists quoted in Landon's *Building Great Sentences* (2013): from Thomas Berger, who sees the sentence as writing's only material reality, even the paragraph being a drastic abstraction; and from Don DeLillo, who stakes his claim to being a writer in his desire to "construct sentences." In vocalic fact, as Stewart lets his students discover, Berger's "a sentence—there you have something essential" seems to bond noun and modifier in a nonetymological yet inextricable assonant kinship. *Mutatis mutandis*—and very mutable, indeed, are these effects in the media he explores—Stewart too "thinks small" at first. On the down-scaled and essentialized model of sentence construction rather than the shaping of paragraphs, and even one-level further in the matter (and materiality) of syllables *before* syntax, his attention gravitates comparably to screenshots before episodes, canvas strokes before painted scenes, material substrates before installation constructs, vocal inflection before lyric sense in song rendition.

In like manner, *Attention Spans* amounts, in no small measure, to a private tutorial with Garrett Stewart—from end to end a sequence of call and response, excerpt and commentary, revisitation and reflexive rein(ter)vention. For those readers unable to attend his classes over the last six decades (that is, most of us), and for the future impossibility of such in-person sessions (mortality being a dictation of finitude that we all must acquiesce to), this volume provides the ongoing navigation, modeling, and mentoring any Stewart fan (or Stewart-curious reader) should want. Taken up in portion, dollop by dollop, or phase by phase, *Attention Spans* releases a high-octane boost to any return to the full measure of his prose monographs as well as the texts he reads—and even those that escaped his notice or are yet to come. With Stewart's transtemporal voice in one's head, the layers of probing linguistic inquiry should provide the necessary and gratefully gifted orientation one seeks or, even better, *finds*, as if by fortuitous accident, a bounty awaiting discovery and yet further investigation.

At the same time that we dwell on the scale and scope of the sentence—a passion for writers and readers alike—we are duly drawn back to exemplars of the form (Plato and Epictetus, Montaigne and Emerson, Proust and Henry James, Nietzsche and Wittgenstein) to get us worked up about just what Stewart sets out to do with his *essaying* "after" his own work and words. Herewith *Attention Spans* is an innovative history of his "attempts, trials" and the like— *essais*, one line at a time, one sentence after another. How delightful for readers— familiar or unfamiliar with Stewart's library of books—to see *Attention Spans* as the author's knowing effort at *practical* criticism (an endeavor that editor and reader can now acclaim accomplished, while Stewart himself must stand by and wonder about our responses to his responses). How fitting that Stewart should be coach—and amanuensis—for guiding our "calisthenic curiosity."

When they are deservedly granted and demonstrably established, how easy it must be to rest on one's laurels. Perhaps the gathered community of readers will appreciate, then, Stewart's counter-instinct. He leaps from the threat (and admitted pleasure) of such prophylactic placidity by exercising instead a vulnerable, unflinching, agile, and reflective approach to reading—that is, *re-reading*—his work, since he is neither wasting his time catching the odd erratum nor holding forth on his accomplishments as a contributor to "the field" (whatever and wherever that may be). Rather, he is submitting himself to his texts anew, including his points of reference, what some are encouraged to think of as "source texts." In his approach, there is an exhilarating accumulation—plaits of time and text—underway throughout the volume: where we find Stewart reading Stewart reading what Stewart was once (and now again) reading. The double play of the book's subtitle emerges for our consideration and pleasure: not just a "reader" or compendium of Stewart's previously published prose, but Stewart as a living and lively reader of the same—like us, *A Reader*, and yet, leaning upon the adroitness of his work, a reader existing at a remove, one whose tuitions we will surely benefit from. For instance, present-day Stewart returns to what early 1970s Stewart had written about Charles Dickens only to find that in his current incarnation, Stewart delights in detecting edifying precipitates from the novels (seemingly once familiar, now undoubtedly remade, reinvigorated, across decades of subsequent reading) *and* from refractions and inflections of his own prior annotations on the same.

What one attends to is one's life, since attention spans and time spans are overlapping magisteria: to speak of what one does, remembers, and thinks is to speak of what one has attended to. An attention (span) is a life (span). Meanwhile, or all the while, as T. S. Eliot writes in *The Four Quartets* (1943), we are "distracted from distraction by distraction." In the present day, the so- called "attention economy"—full as it is of immersive distraction—can call us back to Henry David Thoreau's attempted pursuit of "accounting" for his days and nights; in such a mood, we mean to attend to the hours (the spans of time) we have and to make them count. Could it be, though, that we would rather be distracted, to leave things unaccounted for, to be unaccountable to them— attention *and* responsibility both forsaken? Isn't diversion more pleasurable, more satisfying than breaking out of the trance that defines most of our waking life? In this frame of mind, such as it is, attention—sustained concentration—is discomfiting, painful even; we prefer to skim, to stay on the surface, to look away, to seek the elsewhere. Abundance drives us to distraction, to what Stewart at one point calls "attention surfeit disorder."[13] While admitting that we can't finally solve, or dispense with, our tendency to yearn for and enjoy diversion, we can learn to crave and excel in attention by means of models and their compensatory offerings. Countermeasures in attention are possible, available, such as the tuitions of teachers and mentors; in conversation with them, we may cultivate our attention by attending to theirs—hence the modeling and mentoring. Stewart's writing—an embodiment of negotiated reading—invokes a scene of such edification: when the young American scholar Ralph Waldo Emerson went to visit one of his living idols, William Wordsworth, the elder counseled the lonely, wayfaring man: "you know the matter always comes out of the manner."[14] Thus, we not only glean the "man" from the manner but the matter as well. Line by line, book by book, time after time, Stewart's close-grained stylistics exemplify how the manner of attention gives rise to the matter at hand.

In an "introduction," such as the present remarks aspire to be, I have been aiming to underwrite the reader's easier entry into Stewart studies—to support such efforts to "access and explore Stewart's multifaceted contributions at an accelerated rate," and to assess by experiencing them. Part of that prefatory sentiment naturally includes an editor's proclivity to cite text as evidence of achievement, and, of course, I have done some of that here. But it is worth pointing out why there is not even more such citation and exegesis; it's because Stewart himself has arrived on the scene and has identified the exemplary passages he wishes to place at the mercy of our attention, and, in a very special way, his own. Though it would be a pleasure and honor to belabor the proceedings with highlights from my own—and others'—engagement with Stewart, it turns out he has cleverly usurped the assignment for himself. This generous act—together with the unlooked-for pressure it imposes on him—also provides a lesson for us: a reminder to consider when one's criticism is a rehearsal of work by others and when it is a performance in its own right. Terminological habits that speak of "primary," "secondary," and "tertiary" sources may corrode one's confidence in a given line of thinking—deeming it a mere "subset" of the vaunted instances. But the hierarchy is made an apparition when readers, by immersion, are enabled to make the object of attention their own. Stewart shows us how to do that.

The "expert" who *goes on trying* to refine expertise becomes embodied in *Attention Spans*. The young, I think (and the not-so-young too, if they are mindful of the distorting effects of vanity and pretension), can take heart from Stewart's indomitable willingness to return to (his own) books while others of his ilk are prone to saying "I'm done. I *have* a reading" of such and such. But not Stewart: even as he edges into his ninth decade on earth, he's still game for a fresh wager on what a text might mean. I find this kind of intellectual bravery a thrill—not just because he models the best of a life spent reading, but also because of the rewards *his species of reading* provides. Rewards evident in or as his own books; and also in so far as those instances help us read elsewhere and otherwise. In this respect, the specialness of *Attention Spans* arrives in waves throughout the turning of these pages, as we operate perpetually on a double register: watching Stewart revisit the old haunts of his chosen masters (the great Victorian novelists) and favored media (photography, cinema, book art, etc.) along with enlivening takes on his own earlier commentary on all the above. In such feats of prismatic cognition, Stewart pursues an archaeo-analytic method, culminating in a reexamined stacking of texts receding in time. Other points of reference—name-brand theorists, intellectual movements, highlights from the secondary literature, and so on—are drawn in for further orientation, pushing our sense of familiarity with, or place within, these texts (his, theirs) to new degrees of affinity.

One effect of Stewart's text-techné in *Attention Spans* is a felt sense of proximity to the moment of secondary uptake or renewed takeaway: we are present for a veritable live-streaming of his analysis. From this vantage, as noted, attention spans are complemented by time spans—Stewart's reading, rereadings, and revisitations amounting to a cinematic enframing of temporally situated passages of prose. The effect is far more immediate than a set of scholarly flashbacks. In the way that we might hold up a single celluloid film frame to the light (for further discrimination of contour and concept), so Stewart finds his arena of address—this passage, these lines, those terms and conditions, the rays bleeding through the patches of emulsion (affording recognition of still-identifiable figures as well as ambiguous portions that call out for commentary, for freshly rendered adjustment). And, like Stewart, we can play the frames slowly ... or quickly—at a go—letting persistence of vision take over, therein finding ourselves immersed in the flow of these fast-moving, utterly and irrevocably sequenced and connected selections.

Still more on this occasion, Stewart's "return" to his own texts provides a lesson to adept and newcomer alike: it ain't over till it's over. That is, the sense of unfinishedness one may feel when sending final proofs to press—that there are still so many things to say; that what has been said could be said better; that more auspicious examples may any day, belatedly, come to light; and doubtless, with chagrin, that errata will be found to mar what was thought to be burnished—need never end. If one cares, it cannot. Ever so, as Stewart models for us, text can be called back from its time of debut, placed before new eyes and a mind alive to the times. The year 1974 is now, immanent again, somehow, its lines suddenly accompanied by a pulsing cursor ready for the next, new thought. In this way, Stewart revisits his former selves—draws the myriad doppelgängers into his circle—and in his reencounter tutors them, and us: here is something still worth our time; here is something we missed; here is something that we can let go of, not quite delete so much as notice as a false lead or infelicitous phrasing. We did our best, folks, is the mood of reunion, and still more refinements await.

Yet a further lesson—beyond structure and stylistics—can be found in the tone of what amounts to master-teacher Stewart's "re-grading" of his prose (both in the sense of an instructor's red pen poised above the page, however forgivingly, and in the sense of a Zen master's smoothing out of his garden comprised of a million individuated stones, all placed with care, intention, and yes, love). His genuine generosity with his students is extended, graciously, to himself: he is neither nostalgic nor apologetic about what was written, and thus neither maudlin nor defensive. Rather, he is persistently intrigued by the way a time of encounter (then, now) and the conditions that underwrite it (what has been read, what has been written) shape the mind's capacity to be alive to the text(s). Stewart—always the student—performs his "purposeful rereading of analytical work" with the zest of a fledgling and the wherewithal of a dominant peregrine. Throughout *Attention Spans*, he is very much in the classroom risking his earlier thoughts on a book or passage or claim, willing, in effect, to hear out his present-day self—with all that it has accumulated over the years, with all that was missed and now given a chance to speak, to be marked out, (re)submitted for our shared consideration. Stewart's transtemporal access, as it were to his own mind (What *was* I thinking? What was I *thinking*?) is made manifest in these pages, a rare gift to all his students, all his readers—known and yet to come.

From the first pages of the book, Stewart appears on guard against any charge of vanity in this undertaking, wary of a slippage into grandiosity, or allergic to self-indulgent autobiographical reflection. These are all misplaced worries, of course, felt by someone who needn't fret. Rather, Stewart appears, phrase by phrase, sentence by sentence, paragraph by paragraph, to continue the practice Stanley Cavell once described to me as noting only those moments of auto/biographical detail that "rise to the level of philosophical significance."[15] Stewart's invocation of a former teacher or mentor, his allusion to a book that influenced the course of his thinking, and, more prominently still, his necessary, structurally imposed turn and return to his own writing, all operate under the banner of this standard—one he is doubtless naturally, spiritually we might even say, suited to bear and exemplify. We readers, to be sure, crave such models, especially as they continue to vanish from the field of view.

In an editorial effort to give readers a sense of not just who informs Stewart's readings and writings, but when they lived and did their work, one will notice the pattern of recent years in parentheses that signal nothing less final than death. Some of our best readers—our finest companions before the page—are disappearing. "It was collection time for an entire generation," as Saul Bellow wrote—or two.[16] Thus "time spans" in yet another sense: our *mortal spans* (the time of one's life, no more no less). And yet, the trick is ever a matter of earthly talents turned to good uses. As an acolyte attuned to the achievements of "[t]he departing contingent," I must hedge my own melancholy and nostalgia for these losses (including among them, friends), to recapture the point: that *Attention Spans* is, and will remain henceforth, a series of lessons in reading: inimitable clinics (braced for the onslaughts of a fraught future laced with artificial intelligence) in how a writer reads, rereads, and rewrites his own prose—in effect confirming his own *unsettled* relationship to a lifetime of readerly encounters. In these respects, among other virtues noted, the volume must be a valuable, and lasting, contribution to our present and future tasks of reading and further composition. *Attention Spans* is not an instruction manual, still less a last will and testament, but it is a testimony to the power of intellection turned back upon one's own best efforts at consecutive prose. That is a lesson worth noticing, heeding, emulating, and enjoying.

AMONG THE MANY PROPITIOUS REACTIONS I have had to Stewart's "Inventory as Itinerary"—and its book's worth of TexTcerpts and crisp commentaries that follow it—an endearing one abides, namely, how much I wish every one of my (and your) intellectual heroes had undertaken such a project with a devoted amanuensis, created a *florilegium* of their work with new and novel commentary interlineated throughout. For such is the opportunity that awaits us here: a self-generated "director's cut" (with DVD commentary of a sort duly included not as a "special feature" but rather as the marquee event), imbued as it is with characteristic subtlety, wit, and illumination. And yet, we are still permitted to imagine the companion collections by others that don't exist (because they can't), or that don't *yet* exist, but may, perhaps, one day, if this scheme catches on with those who remain and those who are to come.

In our day and age, with the proliferation of M.F.A. programs—especially prestigious ones, such as that housed at Stewart's own university—there is a recurring question about whether students can be taught to write. Down the hall, we find Stewart asking a different but related question, the question that naturally suits the other side of the newly submitted manuscript page: can students be taught to read? *Attention Spans* is an answer to this question, at the very least in the virtuosity of *Stewart's* achievement, but it is also an invitation to the rest of us, (mostly) apprentice readers in search of masterful insights. Pulling the text closer, we may become "close readers"—nearer to the text (this one and any others) and thus, with effort duly applied, nearer to our ideas about what's going on with it. As Stewart himself has discovered, "at least a few students always get addicted to this scale of fascination." The cathecting is its own reward, assuredly, but might it also proffer its own yield of compelling, perhaps even productive, analyses?

Like many others, I have been told and trained to be on guard for the "lectiocentric."[17] According to this critical (suspicious? paranoid?) *reading* of reading, things that can't or shouldn't be "read" are, in fact, deciphered according to that term. As long as a century and a half ago, Dickens was wildly funny on this very point in a passage dear to Stewart's heart. Not reprinted here from his commentary on it in *The One, Other, and Only Dickens* is this lampoon, in *Our Mutual Friend*, of just such an always-pertinent cliché—a wilted usage travestied through personification in the satiric wit of Eugene Wrayburn as "ever youthful and delightful," even in its promiscuous dispersion:

> You charm me, Mortimer, with your reading of my weaknesses. (By-the-by, that very word, Reading, in its critical use, always charms me. An actress's Reading of a chambermaid, a dancer's Reading of a hornpipe, a singer's Reading of a song, a marine painter's Reading of the sea, the kettle-drum's Reading of an instrumental passage, are phrases ever youthful and delightful.)

In our contemporary discourse as well, a painting is "read." Film sound is "read." And so on. If there are resistances to this colonialist "spreading" of reading—a certain caution about category transgression, of courting the untranslatable—Stewart offers us good reasons to think again. For him, the purity of literary text isn't diluted, but concentrated by medial contrast, under shared investigation with the other media whose artifacts surrender to the legible. One might go so far as to suggest that Stewart's work infers a deep transformational grammar by which paintings as well as books, and not least paintings *of* books (see *The Look of Reading*, 2006), movies as well as vocal performance, installation art as much as Romantic poetry, participate together in structures of signification made differently visible and audible in the medium's own separate vocables and vocabularies. To judge more fully of this, you will have to, yes, "read the map" offered as charted itinerary here in Stewart's own words, where, in his literary study, one might say that the sentence is the upper level of "usable" first reaction in critical response.

But disciplinary trends have tended otherwise. "That very word reading, in its critical use," again quoting Dickens, has in fact suffered notable attrition. For as academic fashions in recent decades encouraged a constant updating—of curriculum, of disciplinary boundaries, of the canon, and so on—certain skills, even talents, have often been left behind, allowed to atrophy, or been marshalled to serve questionable ends. Exhibit A: reading. Exhibit A_1: close reading. The sheer temporal expanse of Stewart's life as a reader provides a bulwark for younger generations, if only—and not *just* if only—to note and acknowledge a reader who has "seen it all." Like the author himself, the sequence of his books gives firsthand witness to trends that take us from one era of scholarly leaning or bias to another; as for leanings, note the difference between a cultivated and worthy posture and a mere posturing. *Attention Spans* may be read, in part, in no small part, not just as Stewart's proof against planned obsolescence in institutional paradigms but, positively put, as proof of the sustained and sustaining significance of reading-as-act, reading-as-art.

In framing Stewart's extensive new contribution in this volume most broadly, one could borrow, as its own, the subtitle to his latest book on theatrical cinema, *Cinemachines* (see Phase VII / 16), namely, "An Essay on Media and Method."

This would recall, in turn, the summarizing epilogue to *Novel Violence* over a decade before (see Phase IV / 8), "Novel Criticism as Media Study." And this is just where, by counter-case, the notion of "demediation" comes in—and I need to say more about this shortly—as the ultimate test of a reading impulse that survives even the former place of words. Garrett had recently mentioned to me his surprise at a visit to the US post office, when sending a colleague a copy of his latest book, that "book rate" is now subsumed to "Media Mail" (registered trademark). "That is not what I meant at all," he added, spoofing Prufrock. His emphasis on a book's medial basis has always had something less generic in mind, something quite differently weighted, something with genuine gravity that students could learn to appreciate and uphold in their own work.

In a most welcome note struck some time back, one of the press referees for this manuscript, when still a proposal, mentioned a particular eagerness for its realization based on having shared passages from Stewart's work with undergraduates—who became interested in the broader scope of the approach, and would have benefited from such a compendium for reference, context, and further inspiration, curious to know more about not just what Stewart reads, but how. Welcome indisputably, that referee anecdote, and I was every bit as much energized by the prospect of an actual new-generation audience out there for commitments I share with Stewart as I was by this timely "selling point" at the acquisition stage. Context we were certainly prepared to give, along with lots more reference, and inspiration to hope for as well. But the last without blinking, so to speak, at the flickering 24/7 threat to close reading posed by the nonnarrative screens on which, and sometimes partly by which, younger generations of students have been reared.

In this respect, and in view of his work's full mediatic parameters, one seemingly anomalous strand stands out. For all the intense density of his close readings, Stewart is perhaps never more revealing about his interpretive mission than when he confronts nontext "bookhood," first in 2011, then again in 2020 (see Phase V / 11, then Phase VI / 15). His notion of the *bibliobjet* enacts precisely the expansion (under duress?) of reading, since it provides yet another object/artwork that is (emphatically) *not* a traditionally legible book. Thus, as art critics, as literary critics, we arrive in the gallery as if to a morgue or anatomy lesson screeching (to a halt) in panic at how the codices have been chopped; spines stripped from bodies; skin (once vellum) torn, cut, sliced, sewn-up, and stitched postmortem to leave out and to hide (as the case may be). The attack on the body of the book seems a scandal, yet what are art critics and literary critics to do but … read, but offer "readings" of what is happening to reading? So, the core question, in brief, asks after the *tension* between *bibliograph-as-codex* and *bibliobjet*. What is bookwork now? What is the work of books to come … if we are to be but passively read to by machines (as Stewart, you'll learn, in his not-yet-literate infancy was instead read Dickens by a savvy babysitter)?

But the question of pedagogy, so central to Stewart's production, and so much shared by some of us a generation or two or three behind him, if thought of as an actual question, has no clear answers. I speak collectively for those of us still caught up in a fond bibliophilia and ineluctable lectiocentrism, wondering about our vocational status. There is the work—the proceeds of labors—and then there is the culture that celebrates, accommodates, or neglects it. Among a range of fates, are we the astrophysicists of our age (sending rockets into space to slightly change the trajectory of massive objects, whose deflection may in fact be world-saving, species-preserving) or the alchemists (a figure fitting for Stewart's reflections below, in Phase VI / 15, on the baroque chemical reductions of print text by Alexander Rosenberg): marginals who, with each passing day, become less comprehensible to our peers—even if we become surer of our methods, commitments, and findings; that is, the smallest of observable objects, which are, in fact, easily swatted away, or smaller still, not even making an appreciable impact, one worthy of care or concern? I see that the trope is forcing a science/magic divide (even if "white magic"), but maybe that's not far off—if reading (of the sort we're still aiming at) is as rare as I think it is. Has the postwar academic industrial complex (so instructively sequenced in the methodological timeline Stewart steps through with his graduate students, as rehearsed in the "Inventory as Itinerary" to come) left the actual readers among us rather like a troop of artisanal mendicants, yes *itinerants*, more vagabonds than mavericks, with wares on offer that no one knows what to do with? The question otherwise: Is there a pilgrimage left to tread and chart? A report or epiphany to share? Or a peripatetic curiosity still to exploit? The simple fact: it's not all over while some of us, Stewart's age, my age, students' ages, are still all in. However declining the numbers, numbness hasn't won out. So that the uphill spirit of this endeavor—sincere, not cynical—is a far cry from the crusty lament "kids these days!" No, they're its hope—and so, ours. The impulse is to cultivate what I think of as the patrimony of important things, serious matters.

No matter where one finds oneself today, there is likely some measure of benefit from a season of close reading (even if set in contrast with such provocations as surface reading). Take note, then, that there is nothing self-involved or narrowly memoirist in Stewart's reflections to come—for in themselves they are always looking ahead as well as expansively back. In his pending "Inventory as Itinerary," the biographical diachrony charts a movement through phases of disciplinary debate and breakthrough to which the synchronic groupings of the books in bundles, or Phases I to VIII—under the variant (almost kaleidoscopic) facets of Stewart's attention—give weight and illustration. What unrolls is less a chronicle of accomplishment (though it certainly is that by sheer depth and extent as well as caliber of realization) than a map of intellectual trajectories and their frequent intersections, highways, and byways alike. With disciplinary coordinates vehemently girded, and longitudes visibly gridded, there remains, you shall soon see, a fit leeway in all the latitudes Stewart's writing traverses.

The temporal sweep of this one critic's practice—including a periodic encounter with new methodological contenders, and this in his inclination onward as well as inward—reminds us of what a blistering pace we have been held to. Notice how the acceleration of publication reflects a heightened urgency in Stewart's maturing thought, the rising arc of the asymptote in a life well-spent in criticism: one book in the 1970s, another in the 1980s, three in the 1990s, three more in the 2000s; four in the 2010s; and count'em, six in the first half of the 2020s. Including his latest literary arguments concerning a post-postmodernist reflexivity in contemporary American fiction (*The Metanarrative Hall of Mirrors*, 2022; see Phase VIII / 19), all of these books were paced on the way to the printer in at least indirect response to the juggernaut of methodological usurpations operating with even more exponentially rapid turnover across his writing career. From New Criticism to object-oriented ontology in half a dozen decades. The point is: despite the differences present in the interstitial phases of contention and periods marked by transient concerns, there abides—as this volume embodies in form *and* content—a grave need for attuned, attentive readers. No doubt, the audience of *Attention Spans* may feel how it, like the intent of Stewart's classroom pedagogical practice, "ignites critical energy" (with the doubleness of "critical" throbbing with a charge of its own). In an age of distraction, with attention spans attenuated, a little lectiocentrism might be a good thing—a corrective in the form of a restoration. This one's for the readers. If you dare.

Notes

1. Roland Barthes, *The Grain of the Voice: Interviews 1962–1980*, trans. Linda Coverdale (Evanston: Northwestern University Press, 2009; originally published as *Le grain de la voix* [Paris: Éditions de Seuil, 1981]), 115.
2. Garrett Stewart, *The Deed of Reading: Literature * Writing * Language * Philosophy* (Ithaca: Cornell University Press, 2015), 1, 3.
3. Ralph Waldo Emerson, "Self-Reliance," in *Essays: First Series*, *The Complete Works of Ralph Waldo Emerson*, Concord Edition (Boston: Houghton, Mifflin and Company, 1904), 2:144.
4. Garrett Stewart, *The Value of Style in Fiction* (Cambridge: Cambridge University Press, 2018), 1–3.
5. Garrett Stewart, *The Ways of the Word: Episodes in Verbal Attention* (Ithaca: Cornell University Press, 2021), 2–3.
6. Garrett Stewart, "Open-Circuit Narrative: Programmed Reading in Richard Powers," *Novel: A Forum on Fiction*, vol. 55, no. 3 (2022): 547–65.
7. Garrett Stewart, *The One, Other, and Only Dickens* (Ithaca: Cornell University Press, 2018), 2.
8. Garrett Stewart, *Book, Text, Medium: Cross Sectional Reading for a Digital Age* (Cambridge: Cambridge University Press, 2020), 125.
9. Stewart, *The Deed of Reading*, 214.
10. Garrett Stewart, *Between Film and Screen: Modernism's Photo Synthesis* (Chicago: University of Chicago Press, 1999), 272.
11. Stewart, *Between Film and Screen*, 349.

12 Stewart, *The Ways of the Word*, 90.
13 Garrett Stewart, "Attention Surfeit Disorder," in *Novel Violence: A Narratography of Victorian Fiction* (Chicago: University of Chicago Press, 2009), 61–89.
14 See Garrett Stewart, "The Avoidance of Stanley Cavell," in *Contending with Stanley Cavell*, ed. Russell Goodman (New York: Oxford University Press, 2005), 142. See also David LaRocca, *Emerson's English Traits and the Natural History of Metaphor* (New York: Bloomsbury, 2013), 76.
15 See David LaRocca, "Must We Say What We Learned? Parsing the Personal and the Philosophical" (1–48) and "Autophilosophy" (275–320), in *Inheriting Stanley Cavell: Memories, Dreams, Reflections*, ed. David LaRocca (New York: Bloomsbury, 2020), esp. 11, 301, 312.
16 Saul Bellow, *Ravelstein* (New York: Penguin, 2000), 130.
17 Emily Apter, "Untranslatable: The 'Reading' versus the 'Looking,'" *Journal of Visual Culture*, vol. 6, no. 1 (2007): 149–56. See also David LaRocca, "From Lectiocentrism to Gramophonology: Listening to Cinema and Writing Sound Criticism," in *The Geschlecht Complex: Addressing Untranslatable Aspects of Gender, Genre, and Ontology*, ed. Oscar Jansson and David LaRocca (New York: Bloomsbury, 2022), 201–68.

INVENTORY AS ITINERARY

Garrett Stewart

THE SURPRISE PITCH was, at first, not quite as irresistible as it was generous. I had recently finished my third contribution to a David LaRocca anthology when the intrepid editor wondered in an email whether it might not be my own turn to be collectively anthologized, given that I was nearing the twenty-monograph mark.[1] Wasn't it time for the crowded shelf to become a manageable sheaf of rebound excerpts? It had never occurred to me. But David was suggesting more than a mere cut-and-paste project—not just a best-of "reader" in the classical sense. He had in mind something more distinctly pedagogical in nature, and thus attuned to my particular penchant for making my writing available as a prompt for the classroom as much as a reflection on its events. One encouraging difference from the standard reader model was his invitation for the author to participate not just in the selection of his own work, but in documenting its situatedness within both classroom dynamics and shifting critical trends over the years. Envisioned was a compendium of selected writing (across a span of some five decades and counting) to be complemented by two crucial, novel attributes: fresh, present-day commentary by me *and* a supporting critical apparatus designed to make the texts *useful* after a fashion (or some further fashioning) to familiar and unfamiliar audiences in and out of classrooms (e.g., discursive endnotes, a distilled glossary, a topographical bibliography, and so on). The ingenuity as well as generosity of the pitch remained foremost even as I contemplated what its particular form would entail for—and from—me. In a word, work.

With the thought suddenly there to conjure with, the very volume of these volumes made for one, if just one, of my hesitations. And not even first among them. Any question of what was to be carved out was preceded by the *why*? Which is largely to ask: for whom? What imagined "readership" for such a Reader? Students first of all, presumably, but with—and to—what new, or further, purpose? What would be the "value added" of extraction when there was too much backlog for any true cross-sectional view? What would sustain curiosity—and hence momentum—across all those reopened books? You certainly wouldn't be hearing it there first in such an anthology: "one thing leads to another." Yet what else might emerge in stepping off again the disciplinary zigzag of those publications?

Asked of myself, rather than David, when first sleeping on the suggestion: Would the point be just to render more readily accessible, in spotty overview, an evolving literary critical and media studies commitment? Or, more forward-looking, to energize some fresh enthusiasm in its readers, or at least curiosity, regarding a recurrent—if continually readjusted—emphasis? An emphasis, that is, on the legible measures of aesthetic *materiality*—the underlay of any formal patterning—as in fact a zone of textual function in its own readable right. If so, how to organize productively the shifts in focus from the linguistic texture of narrative fiction and poetry to the syntax of celluloid film, from the pigmented field of a reading body on canvas to closed circuit surveillance monitors in narrative deployment on-screen, let alone the rest of an expanding range of my topics from conceptual book sculpture and digital special effects through popular song recording to the laser holography of virtual reality in both fictional treatment and gallery installation? These were the kinds of questions around which David and I together workshopped the eventual format of the volume, always with its potential chance for new student impact in mind. How to make visible in all this—that would be the task—a coherent trail of finds and findings leading up to, and then following on from, the equally visual and literary principle formulated in the closing paragraph of 2007's *Framed Time*: that, in a mode of reading I had begun to call narratographic, "the message delivers the medium."

The anthology proposal couldn't, in short, be embraced as just a flattering opportunity. Without looking back more closely at my books in the first flush (or blush) of consideration, I knew that some story would need telling. And hardly biographical in the ordinary sense. Nor, for my part, autobiographical. A literary-historical anecdote consoled and fortified me in this. Asked to comment by his publisher on the origin of his 1893 novel, *The Coast of Bohemia*, for its turn-of-the-century reprint in 1899, William Dean Howells recalled a precedent that deflected further direct reminiscence—while in the process unwittingly anticipating the recent critical interest in so-called object-narration in both literature and film: "In one of the old-fashioned books for children there was a story of the adventures of a cent (or perhaps that coin of older lineage, a penny) told by itself, which came into my mind"—and precisely as a model: "I promptly fancied the book speaking, and taking upon itself the burden of autobiography, which we none of us find very heavy; and no sooner had I done so than I began actually to hear from it in a narrative of much greater distinctness than I could have supplied for it." And "distinctness" is at a premium when distinguishing among twenty talky monographs.

The "burden" of autobiography sits a bit heavier on me, perhaps, than on some. Certainly, I was very glad, from the start, to anticipate deferring gestational commentary to the extracts themselves, letting my own brood have their primary say—as if they were the kind of microphone-embedded codex structures I analyze in their conceptualist ironies for *Bookwork* (2011) and *Book, Text, Medium* (2020). Any number of my volumes might have joined that favored child of Howells in words to this effect: "'You must surely remember,' it protested to my forgetfulness, 'that you first thought of me in anything like definite shape as you stood looking on …'"—looking on, in my case, at either pages or screens or canvases. Howell's loquacious novel, however, puts half the burden back on the writer at this turn. "But previous to this, my motive existed somewhere in that nebulous fore-life where both men and books have their impalpable beginning." Sure, but we don't need to go there with the monographic record of this collection. Still, my own books might serially have added, in echo of Howell's delegated mouthpiece: "The getting me down on paper was a much later affair." And later still for me, all these years later in some cases: the lines of filiation among them.

In any event, I was as glad as Howells before me to let one book after the other take center stage as the main locus of autobiography. With the hope of some feasible through-line, though, what selections could I productively assemble for the editor's further overview? What mappable path through the variable byways of my writing could be found—even with the continuity of their *textualist* road signs, both within and against shifting academic paradigms during these same decades? For only something of the sort would be a plausible motive for such a collection, the books taken up again in light of what they were often taking on. It was, as you guess, by imagining what might turn up in retracing such disparate but often oddly intersecting avenues of investigation that, despite feet-dragging uncertainty at first, I was gradually talking myself through possibilities, past obstacles, and into the shared endeavor, agreeing to authorize this unexpected volume on my authorship.

A volume to be addressed, first of all, to a familiar, but only tentatively "enrolled," student cohort. In regard to the textual immersion to be reviewed on so many fronts at once, the anticipated anthology could hardly pride itself on being an aid either to "catching up" or even to "catching the bug." It would offer mainly a more efficient way, through new adjacencies and correlations, for a certain kind of interested student to catch on—and thus for any number of text-based transmedial possibilities to catch hold anew, long after their first trial runs in one book after the other. It had always been teacherly, the central emphasis of "my method" (to speak with a thud; call it instead my interpretive instinct)—and not least in its trespass across disciplinary and curricular firewalls. Teacherly, but not merely in the way that New Criticism (its true boom peaking in my undergraduate years) had systematized a manageably self-contained classroom pedagogy for canonical literary study, of lyric poetry in particular.

After redirecting such a focus to prose in my dissertation on fiction, my books soon became exercises, whatever their actual grip, in a more far-reaching investment in the meeting of theory and *practice*—if only at the far horizon of a vanishing point where the former is, at best, absorbed by the latter. Short of that, I mean "practice" there in the sense of what used to be called practical criticism: the indubitable utility of knowing how to say what you see and hear at work, at play, at stake, and sometimes (critique in the other sense) even at odds with itself in a vexed episode of print or a dubious passage of screen imaging.

Bibliography as Syllabus

OFFICIAL CLASS REGISTRATION ASIDE in this anthology's intended new "teaching aid," but never far from mind, the genealogy of a practice, rather than the autobiography of a practitioner, was called for—though with the personal given space here and there when "instructive." The editor and I agreed that this was the genetic emphasis I would sketch out in introductory remarks like these, estimating in review a lifelong lesson plan. Book by book, as in seminar by seminar: premise, emphasis, test. Under review: not a consolidated theory of text across media, but a broad disposition toward form's material basis wherever caught in the act of aesthetic realization. How, with time and work, did this disposition on my part, this instinct, come to resemble, with "practice" in the other sense, something like a method—and how contagious could it be made for a younger generation of the inquisitive?

Having experimented over the years with the objects and levels of attention that students, matriculated ones, could be energized by from term to term, I thought of each new class as designed to course-correct the last. The results, slowly at first, then more rapidly, gestated into articles and books that felt to me, in part, like progress reports—or what we've lately come to call, in a narrowly administrative sense, "outcome assessments." In my mind, however, the monographs as "write ups" were just as much course planners for a second shot at the same topic: prospectuses from which to set out *again*. Teaching, like the writing gleaned from and reseeding it, was regularly a butting against limits—including self-inflicted deficiencies—when surveying again certain traversed grounds of literary and aesthetic response. All I could hope for, in the recirculation of this material years later, would be some spur to fresh initiative on the part of students: at least those eager to become "studious" readers within the assumptions (checked by some questioning push-back) of critical allegiances they were elsewhere signing up for in their research. With a sometimes adversarial frame around my textual advocacy, that had always been the only true lesson meant to be imparted: how, if so inclined, you might not merely coast along in the shallows of analysis but instead brave the full force of disciplinary crosscurrents—while keeping your object steadily and intimately in view. The skill variously inculcated, in each new monograph and seminar alike, was, if only implicitly, how to stay afloat, in anything like a committed textual immersion, by retaining both a calisthenic curiosity and a healthy skeptical balance—and to do this while, in almost paradoxical fashion, both cresting and bucking the latest tides at once, rather than buckling under them.

In contemplating a review of this hybrid pedagogic genealogy in anthology form, with all its alternate media touchstones, there was still an extra hesitation to deal with. The books, as implied, were always instrumental in my mind, not in any sense monumental: a series of considered memoranda as pedagogic aids (for me in their writing, as well as for my students, at least in my imagining). Something to draw on next time out, rest on, even eagerly remodel, often refurbishing its central premises in venturing some further and perhaps more decisive extension. So the monographs felt less like settled doxa than like promissory notes toward future exploration. Now, unlike many academics I know, I don't immediately sit down with an author's copy of a new publication (not at least since the first book or two) to see how it sounds in print after all—neither to catch the typos, in the fantasy of a second edition, nor merely braced for them. But the nervous distance I've increasingly kept has a deeper cause, repeatedly burned as I've been on return to a given chapter. Whenever I've had to recheck an argument for some later allusion to it, or for recirculation in class, I've typically wished it had been said otherwise, more precisely. And then there were those favored (and labored over) literary phrases or cinematic images whose additional fascination I now lamented overlooking, not to mention a clinching generalization regrettably stopped short of. I therefore flinched at the thought that working on the proposed anthology would be like reading final page proofs all over again, hands tied by the press for any changes other than typos or factual errors. But what after all is the analytic "fact"? Isn't a missed cue, a dropped interpretive stitch, or a flubbed paraphrase an "error"—or at least lapse in critical judgment—that has misrepresented the textual "data"?

David LaRocca understood my qualms, and we hit on the present format of the volume, where I'd have the opportunity to single out and rethink a wide variety of extended excerpts, rather than simply whole chapters or articles at a time. In doing so, it was agreed that I could interrupt my former self, where necessary, with all due regrets, second thoughts, or *ex post facto* theoretical reorientations; and by strategic excisions in a given stretch of argument, could get more points across than otherwise. So this Reader would unfold for students, as if by vicarious exemplum, as a purposeful *rereading* of analytic work—as with their own strenuous and challenging essay assignments in class. Like them reporting on other critics, I would be reporting on me. A determined second go—but in this case by the author himself. In this respect, recapitulating its own pedagogic lineage, my part in the anthology might hope to borrow twice over from the spontaneity of classroom exchange. For in the seminar room or lecture hall, whenever referring to any of my own previous arguments, I would never hesitate to improve upon them if possible, whether admitting a slip, digging in deeper, or, especially in doctoral classes, trying out a whole new and trending paradigm in an *ad hoc* recalibration of the selected textual evidence, dubiously or otherwise.

But all that was then, even if habitual. Where now? One way forward in this revisitation is to start by reading "reading" itself for its own lexical depth. The infinitive (always infinitely renewable) *to read*, from *legere*, is not just to gather (in a literalized sense) but, as the dictionaries have it, by further macabre specification, "to collect (cremated bones)": to choose, select. Closer to home in Germanic descent through Old English: from *raten* to *rede*—that is, to interpret (as a dream), to guess, or better yet, in critical application, to estimate. So it is that exemplary picking out of details, in picking over the available evidence of a visual or verbal text, may fertilize new offshoots from the pulverized traces of received material. But the question for me has always been how such reading can be taught, or at least modeled. The use of the earnestly Greek-derived "pedagogue" for teacher—a term denoted as "formal or humorous" (I find myself often trying for both in the actual event)—has its own potentially sardonic etymology. Originally, it denoted a slave ("agogos")—call it these days salaried laborer (once, and not so long ago, mostly tenure-tracked rather than indentured)—"who," in the masculinist Greek, "accompanies a young boy to school." So that from *pais* (boy), we derive *paideia*—education, learning. As pedestrian chaperon more than credentialed pedant, this kind of privileged footman was merely a preliminary escort to the site of instruction. And though you can lead a boy to water ....

Any actual teaching, then or now, tends to be more hands-on, a leading to but then drawing out; educative becomes e-ductive. Whether in the form of lectures (etymologically, readings *out*, if not in) or seminars (from the degendered "seminarium," neuter for seed-plot), *to teach* as verb derives, unlike the Latinate "instruct," from the Old English *tæcan*: "show, present, point out," close kin to "token" from the Greek for "sample" (*deigma*). To teach is to show, to exemplify, to point out and up (verb), and thus to offer confirmatory tokens of "a point" (noun, by back-formation). Any such anthology as the one coming, or already underway, I knew early on, would have to be this kind of retrospective show-and-tell, alternating excerpts with further exegetical reflections.

And in etymological terms, there's another way to highlight the "roots" of my classroom fidelity to text and its intensive reading. Although not "public-facing" in the sense of that new institutional catch phrase, my teacherly investments do recall the etymological origin of that activist descriptor in the common aesthetic wealth shared by the *res publica*—as well as in modes of *public*ation meant to circulate it. Beyond a move from private to public universities early in my career, I've maintained a hospitality, hardly universal among my most prolific colleagues, to a quite specific teacherly mode of publication. This has meant compounding my classroom investments with regular essay deposits in the archive of explicit print pedagogy: these in the form of contributions to handbooks, casebooks, companions, and literary encyclopedias. Perhaps I was remembering with sympathy the callow "boy" in me, with so much catching up to do (more on this below), whose *paedia* would once have stood to benefit from any such critical "aids." These versions of the classroom "primer" never seemed to me like water-downed scholarship, but rather like concentrated instruction, primed for the detail that "betokens" what lies *behind* an object of consideration in the constructive (or formative) sense: not hidden beyond it, or even just hinted, but instead openly, legibly, manifested—and demonstrable—in the process of response. So that, in the present volume, picking out "tokens" of this hermeneutic assumption, and its resulting habits, may accrue to a teaching manual in its own right. In a further etymological spirit, one notes that *tome*, before its heavy popular sense today of *magnum opus*, originally meant—from "cut" (*temein*)—a single book in a multivolume work. So be it here: each of my monographs slotted into place as installments in an ongoing pursuit—and assembled in excerpts, one course plan after another, as a kind of metasyllabus.

Though I rarely "teach myself" in class—not wanting to put students on the spot for response—I have been, for the last few electronic years, including on the course website some of my essays and chapters in pdf form. This has seemed especially useful in my mainstay seminar in the history of interpretive methodologies across literature and film, deliberately spanning from New Criticism to the latest critical news. The point isn't to show how my own particular thinking has evolved, but instead to exhibit ways in which any number of challenging theoretical positions from the critical canon could get taken up by the different rigors of intensive verbal or visual notice. I have lately begun that course with the handout of a graphic timeline. Its virtual spreadsheet of limited longevities clocks in, roughly half-decade by half-decade, the leading disciplinary modes of my professional tenure. The chart makes clear, and not without some professional irony, their increasing proliferation and decreasing shelf life, including a turnover so fast in the last couple of decades that movements emerge without the signature status (as reflected in my chart) of a lionized prime mover. Yet the exercises that follow our consideration of these trends do pointedly encourage the class to harvest the best from each "movement," wherever a given partisan perspective would seem still to suit a particular analytic project the student might have in mind for the term's work.

Turnover certainly, and sometimes deliberate overturning—as most recently in the resistance to the long reign of symptomatic (or suspicious) reading, in the mode of politicized critical theory, by so-called surface reading—as if there could be a text without subtext. (Think—as of course you can't—of surface tension without a liquid depth!) Such disciplinary one-uppings have been increasingly euphemized as "turns," rather than just turf battles, each imagined as a heady swerve into uncharted territory. I begin that methods course, therefore, by using my sketched timeline to summarize how, in the postwar institutionalization of literary study, New Criticism began it all by vanquishing both insistent biographical investments and straight canonical historicism as the givens of critical remark. From there my charted timeline—long before eyes-on grappling with landmark essays—serves to helicopter students across

Methodological Timeline

1930s 40s 50s 60s   70s   80s   90s   2000s   2010s   2020s

OLD HISTORICISM / PHILOLOGY / SOURCE STUDY / LITERARY HISTORY (John Livingston Lowes, F. R. Leavis)

    NEW CRITICISM (I. A. Richards, William Empson, Cleanth Brooks, Christopher Ricks, Helen Vendler)

        STYLISTICS and PROSE RHETORIC (Mark Schorer, Wayne Booth)

           SEMIOTICS / STRUCTURALISM (Roland Barthes, Tzvetan Todorov, Gérard Genette, Michael Riffaterre, Jonathan Culler)

           PHENOMENOLOGY and READER RESPONSE (Georges Poulet, J. Hillis Miller, Wolgang Iser, Stanley Fish)

           LINGUISTIC TURN
                DECONSTRUCTION (Jacques Derrida, Paul de Man)
                SUBJECTIVITY THEORY (Jacques Lacan)

              NEW LITERARY HISTORY
                OEDIPAL (Harold Bloom)
                FEMINIST (Sandra Gilbert, Susan Gubar)
                MARXIST (Fredric Jameson)

              NARRATIVE TURN (Hayden White, Peter Brooks)

              DISCURSIVE TURN
                NEW HISTORICISM (Michel Foucault, Stephen Greenblatt, Jerome McGann)
                GENDER / QUEER THEORY (Judith Butler, Eve Sedgwick)

              POST-COLONIAL TURN (Edward Said, Gayatri Spivak, Homi Bhaba)

              CULTURAL TURN / MATERIAL TURN
                POP CULTURE (Jane Tompkins)
                THING THEORY (Bill Brown)
                BOOK STUDIES / HISTORY OF READING (Adrian Johns)

              ETHICAL TURN
                RETURN TO PHILOSOPHY (Stanley Cavell, Martha Nussbaum,
                Emmanuel Levinas, Giorgio Agamben)

              POST-SECULAR TURN (Jurgen Habermas, Charles Taylor)

              COGNITIVE TURN

              NEOFORMALIST RE-TURN

              AFFECTIVE TURN

              DIGITAL TURN

                ECOLOGICAL and POST-HUMAN TURN
                OBJECT-ORIENTED ONTOLOGY

                TRANS TURN

the semiotic and structuralist turn, the phenomenological and reader-response turn, the deconstructive, the psychoanalytic, the feminist, the discursive or epistemic or New Historicist, the ethical, the queer, the postcolonial, the material (including "thing theory"), the affective, the post-secular, down through the ecological turn, as its "reading" of new dimensions in sentient intent link up with object-oriented ontology. And beyond—always beyond: including the sociological turn within the supposed second-wave revamping known as neoformalism. This is a line of thought in which verbal agency itself, its specific linguistic systems, can too readily, in my view, be subsumed to the likes of societally modelled actor–network theory. Yet as a long-standing actor myself in all these competing critical networks, I see my role as teacher to encourage a wary contemplation of models stretched too thin—and textual attention with them. In respect (all due) to that last-mentioned trend, especially as it has been wheeled into the broader orbit of so-called "cultural formalism," I nudge students—it doesn't take much—to wonder some about any such obliterated differentiation of "forms." With enough rich and complicated verbal (formal) examples on the table, apprentice readers easily come to doubt any such leveling of medial coordinates—especially with its theorized refusal to prioritize, for literary study, textual over social form as the immediate and tangible matter at hand in reading. Wherever—beyond (or beneath!) itself—it then points.

So, obviously, I've "buried the lede," as the journalists say. Not at all apologetically. But it certainly is none too soon to say that the agenda of each of my twenty partitioned "tomes"—and the repurposed course plans that keep adjusting to the last one and then refueling the next—have been a career-long experiment in the proverbial (if many times retooled) "close reading." The benchmark of New Criticism, and many times renewed under subsequent dispensations, this was a formerly vital inclination in the academy, now mostly an atrophied habit, reduced sometimes just to a nervous twitch, that has been losing ground in all media study at once, verbal and visual, and at exponential rates. So why rehearse one long and increasingly lonely, or at least uncrowded, path of its application? The attenuation of muscle-memory for any such grip on aesthetic detail is the reason in itself: the chance for rehabilitation, for an overhauled habit of attention. At least a few students always get addicted to this scale of fascination. And so the coming anthology, with first stirrings here, might offer at least some modest holding action against the latest manner(s) of foresworn alertness to media determination in reading. It would hope to do so by rescanning the stamina of an opposite exercise regimen, mine, for a rescued sense of its pleasure over the years. (To the idea of pleasure, theorized, I'll return in a moment—in its obvious pedagogical appeal.)

In a symptomatic way, my own departmental reputation as mentor, increasingly "niche," bears out the erosion of a textual, in deference to cultural studies, emphasis in classroom protocols. Regrettable, I may feel, but no cause for a grudge. Oddly, my instructional contributions have, in something like a compensatory way, been almost increasingly valued lately—in a spirit, at worst, of "diversity" and "inclusion." I'm the odd man out frequently called in—or assumed as prime mover in certain student instances. Never has my named chair as "Professor of Letters," with its charming honorific datedness, seemed so fitting. Not *belles lettres*, in the older-yet sense of beautiful writing, certainly, but in my case an inclination to hear belling ones, sometimes dissonant, always structurally resonant, echoing across texts as phonetic signals—and even across abutting syllables. (Parenthetically, and only incidental to my job title, there is the administrative sense of "writing letters," that is, of recommendation—recommending students for your consideration—a particular genre of moral suasion reliant on the grace of well-placed paragraphs and well-honed arcs of praise for gifted students facing a daunting future, if nearly an impossible present, in the academy.) But back to the more traditional literary sense of "humane letters," I take up again (as I have done so often in practice) my propensity for responding to such intrinsic and incremental effects as the tolling of vowel sounds, including their rough material equivalents in the other media I study, as pressure points that can profitably rivet interpretation. These include, beyond literature's phonetic substrate and its syntactic syncopations, the transitional patterns of film editing to which my eye otherwise gravitates, the graphic displacements of form on canvas, the troping of materiality itself in book sculpture, the computerized self-reference of digital effects in action cinema, and the contours of vocal enunciation in musical comedy on the pre- and post-Dolby screen. To name but a few prods to analytic contemplation.

And prodding is where my mentorship, real or presumed, comes in. Or say nudging. Certainly, on the literary front, undergraduates aren't trained at this tightly gauged scale of linguistic attention in other "English" departments any more often than in my own. And so even doctoral applicants aren't likely to bring that particular "skill set" (grammar, dictional register, figurative rhetoric, etymology) into their writing submissions—or, when admitted, into the classroom—very often either, mine or those of their own undergraduate teaching assistant courses. For those admitted to our program, I have become the go-to mentor on this passingly appreciated if rear-garde front. For honors undergraduates and Ph.D. candidates alike, concentrated textual analysis is not just my abiding allegiance but my middle name on campus. It is sometimes even a mistaken imprimatur on a student's work. Increasingly, whenever a doctoral candidate's dissertation chapter, in either of the departments on whose defense committees I regularly sit, bears down in anything like the intensive analysis of a single phrase or shot—an ironic verbal repetition, say, or the inference of cinematic match cut—some colleague is likely to offer a polite nod to the suspected presence of "Garrett's influence." This can happen even when the chapter's whole turn of argument is entirely new to me. I always, even in demurring, insist on taking it as a compliment. So, it is with just such students in mind, whether or not their thunder has been momentarily and erroneously stolen, that the following pages have been culled. What results is a Reader not so much in medial stylistics as in styles of reading, *actual* reading. Without delusions of grandeur or fantasies of groundswell, the effort is to maximize, hardly "Garrett's influence," but rather the enacted inspirations and influences that his writing has drawn from.

The new sorting to follow is conceived as a filing cabinet of such sponsoring impulses at work. Embedded in analytic response, these include numerous critical flashpoints that did for me, and might still for others, ignite critical energy—of use first of all because students would not be likely to encounter them elsewhere. Logged in chronologically, on this plan, are hermeneutic ventures on my part that rose to meet the peculiar urgency of a critical moment—sometimes well before this book's intended student readers were even born. I revisit these efforts in the faith that responsive gestures of interpretation on one writer's part—such efforts of theory put to practice—might survive the debates of an era (or two, or more) in embodying an aptitude and a prowess still worth pursuing. And, again, a pleasure worth cultivating. So, through it all, two inseparable lessons from Roland Barthes, encapsulated in his title *The Pleasure of the Text* (1973).[2] Speaking there of literature, the pleasure is understood as narrative and phonetic alike, at different levels, what he calls readerly and writerly: a matter of a suspense gratifyingly sustained until resolution over against an alternate sensory bliss in the materiality of wording per se. Added to which is his call, in *S/Z* (1970),[3] for a broader definition of text itself that would dissolve the rivalry of the sibling arts and lift every aesthetic effect into the light of legibility, of textual "reading."

With these provocations and enticements scheduled for highlighting in the projected volume, something else dawned on me in retrospect, in selecting excerpts that might have the most staying power in recharging the "teachable." I realized more than ever the productive triangulation invited by the mixed clientele in my seminar rooms over the years. With theoretical exemplification sidling back and forth between media, I now see clearly how the split commitments, never a divided loyalty, of my teaching across literature and film programs—even, and perhaps especially, as the latter aged in national trends from film studies (celluloid) to screen studies (including TV and video) to media studies (digital)—had a net benefit only instinctively cashed in at the time. In graduate teaching especially, striving to credential students as broadly as possible across disciplinary boundaries, I would filter out what seemed to me transient concerns in each field separately, selecting for discussion those approaches most likely to enlarge not just specialist vocabularies but broader critical faculties. That selectivity is what I will be selecting again from here.

So, it's part of what I meant in dedicating a recent multimedia study, *Book, Text, Medium*, in five enjambed but unrhymed lines, "To and for / the challenging students who keep me / productively off balance in moving / to and fro / between media." Productively unsettled, both on the page and at the seminar table. Let me leave that stamp of debt for this new volume as well. And not just for the inspiration students can bring, but for their very own formulations. In pages I am alternately reading as I draft these lead-in paragraphs, a doctoral student (Benjamin Kirbach) has just completed, also under my "direction," or say my admiring gaze, a thesis on the gestalt tension between medium and narrative in contemporary speculative fiction in the wake of postmodernism. But in his opening chapter on what for him is the last modernist epic, Stanley Kubrick's *2001: A Space Odyssey* (1968), he bears down repeatedly, in the same gestalt mode (now-you-see-it-now-you-don't) on what he wonderfully calls the celluloid "undercarriage" of the film medium: with the hint of platform and carrying motion at once. A deathless phrasing one would have killed for. Chassis as base framework, frame by frame: why in four-and-a-half books on the subject hadn't I thought of that? These moments, when a student's insight and critical wit outstrips their own mentor's will not be logged in among the several instances of chagrin or regret in these pages. Because they aren't. They are instead the entire mission—the intellectual transmission—crystalized.

Curriculum Vitae and the Curricular Life

THESIS "DIRECTION," THE "ADVISOR" STATUS: part of one's curricular paper trail. And like much else, though sometimes less obviously at the time, part of one's intellectual profile. So, if any of the above on classroom practice sounds too abstract or visionary—since we all know there are bad days, botched demonstrations, clumsy uptake on a student guess, fizzled perorations—let at least the foregrounded intellectual enthusiasms be forgiven, or better, taken in the right spirit. Especially, let us say, when they are now to be more confessedly embedded in the ups and downs of a professional (as much as professorial) teaching "job" that is part of anyone's protracted scholarly *Bildungsroman*: a role not easy to theatricalize much less theorize. So, add that to the narrative challenges I'm still addressing as I write.

To begin with, for all the buffeting subplots borne on the winds of disciplinary weather and its high-pressure zones, I knew from the first, in committing to this publication time line, that what I had to tell (however telling I might hope to make it) would be mostly a story of continuity rather than transformation, punctuated not so much by dramatic retooling as by rest stops and refuelings. Sounds a tad flat as plots go. But at least the workaday story would have those moments of triggering disequilibrium inherent to structuralist Tzvetan Todorov's foundational essay "The Grammar of Narrative" (1971) and, thereafter, those nodes of cathexis and binding central to the psychopoetics of Peter Brooks' *Reading for the Plot* (1984)—even if the plot here is mostly just one long history of reading and reaction.[4] Not bad work if you can get it. On Brooks' model, yes, the story would be mostly all "middle," never tending to closure, just a recorded doggedness—knotted up around one particular textual instigation after another. It would track little more, in broad outline, than a dedication to keeping things open: open to curiosity, to the disciplinary seismology of paradigm shifts, as well as to less earth-shaking (but nonetheless career-shaping) curricular needs.

That last matter, the more I "reminisced," loomed large. It became increasingly obvious, as I began to page through the record again, just where intellectual energies were often directed by tactical deployment before they got reprogrammed as strategic research. I began writing seriously about film, for instance, when I was loaned from my home department in English to a struggling and understaffed (now thriving and renowned) film studies unit (not then department) at the University of California, Santa Barbara, where I taught from 1976 to 1993; the course was launched around 1980. This began for me a prolonged engagement with narrative theory, rather than just Victorian narratives, including two Mellon Dissertation Seminars on the topic years later, simply because the chair of English at UCSB, with staffing shortages in mind, suggested a cost-effective large lecture course combining novels and films under its rubric.

Course assignments, even when cautiously accepted, continued to lead the way. In moving to the University of Iowa in 1993, I adapted the dormant "history of criticism" slot in the graduate program to my more targeted look into textualist methodologies dear to my own practice: landmarks of close-reading from William Empson through Barthes to Barbara Johnson and beyond. And then never stopped recycling this heritage in my own writing. The effort was always to question a given method or theory at its edges—for unseen lateral application. "Yes, but": a familiar enough teaching strategy—yet in this case a move less to contest the premises of a particular theoretical superstructure than to test its applicability at the level of literary writing's own infrastructure. Also at Iowa, my work with graduate cinema students has kept me in contact with the latest media thinking as I navigated my own "course"—from auteurism through 1970s film theory to its hyphenate successor in film-philosophy—in moving beyond the filmic altogether into digital studies. At which point, at the height of computerized surveillance-state anxieties a decade ago, I developed a cross-listed course on the spy cam in literature and film, classic to contemporary: Fritz Lang through George Orwell to Tony Scott's metafilmic thriller *Déjà Vu* (2006). Once the dust settled over the attendance sheets and graded papers, there was another book right there—even as the course died in the face of (self-surveillance) selfie culture and a relaxed Instagrammatology, all nervousness about being *unwittingly* seen having lost its hold, or rather been monetized as brand and style.

Further in this curricular plot, the shift in our Iowa department over recent years to a "Literature and Creative Writing" major led me to revamp my "Prose Style" course into a Creative Readings course—and in the process (after two more books on said prose style[5]) to bear down in class assignments on contemporary American fiction. This pedagogic emphasis included Toni Morrison and Richard Powers among the unique but radically different "stylists" I found students could intuitively (and then more exactly) respond to, as I myself had begun doing in print with these same authors. In connection with Powers' epic of forest activism, *The Overstory* (2018), this interest also brought me into connection with the cohort of graduate students exploring the possibilities of "ecocriticism." Entering that conversation in view of object-oriented (nonhuman) ontology and its current critical appeal in matters of vegetal sentience and sustainability, the always tacit pedagogy of my writing sought, once again, to show that even biological systems-analysis need not reduce literature to just one network among others. Instead, the writtenness of a narrative text, when stylistically deployed in patterned wording like Powers', can serve to *interpret* natural filiation through its own "echological" grid (for cues on this, among other, neologisms, see "Terms of Use" at the book's end).

Such is the way, in annual paperwork mandated by a university bureaucracy, that the tabulation of courses taught and student populations served—on exams and thesis committees as well as in hours of classroom contact—dovetails so closely with the publications column on the same in-house CV. My point isn't simply that teaching incubates scholarship, as often happens for academic writers. For me, publication has been less a dividend from the trenches than in itself, as suggested, a kind of conscious investment in future teaching. Each essay, imagined for a later book chapter or not, has come forth as a "token" (that etymology of "teach" again) for further take-up, if only by its own thereby fortified author. Writing has typically served, in my case, as a mode of self-mentoring, filing away ideas and their hard-earned formulation for some future (if phantom) Course Reserve List—even if none of it were ever to rise to the level of "assigned reading." If I could get at least this much down, I kept telling myself, then there'd be a more secure ground to step off from next time.

Given an online dictionary still on tap in arranging this anthology (from the "anthos," the flowers, the blossoms, or at least critical fruits, thus gathered in such a mixed bunch), other lexical encouragements turned up. With no rousing curtain calls pretended, it was at least a minor charm to discover that the word *encore*, a verb in English before it became a noun, is thought by lexicographers to derive, for me arrestingly, from "Vulgar Latin." It does so by way of one of those portmanteau syllabic contractions I've often both speculated about in literature and mobilized in my own answering terminology: in this case, brought back from an earlier instance: "(in) hanc horam" ("to this hour"). And nothing so "vulgar" as an accidental homophonic pun! At times like this, in one language or another, one word may have its own "an/chor" in the next. If you read closely enough, as this bit of folk etymology goes to show, you can sometimes hear even the blank between words activated as a kind of cantilever bridge. Cross-word compression of this sort aside—and reasoning not the need, that element of popular demand we now associate with the term "*encore*"—the motive for the replayed pieces of this collection, with their modest goal of revived utility, is there in all the etymological senses of that word's more immediate French original: "still, yet, again, also, furthermore," where retention and repetition would ideally take on the sense of the additive, the compounded, the reinvested. Be that as it may (be hoped), what to *encore*? What to play over again for what gain in overview?

It seems obvious that the rearview mirror of a writing life may well reveal new features of the uneven ground long ago covered, smooth and rocky alike. But a forward motion aimed always at some kind of provisional advance has also regularly been tracked by adjustable side mirrors and their progressive vistas. These are deliberately set to reflect, both then and now, some peripheral views of the broader professional terrain—the lateral lay of the land—through which a given book plows its way and plies its claims. In my case, at least, such sidelong estimates have served to delineate one leading, student-oriented reason for keeping the pace, even driving forward a little more aggressively where possible. And in this respect, again, the anthology I'm working my way toward here cannot help but take, to some extent, the pulse of one or more disciplinary histories with which it crosses paths.

Then, too, beyond the obvious impact of molting trends and larval paradigms, there was something else I was struck by when looking back with an eye to truncated selections, sometimes only snippets. It wasn't just that the anticipated cutting and pasting recalled the earlier work of trimming (almost every book on the list was at least 25 percent longer in manuscript form, whittled back under orders by the respective presses). It was also that the further present sifting, at the conceptual level, replayed all the winnowing and weeding among the most relevant approaches and critical touchstones, the sieving and filtering, that went into the published arguments in the first place. And this too, of course, had its pedagogic dimension. For the classroom was the laboratory of such preferential decisions and the test run of critical emphases. So, this is what I bore in mind when scissoring in, for this Reader, the most typifying and ideally persuasive examples of a given methodological angle: already a secondary sorting among privately validated "best practices." That's to the good, I guess, since it will make, under the duress of compression, for some further coherence and continuity.

Many histories are thus twisted upon each other in all this. There's (inter)departmental history: not just in my early UC Santa Barbara "service courses" (what else are they ever?), but in my solidified if often marginalized role at Iowa, since then, as "tech support" for the "languages" of literature and film. Entwined with this, too, there is the background of professional and institutional history in the "state schools" and their mutated curricula to which I've devoted my classroom time. There's disciplinary history in the genealogy of critical methods in the half-century of a writing life that virtually coincides with the profession of English teaching as we know it, in so many ways depleted and besieged as I write. In such crosscurrents at macro and micro scale, where would personal history come in? At several points, but only slowly apparent to its historian. Long after dragging them at first, once I dug my heels in and committed to turning over again my pages, a nagging question still loomed, and with a certain metacritical irony at that (the longer I worried it). Given all the debates I happen to have steered graduate students through lately, under the contested influence of analytic philosopher Galen Strawson, on the literary impact of competing models for/of selfhood—"narrative" versus "episodic"—would there emerge from my auto-review anything resembling a genuine storyline? Or just a ruminated checklist of critical episodes? What would those separate spells of sustained attention known as monographs have to tell about some nexus, however loosely linked, of cause and effect in bio-graphable terms?

Deliberately tabling the question as I began looking back, still I was a bit surprised to be reminded, in eventual rereading, of how often I had indulged in pockets of autobiography as the books themselves accumulated, from early moviegoing (Hitchcock) to early literary puzzlements (Richard Wilbur, 1921–2017). Never for a moment were those books, let alone this one, intended to be "about me." Yet it was "I" writing, or at least "Professor Garrett Stewart," no denying it, so there would be some grounds for the biographical subject-formation that eventually issued in those previous book pages, reviewed in these. No resistance here to any notion of the "constructed" or the "split" subject, certainly. But this review, I decided, could only be helped by attempting to answer, where possible, the question of exactly what it was that drew "me," or say just attracted "my interest," to just what in aesthetic experience—and especially if it didn't have to be labored in any separate "memoirist" mode. Instead, selecting moments in the reviewed work where this "introspection" had already been manifested seemed the most expeditious means for putting the life back in the book-crowded bi(bli)ography.

This is where a professional *curriculum vitae* may well find its first if not truest gloss in the author's own early "vital signs" of critical curiosity. Traced there is the first lurch of a learning curve that can be advanced from one set of professional coordinates to the next, including in the long transitional regimen from taken classes to those later given. No one, I fully realize, wants to probe "the man behind" the manuscripts, still less the boyhood influences that "began it all." The point here isn't to align psychology and scholarly output, as if the former had any independent narrative interest, but instead to mark sensitivities, not to mention setbacks, in the shape of intellectual experience that have imprinted some lived incitations upon the cast of the writing—long before some unshakeable disposition has been turned, in scholarship, propositional.

Such is the belated way the past has crept back up on my writing—as will be traced now and then in excerpts ahead. In the couple of years before beginning an architecture program at the University of Southern California as a college freshman, my first high school fumbles at poetry reading in a local California bookstore make their cameo appearances, with Richard Wilbur, the hero, exactly fifty years later in the introductory stretch of 2015's *The Deed of Reading*. (That the penultimate draft of that last sentence read "fifty ears" is one of the phonetic typos, or call them phonos, that such contractually engaged reading would already have "theorized" in *Reading Voices* [1990] under the punning category of "the ear heretical"—and whose phonetic density was pursued again, from its congestion in writers such as Poe and Dickens, in that later *Deed* volume.) Triggered in modest form by my high school fascination with the cadences of Wilbur's verse, the almost visceral challenges—and enchantments—of phrasal and phonetic ambiguity became an enduring obsession.

Along another and equally visceral track on the way to my experiments in media criticism, my lifelong fuss-budget sensitivity to image quality as an avocational film buff, from fidgeting over worn celluloid prints and crude 3D effects through blue screen annoyance and the regrets of anamorphic distortion from Todd-AO[6] down past Cinerama[7] to early IMAX, and on to digital glitches on the home screen (and the conceptual artists who recirculate these[8]): this confessed personal quirk is one that surfaces—to the level, I hope, of a newly theorized image plane—only as late as 2020's *Cinemachines*. Then, too, my high school time as a movie usher and marquee assembler is rendered allegorical the same year in *Cinesthesia*. And my childhood hearing of *David Copperfield* read aloud, alternately in my mother's voice and that of a babysitter, only comes reverberantly back to me, to pertinent notice, that same year—in my second, rather than my first, Dickens book.[9]

No doubt the most formative experience of all, once I switched majors from architecture to English, was being asked to co-author a handbook of grammatical exercises with my USC mentor, Virginia Tufte (1918–2020). My remit to illustrate a wide span of tactical syntactic variety in journalist and literary writing alike (backbone of my unflagging interest in grammatical articulation and its braced spans ever since) took me, as remembered in my latest book, *Streisand: The Mirror of Difference* (2023), to the date-night prose of a Hollywood Bowl program, with its deliberate mimesis of Barbra Streisand's mercurial early microphone persona. I had been given "with the assistance of" title-page credit in *Grammar as Style*, and then was proud to appear as co-author of *Grammar as Style: Exercises in Creativity* (1971), the resulting handbook: style as in part syntax—a feature of my pedagogy ever since.[10] A pattern had been set. I was so much strictly a learner, though, as greenhorn undergraduate co-author, that I've been inclined ever since to list as my initial book publication, fruit of a further graduate education, my actual first monograph, not so much because it was single authored, as because the perpetual student in me felt he had at last a little something to teach.

No doubt, too, in glancing back to undergraduate uncertainties, my formatively torn interest between architecture and literature shows itself in more than one compensatory way. There are the structural metaphors I'm always resorting to for the weight-bearing emphasis of grammatical cadence and the coupling ligatures of its diction, as, in recent paragraphs (as I have recognized self-consciously only in rereading), with the case of "cantilever" and "bridgework" and "braced spans." Quite separately, in the distinct keys of verbal versus spatial invention, there is the imaginary feminist novel whose excerpts—and reviews—I concocted for *Novel Violence* (2009), matched later by the imaginary book art exhibit in Paris that I housed, for *Bookwork* (2011), in the fabricated architectonics of gallery space beneath the book-like four towers of the Bibliothéque Nationale.

A freshman switch in major was, of course, only one kind of new beginning. When my literary interests were more professionally channeled, their expression often chastened, during my hit-and-miss time in graduate school, I was able to spell out the debt, from within the impediments, only as late as a 2013 festschrift collection for my most influential teacher, Geoffrey Hartman (1929–2016). Earlier, it was his acceptance speech for his own eponymous *Reader*, winner of the 2006 Truman Capote Award for Literary Criticism—administered in an interdisciplinary spirit by the Iowa Writer's Workshop—that I was delighted to introduce. Among the already printed autobiographical flashbacks, it is only here now, in framing the treatment of John Keats in *Reading Voices*, that I recur to the cautionary—felt at the time as caustic—treatment I received from the red pen of my colleague, Helen Vendler, in my first job at Boston University

(1971–6). This was a rare case (detailed soon enough, see Phase II / 3) of head butting up-close and (im)personal. Usually I learned from brilliant critics, rather than doubling down in resistance.

And one of the clearest instances of such learning, and resultant pedagogical application, comes from the little-mentioned professional service of referee reading. "Relations stop nowhere," wrote Henry James. Influences neither. I've gotten the scoop on many impressive projects in this way over the years, in the scores of reports I've done for nearly every major university press in the United States and the United Kingdom, and I have therefore been primed to alert my students when the results hit print. But beyond getting this jump on the general critical catalogue, I've always counted myself uniquely lucky to have been called in, within the course of an early and shaping decade (viz., the 1980s), as the anonymous referee of three game-changing manuscripts in my field(s), in order Sandra Gilbert and Susan Gubar's *The Madwoman in the Attic* (1979), next Stanley Cavell's *Pursuits of Happiness: The Hollywood Comedy of Remarriage* (1981), then D. A. Miller's *The Novel and the Police* (1989)—with their respective and indelible contributions to feminist literary history, film-philosophy, and Foucauldian narratology. It wasn't just the empowered fun of having up my sleeve the hottest possible tips for my graduate students when the publication dates came round. These approaches changed, irreversibly, my teaching and writing, urging subsequent steady attention to gender politics, cinematic auto-allegory, and what Miller would later call, in his own crossover work on Jane Austen and Alfred Hitchcock, the slide of "too close reading" into "close writing."

This "urging," this determination, continued, for me, and long after my first book on Dickens, all the way from that imagined feminist fiction contrived for *Novel Violence* to the account of gender irony and screen reflexivity in my hypertuned (as if analytically close-miked) audition in *Streisand*. A circle is rounded out there as well. For the aurality of Dickensian prose—in his role, from his twenties on, as the first best-selling pop superstar of modern literary culture, as well as a legendary stage performer of his own written words—finds its complement in Streisand's daunting longevity, down through her teleprompted return to live performance, as among the greatest natural and sustained talents of the next century's popular entertainment.

One circle closing round, then, within a spreading center of investigations—and taking me back to my undergraduate days once more, with architecture professionally foregone for a related interest, nonetheless, in its first principals across other material forms. If "form follows function," as my early hero, Frank Lloyd Wright, learned from his mentor Louis Sullivan (though hardly adhering to the maxim in his own willfully idiosyncratic designs)—and in the kind of primal alliteration I would come to dote on when changing majors—this was a functionalization of form often tried for in the architectonics of my own monographs, an effort more and more pronounced over the years. In this vein,

I think of the mimetic shaping of my later contents pages—a museum floorplan for *Cinesthesia*, a press packet and festival brochure for *Cinemachines*, a concert "Set List" for *Streisand*—as less an imitative than an intimate form, feeling out an argument from as *close in* as possible to the enacted nature of its topic.

But enough about me, as they say. The point is that traces of this "intellectual biography," not anecdotally, but actionably, have been taken straight back to my teaching, real and virtual, in person and in print. And will be again here whenever implicitly filtering disciplinary evolution through the personal history of one restless *disciple* (Stewart never met an etymon he didn't like, a truth contained right there in *etymos*—from the Greek, meaning "true"). Punctuated by autobiographical flashbacks, a seasoned *modus operandi*—now and then referring to a temperamental *modus vivendi* as backstory—was the intended goal from the first: an inventory vectored as itinerary. (Or was it, is it ever, the critical inventor who must be itinerant—nimble in response to changing circumstances, ears attuned to messages written on the wind?) How then to optimize the published evidence for this plotline, and its parallel subplots, in excerpted form? If this book is partly about Garrett Stewart *as* reader, how to notarize the "signature" effects while marking the attempted departures? How to weigh progression in the unstable balance with digression? That was the serious work involved in a long bout of rereading. With twenty books to choose from, variety was no challenge, in fact was its own kind of problem. But what I really wanted was to maximize the different *styles* of reading, rather than just topics, to which the latter prompted me, now rigorously theoretical and cross-referenced, now loosely exploratory and at times unconventional. In the process, the balance to be struck between "representative" treatments and the broader spectrum of experiments remained for a good while unsettled. Still is, I suppose. Because for me the "typical" interpretive gesture was always a kind of stretch, whether chapter by chapter or in freestanding essays that never found themselves tethered into a monograph.

Not at the planning stages, but only in reviewing and compressing the excerpts in the last phase of arranging this book's composite, did a further potential bonus occur to me in regard to their rapid-fire alternation. Much from one study to the next had always been left to speak for itself about their alternating topics. Moreover, it would have been dreaming to suppose that readers taking an interest in the phonetics of Victorian fiction would have necessarily turned to me on digital special effects in cinema, or that readers in either line would move on to my genre claims for the painted reading scene or the textually demediated book sculpture, still less that any of this would naturally call out to the notice of those interested in what I was finding in the dovetailed media platforms of contemporary Conceptual art. Hard or paper, book covers are partitions that tend to compartmentalize. It was not until the penultimate monograph covered here, in fact, *The Metanarrative Hall of Mirrors* (2022), with its subtitle *Reflex Action in Fiction and Film*, that I had tried to formulate at some length the cross-media hermeneutic—rather than just concentrating on various media artifacts—that has for so long preoccupied me. But since then I have come to feel, to hope, that the reader of this later and present book might end up (and here I'm backdating your cinematic trope for the reframings of this volume to the prefilmic era) like something of a flip-book or zoetrope operator, speeding through and between separate positions (and position papers) at so fast a pace that the mere mechanics of the series would induce the transfusion (not just illusion) of continuity: a seemingly organic movement across stages of a common immersive methodology. It is of course only my current readers who can tell, at the switchback tempo of your own attention spans, whether this imagined dividend actually pays out.

In all this, any residue of the personal in the professional was, as I've said, taken directly into the classroom—and often in the form of a transferential identification with students trying to feel their own way across an enjambed (literary) line break or a (cinematic) shot sequence. In this respect, one last autobiographical point seems as emblematic as any. At Yale, my apprenticeship in Dickens studies was, in any interpersonal terms, that of an autodidact. I was out of sympathy, and certainly of sync, with the way Victorian literature, and especially prose fiction, was taught by senior professors there: in strictly literary-historical terms, part of the ethical register of a very "long eighteenth century." I found myself working instead under the free rein of a medievalist specializing in the history of language, a poet with a popular course on literary style, the revered Marie Borroff (1923–2019), who gave me all the leeway I wanted—and then some. It was from Steven Marcus (1928–2018), miles away at Columbia, with his magisterial book on the first half of Dickens' career, *Dickens: From Pickwick to Dombey* (1965), and from other essayists earlier (Dorothy Van Ghent, Julian Moynahan), hailing from departments farther afield yet, that I took my remote tutelage, as I continued to think of critical writing from then on.

Readers of the present volume are therefore invited to take it (in both senses)—if only auditing intermittently—as an extension-course version of a career-long seminar, the books it samples lined up as summary reports from the thick of earlier curricular iterations. As in the always-improvisatory classroom, so in this compendium. One never stops trying to get things right, if only by finding new things to confirm them. The results are always more a reboot than a *summa*—and here, certainly, with no false promises or chimerical prospects entailed. The point of this anthology could scarcely be, in some wholesale way, to redirect current preferences with the momentum of reprint. All that could be hoped is to ballast the range of possibility with the weight of accumulated experiment. Digging in is always beginning again, so here goes.

Notes

1. See Garrett Stewart, "War Pictures: Digital Surveillance from Foreign Theater to Homeland Security Front," in *The Philosophy of War Films*, ed. David LaRocca (Lexington: University Press of Kentucky, 2014), 107–32; "'Assertions in Techniques': Tracking the Medial 'Thread' in Cavell's Filmic Ontology," in *The Thought of Stanley Cavell and Cinema: Turning Anew to the Ontology of Film a Half-Century after* The World Viewed, ed. David LaRocca (New York: Bloomsbury, 2020), 23–40; and "A Metacinematic Spectrum: Technique through Text to Context," in *Metacinema: The Form and Content of Filmic Reference and Reflexivity*, ed. David LaRocca (Oxford: Oxford University Press, 2021), 63–84.
2. Roland Barthes, *The Pleasure of the Text* (Paris: Editions du Seuil, 1973).
3. Roland Barthes, *S/Z* (Paris: Editions du Seuil, 1970).
4. Tzvetan Todorov, "The Grammar of Narrative," in *The Poetics of Prose*, trans. Richard Howard, 108–19 (Ithaca: Cornell University Press, 1977), originally published as "La grammaire du récit," in *Poétique de la prose* (Paris: Editions du Seuil, 1971); Peter Brooks, *Reading for the Plot* (New York: Alfred A. Knopf, 1984).
5. Namely, *The Value of Style in Prose Fiction* (2018) and *The One, Other, and Only Dickens* (2018).
6. Todd-AO, founded by Mike Todd and Robert Naify in 1953, gave its name to the widescreen, 70mm film format Todd and Naify developed at mid-century for United Artist Theaters in partnership with the American Optical Company.
7. Cinerama is a widescreen technology developed in the 1950s that simultaneously projected three synchronized 35mm projectors onto a single screen, subtending a 146-degree field of view.
8. Stewart's own interest gravitates to the evolution of this mode from the early photogram studies in the work of French artist Éric Rondepierre (b. 1950).
9. Garrett Stewart, *The One, Other, and Only Dickens* (2018).
10. At age eighty-eight, Tufte published a successor volume, *Artful Sentences: Syntax as Style* (Cheshire, CT: Graphics Press, 2006).

TEXTCERPTS

Garrett Stewart

FILE UNDER: Process of selection; or selections from a process. When I began combing through the print record for "representative" passages, I didn't know at first exactly what I'd find in hindsight, find extractable. But, as already stressed, I knew going in—going back—that I didn't want to leave the excerpted commentary stranded to speak for itself, unglossed by summary or retrospect: just mere snapshots of applied critical instinct, matured (or not) over time. Because such writing never did speak only for itself. Whatever its local claims or speculations, it was always part not just of a larger argument, book by book, but of an ongoing penchant across the volumes. Despite my cross-title tendencies, with their underlying links between projects, I often had little print space to dwell upon them from one project to the next—even if such continuities were always clear to their author. So, I'm playing catch-up with myself in this album of clippings. That's what the introductory glosses are here for: to educe linkages and allegiances not just between books but also with (or athwart) the developing "turns" of critical orientation over these same decades. Allegiances, yes, but resistances as well, not always rising to the clarity of a polemic at the time. But I think unmistakable. Never meaning to thwart dialogue, I worked instead in the hopes of provoking various camps of literary study into speaking the same language: textual language in its status as wording per se. And with an equivalent emphasis on medium in the other arts I more and more often wrote about.

"Representative" passages: typifying a method, or at least a disposition, a preference. What really to call it? An inclination—a leaning in—toward a reading that may often feel too close for comfort, too tightly focused to leave the given artifact under examination fully intact. So there is inevitably more *reading* to excerpt than so-called *readings* plural. With quite truncated selections at times, the plan is to make room, in the resulting variety, to touch down on a sufficient number of (material) bases—phonetic, plastic, digital, vocal—in the shifting media spectrum, and its discernible *textual* field, that has increasingly intrigued me. And now and then to venture some speculation on the autobiographical sources of that fascination. Truth to tell, such moments going back to earlier "scenes of reading" (my own rather than those of fictional protagonists in Victorian fiction, the subject of my fourth book) never stopped taking me by mild surprise in review. I had largely forgotten my "confessional" streak. But I found these introspections often worth bringing back here for orientation in the long paper trail this book retraces.

Still, the larger task remained. When thinking what best to use in exemplifying just what, I ended up not so much cherry picking as detecting whole new branches, even root systems, that I was hardly aware of at the time. I grew newly alert to certain curious chain reactions in the smallest scales of focus—with attention ranging from ambiguous grammar, lexical puns, and entwined figures of speech through overlapping syllabic ironies to the not unrelated elisions of filmstrip increments, then on from canvas brush strokes to pixel glitches to sculptural accretions in book assemblages, then back to stylistic microplots in prose and on down to modulated song lyrics in the screen musical. Hence the "sampling" prerogative of this collection. No reason to excerpt whole chapters, since, out of context, they'd neither reflect a book's fuller claim nor serve economically to detect (and usefully distill) the pressure points of its approach—including its oblique continuities with those on either side of it.

All the more reason to feel freed, in reviewing these bound volumes, in not being bound by their own chapter divisions and sequences. Though once cemented in print, extracts here didn't need to be quarried *en bloc*. Taking them (back) to pieces, from whose local perceptions their own arguments were originally built up in the reading act, offers a more accurate gauge of the original engagement—and a more revealing way to reread, not my pages, but those literary (and critical) pages on which my attention was in both senses *trained*. And then eventually a better way to "read" the other rectangles—of screen, canvas, or denatured book surface—that came under discussion as legible text. So, after that last instance right there, I drop the scare quotes around the idea of *reading* from here out. They disappear like those around *text* when a movie or a painting or a song number is understood as pointedly *legible* under the lens of analysis.

As backward glances go, this double-take—with a chance to take up familiar material anew—may sound too neutrally presented. I should add, then, an admission of behind-the-scenes drama: the attempted sampling hasn't always come easy. I found myself revisiting my early books on Victorian fiction with a certain wince at their then-unembarrassed appreciative cast, especially the inaugural Dickens book. With no method but enthusiasm for the excitement of inventive language, my delight in the verbal form of fiction was entirely roving and unformalized there, veering by turns between psychological and stylistic registers—with neither established priorities nor an articulated system of connection. With only, instead, a mostly tacit confidence in language as thematic leverage. Since I peer from a half-century out, though, I take heart—compensation against chagrin—that the early exuberances were necessary for the long and diverse interpretive haul I have made across the decades.

My "approach," whatever it was then, needed work, not just more play. But I do see now, as I must have faintly sensed at the time (but could neither discern nor admit), that what might, and ultimately did, keep me going, studying, rethinking, found its anchor in my once giddy fixation on the fine print of style and the italics by which I could elicit its kinetic energy. That's certainly what later kept me in contact, and sometimes heated conversation, with the mindset of structuralist narratology and the onset of deconstruction: an itch on my part for some metalinguistics of narrative that would get beyond the *ad hoc* notice of thematized form. And, later yet, kept my thinking in active dialogue with media theory, as well as in debate with film phenomenology and its enworlding paradigms—this, when my work, still my *reading*, began its lateral move into the textu(r)al underlay and optic on-screen weave of celluloid, then digital, cinema.

Unlike the greatest hits mode of many scholarly Readers, this isn't the kind of sourcebook digest that offers up a set of duplicates: unadulterated excisions from the first printings, made for quick citation in lieu of "checking out" the original publications. Here, to hone a more efficient uptake of themes, texts, and styles, I've cleared away most of the initial apparatus, thereby smoothing the flow of the discourse by deleting line, page, chapter, and volume references as well as all but the most crucial endnotes. The segments are thus offered up not for working with individually, but for *working through historically*, grouped for family resemblances in Phases I to IX; for those inclined to count book covers as legitimate associates to the long-term project, please add Phase X. Such a "clearing away" only stresses further and again that a narrative educed from this sequence of book excerpts is very different from the localized one each book originally set out to recount, argument by sustained argument. By taking their place instead in *the writing journal of a teaching career*—and by a participant witness to several generations of institutional trends—these newly shaped extracts speak in the other sense to a kind of lineage of critical (rather than genetic) extraction, if hardly a pedigree.

And that's what the current Table of Contents is all about, linking projects not in temporally situated serial progression but rather in a rhythm of varied departures and subterranean pairings as well as in many a spurred return—all best estimated in retrospect. (And with the editor's headnotes offering more straightforward summaries of the volumes as they couple with, congregate, or split from each other, in this first case below stressing the prominence of Dickens in my first two books.) *Attention Spans*—inviting from the reader, by title, something like the variable concentrations on the author's own part that it tabulates—presents a decidedly unfamiliar format (hence the telling shift from the customary product *A Stewart Reader* to the appositional *Stewart, A Reader*). A second look, not just retrospective but sometimes corrective, operates so that new glosses penetrate the extracts, *text excerpts* (hence TexTcerpts), in a mode of almost gestalt oscillation. Things foregrounded need new backgrounding, which then freshly constitutes the elucidating frame in which they are inset. It is as if you're reading over my own shoulder as I move along, thinking aloud, bookma(r)king myself, boxing off passages of an isolated argument worth keeping special track of. The paratextual markers that book studies would normally recognize as marginalia—brackets or checks or asterisks—have come front and center as the new work itself (tome and labor both): a task of self-glossing that naturally can't entirely inoculate itself (apologies in advance) against autofiction in scissoring together this scrapbook, however intentionally candid, of a print career.

I.

DICKENS AS PROMPT TEXT

1 / Deploying "trials" in the double sense of labors and tests, ***Dickens and the Trials of Imagination*** (Harvard University Press, 1974), traces the delegation of Dickensian creativity to certain redemptive pockets of characterization as well as to its perverse misuse in other episodes. After an analysis of bifurcated energy in Dickens' debut novel, *Pickwick Papers*—split between Dickens' high-octane verbal ingenuity, as channeled by Sam Weller, and the feverish ravings "quarantined" in the interpolated tales—Stewart canvases a full range of imaginative affect from the wry comic phraseology of Weller's inheritor Dick Swiveller in *The Old Curiosity Shop* through Micawber's inflated rhetorical vaunts—and vents—in *David Copperfield* to the alternate acerbic irony and intermittent transcendental metaphors of Jenny Wren in the last completed novel, *Our Mutual Friend*. Alongside this compensatory verbalism, Stewart examines the prototypical scene of fire-gazing in which certain "escape artists," not this time in words but in flickering images, warm themselves by projecting alternative "pleasant fictions" to alleviate the weight of their days. In words and invented scenography alike, authorial energy reflects on its own powers by redistribution.

1 / Trials—and Test Sites

Dickens and the Trials of Imagination (1974)

I "CAME OF AGE" AS A READER—long after listening mesmerized to *David Copperfield* read to me aloud as a young boy—in a graduate department prominent for its scholars of poetry rather than prose, at least until the appointment of J. Hillis Miller (1928–2021), just after I left Yale, doctorate in hand, in 1971. A lucky stroke—since he was then fair game as a reader for my manuscript when it was submitted for press review. The pedagogy of referee response had begun, with me so far on the receiving end. More broadly, of course, narrative phenomenology loomed in Miller's Yale recruitment. And its deconstruction was just around the corner. But having been loosely schooled, well before Yale, on a vestigial New Critical method whose closure in the study of more or less short poems was not easily translated to the novel, I had no strong models to build on at the time in writing about Dickens. Too soon for the true Yale School influence, however, another literary watershed did have its impact. Classes behind me, the dissertation looming, I had in 1970 committed to a popular Victorian narrative entertainer in the very year that William H. Gass' influential coinage "metafiction" began making the rounds. If more or less consciously, I had soon solidified two goals in my approach to Dickens. First, to demonstrate as much pertinent verbal density in this "late-Romantic" author as one of my teachers, Geoffrey Hartman (1929–2016), was bestowing on Wordsworth and Keats and Shelley. Second, to venture my sense of a metafictional dimension in Dickens' writing—less ontologically showy, to be sure, than the late-1960s pathbreakers of the next century—but more purposeful and suffused than Dickens had usually been given credit for. *Pace* Miller, in short, the books were for me less built worlds than triumphs of wording's intricate building blocks.

Dickens and the Trials of Imagination: I must, by that title, have been half thinking of my own ordeals, and their throes of uncertainty, in finding my way through the deluge of Boz's verbal ingenuity.[1] Not to mention the blast of new high-profile Victorianist scholarship the same year I began writing, the anniversary of his death. But it was ultimately the contemporary culture of "metafiction" whose postmodernism gave me purchase on the great Victorian, though mostly laddered down to the reflexivity of his own phrasing. That's part of what I deliberately meant by the double sense of "trials" in my title: endurances for the characters whose fancies were often crushed by social fact, even while tests for the prose in conjuring their attempted imaginative facility as "escape artists." And not least when Dickens could sometimes be overheard delegating to these characters a modicum of his own stylistic genius in restorative doses of verbal energy. More obvious to me now—in looking back on a study that put fire-gazing fantasies and near-death fever scenes on something of the same stylistic spectrum—my demonstrations were bookended by two very different characters. Two divergent but equally expressive mentalities—and a resulting verbal attention that gravitated, in and around their contrast, to the paired dominant poles of Dickensian rhetoric: fantasy and melodrama, satire and sentimentality. The names of these eccentric standard-bearers: the tippling demotic fantasist Dick Swiveller (*nomen est omen* for irresolute energy) in Dickens' early novel, *The Old Curiosity Shop* (1840–1), and, in his last finished work, *Our Mutual Friend* (1864–5), the self-named visionary seamstress Jenny Wren (née—nay!—Fanny Cleaver). It was her literal flight of fancy in assonant self-rechristening that I had the youthful effrontery to call her *nom de plumage* (beginning, in a thesis chapter that became my first published article, a career-long lowering of resistance to the risks of wordplay in scholarly discourse).

In assessing at the outset the sympathetic vibrations between the narrator's verbal irony and that of his character (with Dick a marked chip off the Dickens block), my study begins with a prologue called "The Parable the Rosy Wine"—and with Dickens' double trope of hearthside emotional droop and ornithological restoration triggered by "literary" allusion when we first see the irrepressible young Swiveller at home in the seventh chapter: "'Fred,' said Mr. Swiveller, 'remember the once popular melody of Begone dull care; fan the sinking flame of hilarity with the wing of friendship; and pass the rosy wine.'" Description then zooms out to set the residential scene for this inebriate benediction, with prose commentary on hand—redoubled by my own:

> The prose declares its authorship at once. It is in general too finished while at the same time too brisk and effortless, the syntax too ornate yet somehow unforced, offhand, never labored, the diction too heavily ornamental yet all the while too crisp, the tone too facetious though never smug or even flippant, indeed almost delicate in its own histrionic way—all of it too gaily majestic, too self-conscious, too much to be the work of any one but our greatest writer of comic prose:
>
>> Richard Swiveller's apartments were in the neighbourhood of Drury Lane, and in addition to this conveniency of situation had the advantage of being over a tobacconist's shop, so that he was enabled to procure a refreshing sneeze at any time by merely stepping out on the staircase, and was saved the trouble and expense of maintaining a snuffbox. It was in these apartments that Mr. Swiveller made use of the expressions above recorded, for the consolation and encouragement of his desponding friend; and it may not be interesting or improper to remark that even these brief observations partook in a double sense of the figurative and poetical character of Mr. Swiveller's mind. [...]

I see now that, in my interpretive treatment, I was trying to bring my reader into the scene, and into the stylistic texture of Dickensian prose, with longer block quotations than I would ever allow myself later. Unguarded in them was an unabashed fan's approach to Dickens' rolling sonorities, along with his spry wit, that was, on my part, not just stylistically late-Romanticist in its analytic parameters but downright romantic—for all their purported rhetorical analysis:

> The hefty, periphrastic, deliberately inconvenient wording, "conveniency of situation," the linguistic incongruity and anticlimax of the expressions "enabled to procure a refreshing sneeze" and "maintaining a snuffbox," the obligatory twinning of phrase in "trouble and expense," "consolation and encouragement," "uninteresting

or improper," "figurative and poetical"—these are all tags of the Dickensian comic rhetoric, that satiric inflation I will be taking up in some detail with the initial chapter on *Pickwick Papers*. It would seem at first glance as if those conspicuous pairings just mentioned have been carefully pared down to an emphatic redundancy for their last appearance in the phrase "figurative and poetical character of Mr. Swiveller's mind." I suspect, however, that Dickens is quietly preserving there, and in fact spelling out, the distinction implied in "double sense." Because Dick says "pass the rosy wine!" knowing full well that it is only gin, he is speaking metaphorically, "figuratively," as it were; and because he is willing by his very nature to believe in the gin as "rosy wine," he is, in that second sense, dealing "poetically" with his environment, revising the prosaic facts of his inhospitable world. [...]

It's almost touching to see my candor at this stage. I would seldom say "I suspect" again, learning to displace my discourse—as I would of course teach students to do—into the sophistication of textual suggestion rather than critical guesswork. And let me return to the elliptical first citation to pick up the thread, in the elaboration of "the character of Mr. Swiveller's mind," with further stress on the transformative *mind of the character*—making all but literal space for itself in more than architecturally cramped circumstances. Its own brand of allegory, then: with no books at hand, we are comically to find, Dick becomes his own fictionist. In illustration at the time, another block quotation:

> By a like pleasant fiction his single chamber was always mentioned in the plural number. In its disengaged times, the tobacconist had announced it in his window as "apartments" for a single gentleman, and Mr. Swiveller, following up the hint, never failed to speak of it as his rooms, his lodgings, or his chambers: conveying to his hearers a notion of indefinite space, and leaving their imaginations to wander through long suites of lofty halls, at pleasure.

The next paragraph extends and enriches the parable. The "flight of fancy" elaborated upon here is again the plurality of Dick's apartments:

> In this flight of fancy, Mr. Swiveller was assisted by a deceptive piece of furniture, in reality a bedstead, but in semblance a bookcase, which occupied a prominent situation in his chamber and seemed to defy suspicion and challenge inquiry. There is no doubt that, by day, Mr. Swiveller firmly believed this secret convenience to be a bookcase and nothing more; that he closed his eyes to the bed, resolutely denied the existence of the blankets, and spurned the bolster from his thoughts. No word of its real use, no hint of

its nightly service, no allusion to its peculiar properties, had ever passed between him and his most intimate friends. Implicit faith in the deception was the first article of his creed. To be the friend of Swiveller you must reject all circumstantial evidence, all reason, observation, and experience, and repose a blind belief in the bookcase. It was his pet weakness, and he cherished it.

The "deceptive" is here no lie, but a salutary fiction, part of that effort of mind by which Dick's single room is multiplied into "chambers," his imagination thereby more generously and spaciously quartered. [...]

If I admitted too modestly a mere suspicion above, I wish I had suspected more in the discussion to follow about that penultimate cited sentence—or had been willing to say it:

With the transmutation of bedstead into bookcase, that "first article" of Dick's fanciful "creed," practical "reality" again gives willing way to poetic "semblance." Dickens has found here an uncannily neat symbol for the functional reciprocity of the real and the ideal. The seeming bookcase pulls down at night into a bed; the actual lies just on the other side of the imagined, perfectly hinged for the daily changeover from one to the other. In the description of Dick's waking denial of the bed, Dickens' own "figurative" language informs us at unusual depth about the full "poetical" significance of this bookcase/bedstead. For the metaphor "closed his eyes to the bed" hints at a dreaming-away of the domestic appliance designed in part for dreaming. And what replaces it is that item of household furniture devoted in its turn to transcribed daydreams and recorded fancies. These convertible symbols are astonishingly good, the imaginary bookcase as well as the ignored bed. Like the majority of the fanciful men in Dickens' novels, we do not see Mr. Swiveller as a conscious student of imaginative literature. His poetry has come miscellaneously, through a popular oral tradition of sprightly formulas, aphorisms, epithets, ballad lyrics, elegant clichés, high-sounding phrases of all sorts. What Dick has from books he probably has indirectly, and all of his poetry he carries in his head. It is only and wonderfully right that the books in his room should be all in his mind as well.

The expansiveness and profusion of phrase, with concision flouted in sentences terraced crazily with surplus detail, the constant foraging after metaphor, all the tireless flights and flourishes of Dickens' prose become occasions for a symbolic economy unknown to more chiseled and lapidary, less broadly spontaneous styles. With the scene in Dick's room, the glib effusions of Dickens' style become also a kind of prose empathy with his voluble character. [...]

A "prose empathy" so deep that its "figurative and poetic character" knew no bounds. In sensing the whiff of dream in the notion of eyes closed to the bedstead—amid this incumbent sleep of reason owed in deference by Dick's friends—how did I miss its complement: the further play on illusion's waking dream ("repose a blind belief") in regard to bedstead denial? Did I hear a play on "repose" without the courage of my conviction, afraid to risk this slippery slope of free association without the license, later formulated by Christopher Ricks, of the "anti-pun": the spectral energy (from his *The Force of Poetry*) of a diction not fully assimilable to immediate sense? Whether chalking it up to a momentary tin ear or to sheer disciplinary timidity, I don't at all mind copping to either in this present reparation for my lapse. One keeps learning criticism, as well as literature, from criticism.

I certainly didn't bear this scene consciously in mind when, eight monographs later, I turned to faux books and bookcases in conceptual sculpture, *trompe l'oeil* included, for *Bookwork* (2011). But the tendency to find Gass-like "metafictional" allegories triggered by style certainly persisted in my narrative work, in fiction and film alike, down through the specified medial convergence of this reflexivity in 2022's *The Metanarrative Hall of Mirrors: Reflex Action in Fiction and Film*. In its original context, however, "The Parable of the Rosy Wine"—the privileged beverage denoting in fact gin's transubstantiation into vintage—might just as well have been called "The Parable of Invisible Books," with reading matter immanent by popular citational intertext (romantic effusions and the lyrics of drinking songs) in the very depiction of its absence. Along with any such methodological seedbed for further emblematic readings, there's no question that Dick's polar opposite among that first book's imaginists, the death-haunted Jenny Wren, led me rather directly to my next monograph, *Death Sentences* (1984).

As Dick's opposite number, Jenny is an "escape artist" in a higher key, yet whose workaday craft as a doll's dressmaker can never approximate the images flashed upon her in her more than aesthetic visions. Her circumstances are even drearier and more constrained than Dick's. No whiff of tobacco in updraft on the staircase is sufficient to sedate her deprivation, nor would she resort to the alcohol she's watched reduce her father to a belligerent and sniveling child. She must instead escape to the rooftop, above the ashen haze of the city, to feel free—as at other times into the dream of angelic visitations disburdening her crippled back and legs and making her labors easier.

> Jenny soon explains her latest "pleasant fancy" on the roof—how, above the closeness and clamor of the city, "you see the clouds rushing on above the narrow streets, not minding them, and you see the golden arrows pointing at the mountains in the sky from which the wind comes, and you feel as if you were dead." Grammar and definition in the participial phrase "not minding them" are

beautifully loosened, as if set free—the normal tethers of reference, both lexical and syntactic, here disengaged. The verb "minding" registers as both "mindful of" and "troubled by," and complicated by the ambiguity of its referent, makes for an unusual trivalent syntax. What or who is "not minding" what? The clouds pay no attention to the streets; neither, therefore, are they troubled by them. And the darkened streets, of course, pay heaven no mind. "You" too are with the clouds, neither worrying over nor even noticing the despoiled place you have climbed free of. When she is asked by Fledgeby how it feels "when you are dead," this is Jenny's reply: "'Oh, so tranquil!' cried the little creature, smiling. 'Oh, so peaceful and so thankful!'" The adjective "thankful" answers in near echo to "tranquil" (as restated by "peaceful") in the way that Jenny's profound sense of gratitude follows upon her achieved and private sanctity, a condition of the spirit which she goes on to explain in a serene conjunctive series: "And you hear the people who are alive, crying, and working, and calling to one another down in the close dark streets, and you seem to pity them so! And such a chain has fallen from you, and such a strange good sorrowful happiness comes upon you!" Our interest, in the last clause, is drawn by an incremental rhythm through the unpunctuated chain of pre-nominal adjectives to the "strange good" paradox at its end, that "sorrowful happiness" which marks Jenny's attempt to wrest elation from the slavish levelings of melancholy. We have recently seen how the doubled adjectives in "small sweet voice" and "mournful little song" helped imply the quiet parallel Dickens had in mind, and here again his habit of multiplied adjectives is turned to special account. As always in his style, Dickens refuses to rest easy in the habitual, pressing it constantly for new yields. As we are about to see, this pre-nominal loading of modifiers can easily be impressed into imitative service.

To pick up the text where I left off, it is important to realize that the "sorrowful happiness" which Jenny recommends when "you feel as if you were dead," this crucial phase of her escape artistry, is in fact subjunctive, an "as if" hypothesis. This has nothing in common with Little Nell's actual death-wishes in *The Old Curiosity Shop*. Like any romantic, Jenny simply dreams of a finer time, remembered or foreseen. Once again, though, her dreaming seems to approach achievement, for she herself appears to Riah like a vision: "the face of the little creature looking down out of a Glory of her long bright radiant hair, and musically repeating to him, like a vision: 'Come up and be dead! Come up and be dead!'" Here the mimetically elongated phrase "long bright radiant hair," describing what is often her bower, here her Glory, seems to echo—to be "musically repeating"—the adjectival cadence of her divine children's "long bright slanting rows," just as Jenny herself approximates in her own person at such moments, "like a vision," the best she has imagined. [...]

These are the beatific figures of her "fancy"—equivalent to Dick's more obviously metanarrational "pleasant fictions"—that come unbidden and help her bear up, as if operating, through the synesthesia quoted above, in one long luminescent dodge of a cliché like "lighten her burden." So, lodge here another of this encore's many local regrets. Unlike the idea of "reposing" in a benign lie about sleeping arrangements rather than in the hidden bed itself, if I had thought of this later tacit phrase at the time—this lurking idiom (the formulaic "lighten") in the pivotal play on the adjective/noun "light"—surely, I would have said it. I take it to be something that only years since of classroom grappling with the suppressed "matrix" (the peripheral and impinging cliché or truism) in Michael Riffaterre's semiotics (another print mentor along with Ricks) would have spurred me more surely to notice. In working otherwise at the time to secure the oscillating tenor of Jenny Wren's phrasing as part of a compelling verbal motif in the novel, I soon extended this discussion—centered as it is mainly on the verbal cast of her metaphysical escapism—to note the way her forlorn refrain "Come up and be dead!" finds resonance and reversal in the actual death scenes of the novel, especially the final "Come down" of a murder/suicide by drowning.

> 2 / **Death Sentences: Styles of Dying in British Fiction** (Harvard University Press, 1984) is launched from the assumption that the death moment in fiction is always its own "trial" of figuration (versus impossible report). With an introduction named for both the character exit mounted by such scenes and the structuring assumptions from which Stewart's own analysis sets out, "Points of Departure" establishes the abiding facets of death's end-stopped scenario. In its threefold role, the death moment is repeatedly staged as shifting from literal description to trope, thus figuratively summing a life, and often in the process relocating the dying affect in a surviving consciousness, whether mourner or alter ego—in Stewart's triadic terms: transposition, epitome, and displacement. Victorian death scenes inherited by Dickens' narrative legatees—from the Brontës through Elizabeth Gaskell and W. M. Thackeray down through George Eliot and on to Thomas Hardy—come to light, under investigation, as less straightforwardly sentimental or formulaic than usually assumed, more braced by irony and bracketed for structural resonance. Such is the tradition of narrative foreclosure that *Death Sentences* then follows out from the early modernist E. M. Forster through D. H. Lawrence and Virginia Woolf to the involuted and self-referential forms of mortality in the metatexts of Samuel Beckett and Vladimir Nabokov.

2 / *Death Sentencing and Narrative* Parole

Death Sentences: Styles of Dying in British Fiction (1984)

THAT LAST PLAY ON THE FRENCH WORD for "word" was a pun I didn't make at the time. Yet *parole* does certainly suit the emotional release that is verbally compressed into the narrative speech acts as well as faltering dialogue of so many Victorian death scenes. In this more ambitious second monograph, the plan was to place Dickens—definitive prompt text again—within a longer narrative tradition of mortality's symbolic leave-taking that his showstopping passages, at least for later Victorians, had in large part inspired. The unhedged critical enthusiast of the first book was reaching this time, if fitfully, for a more sober anatomy rather than just an appreciation. I was also moving from the proverbial single-author study to an account of over a dozen major exemplars in an effort to conjure the genealogy of fictional dying in its function as a quintessential narrative challenge. Beginning with nearly two dozen instances in Dickens' own novels (fruits of my earliest undergraduate courses in Dickens, later grafted onto more strenuous graduate seminars), I then tracked the literary-historical descent of this *topos* to narratively pivotal death scenes in Victorian writers George Eliot and Thomas Hardy, among others, then on through E. M. Forster to the modernist Virginia Woolf and such later ironists of mortal erasure as Samuel Beckett and Vladimir Nabokov.

How so, "quintessential," the fictiveness of the death episode? Following is the book's threefold premise—confirmed by repeated evidence—that, in death, verbal reference (mimetic depiction) must yield to sheer figuration. In this sense, even outside of any larger narrative context, every death scene is, in its internal engineering, "pivotal."

> Because of death's essentially amorphous nature, however, its actual moment must take form in fiction in multiple relation to other narrative content. I shall label as *transposition* fiction's inherent need to account for death in idioms and metaphors drawn from life. When such an act of figural transference also serves to condense the particular identity whose individual terms it is so transposing, a character's psychology is then being summed up by the mechanism of abridgement or *epitome*, a special case of transposition. From this may ensue the dramatic and sometimes explicitly textual process of *displacement*, whereby identity epitomized by death can be deputized to an alter ego within the text or deflected by cathartic recognition onto a reader outside the perimeters of representation. The drama of death attended by a double can thus in itself enact the drama of reading about death when understood as a mortal encounter outlived and assimilated.

If, in my first book on Dickens, death as motif was signaled in *Our Mutual Friend* by some tacit coming-or-going motif (up or down), I would have certainly felt its bearing on the broader scope of the next book. What at the time I wouldn't have known is how the last metanarrative sentence above, about reading's own survival of the mortal scene, would have buried a seed finding fuller fruition a decade later in *Dear Reader* (1996). This is the case even though my original title for my second book, *Death Bequeathed* (with "Death Sentences" only featured as a title for the introduction), had lain stress on this sense of cognitive transference as well as literary legacy.

In any case, as I found this Victorian pattern of tripartite mortal operation recurring under transformation through and beyond high modernism, where death summed one life while being displaced onto another, I also found my work converging with that of Peter Brooks in his influential *Reading for the Plot*, published in 1986 just as I was finishing a draft of my manuscript. His psychopoetic version of narratology was drawn, like my historicized stylistics, to the privilege of deathbed retrospect in Walter Benjamin's "The Storyteller" (1936).[2] But, given the different scales of our analysis, what I include below is meant to sample the main stress in *Death Sentences* on the figurative and grammatical maneuvers of the death moment: their border equivocations, their linguistic slippage and transfiguration. I give first a stunning idiomatic crisscross at Cathy's midpoint death in Emily Brontë's *Wuthering Heights* (1847), followed in a later novel by the "homophonic pun"—anything but comic—that rarefies one of the many deaths by water, as well as metaphoric drownings, in the novels I examine, in this case at the climax of George Eliot's *The Mill on the Floss* (1860).

> The most famous paired deaths of the period in an unequivocally sexual context, each virtually suicidal and linked across plot by a tortuously sundered *Liebestod*, belong of course to the lovers in Emily Brontë's *Wuthering Heights*. Her heroine, Cathy, whose notorious "I am Heathcliff" is a ceding of identity to erotic fusion—a madness of primal abdication—thus dies by epitome "of what was denominated a brain fever" in childbirth, leaving behind the daughter of Edgar Linton. Death as quintessence, the familiar Victorian pattern, is reduced a chapter after Cathy's death to pure formula in the local doctor's words about the end of her brother, Hindley Earnshaw, who "died true to his character, drunk as a lord." Similarly, both essence and cessation of the self, the death of Cathy comes exactly midway in the novel's roster of fatalities—those of her parents, her brother's wife, and Mr. and Mrs. Linton before her, of Hindley first, then Isabella, Edgar, Linton, and finally Heathcliff after her—and so motivates the transition between the two generational phases of the novel. Cathy's death is at first described in Nelly Dean's running discourse to Lockwood with an unwitting hint, muffled by idiom, of reversion and epitome. The excess of Cathy's passion, we realize, has always been the prophecy of its own effacement. The language of being that would annex identity—I *am* the other—instead predicts its cancellation at the outset. Without momentous last words or any symbolic projection of dying, psychology, still Nelly's style is surprisingly tapped in rendering the interval of Cathy's death; the idiom of temporality broken open into the grace of a negative revelation, of release and appeasement in an escape not only from but back to. Following upon Heathcliff's forced visit and the delivery of Cathy's child, two hours later "the mother died having never recovered sufficient consciousness to miss Heathcliff or know Edgar." A circumscribed temporal sequence of a few hours' delirium seems under discussion, when in fact the prose hints at a recouping if never recuperative delusion that carries Cathy back to an unfettered passion before, by her own cowardice in part, she had been made to "miss" Heathcliff in her life, or to "know" Edgar's misbegotten place in it. Ordinary idiom has been opened by death's stylistic pressure to what we can only call a visionary amnesia, a lapse into reparation. [...]

So yet another second thought. How fine it would have been—hardly putting too fine a point upon it—to have lifted into a metalinguistic generalization at this (in the other sense) epitomizing textual moment. I might have done so, wish I had, by noting that, across this meliorating psychic chiasm, mortal extremity is a force that can turn vernacular perspective—the very language of the everyday—inside out. In any case, the idiomatic verbal hinge of this moment does find, later in the printed chapter, first a phonemic, then a grammatical, equivalent in another typifying instance of paired mortality, this time simultaneous, in George Eliot:

> In *The Mill on the Floss*, Eliot renders the deaths of Tom and Maggie Tulliver not only successive in the text but simultaneous in order to turn the one death into a metaphor for the other—displacement as overlay—and thus to explore the mutual recognition that at the same time both deals out and half heals this tragedy. More than portraying such a mortal convergence, style is also assigned to disclose the way in which the heroine's whole life has been a long delaying of the death moment, existence not only leading up to but led too much in the shape of a dark drowning, airless, desperately thrashing, obsessively retrospective, murky, expressionless, and blind. In this infamous Victorian death scene, unmatched in verbal flourish and nuance outside of Dickens, figurative drowning passes to fact in the symbolism of epitome. With more irony than is usually credited to Eliot's ending, her heroine seems liquidated in the quintessence of her own headlong being, pulled down by frustrated instincts to suffocation and effacement. [...]
>
> Death still serves as vehicle to the heroine's tenor of loss as we near the flood scene. When, in a final interview with Lucy, Maggie sacrifices her passion for Stephen by asking Lucy to forgive him, the words are "wrung forth from Maggie's soul, with an effort like the convulsed clutch of a drowning man." Eliot tries by such means to make the flood arrive as a psychic inevitability. In a preparation of the epitomizing moment all but unprecedented in Victorian fiction, the tidal imagery preceding the storm waters suggests that the heroine is both victim and fountainhead of her own defeat, swept forward by the impulsive rush of her deepest nature. Once she is seduced by Stephen into an irresponsible rowing excursion, the indifferent tide toys with her as an objective correlative for the listless but insistent drift of her own desire, her emotions "borne along by a wave too strong for her." She wishes that she "need no longer beat and struggle against this current, soft and yet strong as the summer stream!". Though Eliot explicitly introduces the threat of drowning as if it were a danger lurking within some destructive "submergence of our personality by another," it is clear that the true threat is a swamping of moral purpose by the heroine's inner turmoil.
>
> We have learned earlier that Maggie's life presents itself to her "like the course of an unmapped river: we only know that the river

is full and rapid, and that for all rivers there is the same final home." When the potentially instructive width of simile is clamped shut to equivalence, Maggie is ready for that long home whose earthly type has been closed to her by perversity and neglect. If the tide that overtakes her is meant to evoke the "awful Eagre" which, when she was a child, "used to come up like a hungry monster" and put her in mind of that symbolic mortal border in *Pilgrim's Progress*, "the river over which there is no bridge," then this premonition would befit the awful eagerness of a life that could only surrender to the element of its own dammed hopes. We do not hear the name of the tide that rises for the final flood, but in the opening paragraph of the death chapter we are told how its first effect, upriver, is seen in the fact that the "harvest had been arrested." Downriver, too; for by the fruitless confusion of her life the heroine is halted, deluged, and engulfed. Style inscribes this in an interval over which there is no bridge, except for the projected gestures of rhetoric meant to traverse as well as render the gap of human negation within a world that endures.

When, driven out on the water, Maggie cries, "Oh God, where am I? Which is the way home?" the question compacts both senses of the noun "home" from that previous simile of the unmapped river. Primarily Maggie hopes she can reach her earthly home soon enough, and just long enough; to rescue what is left of her family. It is clear that she has in mind not safety and salvation but "some undefined sense of reconcilement" with her brother, the dream of leniency come true in the face of death. She does not fear to die, only "to perish too soon." Once she has come upon Tom, his "lips found a word they could utter: the old childish—'Magsie.'" The phrase "the old childish" was added in proof, not only as a reminder to the reader of the long dormant nickname but as an index to the emotional reversion with which the whole scene is concerned. [...]

Stiff, pinched denizen of life's emotional shallows, Tom is launched at last upon those profundities he has never before tried to plumb, overcome by their tidal sway as they "rushed upon his mind." Moments later he is taken down by this thunderous burden, but for a split second of ecstatic illumination he endures "a new revelation to his spirit, of the depths in life"—the unfathomed reaches of his own filial identity and of that life which, knowing himself better, he could have helped make with Maggie, helped her to make for herself. Not unlike the remedial bliss of Maggie's epitomizing last moments of consciousness, Tom's drowning takes place in the depths of his own long stagnant nature. In the brief prelude to this submergence he comes upon what Maggie, in a more prolonged interval of revelation, has striven toward and at last achieved; swept out upon the flood, she "felt nothing, thought of nothing, but she had suddenly passed away from that life which she had been dreading: it was the transition of death, without its agony." The idiom "passed away" is sustained this side of the Victorian euphemism for death just long enough for a visionary broaching of the untraversable. Under pressure of repetition, that "nothing" she first conceives, then feels, inches its way toward voiding noun within the still transitive grammar of living subject and suspended object. The "transition" of such a nearly traversed interval is an encroachment upon the very abyss whose contemplation, by the staying power of "nothing" in its pronominal sense, is held briefly in abeyance, its terrors allayed.

In her reunion with Tom shortly following, Maggie lets this abyss be filled with the retrograde grace of her recovered nickname "Magsie." Style immediately spells out this ambivalent blessing in a homophonic pun heard with a clear ring on the underside of idiom. "Maggie could make no answer but a long deep sob of that mysterious wondrous happiness that is one with pain." Instead of writing "at one with," Eliot phrases this spiritual equivalence so that the phonetic torsion from the second set of double epithets, especially the first syllable of "wondrous," turns the idiom of fusion ("one with") toward the achieved participle of a lethal victory, the triumph "won" only with the reavowed oneness of brother and sister. [...]

I have no confidence, in any recoverable memory, that hearing the sound play of "w/on/e with" was a moment that factored into my thinking ahead toward theorizing such a "phonotext" in my next book, *Reading Voices* (1990). But how could the propensity to listen this way not have been brewing at such a moment? In any case, however much any broader account of "hearing double" was at work in my sense of the literary medium, the "seeing double" mentioned at the end of the last paragraph gets its own further look. In a return to the biblical epigraph from Samuel, the logic is played out linguistically, grammatically, as a kind of reciprocal displacement of two into one. Here is a dying shared—as I wish, yet again, I had been more precise about at the linguistic level—via a death-wrenched grammar of anomalous number (the biblical "their death," not deaths plural):

> For the culminating formal irony of drowning in *The Mill on the Floss*, it is not enough that Maggie succumbs to the retrospective compulsion of an entire life, swallowed with Tom in the very stream of time to which otherwise, and because of him, she resists submitting. The drowning is followed by another burial of brother and sister, this time in earth, and by a chiseled record on their tombstone which also happens to be the book's initiating biblical quotation and inscribed epigraph, "In their death they were not divided." Eliot elects this return of text upon opening text to stress in part the singular noun

phrase "their death," one shared dying entered upon together, even as it is the "divided" nature of each of them separately that death rectifies. At the same time, that widespread ambiguity "in death" is meant to chasten its own lurch toward eternity with the alternate designation as a mere last moment, supreme only in the closural sense. There is an interval traversed, but no eventuality.

That was then, but looking back at this passage now, I take renewed heart regarding my recent sales pitch to mixed audiences of undergraduates in prose style classes. I might actually use this example next time to show how attending to the very rudiments of grammar, in the matter of tense and number to begin with—grammar always a mainstay of my writing courses—is not just a necessary focus in the line-editing expertise to be sought by students in our so-called publication track. It is a useful move in literary criticism as well, not to mention creative writing. As in Eliot's rescinded plurality, a brush with error can score a deeper irony.

Notes

1   *Sketches by "Boz," Illustrative of Every-day Life and Every-day People*, known under the abbreviated *Sketches by Boz*, is a collection of short pieces by Charles Dickens originally published in newspapers and other periodicals between 1833 and 1836, and subsequently as one volume in 1839.
2   Walter Benjamin, "The Storyteller," (1936) in *Illuminations*, trans. Harry Zohn, ed. Hannah Arendt (New York: Schocken Books, 1969), 83–109.

II.

READING IN, READING OUT

> 3 / *Reading Voices: Literature and the Phonotext* (University of California Press, 1990) encounters Derridean deconstruction head on. While granting that there is no authorial voice retained in the phonetic language of reading matter, Stewart moves to demonstrate nonetheless—with a broad scope of evidence from subvocal neurology to the history and philosophy of language—that the act of reading is a subliminal voicing in itself. Examples from Shakespeare to a closing chapter on Virginia Woolf—with numerous treatments in between of Romantic poetry and prose fiction from Laurence Sterne through Dickens to D. H. Lawrence, including chapter length accounts of cross-word rhymes in English verse and the "earsighted" skid-marks of Joyce's phonetic play—make the case for a malleable linguistic medium in which the eye/ear ratio of decipherment is productively unsteady and referentially generative.

3 / Literary Graphonics

Reading Voices: Literature and the Phonotext (1990)

WHENEVER I HAD ADAPTED AND REDEPLOYED, or devised from audiovisual scratch, my own metaphors for aspects of the death scene—as, for instance, "Thresholding" in a chapter title—I thought of myself as illustrating, by instance as well as principle, the verbal skids and elisions that fascinated me in the equivocal grammar of mortality. Inhabited thereby, in my own coinages, was the leeway so perfectly summed up for me by William Empson as "play in the engineering sense." This had by now become habitual in my writing, even three books in. But it was never so much in evidence, before or even since, as in *Reading Voices*: what with the bolding of the section rubric "**Over**eadings" to suggest the dovetailing of syllables one finds in prose and poetry alike. Or with chapter titles playing on the elision of dental sounds ("Rhymed Treason") or floating a cross-word homophonic blur like "The Ear Heretical" for the very "theoretical" doxa my book was resisting. Or in the pushback against a leveling deconstruction in the coda, "Epilogos: The Decentered Word." The book's title itself was meant to have the gestalt effect of a Necker Cube, one reading of its two words rejecting the other—this, despite the fact that it was explained straight off as a clause not a phrase. The title was thus stationed to identify the act of subvocalization that activates written language, the reading that voices— an always "graphonic" phenomenon, or as Joyce would say "phonemanon"— rather than to entertain some mystified authorial Voice present in language, one justified brunt of a deconstructive critique.

In pursuing the hows and whys of the *reading that voices*, this project grew more "scientific" and explicitly theoretical than my previous work. It strove to consolidate the neurology of silent reading, via the philological history of word breaks, not just with the far reaches of structural linguistics (and its lunatic fringe in Ferdinand de Saussure's anagram studies) but also with a confluence of post-structuralist thought from Roland Barthes through Julia Kristeva to Jacques Derrida, including a host of their secondary commentators. What I select here to exemplify the method is a return, in fact, not to Dickensian romanticism but to Romantic poetry itself, as part of the study's historical arc from Shakespeare's sonnets to Virginia Woolf's last novel. Including a few sentences on John Keats lifted from their previous publication, this excerpt throws a unique switch in my professional memory. I well recall how an essay of mine from 1974, on Keats's *Lamia* (1820), was chastised in draft form by my then-colleague Helen Vendler at Boston University. Her own much-published sense of Keats rejected all trace of pertinent wordplay—including his habitual punning, notorious in his letters—in some supposedly purer attunement to his thoughtful music.

Yes, a little therapeutic biographical venting here to brace my phonography. Naturally enough, as an assistant professor, I suffered a good bit from this temporary setback, including Vendler's comment on my draft pages (along with "Keats never puns!") to the effect that it wasn't enough to think you've taught a poem well to justify writing about it. That line sticks in my mind here (if not still in my craw) because it is, quite to the contrary, the feedback loop between writing and teaching to which these collected excerpts are meant to testify. Once I recovered from this lack of a sympathetic audience, I was of course gratified to be invited to "teach" the poem in an article for *Studies in Romanticism*, "*Lamia* and the Language of Metamorphosis." Boosted by this vote of confidence as I was, some of that poem's ironic aural keynotes reappeared, as I say, in *Reading Voices*, one of whose chapters is called "Attention Surfeit Disorder." So, my difference of opinion, of audition itself, with Vendler as legendary close reader was in fact an unexpected stepping stone, gradient tones included, on the way to the more fully audited "phonotext" of the later book's subtitle. With the published exercise in Keats' "metamorphic" language behind me at that point—associated with the shape-shifting eponymous snake/lady of the poet's erotic narrative—the attempt was to bring its mode of ingrown linguistic mutation into productive alignment with less blatantly thematized instabilities in prose fiction as well as other Romantic verse, the latter illustrated below with Wordsworth and Shelley as well, on either side of Keats.

The entirely solemn homophonic puns in these other two poets that flank the Keats material in the following snippets—the Keatsian effects under the rubric of his own famous phrase "Unheard Melodies"—depend, I should add, on a central coinage in the book. The root terminology is borrowed from the linguistic concept of phonemic "segmentation" in lexical structure. It is directed here to recalibrate attention within the syllabic undertow, and sometimes disruptive riptide, of certain stylistic effects—as self-illustrated in the term "transegmental" itself. Attention, when snagged in process, is thus regeared in the silent but auditory note—"evocalized" without being voiced aloud— of breached syllabic (and even full-word) boundaries under the impetus of "transegmental drift" (especially prevalent with just such swallowed sibilant junctures, as alternately with the d/t elision of dentals). Think again, as I "encore" this material, of that verb's own collapsed etymological gap in the radically unvoiced h's of "(h)anc (h)ora." The result, when spanning (and momentarily disbanding) two separate lexical units, is a kind of cross-word play—or splay— that taps repeatedly, I wanted to show, into some of the deepest resources of English as a literary language. With Wordsworth as immediate example:

> The rhetorical question on which the whole consolatory logic of the "Intimations" ode turns—"What though the radiance which was once so bright / Be now forever taken from my sight"—leaves only the least trace of "from eye-sight" in the metrically divergent "from my sight." The (not unwelcome) result is that the difference between "my sight" (figurative as well as literal) and "eyesight" is thrown open to question in the space of an ambiguous lexical juncture. It is, in fact, at exactly this climactic turn of the poem that sight is redefined as a faculty of spirit, paraphrased later as "the faith that *looks* through death." Hence the rhythm of the verse might seem to have muted but not entirely suppressed the earlier transegmental pun, "fro/m eyesight," as an impertinent equivalence to that keener incorporeal seeing which the ode is striving to define even in the midst of its nostalgia for present and unmediated vision. It is the soul's sight, the mind's-eye-view of retrospect, in particular, that permits each of us (as recovered "seer blest") to envision the "immortal sea" of our origin, "And see the Children sport upon the shore." What in the general sense of these lines is there to veto the probability of the antiphonal phrasing "children's port," designating the threshold of life, the harbor of all arriving and unfettered energies? This is indeed the textual equivalent of those "intimations" the ode has set out to trace, failings from us, here phonemic shavings, vanishings. [...]

Unheard Melodies

Rather like the "Eolian Harp" in Coleridge, with its rows (or lines) of latent instrumentation waiting to be breathed upon, Keats's sculptural symbol in the "Ode on a Grecian Urn" may at one point be more directly an emblem of poetry as text, as inhibited vocalization, than has been recognized. Everyone finds in this ode a parable of art and imagination. But when the musicianship pictured on the urn, as in turn rendered by the ode thereon, is characterized as producing "ditties of no tone," there would seem to be more textual auto-commentary at work than just wholesale aesthetic meditation. In texts, as in plastic representation, "melodies" are not less melodious for being "unheard," for keeping the silence of their unspoken vocalizations. Rather than being generated for the "sensual ear," the unintoned "ditties" portrayed on the urn's surface are registered solely in the mind—yet registered as music, not just as the idea of music. [...]

Another pause for second thoughts, ones in this case that at least I did finally have in print (not just here now) when addressing this poem again in *The Deed of Reading* (2015) twenty-five years later. For it shouldn't go unnoted that all the above play between the musically imagined and the textually heard is tacit right there—inflected to the metalevel, the point worth further stress—in the sounded "no t(e)one" that hovers between phonic drift and graphic anagram.

Then, too, Keats has even more in common with Coleridge than this may so far suggest. In his correspondence he is a homophonic punster as well, who gives Coleridge's "anymadversions" a run for its money—for its lexical short-changes and syntactic overdraft—with his complaints about the "{hie}*rogue*glyphics in Moors almanack." In that rebuslike syllable, Keats's drifting phoneme (carried by the grapheme *gue*) doubles by liaison for the *g* of "glyphs" (just as the *r* of "hier") could have been made to operate in this way with the fuller spelling "hier-rogue-glyphs"). Such "rogue glyphs," loosed by phonemic slack, can, as in Coleridge, certainly inflect the graphonic contours of a verse line as well. In the "Ode on a Grecian Urn," for example, there is a transegmental overlay in the very thought that art's idealized and wholly imagined music would not pipe or pander to the "sensual leer," to that fevered gaze of desire that animates the male lovers on the urn. From this we infer some sort of sensory luxuriance apart from aggressive sensuality: a rarefied state which the line, by thematically positing, also phonemically enacts.

In Keats's "Ode to a Nightingale," we have already noted the critically debated rhyme on "sole self"/"deceiving elf," with a potential homophonic ambiguity at the sibilant juncture that returns more unmistakably in *Lamia,* where the title creature is either "some penanced lady *elf*," or, if not, "Some demon's mistress, or the demon's *self*." In the multiplicity and logical contradiction of these lines, an uncertainty turning on identity-versus-possession would readily serve Keats's purpose. So with the proleptic irony of Lamia uttering her first words in the poem "for Love's sake." As we saw in Donne's "Love's Exchange," the elided underside of the possessive "Love's *sake*" sounds a warning of that "ache" which attends the possessiveness of love in the tragic remainder of the narrative: In Lamia's own description of Hermes' nymph, the fourfold repetition of her going about "unseen" also impresses a narrative logic upon transegmental ambiguity: "From bow'd branches green, / She plucks the fruit unseen, she bathes unseen." The virtual redundancy (for the sake of rhyme) in "branches green" is rescued by the sense of it being precisely their leafage which creates the "branches' screen" that provides her privacy (recalling Shakespeare's "summer's *green*" in Chapter 1). Such is Keats's ear for the thickening textures of the literary tradition. In the second part of the poem, well after Lamia has taken up with the hero, Lycius, the climax is precipitated by the appearance of his stern mentor, Apollonius, at the wedding feast. Once within sight of his pupil's bride, the dry rationalist begins to puzzle out the mystery of the snake lady, her embodied ambiguity. The task is described as a "knotty problem" that "had now begun to thaw, / And solve and melt." It is another highly Shakespearean moment in this poem. Keats would indeed seem to be consciously alluding here, and in the process normalizing, Hamlet's famous sequence, "melt, / Thaw, and resolve," while retaining a related pun on resolution in "solve." It is a pun that is submitted in Keats's line to a transegmental drift as well. Holding the place at once of rational "solution" and of metamorphic "dissolution" (as immediately restated in "melt"), the punning lexeme gives out laterally. In a silent voicing of the line, that is, the slight sibilant hiss of "And solve" is all that is necessary for the inner ear to generate, following the dental sound, the near equivalence of "And (d)(i)solve." [...]

The famous fifth stanza of the "Ode to a Nightingale," which begins with the speaker admitting that he has "been half in love with easeful Death," closes with his imagined relation to the nightingale's song once he has given up consciousness: "To thy high requiem become a sod." Without relating it back to Milton's synaloepha (his metrically determined eliding of vowels), Walter Jackson Bate, in *The Stylistic Development of Keats*, notes instead the "extreme and persistent" tendency toward "hiatus" or "vowel-gaping" in Keats's early sonnets. But what of the cross-lexical shunt that moves to span this gape, this gap—or, should we say, threatens to?—even at the expense of meter, in a phrase like "thy *high* requiem"? To have ascribed that song to the nightingale, in the context of the speaker's wished-for return to earth, is to have defined it, by contrast, as "high." In this sense it is fitting (indeed, by a close phonemic fit) that the pronominal adjective seems to entail, to trail off into or be taken up by, the epithet. This is so even as the full measure of "high" (in a kind of kinaesthetic enhancement of the referential elevation) would tend with its "high" vowel to lift away from "thy" in enunciation—against the enforced prosody of Keats's own iambic requiem, where "thy" rather than "high" would take the accent. The inner speech of the body as reading site must negotiate in this way between two contradictory impulses, transegmental and kinaesthetic. If held to metrical regularity, this phrasing thus suppresses that normal hyper-articulation which might otherwise work to offset thematically the languid blurring of "a(s) sod" at the close of the line. Just as the reflexive recognition of "the very word," like a bell, will help the persona recover from his death wish a stanza later, the tension here in both phrases between hiatus and elision, enforced juncture and conflation, might equally be felt to hold alert (even if under constraint) the verbal consciousness (ours by proxy for that of the "speaker"), to keep the mind and body energized at one crucial point of their intersection: in silent as well as spoken enunciation. In this, the self-conscious literariness of graphonic tension encodes the very force of its utterance as a will to (still) living speech.

The subsequent stanza now ends on the belling note "Of perilous seas, in faery lands forlorn," where the subjective admonishment slipping into the phrase through the elision of a transegmental drift—namely, the chastisement of "perilou*s* (*s*)eas(e)"—registers the indolent mood of mind from which the speaker is about to rebound into the chastening echo of the next stanza. Given that the "full-throated ease" of the nightingale has initially led the speaker to his thoughts of "easeful" death—the latter adjective used in Keats's day, both passively and actively, for "slothful" as well as "easing"—the word "ease" has cut deep, always potentially recurrent, grooves in the poem. The lexical risk incident to a sibilant juncture like "perilou*s seas*" is therefore all the more likely to let slip into "production" the text's more telling noun, for which "seas" is part of a figure here anyway. Against the grain of the written phenotext, that is, the phonotext has once again sounded (at the level of a suppressed matrix) the implicit tenor to a metaphoric vehicle operating at the scripted surface of a phrase.

The easy slipping in of the verbal rather than substantive form of "ease," though without the monitory overtones of the "Nightingale" ode, is even more self-enacting in the "Ode on a Grecian Urn," where "ease" carries the sense less of torpor than of aesthetic release. The synecdochic urn, silently inscribed vessel described entirely by the sheer inscription (to recall de Man's terms) of the poem "on" it, is apostrophized in the last stanza as the (quasi-textual) "silent form" which—in a self-illustrating animation of such silence—"dost tease us out of thought." It is just that formal second-person-singular ending ("do*st*"), insignia of direct address (of prosopopoeia in the form of apostrophe), which permits the very slip in inscription that draws off the (in context) synonymous "ease" from its less predictable variant, "tease." [...] In this sense what we find there is a Riffaterrean matrix that could be said to undergo deconstruction by its very apostrophizing inscription—but a deconstruction negotiated in the play between graphic (in particular, here, ekphrastic) inscription and the "sensual ear" of the phonotext. [...]

And then a final Keatsian example, before moving on to Shelley, from the former's late unfinished *The Fall of Hyperion*—stressing in the lexical pressure of the line itself:

the terrible verbal power of Moneta's awesome disclosures. Containing in their narrative the whole englobed tragedy of the Titans, her words seem sculpted by the vastness and devastation on which they report. By a transferred epithet from the mythic sphere whose fallen world they evoke, her language is characterized as "an immortal's sphered words." By elision and another transference, here from cause to effect, the words naming her words thus also characterize the narrator's recoil from this "feared" revelation. Such a wording on the text's part is rounded to contain its own microdrama, its own tension between utterance and response. [...]

In the most luxuriantly plotted phonemic exercise in all of Shelley's work, the "Ode to the West Wind," the speaker, in apostrophe to the wind, imagines a boyhood vitality wound up to the point where "to outstrip thy skiey speed / Scarce seemed a vision." Enhanced by the dynamic of enjambment, the syntax must outstrip its own lineation in order to round out a last strained phrase that may at the same time homophonically regroup itself to "thy sky's speed." Sense would permit this, since the wind's speed is visible as "skiey" only insofar as it pushes clouds on before it. Phonemes too, then, are outstripping themselves there. Against the semantically intriguing, albeit somewhat thick-tongued, metrical regularity of "skiey speed," the no-longer iambic rapidity of "sky's speed" scuds past. This ethereal rush at last comes bearing down on the inspired present speaker for the inverted copulative clauses of "Be thou, Spirit fierce, / My spirit! Be thou me, impetuous one!" With the first comma again "unheard," the enjambment would move to close off one possible, slightly elliptical grammar—"Be thou (a) spirit fierce"—only to have it reopened and adjusted when the tentative predicate nominative is displaced in retrospect to an appositive. The speaker's own "spirit" next takes up the grammatical slot following the equative verb, only from there to be swept up into the second appositive phrase, "impetuous one," across the vernacular solecism of "me" in the objective case. Once again, grammar deconstructs rhetoric by exposing a self still subject to—still object of—the wind with which it hopes to fuse. Yet the wind's spiritualized velocity impels identification, impels fusion— so the speaker dreams. It is an *impetus* that, once scripted as the quatrasyllabic "impetuous," introduces—by way of phonetic rebus— the pronoun "you." That encrypted pronoun is placed, and suddenly played, against the first person authorial plural of "us," though still in the objective case. It thus takes part in a swift but no less emphatic positing of subject and object that—given the spondaic precedent of "Be thou me"—blends into the phonemically lent splendor of *impet/you/us/one*. Such is a desideratum—difference subsumed to unity, lack transcended—written only in the chord progressions of a natural harmony, not traced anywhere upon legible face of things, whether of nature or of poem. Indeed, it is produced as text only by what the next tercet reflexively highlights as "the incantation of this verse"— to be heard and not seen.

Nothing so complex as that Shelley example is needed for classroom proof. Students catch the drift, as it were, of these effects all the sooner when reminded that such phonic throat-catches can often be a commercial hook in the branding logic of advertising, as sampled in *Reading Voices* and later satirized by Colson Whitehead in his 2007 novel *Apex Hides the Hurt*, to which I turn, later still, in the opening chapter of *The Ways of the Word* (2021). In Whitehead's lampoon of Madison Avenue "nomenclature" marketing, we find the syllabically liquefied example "Aquaway" for a water-repellent leather spray, a name that perfectly evokes the flow it would deflect—with the foreign if familiar word for water sloughed off, washed away, before it can threaten the surface of either product name or shoe leather. Closer to home, my Iowa students only need think of the plosive elision (p/b) in the name of the local Cambus. Or, in screen advertising, they can be reminded how the anomalous spelling of "clan," amid the group's other outrages, allows the hated name of the Ku Klux Klan to be invaded by an African American telephone interloper, the plot's improbable but semi-documentary premise, in the very title of Spike Lee's film *BlacKkKlansman* (2018). There is no better example of the kind of lexical flicKkKer effect—internal shutter-stutter and all, as exaggerated there by typography—that I find approximating the glitched frame snags discussed a decade after *Reading Voices* (and indeed in connection with it) in *Between Film and Screen* (1999).

> 4 / *Dear Reader: The Conscripted Audience in Nineteenth-Century British Fiction* (Johns Hopkins University Press, 1996), with its revisionary spin on reader-response criticism, is thus explicitly a study of the audience *in* rather than of fiction: an audience embedded by the figure of apostrophe (the titular "Dear" of direct address) or by enacted scenes of reading as paradigms or counter-models for the mode of reception inferred by a given novel's own rhetorical tone. With the "great tradition" from Jane Austen through Charles Dickens and George Eliot to Thomas Hardy read here for the first time alongside the non-canonical best-sellers of the period, the book gives a revised picture of an evolving readership narrated rather than merely implied: the mass audience conscripted, written with, figured in. Redirecting response aesthetics away from the *a priori* reader function toward this reader *figuration*, the book thereby intercepts two tendencies in the criticism of fiction during the time Stewart was writing: the blanket audience determinations of ideological critique and the thinness of historicizing discourse analysis when divorced from literary history's own discursive field. What might elsewhere be called the wholesale "interpellation" of public response to mainstream fiction is, with unexpectedly rich consequences, subdivided between, in Stewart's terms, the specific "interpolation" of the reading agent and the "extrapolation" of its cued responses from a narrated episode of textual consumption.

4 / Re: Reading Under Address

Dear Reader: The Conscripted Audience in Nineteenth-Century British Fiction (1996)

NO DOUBT, AT LEAST IN THE CASE of that last Shelley example, this nearness of ear (this sustained application of Joyce's "an earsighted view") might seem to a dubious audience a kind of ove(r)reading in the everyday sense—or a case of the dreaded "just reading that in." By contrast, my effort in the next book, *Dear Reader: The Conscripted Audience of Nineteenth-Century British Fiction*, offers, in its return to the Victorian masters of prose fiction, a reading *out*: outward from page to the inferences of its own consumption. Here, too, in a subterranean sense, *Dearreader* was also one earful of a word, one graphonic vaunt: marking an inherent endearment, a latent solicitation, implicit in the very work of narrative. And explicit as audience apostrophe in scores of Victorian publications. According to the double edge of "conscripted" in the book's subtitle, every reading results not just from a drafted (multiple senses) attention but from an applied co-writing in the work of understanding: the construal of meaning earmarked as a collaborative act. In eliciting this inference from certain landmarks of Victorian narrative, I divided attention, stylistic either way, between "interpolated" readers in a mode of direct address that I was tracking in derivation from the salutations of epistolary fiction, including the letter-boxing frame structure of Walton's missives to his sister in *Frankenstein*. That, on the one hand. And, on the other hand, those readers taking their own "extrapolated" fictional bearings from episodes of textual encounter enacted within the plot.

One bracket of discussion in this bicameral approach includes the community of oral storytelling forming the serial frame tale—namely, the monthly publication apparatus of *Master Humphrey's Clock*—around Dickens's novel *The Old Curiosity Shop* (1840). This communality of literary recitation at clockside is set in contrast to a final chapter on the late century "Gothic of Reading." Sampled below, from the latter, is the "trancescript" episode (another of my motivated portmanteau coinages) by which—in a vertiginous regress—the climactic document in Bram Stoker's *Dracula* is not Mina Harker's direct and typical contribution to the "framing" dossier of vampire-tracking data. It is, rather, a note brought out by her own later reading of the otherwise transcribed reading, or deciphering, of her unconscious telepathic antenna, under hypnotic trance, regarding Dracula's whereabouts.

If the contemporary juggernaut of deconstruction had been the prod to a certain corrective retrenchment on the score of triggered orality in *Reading Voices*, discussion here, by contrast, was able to recruit an analytic model to which I could less questionably adhere. In a schematic mapping of this and similar episodes of uncanny transmission in the late-Victorian gothic and its precursors, I found compelling the formalist arsenal of Fredric Jameson's approach to narrative as a "socially symbolic act" (from the subtitle of *The Political Unconscious*, and with a crucial emphasis for me on the descriptor "symbolic" as well as social). This led me to experiment with the structuralist armatures of the semiotic square, encouraged by Jameson's deft and fertile use of this conceptual instrument from the narratology of A. J. Greimas. I should add that I was privately surprised to see in retrospect how fully formulated, in the main, was a distinction in my treatment of Victorian gothic between self-reflective plotting and that concept of readerly "reflex" only to find full theorization more than three decades later in *The Metanarrative Hall of Mirrors: Reflex Action in Fiction and Film* (2022). For this is the crux, below, in my comparison of *Dr. Jekyll and Mr. Hyde* with *Dracula* on the way to an abstractly textualist rather than supernaturally tinged modernism.

> Both Stevenson's and Stoker's narratives do operate with this self-figurative dimension as one armature of their narrative development, with textuality becoming an immanent metaphor for the site of doubling and vampiric renewal alike. Just as importantly, though, the signals emitted by pun and by dead metaphor redivivus, in thematizing linguistic perversity within the respective plots of doubling and resurrection, become the signs of the reader's own dubiety and

second thoughts: the metalinguistic programming of reception itself as a participatory decoding of occulted energy.

Self-referential layering once again induces the reflex of reading. Yet the latent figuring of responses does not stop there. Across the plot of *Dracula*, even as the documents that track the Count's whereabouts are read aloud by Mina to her cohort in detection as a normative exercise in parafamilial transmission, another mode of reception is being progressively thematized—one that bypasses altogether the materiality of the written text. [...]

Trancescription: Toward a Phenomenology of the Vampiric

To be sure, Wilde, du Maurier, and Stevenson each had a way of figuring textuality in scientific terms, chemical (poisonous) and photochemical alike, even while they explored a psychosomatics of reading. Stoker drives their diagnoses one step further in imagining a psychotechnology of reading itself: a wireless circuitry of unconscious dictation which, once textualized, must be reread by its doubly subjected agent—the read character turned reading medium. This clinching episode of the readerly metaplot develops as follows. Mina has been involuntarily hypnotized by the Count so that she might transmit to him long-distance the secret machinations of his enemies. But it is Van Helsing's triumphant stroke to realize that telepathy—what he has earlier called "thought-reading"—can go both ways once the circuits have been opened. The result is that Mina is rehypnotized by the professor to invade Dracula's own mind by using the Count's psychic wiring, even when he is interred in his shipboard coffin, as an antenna to broadcast his whereabouts. While Mina is thus unconsciously engaged, it falls to Dr. Seward, as Van Helsing puts it in one of his telling solecisms, to "be scribe and write him all down"—as if the nosferatu could be translated wholesale and per se to a textual form, Dracula become *Dracula*.

No one could be more interested in eventually studying this text than its unconscious conduit and oracle. Here is Mina, eagerly reinternalizing the narrative at the very moment of its first encounter by the novel's audience: "I read in the typescript that in my trance I heard cows low and water swirling level with my ears and the creaking of wood. The Count in his box, *then*, was on a river in an open boat." In this preternatural access to a temporal simultaneity across great spatial distance, "then" marks the space of present inference rather than the space of the past: "therefore" instead of (or as well as) "at that time." Mina's "reading of thought," once reread, has thus sucked the enemy dry by identification, located his "where" here and now in the psychic field of countersurveillance. The apogee of dramatic irony—the vampire vampirized in his own encoffined passivity—is accompanied by a no less obvious metadramatic irony: the transcriber transcribed in order to read of herself at one remove, read of herself as if she were the other, here and now. At such a nodal moment in the media network within the plot, such a telepathic chiasm and hypnotic switch point of the text itself, the reading of gothic and the gothic of reading collapse upon each other. The "figure" of vampirism as, finally, a baroque but manageable emblem for textual negotiation and its parasitic transfers of psychic energy is thus foregrounded by this regulatory reversal, where invasiveness (of mind by text, of text by mind) becomes reciprocal and liberating. Plot's telepathology seeks its homeopathic cure in the hermeneutics of reading. [...]

With the vampire made male, a role is also left over in Stoker's plot for the energy of the feminine as the worried site of merely glimpsed or *disclosed* rather than incarnate and assailable perversity. In finally tracking the Count to his castle, that is, or in other words hounding the revived trope of vampirism back to its source, the confederacy of male sleuths is in fact *reading the unconscious of the woman*, reading as if in neural code what she herself would never consciously recognize as being shared with or derived from the brainwaves of the vampire: namely, the sleeping secret and nightmarish obverse of the novel's own courtship of domestic idealism in its parafamilial collective. Such is the plot's bizarre epistemological access, through hypnosis, to the horrific reverse nurture of an erotically devouring and solely self-regenerative desire. No parable of reading, I repeat, could be less peripheral to the narrative crisis of its text. Anxieties geopolitical (colonialist), psychosexual (phallic), familial (conjugal, maternal), medical (venereal), socioeconomic (monopolist)—all of them and more, swept up under the rank grave clothes of the Transylvanian invader, converge upon the body of the woman, not inscribed but internalized there: as something that must be deciphered—decrypted—from her mutterings, even and especially by the subject herself, through at once a technology and a necromancy of transmission.

All that remains of Stoker's novel after the summary execution of the Count—where, stabbed to the heart, he crumbles, dust to dust, at prolonged last—is a final textual reflection on his namesake, *Dracula*, after its own consumption. In his closing "Note," Jonathan Harker speaks for the discursive collective when he laments that, with the whole ordeal now behind them, they had little to show for it but the questionable evidence of nonholographic prose, "nothing but a mass of typewriting." They might as well be packing it off to a publisher. Yet the story, we are told, as, for example, with the story of Nell, stays private—becoming in effect a domestic version of one of those male-bonding narratives to which a member of the cadre alludes early on as part of the narrative's own prehistory: "We've told yarns by the camp-fire in the prairies, and ... [t]here are more yarns to be told." When finally unraveled, that is, the Dracula yarn, with Mina its unsung heroine, is putatively to become only a family legend in the Harker household, like the Darnays' story of Sydney Carton's sacrifice. Yet you know better, or else you wouldn't know anything about the story at all. Despite disclaimers of publishing intent—as in the punning "we want no proofs"—any member of Stoker's audience well realizes that, once buried in the lead-lined grave of set type, Dracula can be revived and consumed ad infinitum. This is not an isolated trope of the supernatural genre but, rather, the gothic novel's figurative view of fiction at large in its constitutive rereadability. As we saw at the close of *Villette*, literary characters provide the Victorian novel's running equivalent of the perpetual Undead. But this is only because you vampirize them as much as they you—as they fuse with you. This, then, is the recognition that Stoker's antihero suffers for you. As he lives, invasively, so he dies. Penetration replies to penetration. In *Dracula*, it is the double vulnerability of reading, the penetrability of its objects and its subjects alike, which is ultimately and perilously *at stake*. [...]

In this light, one final emblem of reading as bloodletting lies coiled within the convoluted turns of Stoker's text: the contextually overdetermined means by which Mina decides to bind shut her husband's troubled diary. This is of course the increasingly frantic document that has provided a first impetus to the unfolding textual pastiche we have all along been reading. In a burst of exquisitely quaint sentiment, Mina chooses to seal the evidence "with a little bit of pale blue ribbon which was wound round my neck." If a silenced text would now need its decorative neck ribbon ripped away before it could grant access, then reading is every bit as much like vampirism as it is often figured to seem, here and elsewhere, in late Victorian narrative.

The Gothic Diagnostic: Modernism in the Offing

[...] At just this point in an attempt to think through the transition from realism to its melodramatic critique in late Victorian gothic fiction, one may take counsel from a tacit debate about literary modes within one of the central (central because most self-consciously transitional) texts of the period. I refer to a passing glance at genre theory couched in the defeated discriminations of Harold Biffen in *New Grub Street*. Whereas his friend Reardon, in Biffen's view, aspires to be a "psychological realist in the sphere of culture"— read: George Eliot—Biffen's asperity of technique, as we have seen, struggles for "absolute realism in the sphere of the ignobly decent."

For "absolute," put "vulgar," as in the contemptuous imagination of Wilde's Lord Henry: "I hate vulgar realism in literature. The man who could call a spade a spade should be compelled to use one." But what is the inevitable—or should we say logical—affiliation between the "real" and the "ignoble" (or "vulgar")? And what other categorical distinctions are consequent upon it?

Cognitive mapping can begin here, starting us toward not just an answer but that answer's wider field of inference. Following Fredric Jameson's use of the semiotic square adopted for narrative analysis by A. J. Greimas (see fig. 1 below), we find that an ideological field of interdependent dichotomies derives from a cross-mapping of governing binaries at the level not only of narrative but of genre itself and, ultimately, of reception. One possible quadratic logic would fall out as follows at the generic level, determining narrative construction and its underlying assumptions. Against the ignoble is counterposed the ennobled, which thus stands in preliminary contrast to the real. But what, then, is neither real nor artificially ennobled, and what, if conceivable, is both? Again (as repeatedly in Jameson) the problem of the complex and contradictory fourth term (in this case, the neither quite real nor the wholly unreal) is raised and schematically resolved—here in the oxymoronic mold of idealist realism: the transformation of the mundane into both its aestheticized ideality and its reigning bourgeois ideology. This can occur, however, only after something like the logical (rather than merely tonal) divergence between Biffen's

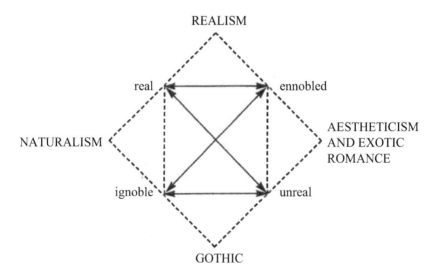

Figure 1 Genre Grid.

literary practice and that of Reardon has served to distribute—to the sectors of a doubly bipolar model—the whole panoply (become grid) of late Victorian generic options.

In charting the ideologemes of narrative (Jameson's theory), not at the scale of conflicting values and the agencies they generate (Jameson's usual practice) but rather at the generic level, the squared ideological horizon ends up inscribing the subject positions of reading itself. [...] The nagging binary that remains, however, is the one whose founding opposition makes dialectical resolution most strenuous and tentative. Setting itself up against its contrary in the gothic thriller (in the diagram's bottom quadrant) is this logical impasse transformed to cultural blind spot. Sharing the aspect of transcendence (ennoblement) but with one foot in the real, that is, stands (in the upper quadrant) the straddling giant of what Biffen would reject as "psychological realism" (his term for idealized, hence no longer "absolute," realism): a literary practice supposedly cleansed of the preternatural—until it returns by the back door of the reader's own quasi-spectral participation. A novelist like George Eliot would, preeminently, represent the distilled form of the realist enterprise. Hardy's skepticism and sociological diagnosis would lean heavily toward the naturalist pole on one end (joined there by certain New Woman novelists, with only the humanist vestiges of his tragic vision holding him back). By contrast, Dickensian melodrama and sentimentalism would edge toward the zone of romance on the other (though not in the particular *fin de siècle* mode of muscular male fantasy).

If this chapter is traveling in the right direction—if generic determinants are indeed caught up with self-enacted orientations of reading even more dramatically in *fin de siècle* texts than elsewhere in Victorian fiction—then we should be able to commute between such a generic taxonomy as sketched there and a correlative model of response, one in which the tenor of the human events represented gives its coloration, not always protective, to the posture of reception. [...]

And at this stage of the speculation I embark upon a second grid in which "identification" with character in the realist mode is contrasted, in the double negation of objectivity and subjectivity alike, with an uneasy sense of psychic displacement: a vicariousness related to such in-plot aberrations as "doubling" or the "vampiric telepathy" of mind reading.

Or related to a very unique case of transference aspiring to a virtual metempsychosis, a soul-mating from beyond the grave, a supernal mind meld. The longest sustained reading of a single novel in this very long book came in chapter 11, "Mordecai's Consumption: Afterlives of Interpretation in *Daniel*

Deronda." The title's double-edged sense of tubercular demise for the Zionist prophet Mordecai, together with the dreamed-of consumption of his vision in and through Daniel's surviving and inspired discourse, was an irony I thought I had followed out rather exhaustively. But then it came time to take this reading back into the classroom, for a not unfamiliar boomerang effect. Some lecturing is just that, reading in the root sense, reading out loud. And it was only in doing so when deliberately reciting the novel's closing passage about what I saw (its own version of "the gothic of reading") as this dying plea for an almost vampiric transmission of the undead—reading it out loud, that is, to a group of undergraduate students who I feared were overdue in finishing this daunting novel—that I was, for the first time, slowed sufficiently to catch an elusive if thematically arresting phonetic drift. The experience is one I had occasion to write up in a collection of essays on the legacy of my onetime teacher Geoffrey Hartman (1929–2016), since an ad hoc explication of it derived for me so directly from his work. Contributors to this special issue of the Iowa journal *Philological Quarterly* offered up pieces with no titles of their own, headed just by chosen quotations from Hartman's writing. Mine was from an essay of his, "Ghostlier Demarcations," titled in allusion to Wallace Stevens' "The Idea of Order at Key West" (1934), and ran this way: "Myth and metaphor are endued with the acts, the gesta, of speech; and if there is a mediator for our experience of literature, it is something as simply with us as the human body, namely the human voice …. To envision 'ghostlier demarcations' a poet must utter 'keener sounds.'"[1] Referring as I did in this short piece to that classroom moment where I overheard myself in a closer demarcation of the ghostly, let me repeat here some of this compressed testimonial to Hartman's influence as long-postponed addendum to my fourth book, *Dear Reader*:

> Mordecai has eschewed textual form for his visionary formulations, hoping they will be in a sense imprinted, in the spirit rather than the letter, on the soul of his successor (as with a memorized Hebrew poem Mordecai is earlier found "printing" on the "mind" of another would-be protégé. Yet the materiality of alphabetic manifestation is of course required for Eliot's narrative climax and its virtual metempsychosis: its transmigration of the racial soul. Springing a microlinguistic allegory of the reader's relation to text, the spectral hold of Mordecai's hopes on his survivor is funneled through an evanescent trace of the word *ghost* itself, sounded out once as an monosyllabic homophone, and then—I suddenly heard myself uttering—insinuated across a three-word trisyllabic cluster where the lexical revenant of "goest" conjures a spiritual recursion *ex propria persona*, the thrust of the future caught on the cusp of last words.
>
> The "tangible" phonic undertow has certainly been prepared for. In the spirit of ethnic liberation, the Zionist prophet Mordecai, dedicated

to rehabilitating what has been called, by one of his Jewish cohort, the walking "ghost" of such a nationalist vision, and who himself, slowly dying, has already appeared as (again explicitly) a mere "ghost" in his father's sleep, insists at last on a supposedly self-effacing transference with the novel's hero that is actually a spiritual power play. In refusing transcription for his own theological and nationalist meditations ("Call nothing mine that I have written"), he hopes instead that, even while wasting away of "consumption," he can breathe his uninscribed beliefs imperishably, because immaterially, into a surrogate self.

The wish fulfillment is not simply, in his last words, manifested in the utterance "Where thou goest, Daniel, I shall go .... Have I not breathed my soul into you?" Of course, aside from the phonetic play in the "ghostlier demarcations" slyly latent here, nothing could be more in the spirit (and in fact Biblical region) of Hartman's intertextual audits than to hear behind this insistence another same-sex affiliation, Ruth to Naomi in leaving her own people behind: "for whither thou goest, I will go; and where thou lodgest, I will lodge" (Ruth 1:16). In *Deronda*, however, Daniel is pledged from here out to reside at the heart of Mordecai's own absence, a perpetual dislodging caught and flickeringly carried by the latter's expiring words. For pressing upon recognition at this point is not just the phonetic overlay of *ghost* in *goest* but (to fill in that heuristic ellipsis of mine) a further bridge phrasing that ghosts its own phonetic tracks with a lexical gesture hovering between an anagram and a near-miss contraction ("Is't not" for "Isn't it?"): "Where thou *goest*, Daniel, I shall *go. Is it* not begun?"—begun even before being spelled out in the very backdraft of another wording. (Not "*Has* it not *already* begun?" but something closer to "Is it not here and now beginning, hence begun, in just the dilation—and liquidation—of my words?"). Mordecai himself has almost seen this textual epiphenomenon coming, when saying much earlier to Daniel that "you have risen within me like a thought not fully spelled." His own last words can still not quite spell it out. But they come close. [...]

It is never too late to keep learning from Hartman. For I was again made keen, in his fine phrasing, to something so nearly and simply "with" me as my own speaking "body"—and this just as the character gives up his embodied will to speech, a subjectivity displaced now from diegesis to sheer exegesis across the very aspiration (both senses) of his own fused syllables. These vanishing speech sounds fulfill the dying prophet's extratextual will by making its forward momentum impalpable in every way, strictly virtual in its possibility—except in the subvocal pulse of our own enunciative engagement, our own physiological sounding board.

At which point I return to certain resonant terms, previously summarized in the piece, from Hartman's renowned essay, "The Voice of the Shuttle":[2]

> In this ectoplasticity of phrase, "ghost" is not at the end said at all, let alone in spectral echo. Rather, its lexical span is seeded, and twice over, as a linguistic, a phonemic, latency, a vocabular shadow. In this way is the character's last breath rescued, by phonetic irony, for a surplus of meaning. About the voicing shuttle's intermediate shunts: "Juncture is simply a space, a breathing-space: phonetically, it has zero value, like a caesura." But as such it "dramatizes the differential, or as de Saussure calls it, diacritical relation of sound to meaning." Which makes all the difference for a reader like Hartman, whose intimate attentions, to vary that same poem of Stevens he mines for his 1965 title, help literature sing beyond the genius of the seen.

At macro and micro scale in *Dear Reader*, Eliot's treatment of Mordecai's intended fate as an authorization without authorship, in its stranglehold on Daniel, was for me a vivid instance of my subtitle's "conscription" in a negative sense, an aggressive co-optation of another's words. But the word itself, a coinage to that degree (see "Terms of Use"), has, in the associative sense of that one chapter's subtitle, another afterlife—in (and beyond) the graduate classroom this time. Yes, I'll explain. Even for those scholars among us hardly likely to join Mordecai in wishing to disown our words, dissolve them into anonymity ("Call nothing mine that I have written"), their survival value is typically uncertain.

This is to say that a critical writer, unless breaking big with some methodological intervention, is likely to have little idea concerning the aftereffects of a given interpretive move. Who, for instance, concerning the later chapter's emphasis on gothic fiction's yet more perverse fables of readerly submission, might have found my shift to the mapping of a genre dialectic at least half as useful as I found some of Jameson's character mappings? I certainly never stopped teaching his application of that method after I myself got hooked—and have certainly seen students able to mobilize its eye-opening potential in classroom exercises, if not so often in their eventual dissertations. Nor do I know how often the interpolation/extrapolation dyad has been taken up in other scholarship. Yet you never know where an influence might catch fire. As I was collecting these materials, I happened to take part in a dissertation defense of a thesis, directed by a colleague, that made excellent use, with no coaching on my part, of the subtitle for *Dear Reader*. Informed only indirectly by work with me on potential applications of Jonathan Culler's benchmark essay on apostrophe in Romantic poetry to prose forms (from a previous theoretical methods course), Konrad Swartz had put a fine spin, explicitly so, on my subtitle in his thesis on resisted patriotic rhetoric in three cases of Romantic prose. His title: "Writing Against an Enlisted Audience: Reading War in Sterne, Barbauld, and Hogg." Where my term "conscripted reader" was a mere metaphor for the co-production of attention (if sometimes its co-optation) by literary rather than martial *draft*, his "enlisted" (a third meaning extending the two I was mostly moving between) brought new point—and historical pointedness—to the operations of address, explicit and otherwise, in the war rhetoric countered by his writers. That students sometimes come to see, to hear, how literary criticism can have its own literary dimension, can ask more of words than they superficially give, is always encouraging. It is this pedagogical gratification, among other gravitational pulls, that would draw me back to writing about writing before long, with another book on Victorian fiction (*Novel Violence: A Narratography of Victorian Fiction*, 2009). But not before a threefold turn into books on the visual, with the common denominator among them—or say instead the continuous medial stream they attempt so differently to ford—being the sense of image plane as textual field.

Notes

1 Geoffrey Hartman, "Ghostlier Demarcations," in *Literary Criticism—Idea and Act: The English Institute, 1939–1972; Selected Essays*, ed. W. K. Wimsatt (Berkeley: University of California Press, 1974), 226. See also Stewart, *The Deed of Reading*, 2.
2 Geoffrey Hartman, "The Voice of the Shuttle: Language from the Point of View of Literature" (1969), in *Beyond Formalism* (New Haven: Yale University Press, 1970), 336–54.

III.

DISCIPLINE BRIDGING

---

5 / ***Between Film and Screen: Modernism's Photo Synthesis*** (University of Chicago Press, 1999). As indicated by the subtitle, film operates in and by a continuous dialectical contrast, as Stewart "sees it," between fixed photo imprint (technically known as the "photogram") and its self-displaced serial manifestation as motion picture. Stewart discusses the photogram not only as the undertext of screen imaging but also in its unexpected links to the early modernist writings of Henry James, Joseph Conrad, E. M. Forster, James Joyce, and others. Engaging the work of such media theorists as Sergei Eisenstein, Walter Benjamin, Sigfried Krakauer, André Bazin, Jean-Louis Baudry, Stanley Cavell, Gilles Deleuze, and Fredric Jameson, this study pursues the suppressed photogram as it ripples the narrative surface of several dozen films from Fritz Lang and Charlie Chaplin through Ingmar Bergman, Francis Ford Coppola, and beyond. To locate the exact repercussions of such effects, the book's three-hundred-and-some frame enlargements are drawn from genres as different as science fiction, film noir, and recent Victorian costume drama, where photography is either historicized in the dazzle of its advent and rapid innovations, rendered evidentiary by association with the fictional track itself, or projected into future optic marvels, including holographic virtual environments.

---

5 / From Imprint to Motion Picture

Between Film and Screen: Modernism's Photo Synthesis (1999)

I HAD DONE A FEW REVIEWS and journal essays on film to this point, including a comparative piece on "Coppola's Conrad: The Repetitions of Complicity," examining the transformation of Conrad's *Heart of Darkness* into its loose film adaptation, *Apocalypse Now* (1979, dir. Francis Ford Coppola). With this momentum behind me, it seemed time for a full-throttle lane change in my analytic itinerary, though still travelling by much the same route—or say at the same level of rubber-meets-the-road traction in the closeness of analysis, even if in an altogether different medium. *Reading Voices* (1990) had unleashed a more exacting tenor of attention—involving a deeper than previous investment in media theory. I had always been interested in the technique of film, especially in the composition of its cinematography. But it was the 1981 appearance of Roland Barthes' *Camera Lucida*, with his reflection on the fixed imprint as quasi-mortal arrest—crossbred with my work on the literary death scene—that, in slow gestation, sponsored my early teaching, and then my first book, on the cellular composition of narrative cinema as time-based medium, a study scaled in attention, like *Reading Voices*, to the level of constituent increments. Combined with André Bazin's famous emphasis of the "mummy complex" inherited from photography by cinema, such emphasis sent me forward from a preoccupation with the constituent "phonogram" (my coinage for the effects probed in *Reading Voices*) to the comparable serial basis of the film strip. I wanted to explore, for its on-screen inferences, this parallel baseline in differential photograms (received term) in the overrun partitions of their filmic framelines. I set out to assess those moments when film seems inflected by some "optical allusion" to the photo imprint as its own motor and modular condition—and its own lurking cancellation in strategic arrest.

With its title and subtitle flipped by the press' marketing department—to avoid, I was told, the book's "being shelved in the botany section with tomes on photosynthesis"—*Between Film and Screen: Modernism's Photo Synthesis* (1999) concentrated in equal part (or, better, in complementary measure) on two prongs of the issue: optical episodes when photographs, filling the frame, are "narrated" on-screen like miniature framed tales of their own; and when, alternately, narrative becomes sheer backlit photograph (freeze-frame). Such a reciprocal "deconstruction" of the moving image, as with my sense of the disruptive phonetic underlay of wording in verse and prose, wasn't bent on jettisoning the ruse of continuity. Rather, in case after case, analysis disclosed the grip of visual sequence thrown into relief by exceptions actively remotivated for stylistic effect—and these in the (thrown) light of constituent elements latent all along in the file of frames on the strip. Rounding back to the comparable phonotextual waver of prose and poetry, this first of my several books on film closed with a chapter on the equivalent "flicker effects" of modernist writing.

In paving the way for these transmedial claims, the theoretical reading I had done in the move from phonic slippages on the page to the photogrammar of screen sequencing allowed me to venture an amalgam of perspectives from Walter Benjamin on the photographic "unconscious" through Gilles Deleuze in his debate with Henri Bergson on duration and the "time-image," along with several of the scholarly commentators on each position. With dozens of films adduced in evidence, the historical span carried discussion from Charlie Chaplin's *Modern Times* (1936) to Terrence Malick's *Badlands* (1973) and Stanley Kubrick's *The Shining* (1980) alongside such benchmarks of European high modernism as Michelangelo Antonioni and Ingmar Bergman. And yet again, the telltale segue between literary and film projects: a chapter on "Deaths Seen," and, following it, on "Cinema's Victorian Retrofit." The latter chapter concerned the seemingly all-but-mandatory reflexive allusion to turn-of-the-century mechanical reproduction offered by such quite recent efforts at literary adaptation—in the spate of so-called heritage films—as *The Bostonians* (1984), *The Secret Garden* (1993), *The Age of Innocence* (1993), *Jude* (1996), and *The Secret Agent* (1996), including, most Barthesian of all, Truffaut's version of Henry James' "The Altar of the Dead" in *Le Chambre Vert* (1978), each of them turning on moments of photographic imprint in frame or in process.

Late in the book I struck once more a recurrent keynote of this investigation, in its most compressed form—summarizing the inference I was repeatedly struck by: "I have said it before in other terms. The cinematic is modern; the filmic is modernist" (311). Or put it that medial self-recognition turns the screen reflexive. To establish this in the broadest possible terms, I did what my tables of contents have often tried to do, before and since: model the structure of their topics. Here my own title page is preceded by the discussion I "rerun" below, dubbed a "Pretitle Sequence" like the one in the film it concerns—and of course dozens of others. I was exercising there, again, and hardly for the last time, an instinct for smoking out a certain allegorical dimension (as with Dick Swiveller's "fictional" bookcase in my first study, *Dickens and the Trials of the Imagination*, 1974) that turns emblematic medial ironies into a kind of metanarrative: in that initial case, with Dickens' Dick, the vacant place of text as a *telling* sign of the unlettered man of words.

And more pointedly than this general openness to media parables, I've realized from the present culling of extracts, when looking back on my initial shift of focus from literature to film, how certain interpretive logics (and their presentational logistics) die hard. This is to say that the correlation in *Between Film and Screen*—the inherent photogram of film's recursive plastic substrate, on the one hand, with, on the other hand, the on-screen photograph, in all the dyad's structuring complementary across given screen plots—tends to reactivate an organizing interplay familiar from the preceding book, *Dear Reader* (1996). This is the reciprocity between reading's inevitable condition (flagged by occasional address to its participants, often with a stylistic twist that foregrounds such verbal mediation) and the explicit embedding of a synecdochic reading event (resembling the zoom in on a revealing photograph rather than a spluttering or stalled reminder of the film's own photo-file). Those complementary screen variants are there unmistakably and right on the surface, both modes of reflexivity and more, in the pretitle B movie I begin with: narrating in almost madcap complexity the constituent photograph of the Barthesian "death mask" in its photochemical multiplication as death-at-work. In hoping to locate this media allegory as preview to the subtler film work whose implications it would bluntly adumbrate, I was gratified to find that the press was willing to run this thematic "trailer" even before the copyright page.

It is just this rather exhaustive warm-up that I excerpt here. In electing this selection, I have uppermost in mind the ongoing pedagogic syllabus of this volume. I say this because *The Asphyx* (1972, dir. Peter Newbrook) is perhaps the most immediately teachable film I have ever shown to undergraduates. Any student who remains awake will have something analytic to say about it: for there is nothing else to see on screen but an exercise in internalized film theory. The narrative performs nothing else by way of plot except its overheated media analysis. All an instructor needs to do (and even that might go without saying, or simply emerge in discussion after the screening) is to intimate, or more fully lay out, Bazin's distinction between photography as "time embalmed" and cinema as "change mummified"—and the class is off and running. This happens in ways that should be clear without the nine frame grabs that, on original printing, helped pace this lugubrious film—as interpretive prelude—across its unblinking mix of plot summary and metafilmic charge. And another way of placing this segment within the whole arc of this Reader comes to mind. Concerning the hokey and cheapjack special effects, especially of superimposition, discussed below, I was interested, in retrospect, to see myself trying out a vocabulary for reflexive VFX (visual special effects) that would come to dominate my return to cinema theory almost two decades later, in both the last two chapters of *Cinemachines* (2020) and the first two of *The Metanarrative Hall of Mirrors* (2022). Special effects: always teachable in themselves (as I would certainly find in the run-up to each of my later film books) because, sophisticated or cheesy, they remain especially appealing (and effortlessly visible) to the undergrad cynic and enthusiast alike.

> It must be one of the least catchy titles in the annals of popular film: *The Asphyx*. Anyone who could spell it should have been admitted free back in 1972. Yet it is just the film to bring forward here as prelude to an unrolling look at the intersection of photography and film: or more exactly, at the instantaneous cross sections of the former on the swift strip of the latter [...]. In comparing photography with cinema, media theory long ago began worrying about the relation of the preserved image to the death whose fixity it mocks in one case, artificially overcomes in the other. The plot of this gothic potboiler both tropes and negotiates just that difference between deathlike stasis and its overflow in motion.
>
> Like this book, *The Asphyx* too gets under way before its title and credits set in. After an auto accident in modern-day London where two cars converge upon an aged pedestrian, we cut to a bobby's astonishment over the surviving decrepit body of an unspeakably old man. The adverbial double take of "This man's still alive!"—after the crash, after all these years—precipitates the second stage of the prologue, overlapping eventually with the emerging titles. A Victorian laboratory has long ago gone to seed, with cobwebs strangling the four family photographs still arrayed on the decaying mantelpiece as the camera roves past each image: the photographic mausoleum as matrix of the entire narrative. Seen repeatedly in the background of

subsequent retrospective action in this very room, these fixed images from a time long gone identify the four subsidiary characters—and chief victims—in a plot that will concern the protagonist's demonic efforts at immortality.

Peter Newbrook's *The Asphyx* (unknown to buffs and scholars alike in my acquaintance) is a film that cannot be overread, since it is all media allegory to begin with, *Frankenstein* in the age of mechanical reproduction. What the Victorian Lord Sir Hugo Cunningham has secretly connived, in his excessive cunning, is not just an experimental procedure like Victor Frankenstein's but a full-fledged apparatus. It will turn out to be a contrivance of death in perpetual arrest. Cinema itself becomes the overweening scientist's monstrous progeny, with its own access to mechanical immortality emerging—across the baroque details of the fable—as the ultimate revenge against its Promethean creator. If to make a man is to steal God's thunder, to capture eternity in a projected beam of light is to steal the supernal fire of a demiurge.

For this book *The Asphyx* should do three things at the outset. First, it should help sketch a difference in the figuration of visual technology that will necessarily pervade these chapters: between the relation of death to photography on the one hand and to film on the other. Second, it should serve up another distinction: between the vexing temporality of filmed photographs (even full screen) and film's own photograms (separate celluloid imprints on the strip) when these single images are prolonged (reduplicated) in the screen stasis of the so-called freeze-frame. And third, it should begin contextualizing these issues in Victorian photographic experiments and their impact (among other ocular influences) on the *fin-de-siècle* invention of motion pictures, a transitional moment to which the last two chapters will, in different ways, return at length.

The technological fable devised by *The Asphyx* rests on a satire of aristocratic privilege and its desperate attempts at an inbred familial longevity. In his explicit desire that his own Cunningham spawn should oversee all future historical development, the aging Sir Hugo has at first a fairly modest and mainstream plan. As he explains to his son during a chat in the family burial vault, he has decided on a young second wife eager to bear him more heirs. Alas, the fiancée and Sir Hugo's son are killed in a boating accident in the very next scene. It is an accident caused by Sir Hugo's insistence on having them row on the family lake so he can preserve their images with his newest invention, matter-of-factly announced as "a device whereby I can record moving objects." Cut to the laboratory, where he screens the results. These are the world's first home movies, memorializing the dead in a second ancestral tomb. The Victorian craze for spirit photography has been upgraded to produce a kinetic revenant: the ghostly image of ghosts in the making, of death in process. With Lumière and Edison turning over in their graves, Sir Hugo is imagined by this plot to have beaten them to the punch in order, finally, to avoid his own grave—not, as we might so far expect, by preserving life in motion but by entombing the very agency of death. [...]

In the course of his charity work with the dying, as he himself admits, Sir Hugo ended up taking more interest in recording death than in easing it. In photographing the sufferers he was repeatedly able to capture a certain smear on the picture near the head of the dying, as he demonstrates in one scene to a society of gentleman amateurs. Was it the soul leaving the body? Good guess, but Sir Hugo comes to suspect that what he has photographed is, instead, the instantaneous descent rather than the spiritual upshot of death: something like the literalized form of the proverbial shadow of death. To be certain which way that shadow is moving, he therefore needs to invent the moving-picture camera, years ahead of its time, an ad hoc contraption to which he neglects to give a name. Think of it, in one of the terms for early cinema, as a "biograph"—at least until the ghoulish metaplot thickens around it.

We know already of the machine's ill-fated debut. And even there the results were inconclusive, since filming was suspended in panic after the accident before it could be decided whether the shadow was coming or going. Certainly Sir Hugo's unexplained ability to still the frame in replaying this fatal footage doesn't settle the issue of directionality. Where better to try again than at a public execution, a hanging? Says the surviving adopted son, "This can prove nothing—but harmful." Nonsense. Off to the execution, with a newly sophisticated two-part apparatus. Sir Hugo's own moving-image camera is now accompanied by a high-powered—and of all things chemically fueled—lamp, set up right behind the mob at the hanging. Just as the body drops through the trap, what Sir Hugo discovers in action is that the puzzling smudge he has been studying is in fact an ectoplasmic phantom captured—yes, as it *arrives* on the scene—in the ancillary beam of light. This is our long-awaited title figure, the Greek spirit of death, the asphyx itself (associated first with the asphyxiation of drowning, now with the strangulation of hanging).

Among the questions that remain (to prolong the narrative) is whether this figure of fate is subjectively present to its victim, seen from within as well as objectively visible to an onlooker. [...] "There is a widely held belief," Sir Hugo soon recalls, "that a dead man retains the indelible image of death" (alluding, no doubt, to human eye tissue as offering a fleeting *optogramme* of the death moment, a proposal of nineteenth-century ophthalmic science that earlier makes its way, we will find, into the history of science fiction film). If the seeing body, as storage mechanism, is already an instantaneous photograph of its own fate, what might it yield up to a secondary photographic probe? One must find out. Having exhumed his dead son after two weeks of burial, Sir Hugo takes a posthumous image of the potentially telltale body, to be studied later in the laboratory (to no avail). [...] To rephotograph the moment itself as captured on the body's own film, Sir Hugo suspects, you had to have been there sooner.

Yet there may be a better explanation altogether. Thinking back to the execution, Sir Hugo guesses out loud that the resistant will of the hanged man, some residual life force inwardly generated, may have been less instrumental in stalling death's lethal moment than was the objective illumination of the experiment's own chemically generated beam of light, which seemed momentarily able to edge the death phantom away from its victim. The speculation solidifies on the spot to the narrative's own axiom. Detached from recording itself in this schematic setup, and anticipating instead film's destiny in projection, the supplemental beam—the so-called booster light—is of course necessary not only to secure and *convey,* as it were, the moving image but, in this exacerbated case, to trap and transport its deathly essence.

So back to the laboratory once more, for an experiment on Sir Hugo himself. We learn there how the beam that pinions the asphyx in a tubular prison of light must be sustained by the continuous dripping of water on phosphite crystals, a chemistry associated with Sir Hugo's previous cutting-edge laboratory work in the enhanced development of photos. He now nearly electrocutes himself in order to secure the gothic equivalent of cinema's electrical afterlife, halting the current just in time. At the first sign of galvanic spasms and the encroachment of the asphyx, the stepson is ordered to edge the ghoul-laden beam into a coffin-shaped box, screen right, with a small rectangular window to disclose its contents to perpetual view. The father's death spirit is then carried into the family crypt, hence laying to rest the specter of death itself. The encrypted cinematic reference is hardly contained there, however, even though death, lit from within the apparatus, has been turned into a continuous framed spectacle in a wide-screen field of view. Let me interrupt my capsule re-broadcast of this late-night TV rerun (just reissued as a "cult classic" on DVD) to examine the spectatorial genealogy written across the mounting violence of the narrative. We've noted the scientist's inspirational leap from gallows to electric jolts, and that's only the half of it. Two modes of execution down, two to go. It is from the tombstone of his subsequently slain daughter that we know precisely that Sir Hugo Cunningham's invention of the motion-picture camera and projector took place in 1875, twenty years before the historical fact. As it happens, the daughter met her death when a laboratory accident prevented Sir Hugo, after briefly seizing her asphyx, from arresting her guillotine in the nick of time. In the wake of the father's own near death in a makeshift electric chair, this Continental violence *á la mode* is followed by the adopted son's successful suicide in a glassed-in gas chamber, completing a series begun with the urban spectacle of the hanging. Four times over, the techniques of ritualized public violence have been turned to private account. Figuratively speaking—and such figuration is the film's true discourse—the cinematic projector (disguised finally as a perpetually lit coffin) emerges from these commandeered mechanisms of formalized state slaughter not only as an immortality machine but as a new form of mass-cultural exhibition.

While cinema's private manipulation by the mad scientist is being extrapolated to the level of its eventual public consumption, its photochemical essence is also being slyly redoubled at the level of the thrown image itself. The lone "special" effect that precedes this boxing in of the fantastic lays bare a double trick of cinematic specificity. The logic is as simple as it is circular. Turn on a projector with prepared footage of a slithering monster, probably a rubber hand puppet, direct the beam against a backdrop that will permit the imaged creature's hazy materialization (an almost theatrical curtain), and then call the optical labor ensnaring rather than relinquishing, capture rather than projection. Such is the mumbo jumbo of cinema as demonic effect to its own technological cause.

At a similar metamedial level, after the experimental deaths of his remaining two children in further baroque plot complications, his exploded laboratory goes up, not in layers of smoke, but just in the thick of filmy superimpositions that simulate it. Everything is, in sum, has always been, about the actual apparatus for which this fable finds substitutes as its parable.

On the inherent shadow play of the photographic plate, what is that further intrusive shadow associated with death? Intrinsic or contingent? The speculative scientist cannot be sure, in short, whether photography suspends death or in its own right instantiates it (also a problem for the theorists of the medium from the 1840s through André Bazin to Roland Barthes and beyond). So the amateur photographer sets about inventing cinema to find out. [...] Although at the stage of initial imprint the machinated sequence of frame upon frame does seem to capture death in action (the arriving asphyx, as at another level the single arresting and remobilized photogram), it is really the beam of delivered rather than received light, at the other pole of the apparatus, that catches (and detains) death in its true cinematic aspect. This is the death that is always on the way but always postponed, on hold in the same chamber of channeled light that allows for the materialized timeless continuance of a moving human figure—one whose natural aging is in this way photochemically forestalled. Thus does the mad scientist's variant of cinematic technology deflect the visitation of death by rendering its virtual spirit visible within a rectangular viewing frame. The bulky wooden repository is death's prepared coffin, not life's. [...] Filmic mechanism in this sense takes the sting out of the transience it must maximize. As montage rather than narrative, movies show us the mortal in the act of surviving itself, invincible in its continuities. Photographs on the fly, that is, work to manufacture the persistent under the sponsorship of the repeatable. And just as fixity is cheated by speed, finality is outplayed by recurrence.

Doing research a while back at the National Film Institute in Stockholm, I contributed to its mission by buying a souvenir t-shirt printed, in tiny Swedish script, with the following quotation, dated 30 December 1895, from the French journal *La Poste:* "On that day when the public can partake of such apparatuses as these and everybody can photograph their near and dear not just as still pictures but even in movement, with their familiar gestures and lips formed to words, death will no longer be terminal." Real enough, but no longer *terminal;* no longer *quite* over. In its own gothic code, this is roughly what *The Asphyx,* too, has to say—as well as show—for itself on the matter of photography, cinema, and the alternative valences of death that drive them: the mortal versus the endless, each equally of a piece, as it were, with lifelessness. So has a single mixed exercise in popular narrative genres, fictional science crossed with the supernatural, served to depopulate the entrenched humanist dimension of a whole school of film theory. If cinema intercedes in the deathwork of photography to do no more than defer its fixity indefinitely rather than to transcend it, so much for phenomenology's sense of cinema as lived duration under the sign of becoming. So much for animation as more than an effect of stasis and its motorized traces. Encapsulated and encoded in this one frail film artifact, the metaplot of cinematic history has come to the corrective rescue of the apparatus' own mystification. If not exactly a good movie, it's not a bad ghost story, after all. [...]

Keeping in mind both the vanishing trace of the photogram and Sir Hugo's weird science, each seizing the onset of an absentation, we may leave it for now as follows: Photography is death in replica; cinema is a dying away in progress, hence death in serial abeyance. Lined up in rows, pieced out, flicked past, then thrown forward toward the lit screen, the elementing photographs on the film track vibrate before us as the death throes of presence succumbing to a temporality not its own, world time transposed to screen time. This is to say that cinema exists in the interval between two absences, the one whose loss is marked by any and all photographic images and the one brought on by tossing away each image in instantaneous turn. The effects are different enough to make for two separate media, two distinct powers of mortal mediation. Whereas photography engraves the death it resembles, cinema defers the death whose escape it simulates. The isolated photo or photogram is the still work of death; cinema is death always still at work. That should certainly be enough to get us going.

In introducing this "Pretitle Sequence," I hedged in calling its screen exhibit "perhaps the most immediately teachable film I have ever shown to undergraduates." It certainly has its close competition in Michael Powell's 1960 *Peeping Tom*, at least once I discovered Laura Mulvey's splendid Criterion commentary on it. And only then, in screening that voice-over track for students in my recently devised class "Reading Movies for Prose Writers" (Mulvey's own exegesis an incomparable one-stop analytic and theoretical primer for screen analysis), did I realize something I had failed to remark on, let alone notice—or if noticing, failed to *pay attention to*—in concentrating on the film's surveillance motif for *Closed Circuits* (2015). My only consolation is that Mulvey didn't call out this salient effect either, despite her searching treatment of the scene in question and her scrupulous connection, elsewhere in the commentary, between Eadweard Muybridge's precinematic chronophotography and the fixities of the photograph as symbolic corpse. Such is the anatomical figuration she varies Bazin to call "fossilization" rather than "mummification"—and which she finds operating in the film as a whole via a psychotic screen reanimation of the already slain.

So again, let me play catch-up with myself. For in this preliminary scene—entailing the first image of processed film in the main body of the narrative—a sheepish middle-aged gentleman has wandered into a newsstand/porn shop for some "views," ogling a number of black-and-white girlie shots before deciding to take "the lot." All of this transpires in earshot of the eponymous pinup photographer himself, we soon discover, staring down at the black-and-white tabloid cover photo of the prostitute he has slain the night before, as we know from this film's own pretitle sequence. Her image appears on the stack of newspapers that he now, all caution momentarily thrown to the wind, accordions out to a row of serial duplicates tacitly associated in his mind with the coveted and fetishized film strip he has made of the killing, one sadistic frame after another. For the chance of such an afterthought I do remain truly grateful to the delayed-fuse structure of these TexTcerpts.

> 6 / ***The Look of Reading: Book, Painting, Text*** (University of Chicago Press, 2006), another lavishly illustrated text, appends again a telltale subtitle, since the book in painting, both held by its reader and holding attention there, turns the canvas itself into a text of reading's projected ambience or formal articulation. Across five centuries of this recurrent painterly scene, which Stewart's evidence renders unmistakable as an ongoing genre, the internalized impact of unseen words is made visible, by compositional displacement, in the architecture or landscape that embeds the reading body—while reembodying its mental response. From Rembrandt through the book-like folds of the cubist reading body to the mangled newsprint crushed underfoot by Francis Bacon's twisted corporeal forms, the scene of reading helps read the history of art—until, with the outmoding of figure painting altogether, the internal surface of the page comes to fill the canvas altogether, in varying developments from Lettrism to a conceptualist movement like Art and Language.

6 / *Pages Painted, Writing Withdrawn*

The Look of Reading: Book, Painting, Text (2006)

THE PREFATORY COMMENTS I've been offering in this dossier of homecomings have never been so sure of the gestation of a project, rather than just of its filiations, as they are regarding the crash course in art history and art theory leading to *The Look of Reading*—a book I never dreamed I'd (need to) write. The sponsoring question had survived the lengthy preparation for *Between Film and Screen* in the form, time now permitting, for a finally scratched itch. In *Dear Reader* (1996), among the frontispieces of reading scenes I had selected for each chapter from a growing collection of my own, was the anonymous Victorian photograph of a skeleton at a wooden schoolroom desk for the previously excerpted chapter "The Gothic of Reading" (XIII). That seemed, as "posed" image, not just a macabre gimmick, but intuitively thematic: one of art's litmus tests of interiority stripped to the bone on the canonical spot. Other images in my collection of reading scenes included more traditional live bodies lost in the otherworld of text. What, I was curious to find out, did art history have to say about this canvas topos? Except when it could identify the sitter-with-book in such scenes, Rembrandt's mother, Cezanne's father, one of Picasso's mistresses, or some mistreated and in fact illiterate hired model, the record was weirdly silent. No mention of formal patterns projected in recess from the disappeared content of the inner paper field within the enclosing canvas rectangle. No claims for the prevalence of this scene as what art historian Michael Fried might call an "absorptive" subgenre in itself, in contrast to the unpeopled still life with books.

At once balked and tantalized, I had too many leftover examples to be satisfied with this categorical indifference. Tantalized, yes, and soon something more like obsessed. After a decade-long search through the museums of eleven countries on three continents—all this before the ubiquity of museum search engines and their digitized holdings—my bulging catalogue was complete enough to prompt some, I hoped, more or less definitive remarks. And not just on the painted woman reading, prototype of the genre, in connection with the generally illegible surface of her pages (prompting the titular play on "Facing Pages" in my introductory "Overview"), but on the evolution of this surface into what I dubbed the full-frame "lexigraph" of Conceptual art, from Picasso's "imaginary alphabets" to the "deconstructive" Xerography of Mark Tansey's figures-with-words. Excerpts from *The Look of Reading* are at a special disadvantage here. Losing the illustrations in this reprinting is even more of a hurdle for sampling than the lack of frame grabs from the film books. I'll set the pattern, therefore, with an easily described pop example (quickly ascertained with an online image search: *New Yorker* cover, December 28, 1998), where a limited ekphrasis can get the point across. Then—passing over the extended descriptions of what I call "reverse ekphrasis" (the painterly representation of a verbal experience) from Bellini to Balthus—this sampling will jump straight to the conceptual ironies of an evacuated figuration in sites (rather than scenes) of mere brush-stroked or stenciled inscription, easier by definition to describe in words.

> Like many scholarly plans in the humanities, *my* idea for a next book (this one) was partly scooped at the late December convention of the Modern Language Association—not in the lecture rooms or new book exhibits, as often happens, but on the hotel newsstands. The *New Yorker* of December 28, 1998, had just come out, and Art Spiegelman's cover seemed to say it all. It did so by offering its own compact version of an art historical format. A buttoned-up snowman may look at first glance to be doffing his bowler at a bikini-clad blond. But since he is armless, like most snowmen, he is more likely to be popping his cork at the uncanny sight. The female figure is sunbathing, outdoors, in the dead of winter, or seems to be—or feels like she is, with her book (more than her beach towel) providing a magic carpet ride to a cheap winter vacation. For she is reading a volume called *Fiction*. We quickly catch on that it announces in miniature that annual fiction issue for which she is the year's cover girl. We get this twist of the joke as soon as we notice the dapper gent, rather than flabbergasted snowman, on the cover of her volume (boasting a top hat rather than a bowler) and recognize him as the emblematic figurehead of the magazine. In more generic terms, within a long pictorial tradition of undraped female readers, desire seems once again redistributed in ratio: the book as alluring to the buxom reader as she is to the potential magazine buyer (as well as to the on-site man of ice). And

gender aside, this image also takes its place in painted reading's centuries-long campaign to advertise the virtues as well as the thrill of readerly surrender: everything from literacy training and domestic sentiment through information gathering and spiritual improvement to the accoutrements—or even surrogates—of winter tourism.

With its exaggerated digest of the tradition, Spiegelman's jaunty takeoff left the scene of reading precisely where I had planned to take it up. Looking ahead to the research involved, I had braced myself for a considerable backlog of commentary. Instead, only museums, not libraries, would turn out to address my questions and, now and then, confirm my hunches. I had instinctively begun with what I took to be the simplest premise of such pictures. From the look of it, the moment captured in the painted scene of reading has already carried the mind away. Only paradox could do justice to the simultaneous focus and dispersion of the scene. Reading is where you go to be elsewhere. In taking in a page, readers are themselves taken in by it—and out of themselves. With this in mind, I wanted to investigate the specific art historical and social developments under whose auspices the scene of reading has been painted over the centuries, as well as the persistent mystery of transport that such painting thinks less to capture, exactly, than to release.

The appeal of this scene has certainly not slackened for the contemporary imagination, as we know from all those point-of-sale art calendars and notecard sets of nineteenth-century reading women flooding museum gift shops at the turn of our digital millennium, with their images of unplugged textual pleasure. Why a potentially diminishing breed of modern book lovers (often ordering their volumes on the internet to begin with) may hanker after the image trove of their literate ancestors—the reader at ease in an easier chair and time—may not seem so puzzling. But why in the first place did painters offer up so much unwitting fodder for this eventual nostalgia? And much there is, in one metropolitan museum after another. On an average day, there may be almost as many readers on the walls of the Tate, for instance, as there are across town in the chairs of the British Library Reading Room. What's the insatiable appeal for the painters? Why labor so intensely to evoke the unpicturable space, and often the illegible page, of textual fascination? For long after the image of page-rooted attention had passed beyond the closed circle of the Logos in biblical art, where the Word subsumes all read text, the formidable challenge to painting raised by the secular scene of reading is hard to deny. Stasis, blankness, introversion: these are not normally the stuff of scenic drama.

The representational hurdle faced by the painters would have seemed almost insurmountable—unless it could be turned to a sly advantage. This is because, as with other forms of gradually satisfied desire, with reading, too, you really have to be there. Reflection isn't enough to call up the exact contours of its gratification—let alone representation, least of all a fixed image. Though painting may induce any number of desires, it cannot convey the sequence of their quenching. All it gives, borrowing from Keats, is the feel of not to feel it. That's the thing about reading in painting. Even while casting its spell in absentia, it withholds the duration of its pleasure. So why doom the canvas to such recurrent frustration? This first and recurrent question has led, very slowly, to a main claim of this book: that painted reading can, in its most ambitious instances, recruit narrative energy even while removing it from view. But removing it where? There, again, is the real consideration. I have asked what painting saw in reading. But this question may seem to narrow the field to a largely compositional matter. Answering only in these terms could well miss the cultural system that figure painting at large both reinscribes and, perhaps more than any other medium, helps naturalize. [...] What such investigation comes to, in sum, is as much an ideological cross-examination of the reading scene as a compositional one. How does the visual discourse of this loosely constellated genre resume from period to period, at once summarize and renew, an abiding definition of the "inward" human subject? This is a subject whose inwardness is not just proven by invisibility but incidentally vouched for by the graphically imagined force field of its cognitive energy. And this is an energy, in turn, that comes to include, under developing discourses of literacy, the full psychosomatic contours of a subvocal, respiratory, and emotive participation in the silent manufacture of textual meaning. Whatever the time frame covered by the story or treatise being read, and however much the subjective horizon may be expanded by it, reading is always a putting in of body time as well, including the prolonged, fluctuating engagement of the nervous system and its multiple affective and physiological registers. It is just this vulnerability to sensation, of course, that makes textuality such an insinuating force in social programming, even under the guise of leisure indulgence.

Art criticism, however, had taken little interest, I soon found, in anything concerning the painted scene of reading [...]. So it was back to the drawing board. [...]

With that turn of phrase—and routing of research attention—I moved through the main thoroughfares of the canon, as well as the sideroads of its sprawling suburbs, in a manner that ended up aligning the history of canvas figuration with the history of subjectivity down through the kinetic fractures of cubism and beyond. Long after Art Spiegelman's broad *New Yorker* comedy as launch,

I turn to the non-magazine work of caricaturist Saul Steinberg late in the volume. His marvelously enticing faux documents, with their fluent script of loops and furbelows, offer a way into the related tradition of asemic writing that Roland Barthes called, and himself practiced, as the "illisible"—this under the influence of Cy Twombly's graphist scrawling. Given Steinberg's exquisite simulations of archival documents, one faces his pages by trying to read them, only to be thrown back on mere looking—and then on the vanished difference, in regard to drawn lines per se, between two-dimensional viewing and reading. In my account of recent word art, his high-comic documents find their edgier lexigraphic counterparts in the alphabetic ironies of civil rights activism by Glenn Ligon (b. 1960) and, not unrelated, the deconstructive painting of a world of words in the art of Mark Tansey's metacritical *Close Reading*, irresistible as a sample in this Reader.

> In one of lexigraphic art's most recent innovations, the work of African American painter Glenn Ligon inhabits exactly the disappearing border of the "imagetext" (W. J. T. Mitchell's term again)—or, in other words, the fault line of the figure/ed/ discourse divide in Lyotard. In the partial return to "figure painting" achieved by Ligon's silkscreen palimpsests, stenciled words are laminated over silhouette images, blacks upon gray blacks, in an ironic commentary on the semiotics of race. In a series based on the Million Man March in Washington, D.C., a river of black faces (group portrait as mass icon) seems overlaid, or maybe underwritten, by an intricate grid of shimmering letters enhanced by the onyx glint of coal dust worked into the paint. These are fragments that excerpt well-known bits of text on African American life, in this case lines from James Baldwin. The collaged and neutralized print rows of a former cubist background have been unleashed, instead, to graphic confusion in a figure-ground waver. Image blurs into letter, text into image, so that blackness is as much a meshed discourse as a perception. There is no implied scene of reading here, for reading always comes before looking, screens and partly occludes it. In the cultural critique of Ligon's art, stencil-clean *écriture* and figure painting together find a renewed and deeply motivated alliance. Under the blanket of signage, image struggles with type and stereotype alike. [...]

Pause button again, before moving on to the book's closing evidence with Tansey. It was long after having selected the Ligon as example for this compressed portfolio that I came upon another work of Black politics in the form of wall art, oil on canvas in this case, that operated a comparable logic in terms of remediated digital video rather than overprinted photography. It would, had I known of it when drafting *The Look of Reading*, have seemed to forecast for me, if only in further hindsight, both my next two film books, one on digital narrative

(*Framed Time*, 2007) and one on surveillance video (*Closed Circuits*, 2015), and a third volume in part on pixel glitching in the transmedial ironies of Conceptual art (*Transmedium*, 2017). The large 1990 canvas by African American artist Kori Newkirk (b. 1970) is gridded into roughly six-inch square monochrome pixels in a cluster of brown and blue tones obscurely tracing the artist's own face and characteristic work shirt: abstracted here in evoking the supposedly euphemistic image-censoring, the digital blurring, of suspected perpetrators on TV news. In this painted screen (out), titled *Channel 11*, the artist has represented himself not in a self-portrait, as he insists in an accompanying wall text at the Santa Barbara Museum of Art, but rather as a depersonalized stand-in for "the collective black body today." Such is the suspect body (un)seen by generalization, legally (un)identified in the forensic eye of the Other.

It is an occlusion of another sort, of world by words, that ties the final example in *The Look of Reading* back to Ligon's Black graphic activism:

> The major *écriture* works in question by Tansey, which themselves call into stringent question the relation of the verbal to the visual in any imaging, are his "deconstructive" monochrome landscapes with figures from 1990. *Close Reading* the title of a famous one, offers the conceptual rubric for them all. In this often-reprinted image, a female mountain climber hangs suspended against a vertiginous cliff made all the more precipitous and risky, one supposes, by being scored all over with apparently incised (though in fact Xeroxed) and mostly indecipherable print phrases—no doubt citing the poststructuralist critics that the word-work of Tansey's canvases so often incorporates. On this slippery slope of geological ontology, the crags and streakings of language offer a veritable archaeology of cognition under arrest by the sludge of hyper-legible overprinting. Despite the evasive mode of inscription, and its implied role at the base of pictorial imaging, another fact comes forward in this visual irony—epistemological as much as intermedial. Nature, even at its most rugged, is laced and veined with culture to begin with. Arrive at rock bottom, that is, come face-to-face with the real, and what the human eye may find is a stratification of discourse.
>
> I close with Tansey's lexigraphic splendors—and the paintings are indeed wonderfully compelling in their monochrome cool—for the way in which their late arrival into the ken of the present book can further widen the lens of their own intermedial wit. On consideration, they reach beyond a deconstructor's irony to the adjacent field of visuality studies and its revisionist work in subjective cognition itself. This is because the difficulty of reading nature, in a canvas like *Close Reading*, isn't just a postromantic irony of hermeneutics. Such an image also posits—or at least poses as a question—the inherence of

preconception in the very work of vision to begin with. This question can be floated even when, as in this particular canvas, all linguistic infiltration remains layered, murky, indistinct, or, say, subliminal: beneath clear lineation as print form. All such lexigraphic vistas in Tansey's work, all those monumental land-scripts, thereby converge directly with the genre of reading. They do so by driving the romantic trope of a legible universe into the very ground: the stony ground to any and all figure, but also the material basis twice over (as hinted here by a suppressed lexical wordplay) of their own intermedial execution. That tacit wordplay happens to recall a special sense, in Quintilian, of the figure of catachresis, a sense often mobilized by Anglo-American literary theory. Interested in its functioning as a variant of dead metaphor, deconstruction finds in catachresis the default option (the unpoetic manifestation) of such a figurative use when applied in the absence of a "proper" or more literal term. Such phrasing can therefore stand forth as a reminder in ordinary language of the metaphoric grain, the tacit rhetoric; that always threatens to intervene in even the most transparent language. In Tansey's *Close Reading*, as the averted face of its strenuous reader turns from us toward the features of the cliff face, such inert metaphors of personification may well call up in turn the deader metaphor yet of that typeface that composes and attracts, respectively, the other two faces: those of the inscribed verticality and of the reader clinging to it. Or to put it in an equally double sense, words are always there before us in confronting the world's partly masked image.

Besides that spate of unsaid verbal formulas behind the illegible word paste of Tansey's impacted lexigraphic sur/faces (those of canvas and natural stone "tablet" alike), and thus beyond the way they take me back yet again to the "close reading" (between the lines) inculcated by Michael Riffaterre, there is further connection in *The Look of Reading* to past and future work of mine concerning other media. For while considering lexigraphic art's displacement of the reading body, I had included an anomalous instance of that body's actual scene in the form of a filmed rather than painted scenario. Discussion invited at one point a comparison between Christopher Wool's word art, in this case his 1988 block-letter *Apocalypse Now*, and its unspecified source in Coppola's 1979 film, bringing to a head the slow unfolding of Kurtz's madness—

[...] where the viewer over Willard's shoulder, and the camera with us, comes upon an intercepted note home from his predecessor: reformatted by Wool in five enjambed and erratically spaced lines as "SELL THE/HOUSE S/ELL THE C/AR SELL/THE KIDS."

Not illustrated here, as it is by frame grab in *The Look of Reading*, is a point I had, in fact, only noticed after multiple class screenings—too late for inclusion in my earlier article on the film:

> For, updating the convex mirror of the northern Renaissance, what camerawork allows for in *Apocalypse Now* remains unprecedented, as far as I have found, in the archive of imaged reading. This is the prolonged central episode where Willard moves through the dossier in alternating close-ups of its pages and his unreadable look—alternating but only until the camera incorporates the former into the latter. Not only does Willard end up moving his lips to those fevered words of Kurtz he silently reads, but there is a further somatic internalization made visible on-screen when self and its text (even self and its pictured double in the included photos of Kurtz) are laminated together in the same plane, with the huge closeup of Willard's eye capturing in reflection the upturned file just to the lower left of his narrowed pupil.

And yet another belatedness, though nobody's fault here. The subtitle of this segment, "Pages Painted, Writing Withdrawn," covers the main weight of evidence in *The Look of Reading*, to be sure. But as seen above (if only in word pictures of pictured words), the captured rectangle of the page, reframed by the canvas rectangle, eventually suffers a reversal by which all visual representation is at times "withdrawn" in favor of writing in paint, the canvas reduced to page. There emerges, then, a regret chalked up not to anything remiss on my part, just to bad timing. I wish I had known, via a decade and a half's leap of clairvoyance on the score of "reverse ekphrasis," of art historian T. J. Clark's passing question in "Painting the Poem"—amid his broad critique of ekphrastic poetry as missing the materiality of canvas depiction—about why painters haven't gotten more from poetry in exchange.[1] I might have speculated about a reciprocal medium envy. And more than that, I could have proposed as partial answer to his question the last third of *The Look of Reading*, and later some part of *Transmedium*, where from an evolutionary angle, under the sign of the sign, representational painting gradually disappeared from prominence, passing through "literature" altogether into Lettrism and the conceptual word art of the lexigraph, as evidenced not least, and early on, by the "imaginary alphabets" (I mention again) of Clark's beloved Picasso.

Let the evidence show, as they say, in this respect and others, that I was already primed for a return from a genealogy of text on canvas to my former base of operations in written narrative. I negotiated the return in reverse order, as logged in next: moving from twentieth-century screen textuality back to Victorian fiction in the next two linked monographs (from *Framed Time*, 2007, to *Novel Violence*, 2009)—more committed in each, after my excurse into painting, to account for the particular (often particulate) materiality of their separate modes of time-based inscription. First, I was eager to bring into sharper focus the mutating cinematic substrate—in the surrender of celluloid to digital—under the adjustable magnification of a narrative stylistics I had come to term "narratography"; then, and again under the lens of comparably scaled lexical and syntactic "graphing" of narrative sequence, to formulate a comparable microstylistics for Victorian fiction (ahead in Phase IV / 8).

> 7 / In ***Framed Time: Toward a Postfilmic Cinema*** (University of Chicago Press, 2007), direct sequel to 5 / above, two European cinematic precedents orient Stewart's follow-up study. Where philosopher Gilles Deleuze questioned, before his death, what would happen to the "time-image" in "numeric" (i.e., digital) rather than celluloid cinema, Italian director Michelangelo Antonioni had earlier characterized the question of time as a founding difference between a European humanist cinema and the manipulations of futuristic sci-fi in Hollywood storytelling. Stewart brings the question and the claim together to pursue further how the new self-transforming frame of pixel cinema is differently manifest in the contemporary divide between European "art cinema" (down through the French Extrematists) and the "temportation" plots of current American film. Interpreting dozens of recent movies—from *Being John Malkovich* (1999, dir. Spike Jonze), *Donnie Darko* (2001, dir. Richard Kelly), and *The Sixth Sense* (1999, dir. M. Night Shyamalan) to *La mala educación* (*Bad Education*, 2004, dir. Pedro Almodóvar) and *Caché* (*Hidden*, 2005, dir. Michael Haneke)—Stewart investigates how digital disclosure, in the mode of editing or special effects, is recruited to theme by way of an optically marked "narratography" operating quite differently in the two separately developing cinematic traditions. While Hollywood movies in this vein tend to revolve around ghostly afterlives, psychotic doubles, or violent time travel, their European counterparts more often feature second sight, erotic telepathy, or spectral memory. How the pixel grid of digital imaging can be raised to analytic consciousness in pursuing this transatlantic distinction is one of the book's sustained surprises.

7 / From Celluloid to Digitime

Framed Time: Toward a Postfilmic Cinema (2007)

AS IS OFTEN THE CASE FOR ME, the title *Framed Time* was marked by an oblique convergence of classroom exchange and critical work, harking all the way back to ambiguities of the phonotext in *Reading Voices* (1990). After many intervening years of teaching both literature and film, I had only belatedly discovered two phonetic uncertainties that had often bedeviled my undergraduate presentations to an easily distracted audience. The first of these hitches, effortlessly explained away at the blackboard once I realized the problem, was the students' tendency to hear "free indirect discourse" as "free and direct discourse." What it took me longer to notice, given the vague climate of confusion that sometimes ensued, was the inability of certain students to distinguish container from contained in the dental elision (*d/t*) of framed tale versus frame tale. That too I learned to correct in writing, while harboring the phonetic snafu as pedagogic fable: emblemizing the way one can learn from one's own slips, and even capitalize on them elsewhere.

For what I eventually would intend by the (this time) *calculated* elision (*d/t* again) of the titular *Framed Time* was precisely a condition at the microlevel of image generation that is sometimes rendered more than just subliminal by narrative. I refer to the material difference between the clocked strip of fixed photoframes spilling over to movement's own duration on screen (in the celluloid or filmic "moment") and the radically new framing of screentime as a mutable pixel mosaic with no serial pressure from off-frame space. In calling attention to moments when this process is made legible by plot, I renew my career-long sense of the textualist fabric of narrative and plastic art—this time via the Deleuzian "opsign" in its role as "lectosign," as summed up below in transition to a digitally shot narrative about analog tape (in the form of the now defunct VHS cassette) and its coercive invasion of privacy. This is Michael Haneke's masterpiece, *Caché* (2005), to which I'll inevitably return again in my book on "surveillancinema," *Closed Circuits* (2015):

> Much depends, for Deleuze, more than is often noted, on the concept of the *lectosign*. This is where movement, no longer self-sufficient, drifts over into meaning, hence into interpretation. Nothing more clearly locates Deleuze within the "linguistic turn" of cinema studies after all, despite the apparently irreconcilable standoff between his phenomenology of immanent motion and Lyotard's insistence on cinema as, at base, a "writing with movement(s)." Deleuze's indifference to filmic cinema's tactile substrate in the photogram is in this sense entirely tactical. For he puts to brilliant use his conceptual—as well as material—blind spot with regard to the underlying discontinuities of filmic motion. And he is relentlessly polemical in setting this out. Movement is *given* in cinema, to it and by it, rather than constructed. It is only when cinema puts some distance between this raw matter of duration and mobility that it finds its will to art in a modernist impulse to resist this automatized medium of sensorimotor images. Only then—though Deleuze never quite puts it in either Lyotard's terms (discourse subsuming figure), or in Metz's (the imaginary signifier)—does cinema begin to write time, to write in and with it. The *lectosign* appears when movement no longer simply is, but means—means something other than itself: where it passes absolutely from the imaginary into the symbolic, turning its picture plane into *figures* rather than instances of duration. When cinema is found asserting its sign function over against its recording function in this respect, it becomes text by any other name. Fictive text—which is (as Todorov stresses in genre terms) synonymous with the virtual. Under this dispensation, time is there on the film screen not just to

be experienced in and as action, or inferred from it, but to be read—and read into. Narratography is one way in. [...]

Brought to Light: The Ethics of Real Time

Such a narratological thematics of time consciousness as an ongoing reading act has never been more pointedly used to refigure a life of self-spectation (the movement-image stalled in the time-image) than in the layered temporality and real-time hypermediation of Michael Haneke's latest film ... an Austrian, German, French, and Italian collaboration that tacitly implicates the colonial and genocidal pasts of the New Europe in a violent historical uncanny filtered through the new rootless telepresence of video mediation. Whereas films from *Peeping Tom* to *One Hour Photo* imagine the psychoanalytic trauma of a patriarchal gaze, *Caché* suggests, in its remorselessly ambiguous ending, a more ethical trauma—and a more historiographic panic. This is the gaze of the son rather than the father, so that the sins of the past become a cross-generational primal scene. Here is humanist "temportation" at degree zero, where the past must be "visited" both by and upon the present.

Haneke's riveting (and often visually riveted) film establishes its optical tenor straight off with a mysteriously inert liminal shot, its fixed frame held for the entire length of the credits and beyond. The narrative later closes with a "switch" ending that involves a similar camera setup, across whose fixed field underspecified explanatory events come and go. In the mode of a trick beginning, the prolonged first shot turns out to be a surveillance videotape being watched not at the moment of recording but in subsequent playback on a domestic TV monitor, where we see its image variously degraded—in a baffled search for its purpose—by the horizontal striations of fast-forward and rewind functions. This first several-minute shot is therefore focalized, even before its temporal manipulation, not from the POV [point of view] of a hidden camera but from that of the subjects whose house is under surveillance, the so-far unseen couple heard only in voice-over. ("Well?" is the film's first word, interrogating the event-free exterior shot still in front of us.) The trick at the end, with an answering last shot of their son's school steps—in all its comparable fixity—is that we can no longer confidently decide whether we are watching just filmic narration or some continuing, subversive remediation via surveillance. There's every reason to wonder, but no telling. In this sense, the revelation we may have expected from the prolonged detective plotting—who has been videotaping their world?—is emptied out by the final turn. By now, the whole distinction between being and being filmed has been worn thin by the allegory of political denial: the flight from self-inspection.

In semiotic terms, that initial model shot—a deceptively present street scene twice remediated in taped replay—has installed an unsettling subtext in which we are never immediately sure, from then on, whether we are watching a narrative film or an inset video. In the context of family shame, what develops is almost a running metafilmic pun on the political ambiguities of first- versus second- "generation" imaging.

The backstory, in short, won't stay back. Georges Laurent's farm-owning parents had wanted to adopt the bereft son of two of their immigrant laborers, who were killed in a political massacre of Algerians in Paris. Jealous, the natural son "lied about" his would-be stepbrother (he admits years later to his wife) until Majid was sent away to an orphanage. The triggering moment was telling Majid that his parents ordered him to kill the family rooster with a hatchet, only to report instead that the adopted boy did it to scare Georges himself. Not accidentally, in the film's contemporary historical context, the childhood transgression takes the form of an empty charge of terrorism as preemptive strike. It is this "lie" concerning the subaltern threat that is perpetuated into adulthood in the attenuated but no *less* poisonous form of a willfully erased conscience, at which point a cauldron of trans-European uneasiness is stirred up by Haneke's plot.

The native son, pampered in solitude, has grown up to be a famous media "personality," host of a literary roundtable, whose intellectual chat is televised against a wall of simulated, title-free, backlit books. Off camera, Georges is impersonal, nearly mute. On camera, he mostly moderates interpretation—while privately avoiding it. Cued by the blank spines and illegible texts, this film's ongoing time-image unfolds as a true Deleuzian *lectosign*. When the mysterious series of videotapes starts appearing that show Georges' house under exterior surveillance, his wife's first thought is a stalking fan: the video personality cornered as such in his private life. So far, the uneventful time loops of these rewound and uselessly scrutinized videos only force upon him the replay of his immediate, colorless past, the diurnal round of driving to and from the office. But when the tapes begin to display scenes of his boyhood home, and then a lower-class Parisian neighborhood, the frazzled hero tracks down his childhood victim in the latter and accuses him of criminal threats to his family, a "campaign of terror." [...]

In scene after scene of the film's reflex hypermediation, its diegesis is regularly one step ahead of us. In this sense, it taps the founding narratological paradigm of the detective plot, going over again the tracks already laid down. At one point, the image we've been watching as a development of our screen narrative is abruptly fast-forwarded, so that we realize we are privy only to its secondary replay as evidentiary trace, under analysis by other spectators. At a later point we see Georges' television show, full frame, as if we have just cut to the studio during taping. Or we might guess that we are actually seeing the show being broadcast in some as-yet undisclosed diegetic space, perhaps back in his own living room. But suddenly a stop-action image interrupts the dialogue. We find ourselves, instead, in the digital editing room, where Georges is ordering technicians, after a fast reverse, to splice out remarks by a guest that are becoming "too theoretical." Yet were we altogether wrong in associating this image with his real-time existence? Even in the main film we have been watching, his laconic character is always exercising veto power over expression whenever it might cut too deep. Once again, hypermediation folds back into allegory. It is in this context, too, that digital facility puts analog recording at a narratographic distance, so that the dated "home video" quality of the tapes, with their streaked indication of tampered temporality, can be taken to assault the media professional as the clumsy return of a technological repressed. Every past has its residuum.

Yet allegory, as we know from Todorov, is the enemy of the fantastic. All that is genuinely uncanny (certainly not marvelous) about the tapes—namely, their indiscernible point of origin—is matched by an entire failure to search for the hidden camera with anything like normal curiosity, either in the street across from his townhouse or later in Majid's apartment. For the contemporary teleconsciousness of a broadcast star, perhaps, the ubiquitousness of visibility seems less an issue than the mystery of its local intent. Then, too, problems of intent are not easily contained by plot. What does it all mean, this aggressive haunting by his past? The issue isn't so much a matter of guilt and reparation as of recognition, acknowledgment. Hence the emphasis on seeing. The postwar modern hero as "spectator" rather than motor agent of his own life in time: that ultimate Deleuzean prototype has boxed itself further into a hall of video mirrors, where virtual replay is indistinguishable from immanence itself.

Where is the abiding blindness in all this watching? As a defensive six-year-old boy, Georges was too young to take full moral responsibility for the exile of his nemesis. To this extent, he's right in his belligerent defensiveness. The chain of incrimination does not stop with him. It is the parents, surely, who should have been more cautious, asked more questions, looked through the lies, exercised less racial prejudgment. For the young Georges, there was mostly self-protectionism, not maliciousness. But the consequences are no less real and disastrous. Solipsism may be forgiven, but only in remission—only if its effects on the Other are admitted, only if the Other is finally seen in light of the self. No longer accusatory, Georges' lies persist nonetheless. They take the form of denial now, a refusal to feel. And to see. That's the real governing irony. Surveillance is not just an invasion of privacy but a punitive inversion of it. Georges must replay tapes of himself because the whole point of the exercise is that he should recognize his actions from the outside at last—and hence see his way, via historical response if not direct responsibility, into the place of the Other.

Majid, denying all notion of the tapes (which may have been made by his teenage son), is only trying to force acknowledgment. His final act is to repeat the decapitation of the rooster, as scapegoat ritual, by slitting his own throat in front of Georges (recorded in turn on video—as we assume even at the time, given the fixed camera position). His last words: "I just wanted you to be present." For presence is no defense against the past. The time-image makes all duration virtual in the now—and this as an ethical as much as a psychoanalytic imperative. If mediation has been keeping reality at a distance, only real death can cut through it with a single swipe of the penknife. Instead of remaining present in the wake of the suicide, however, and without even looking for the camera which he must surely suspect, Georges flees to a movie theater, as do the murderers in *Bad Education,* and again implicitly to "kill time." But from the marquees at the cineplex seen as he exits, we would guess it to be less than a fully escapist venture. For at least two of the film titles bear down on his situation with another irony unspeakably blunt, were it not fortuitous: *Ma Mère* and *Deux Frères* (each in release in 2004, just when Haneke was filming the exterior locations in Paris). Despite Georges' attempt to escape the gaze of the Other in the form of its fictional dispersion by screen projection, what asserts itself against him at this turn is the uncanny of the real itself.

What there is certainly no escaping is the optic of the unconscious. Even in the closing moments of the film, when after a double dose of sleeping pills Georges goes naked to bed in broad daylight, he dreams his way back into guilt. His nightmare replays the forced exile of Majid—after the boy's last-ditch attempt at running away from his institutional captors, screen right. The long-held image is shot as if spied upon by a fixed camera locked into place at the back of the barn, the incriminating hatchet still resting on a stump at screen left, other barnyard fowl awaiting their time. We don't have to assume that the young Georges was in fact hidden (*caché*) there as the scene originally transpired. The camera angle is itself a trope. Narratologically, it is a flashback coded as nightmare. Narratographically, it is a victory for the POV of the Other in the mode of surveillance, a new and suddenly inverted ethics of the gaze. Georges' own recording by an unseen camera has by this point been wholly internalized, dream deep, as an ineradicable time-image. For the screen viewer it is the *lectosign* of repression in its inevitable return: the fixed frame, in short, of an unshakeable fixation. Majid's revenge has been presence itself: presence in the face of disavowal. The ultimate work of the tapes is thus to model, for Deleuze's "spectatorial" modern subject, none other than the haunting recursions of the time-image—and to do so precisely by "projecting a camera" into the unconscious itself.

Mediation is always to be historicized, in class as well as in print. Between video tape and digital cinematography: the narrative abyss of Haneke's film. Between onetime film stock and screen: the synchronous s/pace of original cinematic projection. Between revolving celluloid projection and its digital overthrow: a revolution in the engines of traced and thrown light. Still, amid all the tardy discoveries, or just timely but too late, that I'm eagerly logging in from revisited book to book, the latest below causes the least regret—since it has more promise for future teaching than it would have had in printed argument (where the film's own wordiness could only have been rather laboriously reviewed). As an economical film clip, however, it will become part of my classroom toolkit when laying the celluloid groundwork for the textural, become textual, implications of postfilmic cinema. Though recent students harbor no nostalgia for, and mostly no memories of, 35mm projection—so that the nature of celluloid "animation" is now a required lecture insert—the projection booth scenes from the latest Sam Mendes film, even in "digital versatile disc" format, should make quick work of it. *Empire of Light* (2022) is named as if for that etymologically "purest" of pyres: the struck ignition demonstrated by an exuberant projectionist when the two carbon wands of the arc light converge. "And there is nothing without light." In the plot surrounding this paeon to illusionism, former stage director Mendes seems all but deliberately backdating by almost three decades Annie Baker's Pulitzer Prize-winning play *The Flick* (2013), whose young main protagonist is a racially stigmatized black theater usher who rails against the coming of digital projection at one of the last holdout theaters, and on his exit, when fired after scapegoating by his own co-workers, has bestowed on him the now obsolete 35mm projectors that he drags off stage—and back to college, where he belongs. In *Empire of Light*, set in the early 1970s of Thatcher's Britain, another young black theater usher is shown the wonders of celluloid by a devoted projectionist, digital conversion not yet in sight, on his way through a gauntlet of more brutal racial violence toward his own college admission to architecture school at the film's end.

In the second week of 2023, coinciding accidentally with a research trip of mine, the film arrived at London's British Film Institute (BFI) for "preview" screenings—in, of all things, actual 35mm—though with no thematic fanfare made of this now-rare celluloid substrate for theatrical projection. The film's own dialogue, however, works itself into a lather over it. In the days of multiplatform digital imaging, a rather academic scene of explanation must have seemed all but mandatory to Mendes in recalling the obsolete photogram medium, this in the projectionist's overexplicit monologue about "static images interrupted by blackness," even while the viewer's fooled "optic nerve" defaults and so "brings them into motion, into life. All they see in the theater is a beam," whereas it's these "big machines" that are responsible, with their "pulleys"—and, yes, his very word, "intermittences." Even the "phi phenomenon" and its illusory motion is explained by name. Down the road, all of this, though narratively inert in context, will nonetheless be more fun to watch, through Roger Deakins' majestic lens, than hearing Stewart lay it out at the lectern. But what I will never be able to show to students, or even confirm to my own satisfaction unless I can come upon a 35mm screening in the future, is for me the most intriguing wrinkle, or blip, in the intensely cinematographic and indulgently explicated visual experience. There was indeed a sheen, a soft shimmer, in the projection quite foreign to the sharpness of digital, and, because of the viewer's ongoing consciousness of this retro mediation, a suspected rich twist I wish I could be sure about. Long familiar from my own usher days in the previous decade (see Phase VII / 17), the little blot, or luminous bleep, in the upper right hand corner of the frame, flaring up to signal the change-over to the next reel—a precision process made much of in a transitional scene of demonstration within Mendes' narrative—was actually, I'm almost certain, *exaggeratedly* visible (digitally tweaked?) earlier, well beneath the diegesis, in a blurted (hardly subliminal) optic cue I was surprised to notice so starkly (maybe just because I'd become inured to electronic seamlessness?). Yet over-emphatic or not in Mendes' treatment, such is the passing on-screen glitch as the very switch of motorized celluloid in action.

Even if my eyes played tricks on me in that enhanced blinking wink at the once-acclimated viewer of 35mm stock amid its explicit celebration, the film's most interesting metafilmic shot hints unequivocally at the longer media view. And this, had the film appeared in time, *would* have been worth writing about, not just saving for class, in either *Framed Time* or the later *Cinemachines*. On New Year's Eve the storyline, such as it is, finds its two principals looking out, screen right, from a lower rooftop of the tiered and crumbling deco theater, its already digitally reconstructed tower framing—squaring off—the image from the right. As reproduced in most of the publicity posters for the film, the two figures are thus silhouetted in delight against an open rectangle of sky scaled to the shape of the giant cinema screen we've not even glimpsed as yet in the extravagant set design for the theater's interior. The backlit couple is awash in what registers as most probably the VFX of midnight digital fireworks— or their computerized green screen: in either case, an electronically enabled movie-within-the-film movie that in fact historically outdistances its own narrated and even (in London) projective 35mm technology by a higher-tech video insert. With its pixel-like empyrotechnics (a coinage too site-specific for the glossary in this volume), the slack sentimentality of this narrative moment nonetheless sees the technological future coming in the addressed sensorium of its bracketed public spectacle.

Note

1 T. J. Clark, "Painting the Poem," *London Review of Books*, October 6, 2022.

IV.

CONVERGENCES: MEDIATION REVISITED

> 8 / In *Novel Violence: A Narratography of Victorian Fiction* (University of Chicago Press, 2009), Stewart builds on the structural "violence" attributed to deviant literary phrasing by such different theorists as Roman Jakobson and Roland Barthes, backdating their claims to the seldom appreciated texture of Victorian narrative phrasing in episodes of psychic extremity. Finding in such verbal condensations the "microplots" of larger narrative patterns within what Georg Lukács calls the "extreme violence" of romantic disillusionment in the novel as genre, Stewart distinguishes his method from the broader-gauge "science" of narratology. Conceived more in the sense of cartography than geology, the interpretive purchase of his "narratography" is exercised by mapping the terrain of narrative, as well the linguistic ground it plows, in scenes of ironic upheaval from Charles Dickens through George Eliot and Thomas Hardy to Joseph Conrad, with a chapter, situated by contrast, on the anti-novelistic prose explosions of Edgar Allan Poe's frenetic sound play.

8 / Mapping the Narrative Substrate

Novel Violence: A Narratography of Victorian Fiction (2009)

THIS NEXT BOOK WAS CONCEIVED to follow out some of the many lines of connection from Marxist critic Fredric Jameson back to his own textual mentor in questions of formal "totality," Georg Lukács. And to do so while prosecuting a claim, as the epilogue entitled it (both senses), to "Novel Criticism as Media Study." If *Framed Time* (2007) was "my Deleuze book," this was "my Lukács book," from whose *The Theory of the Novel: A Historico-Philosophical Essay on the Forms of Great Epic Literature* (1974) every chapter's epigraph is drawn.[1] But another pedagogic moment leaves its immediate impress on the opening chapter, with its reading of a stunning "lacuna" in Charles Dickens' social critique in *Little Dorrit* (1857). Calling the attention of undergraduates to the editorial resource of the novelist's monthly "number plans" printed along with the main text in the Penguin edition, I had often stressed his tendency to expand on the sketchy plot hints he jotted down. If, ordinarily, thousands of crafted comic or melodramatic lines of prose connect the dots of his sparse and often revised outlines, in one signal instance the novel gives us markedly—I would say momentously—less than it planned. Students could see this at once. There was, it turns out, to have been the peripheral force of a good, rather than a notoriously bad, mother for the middle-aged but psychically unmatured hero of *Little Dorrit*. I well remember, after pointing out this unfulfilled plot intent in one iteration of my Dickens survey course, how I stressed the absence of this intended narrative material by spontaneous allusion to Jean Rhys' *The Wide Sargasso Sea* (1966), in the days when most students of the period would have read Charlotte Brontë's *Jane Eyre* (1847) through the lens of that famous backstory novel. (Remember postcolonial studies when they still had one foot firmly in the traditional canon.) Well before our departmental major had shifted from literary history toward creative writing, I nonetheless had the notion to ask what kind of book you could write in that gagged mother's voice. Responses were thin and sporadic at the time, but I knew on reflection where I wanted my next book to begin—with the unnerving stylistic fallout from this remarkable exclusion.

For an opening chapter titled "Little Dorrit's Fault," based on Dickens' original idea for the novel, *Nobody's Fault*, the first Lukács epigraph was installed (shortened here) to tap into one of his major themes—the prison house of social alienation in a capitalist world: "Estrangement from nature … the modern sentimental attitude to nature, is only a projection of man's experience of his self-made environment as a prison instead of a parental home." Under impetus from this prison master trope, I for the first (and so-far last) time eased myself from criticism into metafiction (or meta-metafiction, if you will)—and with a feminist argument that in a sense reversed others of the sort meant to rescue the eponymous heroine from charges of passivity and diminishment without recognizing her manipulative last move. In the resulting fictional experiment, once I had left the classroom for my desk, the main drive was to distinguish the scale of narratography from that of a more familiar narratology. I'll cut in here just as I was picking up on implications of the prison metaphor from the Lukács epigraph:

> The "self-made environment" of domestic life in the modern social field is repeatedly mistaken for given, rather than for constructed, in the very vocabulary of its regrets. Though pining for a lost naturalness, so far from a quester is the protagonist of Dickens' eleventh novel, so little prone is the "dreamer" Arthur Clennam to actual quixotic errands, that constraint and denial seem like "second nature" to him. That's exactly the double-edged phrase used by Lukács in *The Theory of the Novel* to isolate a sense of the pervasively artificial in modern

experience—once it has undergone its deep naturalization, and thus first stage of denial, as the simply conventional. While the novel we know as *Little Dorrit* (1855–57) was still in the planning stages, Dickens' provisional title, *Nobody's Fault*, would have (ironically, of course) deflected all ethical responsibility onto the cruelly inevitable and the socially enforced. Ultimately, though, in the most "sentimental" of all refamiliarizing gestures, the book that later emerges under the name of its marriageable heroine does attempt turning back to the poetry of earth—and, in connection with it, to a human wedding supposedly natural enough that no plot-long barrage of artifice could ultimately prevent it—so as to redeem the world.

What arrests attention at the close of *Little Dorrit*, however, is partly the labor it takes to arrest the unspoken violence of that final plot turn into matrimony. Prose works phrase by mellifluous phrase to staunch the flow, to pull tight the tourniquet of marital closure before the last emotional bloodletting of desire. This rescue action is not a matter of rhetoric divorced from narrative, style from plot, but rather an enlisting of the one in service to the other: the requisition of writing by the agenda of represented event, herein a bridled and (in its own way) constrained march to the famous finish lines. Where narratology concerns itself with the structural formation of story, narratography can note the marked prose of such deformations. Its heightened (rather than elevated) level of attention can register a dissonance even in those superficially serene, legato cadences that bring *Little Dorrit* to rest amid a surrounding fretfulness. It is there, in a descent from the wedding chapel into the jostling Victorian cityscape, that hero and heroine begin taking their no longer solitary way even as, by frictional evocation, "the noisy and the eager, and the arrogant and the froward [sic] and the vain, fretted, and chafed, and made their usual uproar"—an uproar into which the new couple, five times reiterated, accepting their lapsarian condition, "went" bravely "down." Plot itself subsides into the tapestry of social acceptance.

Until then, however, parallel plotting has worked overtime to throw its trajectory of mystery and disclosure into relief against various backdrops of communal indifference. The quester hero has withered into the detective; all energy is retrospective; the police keep to their beat by patrolling the self entirely from within its own diurnal rounds. While Arthur Clennam, guilt-laden son of a grasping mercantile "house" that has been his only home, has been seeking all the while to know the nature of the crime for which his father, before dying, had hoped to cleanse his conscience, in the counterplot the prison girl wronged by Arthur's parents is edged into position to accept his hand in marriage. Without solving the crime, he marries the victim. But this convergence of plot strands in the love-knot has allowed the detective line to slip away entirely—or, more to the point, to be summarily truncated. How so, and at what emotional cost, is the focus of this chapter. How we go about noticing such repercussions is the methodological topic. The argument is inevitably twofold: a case for something all but insufferable at the close of this vast, troubling novel, something whose brunt is borne by the medium of prose itself, and a case for the exemplarity of this burden as a proving ground of narratographic attention. [...]

Narratography is a term of engagement for the way we might sample and decipher that underlying excess, might enter into imaginative transference with its reticences as well as breached repressions at the level of wording itself, might let that wording tug at the thrust of story—even if it offers an intractable snag in the fabric of the supervening rhetorical design. [...] Narratology tends, in effect, to diagram structure, however dynamic. Narratography would come closer to graphing a process—and its local machinations. It offers, in progress, a reading of style for its own plot. [...] Narratography isn't regularly concerned, and certainly not by definition, with the return of the repressed in so blatant a way as the coming fantasy novel imagines. Its response isn't, as a rule, counter-narratological at all in this encompassing sense. But it does involve, in conception as well as in practice, a way of reading the textured pace of the *written*, with its unruly skids and jolts, against the overriding—the more abstract and immaterial—force of the *plotted*.

I hope I have said enough to license in advance the present experiment, even though—in its test of such deciphered latencies— its operation lingers far out in left field before coming to bat for any direct attention to the text as we have it from Dickens. Conceived as if from behind the bars of one virtual prison, with the general tenor of its violence debarred from disclosure on the main stage of Dickens' final volume, the invented novel will appear in what follows via the italics of a foreign and alienated English voice. [...]

Barred Narrative

Even with long-dead authors, criticism traditionally favors a grammar of the historical present. But bear with me, instead, for an exercise in the hypothetical future—as we skim through next year's heralded "backstory" novel, or literary prequel, hatched some years before in the Manhattan office of a rather middle-brow but decidedly high-profile literary agent. The scene is no more conjectural than it is probable. It was there that a minor British novelist with some modest popular following even in the States, and a respected Oxford lecturer in fiction as well, specialist in the English and Irish novel, had the seed of a new book firmly planted. "Can't you of all people think of another great novel, Victorian would

8 / Mapping the Narrative Substrate

be just the ticket, deserving that Jean-Rhys-style 'other side of the story' treatment? Tales from the madwoman's attic, you know. Hey, maybe three crazies at once. *Dracula* through the glazed eyes of those Transylvanian brides: a fugue of erotic soliloquies, how about it? *The Wide Black Sea?*"

The agent's pitch, well rehearsed, was amiable and ingratiating at first, then a bit hectoring. "You know: a Lolita's *Lolita*, that bit. Maybe *Sue Bridehead Revisited*." He was visibly proud of that one. "Just kidding, but you catch my drift. A gimmick, sure, but what isn't these days? Just don't give us *Middlemarch* by Dorothea's maid. Hey, maybe *Casaubon in Love*. Okay—but I'm serious in principle. It's almost foolproof. I know, I know, but it's fail-safe just because it *has* been done. Doesn't mean the idea's done in. It's just become a recognized subgenre: girls with pearl earrings and all." That, too, got a frown. "Yeah, yeah, but I mean something bigger, more powerful, as I say, more Victorian. A character whose melodramatic story would be so gripping it would eclipse the original, pull the rug right out from under it, turn it inside out. People love that. Canon aura plus oneupsmanship all at once." Our author-to-be was growing exponentially defenseless, seeing his future unfold before him—if not yet the rave reviews.

The upshot, and to instant fanfare, will hit the shelves under the title *The Story Left Behind*. An advance blurb on the jacket, from Dame A. S. Byatt no less: "This stirring epistolary novel seizes upon the repressed underside of Victorian sexuality, and the covert sadism of its puritanical norms, and lets out the full wail of jailed desire." Reviews follow suit. [...] So what lost story has been lucratively restored this time? It hadn't, in fact, taken our lecturer-novelist long to land upon just the right source text. An unlikely candidate maybe, with so little to go on in its own pages. But that was exactly the hook—at least once the agent's prod had been administered.

It had everything, *Little Dorrit* did—everything and then some, its excesses cloaking a final suspect reticence. The black hole (the hero's real mother's real backstory) was just waiting not to be plugged, as Dickens did, but to be plumbed—and plundered. The trouble was mainly with the dense event horizon of the plot surrounding it. Even committed to the agent's idea, how could he ever get past that final massing of histrionic disclosure while at the same time get its unsaid consequences across? Whenever our imagined author had braved the novel in lecture, even with students who had kept up with the reading, his strategic eleventh-hour summary of the thickening plot always seemed like a shock tactic: an assault on memory and credulity at once. The mold is set at the outset, he always wanted the class to see. It all begins, dozens of chapters back, with that sadsack midlifer in crisis, Arthur Clennam, en route to London after two decades with the China branch of his deceased father's under-specified colonial enterprise: vague money, bad vibes.

As my imaginary academic novelist has to rehearse it carefully for his students, the plot barrage in question is laid on thick to explain how the frigid Mrs. Clennam, not Arthur's mother at all, has married Clennam only on condition that his young unnamed mistress be banished if the betrothed religious zealot is to accept his out-of-wedlock child. Yet Arthur goes to the altar at the end without learning this.

> Even that sizeable majority of his students with no allergies to happy endings still can't help but see the forced march to a marital closure. By contrast, all a new and oppositional novel would need to do in answering back to all this would be to dust off that secret of the real mother and let it breathe at last—breathe long enough to feel its own final asphyxiation. It wouldn't be easy, but the choice of novel seemed just right. In the event, not a single review would doubt it, either. The *TLS* is wholly enthralled. [...] *The New York Times* quickly weighs in as well, lending the achievement an eye-catching contemporary slant: "The poignant search for the birth parent in so many recent novels and literary memoirs, as in so many real-life stories—with their often thinnest of paper trails building slowly toward tentative letters across the gulf of years—is devastatingly reversed here. What happens, with an unholy sense of suspense, is that the hero's mother, banished to little more than a footnote in the original, rages her way back into plot—through her unmailed rants alone—to remake the whole lumbering thing in the battered image of her own accursed, accusatory words." [...]
>
> At just the point in Dickens' outlined plot where all the madwoman's writings are to be finally discovered in a stash of letters, Dickens reminds himself to work this up in the actual drafting of the chapter. The note reads simply, resonantly, with that rhetorical resonance Dickens can lay claim to even when jotting notes to himself: "She had left her story"—with a careted insert after the first word, expanding the scant indication to "had implored to see her son." In fact, this brief telegraphic reminder is more than the novel itself makes good on. The mother's craving for a visit with her child is replaced by a capitulation to guilt, confession, and a plea for forgiveness. It's just as unlikely as it sounds, this sense of penance rather than victimage—and just as briefly dispatched amid the other strained and improbable turns of the denouement. The missing mother's story itself goes missing, left in the dust by the momentum of the requisite marriage plot.
>
> There it is, then, the new title needed: *The Story Left Behind*. The wordplay wouldn't be too arcane for the trade press reader, nor too

blatant either. Now you see it, now you don't. The whole plan was crafty enough. All depended on whether our novelist could really pull it off. Or put it over. Along with the abandoned mother's own traumatic memories of the doings back in London, enough rumors reach her through Flintwinch that eventually a spectral form of Dickens' main plot should also seem to have bled through between the lines of her own letters. Famous details ought to come across as the shadow story of her own emptiness and dementia, the dye stain that throws her own unslaked cravings into contrast. "Great stuff ... keep plugging," shot back the agent's email. And then the real inspiration struck.

Right from the start, this unearthed epistolary underside of the omniscient triple-decker had seemed a canny enough move. But as the writer plowed forward only by burrowing deeper into the pangs of the suppressed story, a wilder idea had slowly dawned. And couldn't be shaken. Our novelist-critic had decided to go for broke, cashing out his whole idea at the metafictional level. It wasn't just that the source text in Dickens holds back more than its form can tolerate, and is rather drastically warped out of shape by this containment action. It occurred to the writer that no reader would recognize this sooner, or with more ferocious eloquence, than the plot's own posthumous lover and mother, if only somehow she could be resurrected—or, that is, would not yet have died—when the novel arrives in print. She would make the story's ideal "against-the-grain" reader. What an idea: the madwoman reading *Jane Eyre* in her own attic! And the longer this idea got brooded over the more it seemed to have driven straight through gimmick to masterstroke. Textual empathy always approximates identification. Here we go the whole distance: the reader lost and found at once in the book that delineates and elides her own life. [...]

After all those years expended in the feverish penning of an already smudged-out life, the heroine learns to her horror—the first hint dropped in a garbled remark by Flintwinch one besotted midnight—that it has all been for nought. She quickly teases out of him that her words were never in fact posted at all, were shown to his twin brother instead, secreted away in a locked box by that infernal mirror image of her jailor, and then somehow returned to "her" Flintwinch for sequestering. And why did the other Flintwinch's wife, the cowed Affery, servant to Mrs. Clennam, not see that what she thought she saw was really in fact happening, all that midnight funny business? Why did she let her husband beat the truth back in her? Maybe the letters should have been written to her instead all these years, to Affery, to wise her up. And more awful yet—here's the terrible twist, leaving the source novel far behind—their writer learns now from her own Flintwinch that those letters had been lately sold for a song (a drinking song at that) to a respected gentleman who made up part of a large party one evening at the local ale house, and who, having heard the merest gist of her grief, wanted the whole chest of letters shipped to London. She learns, too, that this gentleman trafficker in recorded lives happens to be the famous novelist Boz, in town for some public appearance. Flintwinch had somehow horned in on the long round of toasts and grown talkative with the famous man, who let him know just the use he was hoping to make of these letters. Ephraim was assured on the novelist's departure that, if that poor unfortunate's tale is half as strong as he makes it sound, the good chap might look for the story of his mad female charge in a serialized fiction a year or so later: under assumed names all round of course (the great novelist winked), and backdated—the latest fad—into the recent past. Looking for a big finish to a novel he'd been planning, Mr. Boz hoped her crazed tale would turn the trick. And in leaving he raised a glass to her, after ordering Ephraim's filled yet again: "Count on it, my man, the madwoman will have left her story!"

This is to be the last chance, then, for her stolen and now resold life—its last chance for release from all this manacled, mangling silence. Time is a sickly blur until the novel numbers begin appearing. Even Ephraim is interested after his sluggish fashion, and brings the first installment up to her after showing it round the pub in one of his stupid boasts. But wait. Little Who? What did any of this have to do with her? Marseilles? That prison isn't *her* prison. Not that next one, either. As the numbers drag on, it comes to her ever so slowly. Comes to her that there, burning through all these aliases and inventions and irrelevant digressions, there is her own story blazing out at her after all—as if through a chipped prism, facet by facet, time and again. Never by name, or even in person, nonetheless she sees her own poor self everywhere. From early on, she is the secret fact behind every deprivation of the hero's life, every jaded feeling with which he turns from the world. *She is what is missing in him.* Surely, then, she is what the novel will have to make up for, bring forward in the end. [...]

Strange how Affery's affrights are always real, straight through to the end. She thinks I'm alive. Boz gives her that one last hallucination, which he knows to be true as well. She thinks I'm the force that's bringing the house down, not a ghost but a real presence. True enough, I'd gladly think. Listen to the way Affery begs Mrs. Clennam to let her take over my keep: "Only promise me, that, if it's the poor thing that's kept here, secretly, you'll let me take charge of her and be her nurse." But no, they all seem willing to agree, I've been "dead a score of years and more." Not just that, for they say my dying coincided exactly with the moment "when Arthur went abroad." Do they mean, does Boz mean, that in turning his back on his motherland—to join his father in the business out East—he as much as did me in? Or that without me here, even unknown to him, there was nothing left for the son on native ground? Even in their lies, they're never all wrong.

And certainly not in their worst fears. I must copy it out, this passage, just to make sure I've got it right. What I hear is Affery shivering to the bone with a sense of my frightful claim on them all:

> "So much the worse," said Affery, with a shiver, "for she haunts the house, then. Who else rustles about it, making signals by dropping dust so softly? Who else comes and goes, and marks the walls with long crooked touches, when we are all a-bed?"

Affery really believes I'm lurking somewhere there, stirring or scratching, like the sound of my own quill maybe, trying to make myself heard. In all that sifting and silting and crumbling, she hears me gnawing away at the rotted fortress from within. But my raspings are not really "signals," since no one can decipher them. No one in the house but that twitchy servant woman has ever taken the least notice of those scraped traces and scraps of me. So those crazings are only silent scars all up and down the plaster. The writing on the wall, I'd like it to be: a prophecy and a doom. Dust to dust for them all! But no, there's no reason to hope that I alone could bring them low in their lies. So I suppose those muffled sounds Affery's so afeared of are more like me turning the very pages of the book that erases me. She's right in one way, I guess. While I read about it, read my way into it, this disintegrating Clennam world is my only abode. But knowing better, I can't abide it. [...]

Oh, wait, bless her: here comes Tattycoram, who steals the chest from the icy, man-hating Miss Wade, who could never have known what to do with them, my letters, anyway. They scream of everything she has choked to death in herself. Of love not wanted, therefore not wanting. Now they are to be turned over to my boy's wife-to-be. How will they at last come out, those words of mine, of me? I could almost write it myself, what I guess they call the "revelation scene." Let Arthur learn of love's price from the written words of his own lost mother, voiced by his new motherly child bride—a final reading to him in the prison, where he has long been too weak to read for himself.

But no, when the opportunity comes, she never says a word. She takes up that other unidentified book instead, reading aloud just to kill time—and from some irrelevance not even named or summarized. But what will Boz's own reader think, or those who listen to his book *read aloud? Without even telling him what the papers are, Amy asks Arthur himself to destroy the will, to burn it up—of all places!—in their last cozy prison fire on the eve of their wedding. What kind of prenuptial vow is this unspoken vow of silence? Why can't he know about me, my Arthur: about his mother who loved him, or at least the idea of him, loved him to melancholy and to madness? Why must he go to the altar still believing that the Clennam woman was his closest blood kin, thinking still that what was forbidden to him in her heart was actually a mother's love? So he'll appreciate Amy more? This is insupportable. [...] And so I don't leave my story here at all. I only leave behind the hope of its ever being told. Is this what novels always do to life, tear its heart out? Little Dorrit! What a weak, mean title. How much it hides away, how much it buries unmourned. Thinking of my stolen letters, then, and my baby taken, and my motherhood undone, I'd have called it* The Undelivered. *And then I'd know it was my story, and others might too ....*

Breaking off with its last epistle into the void, off the book went to the agent, then in quick succession to press, print, and wide transatlantic acclaim. Everyone hears the heroine's story at last—and comes to see her point about Dickens' ending. Quoting *The New York Review of Books:* "All those unrewarded lives that the ruthless plot instinct keeps at bay in the juggernaut of Dickensian romance, all the deflections and submergences on which it fuels its progress, come back to haunt it in this searing tale of denied desire." [...]

Dysclosure

As indicated at the start, there is a methodology behind this portrayed madness, which a few pages of more familiar reading should be able to bring out. In this case fantasy is only a prelude to narratography. I've tried prying open the gap between Dickens' jotted plans for his finale and the actual pages that got sentimentally worked over and flattened out. One can virtually hear his implied italics first time around, his rousing emphasis on "She had left her story," and then the friction of its erasure later, turning the banned mother first penitent, then silent. And even without this recourse to his number plans, we sense a tension in the plotting itself, as well as in the writing. Surely there is either undue scrupulousness or covert self-interest in Amy's last act before inscribing herself in the marriage book, where she becomes a Dorrit no more, but now Mrs. Clennam the second.

What, then, is really at stake in her destruction of a private legal document before the signing of a public register? Perhaps she is acceding to Mrs. Clennam's wish to keep the secret from Arthur if, on reflection, she agrees that the truth would do him no particular good—and this merely to help the woman save face in the suddenly opened eyes of her victimized charge. Or perhaps Amy herself is filling a void in his life without the risk of naming it just yet. Why *wouldn't* the truth have done him good after the long lie? And anyway, do the dead have in their own right no claim on the living? Didn't Dickens for a moment see otherwise, in a flash of notebook inspiration potent enough to justify the contortions of the denouement, even while he later contrived to smooth over that claim with a meliorative vision of continuity rather than of rupture and return? What I am calling narratography is a way of listening in on these *final* exertions of the prose, transacted at the far margins of plot—and of eavesdropping, indeed, on their own scrambled figuration.

As the chapter "Gone" executes its wrap-up and wind-down, the autumnal Clennam "sat listening to the voice as it read to him" and "heard in it" much of comfort—Amy's voice, of course, the only voice let through to him now. We notice that he is not said to have heard her exactly, let alone her words, but instead to have sensed in the sheer aura of her voice, heard *in* rather than from it, "all that great Nature"—in its decisive assonance—"was doing, heard in it all the soothing songs she sings to men." Across this phonic slope of vocalic descent, harmony is sealed tight with the inverted cognate object of "songs ... sings." But no rhetorical singsong can keep a certain psychic dissonance at bay, one that can be more closely calibrated by narratography. "At no Mother's knee but hers"—nature's, not Little Dorrit's; careful now, she's a fiancée, remember, not a mother—"At no Mother's knee but hers, had he ever dwelt ... on the harvests of tenderness and humility that lie hidden in the early-fostered seeds of the imagination." This is Wordsworth by the numbers, recalling *The Prelude's* "Fair seed time ... / Fostered alike by beauty and by fear"—including that secondary intertextual slide, given the Clennam family context, toward the "Foster-child" and, yes, "Inmate Man" of the *Intimations Ode* and its mortal "prison-house". [...]

But this is really to say that the brief remainder of Dickens' last chapter has a major piece of psychological work to accomplish, whatever its other attenuated narrative tasks. Having desexed marriage, it must now unsex maternity. This figural task, defusing the cruel fate so lately revealed under its heading (the abandoned, maddened mother), is required so that the spectral shadow of the motherly does not swallow up Little Dorrit's marital role entirely under its symbolic rubric, or at least not hers alone. In order that Arthur should not be compromised by marrying his mother, he is turned into a feminized nurturing agent as well, his masculinity absorbed by new connubial purpose. In leaving off, the chapter goes about this work quite unobtrusively, in its very last paragraph, after holding us suspended on the threshold of the penultimate one. No sooner has the couple signed the marriage register, that is, than prose takes a deep breath for them before descending into their life of selfless service, a shared life fused in the final paragraph, by assonance and alliteration alike, in a coupling "inseparable and blessed." Just before, "they paused for a moment on the steps of the portico, looking at the fresh perspective of the street"—that painterly dead metaphor giving way to trochaic, then spondaic stress—"in the autumn morning sun's bright rays, and then went down."

In escorting the couple down across a magisterially cadenced passage, the prose takes off. In a bravura run of syntactic terracing, that phrasal verb, "went down," cleansed of any condescension in its stairstepped descent (and massing its music, as noted earlier in this chapter, against the coming din of "uproar"), strikes the keynote of four more clauses pivoted on it. The first two are fragments: "Went down into a modest life of usefulness and happiness." Not "modest lives," plural? No, their reward, if also perhaps their atonement, is to be at one. So it continues. And remember that the detached subject is not so far back as to have been forgotten: it's the newlyweds together that the prose speaks of still. "Went down to give a *mother's* care, in the fullness of time, to Fanny's neglected children no less than *their* own." Modest utility has been subsumed to a single gender paradigm. Against such a figural conflation, it is hard to retrench.

Certainly the next sentence alone, even if it tried harder, couldn't set the trouble right, with its mention of that further "nurse and friend" (plural this time, unless synonymous) they also "give" to Tip. Sprung from "give a mother's care," parallelism all by itself has grown derailing. Give a nurse? Give suck or succor? Further, too, the feminine dominates as sole antecedent in the pick-up clause, where Tip is "never vexed by the great exactions he made of her." Whether Arthur is tacitly slotted in as bedside friend and brother-in-law or male nurse in this loose and dubious syntax, there was, as we saw, no ambiguity at all in the pronominal grammar of the preceding sentence, where, tendering along with Amy "a mother's care," he has inherited the same maternal role from which he in his own right never took solace. He has answered the lack by embodying it—and not as psychological diagnosis any longer, but as cadenced moral uplift within the last distended cadenza.

For the protagonist to become his own lack, of course, is only a felt castration if he feels he has something to lose. And thanks to Amy, Arthur doesn't realize that anything has been lost, that there has been any story to compare with hers, any love like it, or even as strong in another and more fundamental way. [...] And not being able to love the mother, or mourn her, *the son has become her.* Here lies the keenest if quietest violence of the novel: the double silencing of male as well as female energy even in their most defining of adult relations—and the foisting-off of all connubial desire onto a life of communal duty instead. [...] Oedipus is the least of it. Sure, Amy mothers Arthur as well as just nursing him. To this extent, at least, he may be getting what he wants. Amy as well: if her adored father was a child, why not her husband too? In structural terms, the necessary death of Amy's father in advance of the marriage would be narratology's way, one way at least, of tracing this pattern.

But narratography's more tight-strung reaction is jarred, as we have seen, by a further dissonance in the conversion of roles. What sets in as a result is articulated not so much by enlisting narrative grammar as by twisting it out of true. The unspoken psychic pressure on Dickens' stylistic cadenza reveals itself only by inference in the novel's final sentences—but an inference having precisely to do with the inertial momentum of narrative to this point. On the other side of the destabilized marital equation in which a lovelorn man finds a second mother in a wife, the false mother in *Little Dorrit* is not (not yet) dead. So the new stand-in mother keeps the false mother's secret, rejecting the dead father's will (even in its intended financial benefit to her personally)—and thus accrues instead a huge but inert power in her harbored knowledge. Discharged all but unconsciously as the end draws near, the banked power of this withheld knowledge can seem to backfire into prose. It isn't just that Amy implements (or even incorporates) Mrs. Clennam's manipulation of Arthur's consciousness. Given the hero's unsexing by both the syntax and figuration of the couple's envisioned future in the last paragraph, narratography makes its way, despite the greased wheels of closure, along the not-quite-covered tracks of wording itself, with its elided antecedents and collapsed grammatical identifications.

The onetime smitten author of *Dickens and the Trials of Imagination* (1974) and the future celebrant of *The One, Other, and Only Dickens* (2018) does, I hope it is clear, no disservice to the verbal intensity of his favorite writer in (and of) English by close reading not just the unwritten plot plans, but even the novel's notoriously glorious last sentence, for vital signs (or symptoms, yes) of the sociopolitically unsaid.

> 9 / ***Bookwork: Medium to Object to Concept to Art*** (University of Chicago Press, 2011), in one sense a companion volume to the *The Look of Reading* (2006) (see Phase III / 6), charts, as the subtitle indicates, the denatured book object in the conceptual rather than artisanal treatment of artists' books. These are works—constructions, really, and at times, de-constructions also—that rose to prominence at the advent of mass digitization, both as an act of mourning for the reign of print culture and by the availability of library discards for stacking, carving, shaving, singeing, and other modes of figurative disuse as text. The "demediation" that results (following the causal sequential nexus of the subtitle) turns one or more novels, for instance, first into a sculptable object or increment of an assemblage, then into a conceptual refiguring of its former status—telling a newly-coded story of its own "bookhood"—and hence into the estrangement of a new aesthetic form. Such conceptual objects—whether motivated by nostalgia or merely an opportunity to interrogate literary objecthood by other means than further linguistic analysis—have become a new minor mainstay of gallery art, whether simply on plinths or in complex wired installations. Such are the radically "detourned" codex works—illustrated by Stewart with dozens of examples from London to Los Angeles, Berlin to Beijing—that nevertheless return to their own kind of textuality through the metaphors and puns they seem to sculpt out of their former cradles of discourse.

9 / Reading Foreclosed/Text Reinvented

Bookwork: Medium to Object to Concept to Art (2011)

My sifting below from the "Prologue" of *Bookwork*, with its double-edged title, "An Exhibit in Mind," turns soon into a set of conceptual book pages in its own right. This is because the exhibit described is only imaginary, including the kind of descriptive reviews I had experimented with in the strictly imaginary novel I folded into the *Novel Violence* excerpt. The virtual exhibit to come even includes an imaginary artifact (and real drawing) by the momentarily transmedial author himself. This is the abyssal work by "an American theorist-practitioner from 2010 called *Attempting to Read the M. C. Escher Catalogue Raisonné*." With the lapsed graphic designer in me rearing its undergrad head again, a single line, angled back on itself at repeated right angles, etches out in optic puzzlement five or six indistinguishable verso/recto sheets of a free-floating transparent folio. More broadly, aside from this creative outing of my own, it occurred to me that in the absence of illustration again in these pages, as with excerpts from

9 / *Reading Foreclosed/Text Reinvented*   131

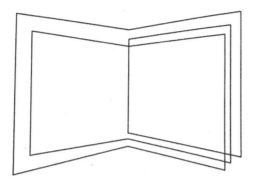

its predecessor *The Look of Reading*, this time the ekphrasis entailed has an extra twist of justification. For analysis can seem just as accurately illustrative of its "conceptual" artifacts, I found, alongside the ones I actually did find, when it conceives them out of thin air—with no duty to an existing instance of the *bibliobjet*. In any case, that was the gamble of this opening gambit. So I include the lone illustration again here. Rewarding the mental picturing on the part of my new readers with a formal complement in two dimensions, that floating folio's unlineated line drawing can install the sense of at least one fanciful exhibit in the imaginary Paris exhibition. On the way to this self-scribed nonbook, my actual book on the denatured codex began this way:

> There they rest, inert, impertinent, in gallery space—those book forms either imitated or mutilated, replicas of reading matter or its vestiges. Strange, after its long and robust career, for the book to take early retirement in a museum, not as rare manuscript but as functionless sculpture. Readymade or constructed, such book shapes are canceled as text when deposited as gallery objects, shut off from their normal reading when not, in some yet more drastic way, dismembered or reassembled. Painting, of course, has often put unreadable books in the hands of a pictured body or left them open on draped tabletops in still life, all text inactivated. Real, or at least three-dimensional, books can instead be negated by becoming installation objects on a real table, if not hung on the wall as bas-relief—even as they remain resident aliens in the sphere of exhibition.
>
> In question here is not the illustrated *artist's book*, the prestige limited edition that may turn up for sale in a specialty bookshop or the handcrafted artisanal book, often wordless, that is more likely to be shown with works in (rather than on) paper. This study has in view, instead, the orphaned codex form—stolen from normal exchange or sculpted from the ground up: the codex as abstract or conceptual *book art*, increasingly to be seen on display in galleries worldwide. Solo or in group bondage, such books are often abandoned on a

display pedestal—if not drawn and quartered, or perhaps scattered or banked, on the museum floor. Whether they are culled from libraries or carved from foreign matter, these retreads and effigies are bookworks that—in collaboration with viewer rather than reader—do bookwork. Whatever we decide that is. In such forms, the idea of the codex survives its use. The bookwork—as material object—once denied its mediating purpose as verbal text, can only be studied for the bookwork—as conceptual labor—it performs. [...]

This study is therefore about the book itself as "study" rather than as functional object: the book as approximation, heuristic double, or—when found rather than faked—piled with (and shut tight by) so many others like it that there's no way in. Appropriated but dysfunctional, the used book appears in this case under conditions of disuse. Either way, reclaimed or fabricated, the demediated bookwork, as we will come to understand it, is a conceptual object: not for normal reading, but for thinking about. In the realist tradition of making and matching that raises the cult of expertise to such heights in painting and sculpture, one of the thrills of mimetic art is always its recognition value. Conceptual art replaces that alluring visual passivity with the deskilled rigors of cognition value, elevating information over image—or isolating information *as* image. And whereas the wordworks of conceptualism often substitute discursive address for visual pleasure, bookworks, blocking discourse, substitute for any and all verbal pleasure a reading of their shape as such—if only through the back door of form and the closed door of the illegible page. So from this halt to all data flow in such castaway shapes, this denuded use, why the potential for jolt, hilarity, exhilaration?

As so often, idiom hits home. We approach the very essence of the experienced book—our access over time to a referred world both elsewhere and inward—when asking, for instance, if you brought "your reading" with you in the car or suitcase. This is to say that a book, conceived as text, is virtually coterminous with its activation. Not so with book art, conceptualized instead as sheer physical object rather than released to linguistic transaction. Reading is divorced in such book forms from its transmitted referential matter, suspended by a more plastic apprehension of its material conveyance. No longer opening within us, museum books close in emphasis upon themselves. In our contemplation of such dysfunctional forms, what we can often only imagine, rather than actually see, is text itself, isolated under arrest—not what it normally helps visualize for us. Such book objects—plastered, slashed, trashed, or otherwise unusable, piled up, pinned down, or disintegrated, nailed, scaled, or raked, pummeled or simply dummied—are volumes not awaiting return to a library's stacks. They often appear merely as stacks in the other and everyday sense: squat towers, faux stairs, textual dumping grounds. They are taken out of circulation for sheer pondering as objects, *reading matter* reduced to cubic inches or feet of worked surface, all verbal mediation disappeared into its physical support. It's hard to overstate the frequent blend of low comedy and high concept in these privations.

We know about bookishness, odd nomenclature that it is. It's what certain readers bring to an abiding cultural form: a thirst for the medial immersion in textual experience, a craving lifted free, however obsessional, from the object that backs it. And, truer to the book as object, we also know about the collector's bibliophilia. But what is bookhood itself? That's what the artistic distancing of bookwork shows forth through the work of demediation. Weightless text disappears into the now-functionless revelation of its suddenly overmaterialized support. Sometimes these bookwork shapes are skewered through the middle and bolted shut. Sometimes they are the proverbial steel traps to begin with, or more specifically lead layers inscribing nothing—nothing legible, that is, as in the funereal tomes of Anselm Kiefer. Oppositely at times, in the work of American book sculptor Doug Beube, for instance, the book returns to its fibrous origins. As one of several book artists in a line descending from the pioneering work of Buzz Spector, Beube goes so far into materialist oddity as to evoke the organic basis of the book object in a variant whose stock is actually made of seeds pressed into rag paper. With pages that therefore, when dampened, sprout over time, in some bizarre punning sense *exfoliated* from the swollen volume, this deviant book can seem to spread itself open by itself, without a reader: a nonmechanical automaton.

Odd, yes, and often motored by unspoken punning, conceptual if not strictly verbal: an ocular troping. [...]

From which one can speculate in reverse, concretizing an idea in only an imagined material form. Hence the double sense of the prologue offered by my opening chapter, "An Exhibit in Mind":

> The books in this prologue—prologue as imaginary catalog in the orbit of contemporary museum display—are not really books as we know them, but rather conceptual sculpture. Entirely conceptual. No pages to turn, no paragraphs to read—except the ones describing them here. As gallerygoers, some of you may think you're used to this. But in this particular case, the book objects, these nonbooks, are not really there at all. So there's no need for the obligatory "Do Not Touch" sign. My sense is that the theoretical insistence of all such

works, their claim on a postwar genre of textual demediation, requires no existence in order to prosecute the ideas they conjure. They are so fully conceptual that they need no perceptual basis except in the mind's eye. Which means that they can, if you're in a cognate frame of mind, pass directly from fantasy into ironic force.

It is this available ease of manifestation that I trust justifies beginning with them in this real book about others like them in real museum spaces. And beginning with a brief definition as well—drawn from them. For now, suffice it to say that demediation, as an active function of such works rather than some a priori condition, names *the undoing of a given form of transmission, now blocked or altered, in the medium of its secondary presentation.* Where in Marshall McLuhan's well-known sense of the form/content dyad, the content of a new medium is always the lingering form of the old, in the art of demediation the *absence* of the old medial form becomes the content of the new work. The actual book objects to come (sculptures, appropriations, composites) often appear, like these first virtual or fictive ones, as abstract volumetric forms—demediated in just this sense, no longer broadcast from within as explicit textual signification or legible message. So that their point, too, is one we must in the best of cases half *make up* for ourselves; or, as we say, make up our minds about. That the display space we're about to survey should house an exhibit whose works are held in mind alone is a testament to that category of bookwork so thoroughly demediated that it needs no real matter, only conceptual material, to be understood. But to have true impact, that's a different thing. Soon enough we must turn to the real executions that bring it about.

To begin with, though, imagine the world's largest composite piece of book sculpture. More than 1 million square feet of quadratic geometry composed of four identical open folios, twenty-four stories each in elevation, facing into each other at separated right angles: durable limited editions in steel and glass. Below them: a cavernous system of "sub-texts" in the form of a vast fantastic warren of a library, accessed separately from each single megatext. A Borgesian dream come true—11 million volumes and still counting, each the fractalized image of the whole. To encounter such a conceptual book sculpture, undergirded in just this infrastructural way and not imaginary at all, see the real thing standing—and burrowing—in no less visible a site than the French capital. Its proud nameplate: La Bibliothèque nationale, Site François-Mitterrand.

The structure's four-towered profile rises from a sparse urban esplanade even while hiding within its deep-dug atrium the symbolized forests (a huge stand of fifty-foot trees) that have never been, nor ever will be, denuded and milled in the service of book production.

Nature meets culture at a mutual point of no return beneath this most abstractly grand of Mitterrand's Grands Travaux, each gargantuan codex like a high-rise work in the bibliographic as well as the architectural sense. And imagine deep at the underground glassed-in core of this work of works, this palace of oeuvres—open to readers between trips to the stacks—numerous *mise-en-abymes* of its overarching formal vaunt. These conceptual miniatures of the fourfold superstructure take shape as handmade, non-industrial microcosms, one after another: in other words, book sculptures in several media beyond conventional paper forms. For there in the central gallery space (ordinarily devoted to rotating traditional displays in the history of the book) is a winter exhibition not of artists' books—that was last season—but of conceptual book art, with an international selection of contributors. Beneath the superbooks of the building's four towers, then, the meta-books of aesthetic reflection. Why not? How long before such a show does actually get mounted?

Let's imagine it's called *La Joie des Livres: De Codex á Biblio Tech*. A half-page press notice in the English edition of *Pariscope* reports that "this bibliomaniac carnival features—and disfigures—the book in all its forms and functions, from sacred to secular object, impenetrable script surface to plumbed receptacle of culture. The show is at once funny, fabulous, and frightening. Not content with the display of artists' books in the decorative or artisanal sense, the curators have arranged instead a multimedia compendium of that mixed medium known as the book, capturing by sometimes comic sample the whole spectrum of its historical force from the ancient illuminated codex to the postmodern PowerBook. By estranging us from one of our most routine tools, postconceptual art has found a new springboard in these familiar planks of culture. We are invited to think again about the too-familiar book, conceive it anew." [...]

For all the diversity of the displayed works, including their purposeful disorientation as bound volumes or isolated pages, a few discernible patterns emerge. In this respect, these bookworks sample the whole neo-conceptual field of such contemporary practice, everything from *écriture* art to pulp sculpture that has followed from the text-work of Conceptual art since its flourishing first moment in the late 1960s. Some book shapes are more concerned, even if illegibly, with content, some with form. Yet any one of them is liable to leach from the blocked, suspended, or effaced textuality that defines it, or from its materialist exaggerations as felt surface, a certain verbal self-consciousness, after all—and to do so precisely in order to play (or even bluntly pun) on its own aberrant mode of legibility, whether occluded, deflected, or redefined. This frequent, obliquely verbalized gesture feels meant, in other words—and sometimes in no actual written words at all—to give back to us, whether by title or associated lexical irony, at least some modicum—and maybe even some strange epitome—of the "textual" pleasure these negated books would otherwise deny us in their frequent sculptural occlusion of reading matter by material form.

"From Guttenberg to Google"

That's the historical span identified by the four-page flyer free on entrance in lieu of the full illustrated brochure that the library, one finds when inquiring, regretted having no funds to publish. (As above, I'll be giving text and titles in English unless some play on words in the imaginary artist's original language cannot be retained in translation.) Gutenberg is one benchmark moment, of course, even while the flyer acknowledges that the pre-print codex hails from sometime between 100 BC and AD 50. Yet the historical scope of the "concept book" goes back further yet in this exhibit, by Old Testament evocation, to a bulking stone tablet in the anachronistic form of a bound codex. An oversize drab form in poured concrete by a Berlin conceptual artist, about four by five feet and six inches deep, is scored like page edges on three sides, rounded off like sewn binding on the fourth, and leaned against the wall next to the faint pale-gray label *Rock of the Faith*—complete with a red satin bookmark emerging mysteriously from the impenetrable density of the bottom edge and lolling on the floor like a silenced tongue. [...]

Early in this imagined exhibition, then, the book form [...] is enlisted by disuse, alteration, or other irony into the roster of art history—which is to say, placed on display as such: turned from instrument to artifact, in other words to object d'art. The theme is set. On another wall of this first room, by a Belgian conceptualist this time, is a lectern with attached podium light shining down on an antique diptych frame. Behind its hinged pair of opened glazed surfaces are the copies of two apparently facing pages—though in fact approximately twinned from separate editions—of Michel Butor's 1960 collection of essays called *Inventory*. Each page is "masked" by a beige plastic overlay—except for the rectangular slits through which appear, in different locations and typefaces on each page, Butor's famous remark about the common material basis of print and painting: " ... all books are diptychs." The whole point of which is meant to be resumed by the spatial overexplicitness of just such a textual assemblage.

Biblio Tech: Re-Medial Reading

Granted, all books are diptychs: framed adjacent fields of marking. They are also machines, technologies. In this mode of bibliographic irony, a seasoned California video artist has branched out into "book sculpture" with his *Books on Tape*, hung on the far wall of the second gallery space. The work consists of two six-inch-high, eight-foot-wide translucent plastic bands, rolled and tucked away at the ends on wall-mounted spindles, one horizontal scroll thus stretched above the other. The image strips are then overlaid with a series of separate photographic negatives, "life-size" and discretely taped together, of pages from published books—their white lettering on a dark gray translucent field legible against the backing and brightly lit white wall. This ironic send-up of magnetic tape marks out the refused, rather than embraced, mediation of a print technology by an audial one, as accentuated by the fact that these photo strips are flanked by small shelf speakers. To complete the joke, the titles of the books thus purveyed for "easy listening" are none other than *The Sound and the Fury* and *The Silence of the Lambs*. Or almost complete it. The ultimate historical irony of this 1987 work, escaping its own direct intermedial comedy, only hits home when we realize that the long genealogy of the scroll in Western culture, ancestor to the codex, has finally seen its day, since even the spool of audiotape has been replaced now by CD technology in the marketing of recorded books. [...]

On and on the fantasy emporium unfurls. But to cut it short here, we can jump from pre-CD audiobooks to digital "readers" in the case of a last example:

"Alas" (*e-texte*) by a Zurich artist reworking that maverick British instance of postmodernism avant la lettre, Laurence Sterne's *Tristram Shandy*. Here we have another new-media irony carried back beneath a print surface to its underlying typographic codes. The original novel is shown open to the black rectangle opposite the mortuary allusion "Alas, poor Yorick!" at the end of chapter 12, the three words themselves outlined at the left, by Sterne's own design, in a horizontal frame like a coffin or a blank funeral card. In the equivalent e-text version alongside it on the display shelf jutting out from the wall, we find two unbound pages side by side. Whereas the first is a dot-matrix printing of "Alas, poor Yorick!" in full legibility, the facing page offers not the solid black of an unlit grave or onyx tombstone, as in the novel, but instead one of those crazed densities of algorithmic breakdown into computer code, breaching the articulatory maintenance of the system as if by elegiac capitulation, seizing it up in going dead to decipherability.

Enough imagined "fabrication," at least here. The dozens of real objects (if unreal books) that this monograph does in fact go on to picture and analyze establish a double pattern—of material insistence and textual "demediation"—that is explored further in *Book, Text, Medium* (2020) ahead (see Phase VI / 15). But first, another extraordinary multifold *objet* in the conceptual book-art folio my own samplings have assembled. Even compared to the mood of that sad algorithmic gravesite—and gravitas—in the high *triste* of *Tristram Shandy*, my wildest fantasies have been outdone in physical fact. I just got news when completing this "entry" (rather extreme coincidences, with more tabulated ahead, seem to be losing their surprise, if not their savor) of a book even I, in my imaginary Paris curatorship, couldn't have made up—but that a French publisher has actually made. And successfully marketed. The gratefully received news comes from a gifted former dissertation student of mine, Michael Sarabia, who arrived to our program with a law degree, blazed through his doctorate, and returned, analytic skills redoubled, to a successful legal practice. And who, on the eleventh anniversary of 2011's *Bookwork*, sent an article just now (September 20, 2022) from *The Guardian* about a high-priced artifact that he thought "might serve as a nice addendum to that book of yours." Little did he know that a sequel of sorts was being drafted even while he wrote—and with, yes, this resulting happy add-on.

His timely email attachment was calling my attention, in effect, to what seems the historical reversal of the dumpstered, pulped, or carved-up books that facilitated the estrangements of book sculpture from the 1980s on. For what the Greek artist Ilan Manouch has done is to return—from their digital proliferation to the original collector's-item materiality of pre-Web comix culture—the spectacularly best-selling online "volumes" of manga artist Eiichiro Oda, in his long running series *One Piece*. Under the metacompression and bulking caps of the title *ONEPIECE*—at over 21,000 pages stretching (a Smithsonian publication further glosses) to almost three feet in width and almost forty pounds in weight (one-fortieth of the British pounds it sells, and is actually selling, for), these paginated graphics are lashed together—whether glued or stitched isn't specified in the illustrated article—so that they cannot be wedged more than minimally apart between "binding" covers: covers that operate in fact more like a wide-spaced vise. Unlike many similar bookworks, this construct can't be construed as nostalgic for a mode of dissemination that, in the case of these born-digital web artifacts, never was. Subject to no charges of copyright infringement either, since none of the artist's graphic drawings, now pages, is legible, the ponderous *ONEPIECE* volume reads more like the tomb of paper culture—while also, and more importantly, a platform for a new transmedial recognition in the orbit of Digital Humanities. According to the publisher, according to *The Guardian*: "Ilan Manouach's *ONEPIECE* proposes to shift the understanding … from a qualitative examination of the formal possibilities of digital comics to a quantitative reappraisal of 'comics as Big Data.'" Convertible media ironies never cease. If a review volume like this present Reader must scramble to demonstrate, rather than just admit, that it's never over till it's over, with Conceptual art it's never over till it's begun again at an entirely new metalevel. But back now from text as big data to the local datum of the visible image as well as word at work.

> 10 / **Closed Circuits: Screening Narrative Surveillance** (University of Chicago Press, 2015). With its typically revealing title circling round on itself—re: the narrative function of embedded spycams along with a reference to their frequent CCTV manifestation—and with its subtitle then operating as three topics and/or one phrase, Stewart enters the public discourse about technologically invaded privacy, provoked by recent NSA revelations, and does so with examples from the medium out of which video, then digital, surveillance circuits had evolved. The book analyzes a broad spectrum of films, from Fritz Lang's *M* (1931) and Alfred Hitchcock's *Rear Window* (1954) through *The Conversation* (1972, dir. Francis Ford Coppola) to *Déjà Vu* (2006, dir. Tony Scott), *Source Code* (2011, dir. Duncan Jones), and *The Bourne Legacy* (2012, dir. Tony Gilroy). These are screen narratives in which cinema has articulated—and performed—the drama of inspection's unreturned look. As characteristic features of the thriller, both the act and the technology of surveillance speak to something more foundational in the very work of cinema, Stewart argues. The shared axis of montage and espionage—with editing designed to draw us in and make us (mostly) forget the omnipresence of the narrative camera—extends to larger questions about the mechanics as well as the politics of an oversight regime that is increasingly remote and robotic, automated and governed by algorithm and artificial intelligence. To such a global technopticon, one popular litmus test of response is just the proliferating mode of digitally enhanced "surveillancinema" on which this book concentrates.

10 / *The Narrative Optics of Surveillancinema*

Closed Circuits: Screening Narrative Surveillance (2015)

AFTER THE DELIBERATELY EXAGGERATED GAMBIT of its opening sentence—"All montage is espionage"—this next book, born directly from an interdisciplinary course for undergraduates, investigates the metafilmic force of surveillance camerawork from silent cinema down through the weaponizing of aerial optics in contemporary films of wired war and remote drone technology, with some of its down-to-the minute material reworked from my then-regular reviewing in *Film Quarterly*. Casting much farther into the past, it was also the first book in which I let autobiography—my earliest pre-teen film going in this case—carry me back to an original summer screening of Hitchock's *Rear Window* (1954) in setting forth, in the first paragraphs below, an establishing point about reframed optics in that famous film of the mostly cam-less spier. Recovering below what the screen-loving young boy in me, fresh from the excitement of our family's first TV set (*c.* 1952–3), might have sensed about the establishing mass media context of voyeurism versus detection in Hitchcock's film may well have encouraged, in the adult scholar, the further reminiscence about my later teen job as movie usher, two scholarly years later, for *Cinesthesia* (2021; see Phase VII / 17). In any case, boyhood recollection in *Closed Circuits* leads analysis forward, in the second half of this excerpt, amid a much fuller treatment of the Hitchcock film, to my adult fascination (from 1999's *Between Film and Screen* forward) with the screen's disclosed substrate in the photogram, mobilized here as a kind of mobile photographic proof sheet in the suspected presence of a buried body part.

Windowed Pictures: Tele-Visioning and the Fourth Wall

Rear Window: one of the essential film titles. Even the timing of its initial commercial distribution confirms the logic of internal framing by which its encompassing irony is developed. In its day, it was a summer thriller. I saw it first—or, say better, I stared intensely at it—in downtown Fort Lauderdale, then my home town, in the first month of its national release in a sweltering August (they all were), escaping with the rest of a theater-going populace into an "air-cooled" space from a routine heat and humidity at least as bad as that with which the film so topically (and tropically) opens in a New York City summer. Most anywhere in its August screenings, in fact, the spectator would have known rather intimately what it means to distract oneself from body heat by ocular fascination. But then or now—whether seated before the *Window*'s wide-screen purview, or sharing the video with students by way of a miserable overhead projector, or watching it on home monitors—in every case a strange sense of optic recession always sets in, quite beyond the first rectangular threshold of its "interior courtyard" view on which Jeff's own curtain goes up with the titles.

I don't imagine I'm alone in this. How long does a viewer have to stare through the frame-coincident big-screen rear window, as if at (and into) a projected world not so much of occupied cubicles as of framed rectangles crowded with visible human motion—how long does one have to stare through the eyes of a chair-bound media-savvy commercial image-maker, our incapacitated photographer-hero, often with a secondary lens in front of his eye, before beginning to suspect those frustratingly distanced subsidiary spaces as stand-ins for inset mediations in their own right? This isn't a directly metafilmic effect, as if we (and Jeff in our stead) were watching an overstrained parallel montage distributed instead across a collage of separate movie-like portals (like a stacking of outdoor though not exactly drive-in movies). Rather, with or without the hero's tele-vision lens in hand (his huge telephoto supplement to a broken camera), these facing rectangulated scenarios, each with its own "broadcast" if muted sound, come to resemble just the sort of smaller screens not only that one leaves behind for a night at the magnified movies but (the more interesting inference) that so many of these 1954 apartment-dwellers would themselves have had, and had visibly turned on—Jeff not least, in his long weeks of recuperation. [...]

Nonetheless, the evocation of TV—as "structuring absence" within (as well as the figure for) each rectangle opposite Jeff's optically enhanced perch—by no means overrules the cinematic reflexivity it miniaturizes. [...] No visual recording on Jeff's part—I mean no *visible* moment of photography—takes place in this film about a once avid, now frustrated photographer. It is as if this absence is designed to narrow the distance, for plot's duration at least, between his experience and ours, each equally visual, neither actively recorded: say passive, submissive—until we later learn that he had in fact, at least a couple of weeks earlier, been taking voyeuristic photos after all, which he cops to, under his breath at one point, as "leg art." [...]

From Oculust to Documentation: A Return of the Photoscopic Repressed

[...] The scene in question is studious, verging on laborious, in delivering its point. Jeff is finally able to convince Stella and Lisa that something is decidedly wrong when he gets them to hold up to the light a slide that, before the film even begins, he has taken of the courtyard flower bed. Spurred by a hunch, he has asked Lisa to fetch for him from the shelf a "viewer" along with a box of slides taken "about two weeks ago." Rifling through them, he mumbles to himself that he hopes he "took something else besides leg art." Soon he finds what he's hoping for, as a yardstick of the present evidentiary setting. But he needs to teach his secondary witnesses how to read it. He asks Lisa and Stella to alternate the slide in question with the unaided view of the current garden from the same angle: "Now take it down; look again; now take it down." Each woman complies. What results, filling the narrative screen in the process, is that the recorded image (of time past) enters into a heuristic oscillation with the seen present—as if in the minimal differential of a filmstrip, one frame edged away by its seemingly real-time successor—so as to reveal that certain flowers appear to shrink rather than grow over time, the garden plot therefore having been obviously disturbed by digging and rebedding. The surveillance plot is directly affected as well. But so is the mechanism of framed sighting at large–and its substrate of photograms. Lifted from narrative burial for the first time—and associated indirectly with the photographer-hero's stock in trade—is the underlying logic. If in normal cinema, by the frame line's infinitesimal progressions, motion comes into being before our eyes, it is only the same means that would allow, for its mechanical reversal—a reversal (ungrowing flowers) matched for once by a clue in the real.

This curious epistemological episode, in its photomechanical basis, clearly exceeds the necessities of plot. Yet the wavering between then and now, full-frame photo transparency and full-frame screenshot, is a definitive balancing act at the plot's true filmic turning point. Apart from establishing shots of the women's gazes as they peer at and past the slide, what we see more prominently, and dramatically, in the POV framing of the garden is more like a filmmaker himself running a sequence back and forth through an editing machine looking for continuity errors, whether of lighting, framing, or mise-en-scene. With this moment explicitly motivated as optic decipherment, put it that close reading may become, as D. A. Miller demonstrates elsewhere and otherwise with Hitchcock, indeed "too close"—so close that, in this case, plot dissolves into its own undertext, the photochemistry of its own serial imprints. That's Hitchcock for you. Such is the mastery of a suspension, rather than merely a suspense, that remains hovering between process and product, filming and telling, medium and narrative turn. [...]

In the exhumation of a single photograph in proof of an exhumed garden plot (and complot), the foundational transfer between recorded world and its populated gazing in distilled to an on-camera, rather than typically in-camera, splitting of the difference. Narrowed to the same ocular scale and shuffled as if to the point of a rudimentary animation effect, the two-frame view undergoes a radical back-and-forth not just between frames but between narrative space and medium. There, screen-wide before us, a photochemical image made visible; there, now, the world being seen by participant witnesses. Narrative cinema in embryo. Suture has been put on exhibit from within an otherwise inconsequential shot and its reverse shot (staring women, external view and its previous trace). Such a displacement of camerawork by enacted gaze is exactly the fiction of immediacy that this one interactive moment of mediated spectation in *Rear Window*—slide trace versus immanent vision—drags back by association to the action of the track rather than the mere tracking of a villainous action.

Many examples follow in the wake of this 1954 classic. It would probably be no surprise to other admirers of what still seems to me (so far, more than two decades in) the most brilliant film of this century, Michael Haneke's *Caché*

(2005), that attention to it in *Framed Time* (2007) would by this later point seem to have left much unsaid. Hence my return to Haneke's metafilmic structure in this later study, especially given the way its involuted play between secondary video image track and narrative tracking tightens even further the knotted functions of my subtitle in the plot's blistering version of "screening narrative surveillance." But, recursive attention included, we keep moving on.

Note

1 Georg Lukács, *The Theory of the Novel: A Historico-Philosophical Essay on the Forms of Great Epic Literature* (Cambridge: MIT Press, 1974).

V.

MEDIUM, PHILOSOPHY, CONCEPT

---

11 / The argument of *The Deed of Reading: Literature * Writing * Language * Philosophy* (Cornell University Press, 2015)—closely equilibrating the four terms of its subtitle to suggest how literary language can be found to philosophize its own condition—begins with a rethinking of Walter Ong in light both of Stewart's previous work in *Reading Voices* (1990) and of Giorgio Agamben's philosophical account of linguistic "potentiality." Stewart's innovation emerges in the pursuit of a "secondary vocality" instanced in readings from Romantic poetry to modern prose. The philosophic net is cast more broadly yet for a chapter on Stanley Cavell's view of the skeptical abyss of subjectivity undergirding—or more like undermining—the wordplay of Edgar Allan Poe. A chapter on the unique metalinguistic leverage offered by the trope of syllepsis—with its off-kilter balancing act between literal and figurative predication, sampled from Jane Austen through Charles Dickens to Toni Morrison—leads to a final chapter on the stylistic anomalies of prose discourse and dialogue alike, as well as on the melodramatized agon of writing, in a much-cited chapter addressing Morrison's late novel, *A Mercy* (2008).

---

11 / Textual Act as Contract

*The Deed of Reading: Literature * Writing * Language * Philosophy* (2015)

GIVEN THE GLACIAL VAGARIES of university press schedules, it should be no surprise that two separate lines of investigation, each derived from a philosophy of mediation, should have arrived from different presses by quite separate paths in the same year. But not by routes previously untrodden. Just as *The Deed of Reading* traverses again the stratum of linguistic productivity at the springs of literary language, calling for an "ethic of reading" (a kind of contractual responsibility) as well as a politicized "ethics," so did *Closed*

Circuits (2015) partly name, as well as frequently entail, the effects of medial recess within screen narrative that had often served as nodes of metanarrative intensification in my preceding film books—though now reframed in the context of international surveillance, its politics as well as its ethics. Same again with the conceptualist penchant of *Transmedium* (2017), continuing as it does lines of inquiry first laid down in the closing chapter of *The Look of Reading* (2006)—and followed out in the subsequent *Bookwork* (2011). Nor was it far from mind that the gallery works intriguing me in these ways operated in contrast to what I was elsewhere lamenting as a "post-medium" negligence in literary study. That's the deepest synchronic link between the two projects seated together in this fifth phase. But in *The Deed of Reading* I again permit myself some foundational diachrony, stepping off the footprints of a poetic influence by harking back to the mid-1960s, a decade after my sweltering Florida summer encounter with *Rear Window* (1954, dir. Alfred Hitchcock) in *Closed Circuits*. Situated in a beach town on another coast, this biographical indulgence regarding my late-teen literary curiosity adds special piquancy to an odd marketing pitch I recently stumbled upon in finding that Amazon designates *The Deed of Reading* (no doubt among my most difficult theoretical experiments) as "Reading Age: 18 Years and Up." My former self was only just short of such a threshold in that first serious poetry reading to which, in proposing just now to "hark back," I was indeed thinking of—in etymological terms—as an initiated listen: a first hearkening to the echo chambers of verse wording, where even surprise twists of syntax may seem to pause for audible breath when read. The scene, Laguna Beach now, rather than Fort Lauderdale—and the site of a true aesthetic uprooting as well:

> I go back in memory, then, to my hometown's well-stocked and long-gone local bookshop, with its fuss-budget and anything but avuncular owner, at least as inquisitive as his patrons, who was always seeming to scope out your roving interests over his bifocals. It was the California of the Beach Boys, not yet the Beatles. And there in Laguna Beach, a newly transplanted and misfit high school student from the other coast, I began my first sustained bookstore romance, a few blocks walking distance from the family house—and continents away. A rather desperately compensatory romance? Sublimated teen solitude and angst? What else was literature for? Then as now, Laguna was a resort town never known for resorting overmuch to books, even beach reading; I was mostly alone there when I stopped at the bookstore; rarely saw anyone I knew; hardly anyone more than once. For me it was a zone apart—and twice over. Planning to be an architect from early in high school, I started looking to literature for something else—but something no less structured, no less a built environment, as I soon realized: a world of distant and shifting horizons, certainly, but also a crafted shelter.

Then, too, the wannabe designer in me loved the graphics of the covers, among them (as it happens) the giant 7 of that ambiguity book. And, a little later, the newly venturesome reader in me came to love ambiguity as a name for my own uncertainties and second thoughts. Who knew this poverty of confidence could be thought of as philosophically rich? I can still spottily document this first flush of serious reading with mental sales receipts, from Tolstoy to Faulkner to, among the philosophy books in the next alcove, E. M. Cioran and those heady answers of Sartre's to *What is Literature?*, including the first books of poetry I sparingly bought. If this last indulgence in particular felt, on a movie usher's salary, almost like paying by the word, maybe that's part of why they counted so much for me: those word-by-word productions.

Because will and wallet knew their limitations, the bookstore was more a guilty pleasure than edifying, all that browsing with so little uptake. Like over-indulging, with no intention to shell out, in those record-shop listening booths a few doors away. Back down the block in the far less busy bookstore, it often seemed like snooping rather than perusing. So I felt obliged to buy at somewhat regular, if carefully spaced, intervals: stabs in the dark for the light. While, all the while, I kept on combing the seemingly endless shelves. Existentialism looked fiercely important whenever I looked into it, and I loved the big novels, not the small ones. But poetry had its special scent, and there I wanted the small books and, in them, the short poems. Challenges one might come up to—or wouldn't have to fail at for long. Some purchases didn't repay my arbitrary selection. I remember having a go at scaling the smallest (and cheapest) book of poems I could find, the diminutive format of *Lord Weary's Castle*, and though I could tell Robert Lowell had something, I wasn't sure what, and I further suspected, in my callowness, how the lord of that keep must have come by his name. My experiments were hit and miss, to be sure, and the misses not always near.

But sometimes the earth moved. I must have been just the right age and temperament to be smitten. In any case, the next collection of poems I cottoned to and took home, very much *despite* its blandly designed paperback cover, had hooked me by its title alone—the first and interesting half of it, that is, but as contaminated grammatically by what followed: Richard Wilbur's *The Beautiful Changes and Other Poems*. Two plurals, I at first assumed: something about changes and then a batch of other poems. Much to explore. Skimming through it, I loved right away the sound of the bunched phrases, that tuneful diction and rhythmic pattern, its lucid music. A rapid caveat, though: If the once-celebrated Wilbur—mainstream, accessible, *New Yorker*-friendly, Pulitzer Prize-winning, and Laureate-aureoled—is no longer to anyone's exact taste, that shouldn't deter the experiment in recovered literary memory I've embarked on. I don't choose Wilbur now for any reason except that I chose him then, hoping to show here how writing like his, as with greater and more demanding poetry, can work its quiet magic on an unjaded imagination. It doesn't have to be a triumphant poem, just a good enough one, and certainly not necessarily an edgy one, to plough certain willing furrows in the topsoil of the teenage imagination (or, say, the student sensibility). For our present use, the single poem lifted from memory, no matter how dated in its aesthetic, how over-polished, needs only to be demanding enough to sustain a rudimentary ethic of attention. Wilbur's short poem certainly is—and does, especially in its difficult last moves.

Back then, the issue was simpler. I was just curious. Was the first half of the title the key to it all? The beautiful changes—as opposed to the other kind, the ugly or sad or defeating ones? Which particular transformations does the poet have in mind? Will each of the poems answer, one by one? These are the sort of questions those three words set going as I parted the volume, well before I looked for and found the title verses waiting at the end as capstone. So why not begin with that, even if Wilbur didn't? Temporarily moored in my room for the foray, I hoped such a last but surely not least poem, given its status as volume title, would be an economical place to start in sating those first curiosities about the title. It did answer some of my questions, but only by undoing the very language that prompted them—only by in fact *changing* the title not once but twice at least in the self-adjusted lens of the poem's unfolding grammar. Long before I would hear the prefix in a college literature class, and learn gingerly to deploy it, I was about to have my first rendezvous with the *meta*.

But every way I put this sounds too cerebral, I realize, even when I stress my tendency to be flummoxed at first with certain literary densities. In my routine teen alienation, taking up (with) poetry was neither a program nor a mission. I was just there *for the duration*, so to speak: the respite from pressures less appealing than abutted words and the time it took for their sorting out. The tugs and drags of dailiness weren't, of course, shut out at the closing of my door, let alone by the opening of my poetry book—much as I might have liked them to be at times. But amid the idiocies and anguishes of a teenage commerce with the world, and most of all its gnawing uncertainties, here was some restorative "time out": call it a way of doubting oneself productively, where missteps might feel like a circuitous progress. To put stress on the stresses and strains of reading, then, by way of generalization: whatever refuge it may be locally used for, the supposed escapism of literature can be just the opposite—given the demands it makes, the regimen it inflicts.

So let me, as it were, cut to the chase—amid the fuller teen reading, line by line, that I reconstructed in this (introductory) "Induction"—by latching onto what seemed at first the grammatical run-around whose paces my teen self was being put through in the poem's closing grammar:

> ... the beautiful changes
> In such kind ways,
> Wishing ever to sunder
> Things and things' selves for a second finding, to lose
> For a moment all that it touches back to wonder.

With these lines in front of us, I began a new subsection to excavate my original digging in:

Changes Wrung: A Mutability Canto

Though soon taken by grammatical surprise in the Wilbur poem, I was in some sense emotionally prepared for it. For it was indeed the quick-change artistry of literary writing that I was developing a hankering for. With such a fondness for instabilities, it's a good thing I didn't in fact become an architect. As "The Beautiful Changes" did its work on me, its relish for the kinetic and unsettled is what seemed epitomized at the smallest compass in the poem's now phrasal, now clausal title (a distinction that came easy enough in junior high grammar class). [...]

To what extent one needed in high school to be good at grammar in order to register these waverings and undertows, I'll never be sure. Years of teaching since do suggest that it is easier to get students to notice something out of the way if they have clearly in mind certain norms by which to compare and annotate its departures. In any case, it must be admitted that if I really excelled at any one thing in those secondary school years, curricular or extracurricular, it was the lost art of sentence diagramming, which I could execute with a sure and practiced hand the way other kids did trigonometry or beach volleyball. (Where some flaunted a great overhead serve, my pride and joy was the backslash of the predicate nominative.) The change from *change* as substantive to *change* as intransitive to *change* as the stem of a past (active) participle may indeed remain only dimly felt if one can't tag it through some kind of familiarity with the categories, if not exactly by name. [...]

"Wishing ever to sunder / Things and things' selves for a second finding, to lose / For a moment all that it touches back to wonder." What? Where has the poem brought us in closing? In the penultimate phrase, has the rhythmic wording carried into the crevices of designation a subliminal hint of "severance" across the metrics of "wi*sh*ing *ever* to sunder"? While I wouldn't have known then to call the hatchet-like onsets that propel these syllables a trochaic effect, I did no doubt catch the perseverance and the divisiveness alike of the beat. Evoked in this way is that differential severing, in fact that designated "sundering," that comes from within the things of this world when blooming anew to themselves under the sensitized eye, things echoing their essence against preconception's sounding board. This is the distance incident to beauty when renewed by conception. In nature and art as well. Yet it is language's own unique privilege with relation to this distance that the poem is there to prove—by reperforming it.

Lost and Found

This happens not least in the transient ambiguity of prepositional phrasing across the final two lines—after the severing and reseamed enjambment at "Wishing ever to sunder / Things and things' selves for a second ...." Under description is the cleaving asunder (and together again) that lends the world "for a second" a—no, wait, the real adverbial phrase ("For a moment," not a second) still waits patiently a line away, preceded here by a verbalized substantive: "a second finding, to lose / For a moment ...." My ellipses, here and just above, mark those points as which phrasing spills over the brink into lurching uncertainties and their quick recuperation. What is to be found is beauty's renewed chance of apprehension—not unlike, come to think of it, the eye's wordless equivalent of an optical rereading on the run. Taking it slow, the phrase "things and things' selves" arranges for its punctuated sibilant elision to mark the flecked juncture of a silent apostrophe across the softly delinked objects of that "wishing ever to sunder." Through the lens of the beautiful, there is a perpetual desire not wholly to divorce things from their entity or essence, nor just to deflect the self-sameness of identity, but rather to estrange those things to the point of fresh perception, if only for that restorative gesture that torques "for a second" away from adverbial toward adjectival force in a "second finding."

I keep trying to imagine first impressions of "The Beautiful Changes" apart from the way this poem is now colored for me in reassessment. No doubt I would have been jolted at the time, though perhaps not as a metrical phenomenon at all, by the tongue-twisting "things and things' selves"—and maybe even seen a silly plural "elf" there, with even the overwrought young reader wise enough to dismiss its impish irrelevance from mind. And I might have felt a bond tighter than usual in these words, harder to sunder—having paused, that is, over just that kind of plural apostrophe I was myself confident of having mastered in my own classroom punctuation exercises by then; and having paused especially over how odd and clotted it looked here in poetry. But I wouldn't have known that a "spondaic" double beat made the locked, muscle-bound phrase the challenge to dissociation that it sounds. And if innocent of trochees and spondees, still less was I acquainted with complicated rhyme schemes. Where I sensed echo, it was mostly as a part of a rhythm, not a formal template. Rhyme would merely have kept company with the other changes at play in the beauty at stake. Only now do I see how the last double pair of coupling rhymes in this stanza works to exceed foreknowledge in precisely the muted drum-roll of incurred fascination that is silently played out in the mounting from "says" to unforeseen "ways," from "sunder" to a resultant and intrinsic "wonder." I didn't know about "making strange" then, by name or principle. Or didn't know I knew. Wilbur did. Knew—and knew how to make me feel it.

With "the beautiful" operating still as antecedent, adverbial brevity would have struck me as returning on the wing in a phrased desire "to lose for a moment all that *it* touches ... [back to wonder]." Still in reprise and approximation, here again is the young mind picking its way slowly across the line. Or better put (which is the whole the point of my grammatical stammerings brought back as literary-critical fable in these days of vanishing attention to such things): here is any mind made innocent once more, and avid, by the localized surprise of poetic second thoughts, second chances. One stands back to process this, lets the keywords vet—and resonate with—each other. Such lovely losses: the beautiful letting go momentarily of all that it touches in a universal principle of change. But the grammar continues, with the infinitive "to lose" turned suddenly compound, arcing over its object to revectorize predication with another wavering adverbial phrase. Or even two, it seems. Across the momentarily lost direction of the enjambment, the impacted phrase "to lose / For a moment all that it touches back to wonder" gathers meaning only across its terraced overlaps of idiom in a rolling syntactic increment. Under the auspices of transformation rather than its transience, beauty loses everything it is recognized to touch, but only in the sense of touching it again with, and so releasing it back to, notice.

In the poem's layered natural settings, from meadow to forest and back again, we encounter what linguists (summoned again to the dock) call—as again I will learn only much later—a "garden path sentence," launched upon its own self-correction in the way the title has already surreptitiously been. Permutations are shuffled through on the spot in the closing grammatical transform. The beautiful suffers its losses in order to refind; loses all that it touches, all that it finds embodiment in—until syntax spins out to suggest that the loss is only "back to wonder," as if in a homecoming. Anything seemingly subtracted, abstracted, is reclaimed now for a fresh finding. All this lends force, in turn, to an ephemeral phonetic suspicion (to which young readers of even modestly secure spelling habits might well be prone) of "looses ... back" (frees to). [...]

So that maybe I glimpsed even in that early reading—hung up on the title as I was, just as the poem is so carefully hung from its gradually doubled and tripled senses—how its loaded verbal turn presides even in absentia over the close of the poem. For here is poetry's power of association in a single climactic node. The loss that touches back to wonder in a second finding puts a strain on idiom that could only be righted if rewritten under the aegis of a compound predicate like "changes back" (far more vernacular than "loses back"). One could put the whole transformative idea this way: Change in the world loses all that it touches, and this only by touching back (because metaphorically holding up) to wonder all that it thus anoints (and in words appoints) to the receptive eye in a restored keenness of apprehension—prehensile, haptic, touching. Once it is taken as no longer a nominal form or substantive, and not even just a verbal intransitive, the title becomes in this emergent sense elliptical, with no limits to the objects of its ministry. It is in every sense transactive, transitive. The beautiful changes—everything, you name it. Difference surrenders all that it thereby renews through a mutability internalized: the loss at one with the thing it realienates for fresh recognition. The difference made by this particular brand of loss is not absence but re-presentation. Like the world's unphrased poetry tendered for reading.

With the rest of the book's demonstrations too sustained and cross-referenced for useful excerpt, the compressed flashback here should at least have shown "literature writing language philosophy" for a receptive attention at a vulnerable and formative stage.

> 12 / Where, in *The Deed of Reading*, Stewart engaged more directly than ever before with philosophies of language, in **Transmedium: Conceptualism 2.0 and the New Object Art** (University of Chicago Press, 2017) he enters instead the crossfire of art theory. His evidence is gathered from proliferating international museum work that resists the broadly received sense of a "post-medium condition" in the long aftermath of modernism's fetishized "medium specificity." What Stewart's far-ranging collection of evidence demonstrates is a hybrid materiality, whether plastic or technological, aspiring to a hypermediatic self-consciousness in the dovetailing of medial orientations and means. This includes everything from the openly mixed register of photorealist painting, with its variants in a conceptualist *trompe l'oeil*, through video and installation pieces, "light sculpture," and digital glitch art. The book moves in the end to Stewart's more familiar, if still innovative, interdisciplinary terrain as well as to the relation of death and mediation that has elsewhere directed his readings (for instance, in a closely observed triangulation of landscape painting, photography, and screen framing in Michael Haneke's 2012 film *Amour*).

12 / Material Transference and Medial Merger

Transmedium: Conceptualism 2.0 and the New Object Art (2017)

Its TRANSATLANTIC RESEARCH completed as *The Deed of Reading* was going to press, this subsequent study on transmedial experimentation "began"—before its actual drafting—with all the artifacts and installations tacitly crowding in upon these opening paragraphs, a bursting drawer of evidence pressing for explication:

> At two scales of attention in what follows, at the level of aesthetic enterprise as well as of media theory, the way forward is in fact between. This book joins certain experimental works of the last two decades in resisting both the sweeping antimodernist assumptions of a "post-medium condition" in art practice and the implacable "convergence" in media study that takes as axiomatic a digital vanishing point for all processes. Between these two premises for the material basis of image production (and certain audiovisual projects as well)—between the release from medium specificity and the leveling point of no return in universal computerization, between aesthetic liberation and technological foreclosure—experimentation makes its frequent and, in both senses, *curious* way. Its inquisitiveness is likely to grow contagious in the viewing act. This is to say that aesthetic

encounter in museum space can be, more than ever, a variably cued engagement with a work's own materialized "thought experiment."

But what in fact to think about the enlarged, repainted, and then re-photographed single frame of a celluloid film when ripped from its place not only in an isolated strip but also in the whole cinematic medium? What to think about a prewar film projector found screening, in loop-fashion on a gallery wall, the brief computer-generated image of celluloid's long-forgotten role as the plastic substrate for binary impress in the first primitive computer? About digital landscape photography generated by US Air Force reconnaissance technology and its virtual-reality software when applied to landscape paintings rather than topographic maps? About a drawing, then lithographic rendering, of a film strip caught in every sense-snagged and bifurcated between frames-in its secondary representation? And what about—what to think and say about—an apparent photo reproduction of a classic oil painting that turns out, on closer inspection, to be composed of 10,000 separate computer-searched images? What one can say may depend on how one begins by denominating such effects.

Naming is claiming. It is an attempt to grasp as category, to posit an understanding. [...] To respond transmedium: that's the invitation of such aesthetic provocations, where the heuristic coinage of that term is proposed less as a free-standing substantive (a transmedium) than as a slant or bearing of response—indicating, that is, a directed attention to the where and how of manifestation. Directed by the analytic stance of the image or installation itself, such attention is routed in this way across—and often in and between—the work's own material coordinates. This is the path by which such artifacts seek to bring production and reception into the closest possible alignment across "the concept" thereby put into transmission, often by some unexpected crux of divergent medial procedures. [...] Many practitioners in this line are termed "art researchers," often with the sense of their being archaeologists in action, probing the history of their present means and materials. Art objects tend to become, as a result, fine-grained reports on their own medial constitution.

This is certainly the case in the two instances below, grouped with dozens of others like them under the emblematic typography of my reversibly lower-cased subheads, where the double colon marks a turnstile between—in the cases here detailed—alternate but convergent medial substrates on a single new optic platform. In the radical betweenness or "interface" of their materializations, the two artists instanced here make part of the "Entre'acte" between the study's two main "Scenes," one on the fixed image, one on time-based media, "Image Frames" versus "Motion Captures." As may soon be obvious, I select these examples not because any pair of artists could be reasonably representative of the wide panoply of media experimentation I survey, but rather for their direct ties back to my own earlier work on the motorized modules of photographic celluloid in *Between Film and Screen* (1999).

[cine::graphy]

Widely noted by French image theorists and film philosophers, the research-intensive work of Eric Rondepierre consistently limns such differences (between "image" and "film," "frame" and "motion") as his own version of epistemography. He does so by arresting the very transit from cellular photogram to cinematographed space. [...] Compare this to British photographer John Stezaker's paracinema. [...] In reshooting, for instance, decades of equine photographs from a horse-breeding magazine in their standardized profile format, Stezaker achieves a blur of differential vision that can't help but call up the prehistory of cinema in Eadweard Muybridge's chronophotographs of horses in motion—this time shuddering in place rather than running, an oscillation rather than a gallop. Nonetheless, just as in standard-issue (photogram-tissued) cinema, the seeming movement—rather than being parsed and analyzed—is refabricated: an artifice of activity rather than a direct transcript.

This, too, is the level at which Rondepierre's interceptions of the film strip intercede in the motion effect in order to seize it (up) from within. [...] Time and again, in the arrest of screen time, his detached pictograms exert consistent if varied pressure on the liminal switch between image and its serial machination. In this, his orientation is resolutely transmedium even while his materials remain fixedly fixed frame. [...] For Rondepierre is a photographic printmaker preoccupied with the interstitial force of the cinematic "photogram" (the most precise term for the photo cell on a film strip) both in its isolation from a projected frame stream and in its obsolescence within the newer protocols of digital transfer and transmit. [...]

The most ambitious of his transmedial gestures [...] are Rondepierre's disruptive captures, a decade back, from old-fashioned banner-flashing film trailers of the 1940s and 1950s for his *Annonces* series ("Ads," or in English, more euphemistically, "previews"). These involve rapid overlays of italicized and exclamation-pointed hyperbole sometimes intruding on the illustrative integrity of the advertised narrative sample, slicing open a star face, for instance, with a serrated edge of transitional typeface. In this way, it as if a defacilitated cinematic vision has again been made to render optic testimony—beneath advertised spectacle—to the pre- or proto-visuality it is inevitably built upon. And to which, inadvertently, it here adverts, indeed reverts. With the photogram's occluded operations suddenly made legible by an actual imposition of text, however fractured or blurred, Rondepierre then submits this sprocket-slipped disclosure to a further chain of distancing preservation. He first reduces the photo again to a transparency, projects it as a slide onto a crinkled paper surface to add a new layer of roughened and denaturing texture, depicts anew what he has anomalously seen in acrylic paint, rephotographs it, and, in what is no doubt a further allegorical move, ultimately destroys the painting—that belated trace of origination—on which the new photogrammic simulation, the virtually *trompe-l'oeil* photoprint, is based. [...]

In this way, as I might have spelled out the "allegory" at the time—in fact, I wish I had—Rondepierre's practice is a reminder that the true screen valence of cinematic presence is the ever-vanishing. Not least so when this "celluloid painter" turns to digital imaging and reverses the course of technological advance by producing high-definition photoprints out of the seized digital glitches of famous films in online delivery. As it happens, or hasn't yet, this is an effect I've been on the watch for ever since my work on *Framed Time* (2007) bore witness to the obsolescence of the celluloid freeze-frame as filmic succession degree zero. What, or more like where, are the digital equivalents of this Cavellian "assertion in technique" that in fact decertifies the moving image? Where is the pixel jam at a moment of narrative crisis in post-filmic cinema? Except for the borrowed gameplay aesthetic of a desktop thriller about invasive chatroom violence like *Unfriended* (2014, dir. Levan Gabriadze), where it functions as a metaphor for something like ontological "ghosting" as obliteration, pixel violence is spewed forth, I eventually came to think, and to spell out at length in *Cinemachines* (2020), mainly in the diegetically subsumed special effects of spatial rather than planar disintegration in the collisions and detonations of "action" (call it "computation") cinema.

But that's a case of being still on the lookout for a metamedial trope not yet realized, at least not widely. More common, as this volume continues to make clear—and minimally make up for—are things seen too late. The wistful "wish I had" in the last paragraph about Rondepierre, concerning his medial allegory, applies doubly to his repainted photograms—even more obviously than to his rephotographed and wall-mounted screen shots. And in this "if only" spirit, a totally unexpected precedent for Rondepierre came very belatedly my way. There are always more cross-media manifestations to be, as it were, transcepted than one imagines, and a deeper "mediarchaeological" resonance (one word again for such inbuilt self-instancing) than one might at first expect. So that, not just on the subject of contemporary art, but even regarding established painters in the canon, one is always in danger of going to print before all the best evidence is in. At a 2022 retrospective of the Victorian oil master Walter Sickert (1860–1942), there was a typically tardy surprise for me at Tate Britain. In chronological declension into cinema images from his onetime preoccupation with live theater settings as a secondary scene of representation and display, Sickert the impasto colorist caught up with the subsequent flourishing of newsprint photography in its automatic reduction of a traditional palette to black and white. He then went on from re-presenting (and further de-realizing) such mass imprints—in exaggerated gray-scale oil chiaroscuro (a several-decades jump on photorealism, with an extra distancing twist)—to the further abstraction, even of already colorized movie lobby cards (in one case Edward G. Robinson and Joan Blondell in a starkly lit close-up from the 1936 film *Bullets or Ballots*, dir. William Keighley). This was achieved by the thickening of his pigment in transmediation, dialing the artificial color back toward the realm of touched up sepia. And if there was more than one may have realized of this materialist thinking in images before the cult of modernist specificities, let alone before computerization, there will certainly be more yet in the years ahead.

So I wrote in January of 2022. Already one year ahead now, two further transmedia works from the last decade—at what might seem the far poles of high- versus zero-tech in the objects of their representation—have crossed my path, or I theirs, in a visit to the Danish National Gallery in Copenhagen. Together, by negation and parodic engagement respectively, they put a broad historical frame around the whole media upheaval occasioned by the ubiquity of the digital substrate in current image culture. Marie Lund (b. 1976) expands on the ready-made basis of her sinuous 2013 triptych—its panels recalling at a distant glance some variant of Morris Louis' "veil" paintings—first by stretching (not sketching) out on canvas, rather than simply rehanging in the other sense, the long-weathered monochrome window curtains that constitute her unretouched found images. What we see is faded fabric intermittently bleached by sunlight between its former folds and thus displaying a subtly shaded gradation of its corrugated blue tonality, as if streaked not just by the sun but by the blue of the sky that its purpose was often to shut out. Lund's version of a mere ready-made is overcome one step further, in this transmediation of the fabric's scrim function, by identifying these "works on canvas" with the metafilmic title "Stills" (2013): namely, photo/graphs (sun drawings) that in their years of exposure to light may seem to have reverted, with entitled conceptual nuance in their time-lapse tracing, to the dawn of photography itself in the light-etched, emulsion-free "photogram."

In a revealing medial contrast—by an artist born a decade after Lund and working at the other end of the history of modern technological media—one comes upon, in a meticulous black-and-white treatment, a dramatic mountain landscape by Andreas Albrectsen (b. 1986). Designated *Untitled (Folders)*, this work from 2018 is executed expertly in a charcoal coverage that at the same time seems to have scattered across its "spoiled" surface the smallish all-white (or say simply blank) silhouettes of skeuomorphic file folders in the form of computer icons, their telltale leftmost tabs a titular giveaway. What we have, then, here reverse-engineered to an earlier mode of the pictorial sublime, is a mock-heroic landscape in one of its last vestigial kitsch manifestations. Reproduced in outsize artisanal form, we realize, is the screenshot of a showy desktop image rendered at a dozen times the normal computer scale, complete with its superimposed (in fact materially underlying) image of clutter. Not unrelated to the photorealism of Sickert when draining the garish palette of colorized lobby cards back in closer approximation to the chiaroscuro of their black-and-white screen originals, the graphite mountainscape *Untitled (Folders)* seems indicated as sans title, in part at least, for the blank anonymity of the on-screen files. Albrectsen's display piece has prosecuted its ultimate transmedium irony—beyond the many mountainous rock faces understood as part of a mere *inter*face—when we recognize that, in context, the richly realized slopes, crags, and pinnacles would in themselves constitute, synecdochically, only one (currently uploaded) picture among the many pictured text or image files whose promised searchability punctuate (perforate) its surface. In this case, however, such unclickable blank icons link only to the sheer platform exposure (in an almost touching belatedness) of an underlying drawing material, a paper materiality, instead of the represented trove of pixel data.

VI.

READING STYLE / STYLES OF READING

> 13 / Stewart's most classroom-oriented book, ***The Value of Style in Fiction*** (Cambridge University Press, 2018), demonstrates the value of prose analysis—both appreciative and interpretive in its "evaluations"—across dozens of authors, including Jane Austen, Virginia Woolf, Don DeLillo, and Toni Morrison. Beginning with a state-of-the-field survey of prose poetics, this manual of invested reading concludes with a checklist of terms and definitions drawn primarily from grammar, rhetoric, etymology, and phonetics, but also from narratology and poetic theory: a glossary whose consultation can help cross-map certain verbal tendencies in literary-historical evolution and its separate landmark writers. Serving as a partial primer for Stewart's tightly framed linguistic approach, the glossary is especially useful for the way it points back, with recalled examples, to technical terms bolded in the text on their first appearance.

13 / Verbal Expenditures, Narrative Dividends

The Value of Style in Fiction (2018)

THIS BOOK ON NARRATIVE LANGUAGE was percolated in an undergraduate class on "Prose Style" for English and Creative Writing majors alike. When invited to do a short study in a newly launched *The Value of* series at Cambridge University Press, rendering accessible certain touchstones of literary experience, as for instance (given titles already in print at that point: *The Value of … James Joyce, Virginia Woolf,* and *the Novel* writ large), I offered a treatment of novelistic writing at a smaller scale. It opens with a much-expanded version of my opening in-class pep talks on the matter.

> One may speak of the *richness* of a sentence, the *wealth* of its invention, but *value* feels less metaphoric. Why—and, if so, how deployed here? In what relation to the thread and tread, the texture

and pace, of words in their ordered but not ordained row? And what critical investments are implied by even starting with such questions? How will we end up wishing to posit the *worth* of style in the wording of single sentences by Austen or Hawthorne or Dickens or Conrad or Woolf? Or, more to the point: wanting to ask what *style is worth* in the work of analysis, as well as in the tenor of response?

Style is language in action. Accordingly, these chapters argue for the place of *prose* in our attention to *prose fiction*. Rescuing stylistic consideration of the English novel from an epoch of neglect, the book is intended for a cross section of literary readers interested in the nature and grain of fictional writing, with examples drawn from the whole history of British and American fiction, including the special translingual cases of Conrad and Nabokov. [...] Examples are meant to contemplate not the style of geniuses but the very *genius of style.* From which emerges this abiding sense: that style is a quotient of literary writing, and so literary meaning, at its nearest point of readerly contact. It is the place where writing *takes*, wherever it thereby takes you, or however it takes you in—and thus out of yourself.

The interrogative starting point, time and again: style as opposed to what? As always, the sentence unit is the clearest litmus test in such investigation. But is the style of a given sentence as opposed to its meaning—its form over against what it formulates—a distinction without a difference? Two sides of the same coin? Students often have a hard time seeing otherwise, separating the two, noticing anything special about the former, or at least attempting to specify it. This book is meant to help. [...]

Style is the constitutive first glimpse we have of a fictional scene—and this in either sense: setting or scenario, description or narrated action. Not least when deliberately bland and apparently transparent, style, from stylus, is where prose narrative makes its mark. And at its most ornate, involuted, or multifaceted, when manifestly less a window than a prism, style is still the only way "in." Neither is it something that late Joyce, through travesty, transcends. Nor is it only the very difference between all such writers. It is the difference within: not just across and then between words kept in line by idea, but between the instated phrasing and its latent alternatives. As such, it locates an interplay of choices silenced but not entirely subsided as we read. Without lionizing the individual finesse or panache of a given writer, reading for style is always a reading for how a thing is said—and how it might have gone otherwise, and may sometimes still be shadowed in reception by that alternate possibility. Ultimately, such a reading is on the lookout, and on the listen, for what—by a particular string of words, understood as the active work of wording—a given passage may, above and beyond its meaning, be more intensively saying: in (just) so many words. [...]

As understood, resuscitated, and sampled here, style is not a supplement or adjunct to narrative in prose fiction, some fetishized refinement of its literary form, but rather its operative vehicle: its almost tactile delivery system. Style is the discernible fictional energy of the prose itself, its level of pure invention—in effect, its fictionality in essence. Whatever its "value," it is not some elusive value added, relative in its worth from reader to reader. It's not what we get more of in Dickens than in Trollope, in James than in Dreiser. [...]

All this might well be granted, of course, without necessarily igniting scholarly (or student) interest. This is because the value of style, certainly its academic "exchange value," depends in part, in any one moment of discussion, on the styles of valuation by which fiction is addressed—or, more to the point, on the styles of attention to which it is submitted: political, theoretical, ideological, cognitive, what have you. So let it be said up front. For too long, style has been the deviance, or say the insistent evidence, that dare not speak its name. In prose fiction, it is the marked work of language too easily suppressed in critical remark. [...] Students don't even know it's gone missing from their toolkits. I must have realized, even at the time, that I was mishearing, grasping at straws—victim of an almost literary pun—when I thought I understood a doctoral student of English I happened to meet recently, in response to my initial curiosity about his scholarly interests, to be planning "a diction theory of Victorian fiction." Really? My own energized uptake was quickly exposed as mistaken. "Oh, no, no: addiction theory—you know, in light of disability and precarity studies." One does know. But, apart from the skills of that particular student, what "a diction study" might constitute would mostly elude at least two or three generations of his peers.

In and beyond such cross-lexical ambiguity as accidentally triggered in that brief scholarly chat, the volatility of diction is very much part of the picture in this book: word choice itself, from sentence to sentence, rather than just its showcasing in the celebrated wordsmiths of literary history. This is diction in the sense not of usage (proper or substandard; high or low) but of kinetic use: the lexicon in motivated requisition, vocabulary in process—widely varying, of course, from writer to writer, period to period. And never reduced to the merely useful. Nor to the privately favored. Process is the issue here, not preference. [...]

For this reason, in a heuristic more than a combative or turf-clearing spirit, there is much to be gained from defining stylistic reading against what it isn't: not just hermeneutically *close* rather than statistically *far;* neither quantitative nor in some tendentious way qualitative or hierarchical; neither surface-bound nor strictly symptomatic and intertextual—but instead, once again, a *deep* reading, formative rather than formalistic. This is because the depth at issue is that of the linguistic substrate itself from which any verbal patterning emerges, takes form, and asserts itself, or we might say *fields its force*—often with a coordinated teamwork mapped out in forward moves, lateral relays, and unexpected conversions. [...] In this sense, the value of style can either be cashed out in immediate appreciation or reinvested in apprehending the founding energetics, and sometimes the definitive friction, of the genre we call prose fiction—but whose prose is too seldom engaged with in commentary.

Among the authors elevated to exemplary status in this book's subsequent citations, eight Dickens novels get a brief mention—an instance or two each—amid the deliberately broad historical scope of evidence. For my purposes at least, and those of my students, it was time for another whole book on his unholy way with words, prodigious and irresistible.

> 14 / In *The One, Other, and Only Dickens* (Cornell University Press, 2018), the steady aural undercurrent of Dickensian fiction attests both to the author's early immersion in Shakespearean sonority and, at the same time, to the effect of Victorian stenography—with the repressed phonetics of its elided vowels—on the young writer's verbal habits long after his stint as a shorthand Parliamentary reporter. To demonstrate the interplay between plot-driven narrative and the aural texture of literary style, Stewart draws out two personas within Dickensian textual production: the Inimitable Boz, master of plot, social panorama, and set-piece rhetorical cadences, and a verbal alter ego identified as the Other, whose volatile linguistic, even sublexical, presence is seldom out of earshot in any of the fourteen novels. With examples by turns comic, lyric, satiric, and melodramatic from the whole span of Dickens' career, the famously recognizable style is heard ghosted in a kind of running counterpoint ranging from obstreperous puns to the most elusive of internal echoes: effects not strictly channeled into the service of overall narrative drive, but instead generating verbal microplots all their own. One result is a new, ear-opening sense of what it means to take seriously Graham Greene's famous passing mention of Dickens' "secret prose," whose original application by Greene to the often-delusional dreamscapes of *Great Expectations* is expanded here to a kind of linguistic unconscious across all the prose.

14 / The Dickens Page, In and Out Loud

The One, Other, and Only Dickens (2018)

THERE IS, THIS RUBRIC IMPLIES, the reading out loud of Dickensian phonetic density. But there is also, first and foremost, the silent enunciation that reads back *in*—with full lexical prompting—the prose's vocal repercussions. These are exactly the resonant vocalic sounds that it sounds like Dickens (in the aurality of his prose) never forgot having so strenuously to reconstitute in alphabetic writing after the ellipses of shorthand compression in his early parliamentary transcriptions. It was with the delicious result of all this that I begin this second of my books on Dickens:

> You are reading along, hooked, until snagged by some aggressively arresting phrase. You hold your breath over twisted mysteries and psychologies that breath is taken away by a sideswipe of language far outstripping the needs of narrative. You get in the swing between cliff-hangers until the whole lifeline of plot momentarily unravels in a daft excess of craft. You are left hanging on word forms alone. You

are, after all, reading not just any Victorian fiction, but a novel by one Charles Dickens. Or, more exactly, reading the Prose of one such fiction, which can be Another Thing Altogether.

Words make their own ebullient way in Dickens, rather than just giving way to story. But they've paid their dues to begin with. This foreword charts the path ahead, of course, but only because it traces Dickens' way forward as well—on his own industrious behalf. The double training ground of his linguistic intensity involves back-to-back chapters in a well-documented biographical epic that have never been brought together for the extra origin story they tacitly narrate about the gestation of an incomparable prose. Indeed, like many a later Dickens novel, the formative tension of such an inaugural subplot involves one bad parent, one good—an unyielding shorthand taskmaster, on the one hand, and a looming literary inspiration, on the other hand: namely, the rigors of vowel-scoured stenographic reporting in the Thomas Gurney method versus the contrary aural invigorations of William Shakespeare, devoured by the young Dickens from page as well as stage. As with the vulnerable characters of many a Dickens novel, from such fostering tension something of a dual personality results—but in this case textual rather than psychological: what I am dubbing the One and his Other as internal rather than fraternal twins, secret sharers, inbred shadow collaborators in the rotary vocalic motion of Dickensian narrative prose.

That's the way the foreword ("Preparing the Way" forward) began retracing Dickens' own early verbal endeavors and ordeals. To my surprise and confirmation—regarding the influence from Thomas Gurney's (1705–70) "brachygraphic" method—a book more explicitly on Dickens' shorthand career appeared in the same year as mine, more technical, less broadly stylistic, a study by Hugo Bowles deeply informed and insightful about Dickens' apprenticeship in the shorthand system.[1] Though *Dickens and the Stenographic Mind* didn't extend in detail to the effect of enforced phonetic contraction on Dickens' later sound play, Bowles certainly found the early constraints of Gurney's compressed transcriptions a determining factor in the novelist's later writing life. It is that writing as such, its open sounds and rolling cadences, with which I began my own opening chapter—in recall of having heard such patterned wording sounded out when read aloud to me as a child. What results, briefly enough, is the farthest flashing-back in the biographical sidebars of the present Reader.

To begin this reading of Dickens with a long-ago reading of Dickens, not by me but *to* me, I record that his words were borne in upon me for the first time, unforgettably, from the mouth of a rather ambitious babysitter late in my first decade of existence. "To begin my life with the beginning of my life, I record that I was born." I didn't know "life" in the biographical rather than biological sense back then, but I could surely sense that something at the beginning of *David Copperfield* was swallowing its own tale. I got immediately caught up in such a loop of words answering to each other, *sounding each other out*. My mother took over the task of recitation when time permitted. And in intervals of withdrawal from this addictive listening, I sometimes tried—and surely failed, myself and Dickens both—to negotiate some of the more daunting syntactic hurdles of the print on my own, a prose that I found not just clearer but so much more powerful when intoned. As in fact, when really read, it always *is* intoned.

As evidence unfolds, it is the elision of vowels in stenographic compression and the need to reinsert them later—in effect, to retrieve them by imagined enunciation when transcribing the rapid-fire code into a normal lexicon and grammar—that lies at the heart of my argument:

Certainly, after the former hollowing out of vowels, prose has often seen them come hollering back, or at least whispering, in new silent groupings along the line. After such strictures in the rigorous concisions of brachygraphy, we might want to say (in Jakobson's terms) that the formerly shorn vowels can seem almost militantly renucleated in even the quietest turns of phrase. The economies of elision are reversed in a teeming repletion, not offsetting or redemptive in any deliberate way, but nonetheless—if only at some unconscious level in the drive of Writing—speaking back to a once-straitjacketed syllabics with defiance and abandon. That back talk is the signature sound, beneath the flair of character and plot, of the Other Dickens. [...]

I was pleased here to make common cause again, more directly than before, with William Gass, whose sense of metafiction quite indirectly inspired my first book on Dickens—and who had since written on the unique phonetic quality of Dickensian prose quite directly:

"Between Shakespeare and Joyce," writes William H. Gass in an essay called "The Sentence Seeks Its Form," from his collection *A Temple of Texts*, there is "no one but Dickens who has an equal command of the English language"—and he means by this to stress, as it turns out, the aural dimension of the novelist's effects. "Language is born in the lungs and is shaped by the lips, palate, teeth, and tongue out of spent breath. It therefore must be listened to while it is being written." At attention's trained remove, Gass the novelist hears this overhearing, in a signal instance, as functioning to solemnize—or potentially to assuage in retrospect—David's emphatic sense of abandonment in early life. This occurs in a compensatory music of remembered distress conveyed by a run of mournful hammering negations: "From Monday morning until Saturday night, I had no advice, no counsel, no encouragement, no consolation, no assistance, no support, of any kind, from any one." When the increased phonic concentration of "no counsel" returns by way of parallel exclusion in "no consolation," Gass' ear is drawn in particular to the internalized inversion of the long (and long-drawn-out—as well as lamentory) *o* and its virtual phonetic ingestion by what we might term the dispersed sound-script of *"no consolation."* No solace, that is, except in the sounded precision of this bitter memory and its self-counseled lugubrious sonority. David, the Dickensian persona, drives the point home with the most rhetorically self-conscious of mournful iterations. At the same time, the Other Dickens (the one coming to later fruition, we might say, in David's writerly tongue) effects that extra congestion of negativity within the longer periodic arc of a sentence strung (unmentioned by Gass) between *"From Mon ..."* to the shifted prepositional sense of *"from any one."* All told, Gass' example is perfectly chosen to catch the double valence of Dickensian retrospect at this emotional nadir: a monotony of former desolation alleviated only in the fulfilled tonality of report.

What delving into the young Dickens' brachygraphic traumas—as autobiographically replayed in the person of the eventual novelist, David—adds to Gass' sounding of the prose has immediately to do with Dickens' favored habit of anaphora. For such parallel repetitions, dear to court and parliamentary rhetoric alike, were treated in the Gurney shorthand by the serial strokes of fill-in-the-blank lines: empty underscores to be auto-completed later. One imagines how the mechanics of iteration became second nature to the Other Dickens.

A related effect from the same novel, this time in the throes of David's melancholy rather than depression, is remarked in the recent anthology *Dickens's Style*, offering rare good company for the current proceedings in its fresh attachment to the topic. Gass himself has a tacit interlocutor there as well, since an essay by Robert Douglas-Fairhurst entitled "Dickens's Rhythms" cites David's threefold lexical refrain (breaking cadence with one variant elongation) as his thoughts revert sadly to the deserted family home: "I imagined how the winds of winter would howl round it, how the cold rain would beat upon the window-glass, how the moon would make ghosts on the walls of the empty rooms." As with the interlaced patterns in the Gass example, one senses further, beyond the essay's own treatment of the passage, how the first slant rhyme of *howl* against *how* (graphically even more than phonically nudged from behind by the alliterating *w* in "winds of winter") also reverberates—more as a murmur or moan than a howl—across the rest of the passage, tainting each of the remaining "how" adverbs with an ambient lament. And then insinuates itself again, across a wider phrasal span, when "how ... walls" spells out in plural form that same wailing if waning "howl" one last ghostly time. Such verbal bliss—what else to call it?—is certainly subliminal, but if it constitutes something like the guilty pleasure of indulgent hyperattention in any immersive reading of Dickens, it is entirely quilted in, nonetheless, to the general fabric of Dickensian phonetics and its blanketing euphonies. [...]

On the way to the lyricism under scrutiny in the next chapter, spurred by Graham Greene's evocation of it in *Great Expectations,* consider, then, the first of these two loaded moments of aurality in *David Copperfield.* It comes upon us as if triggered by David's mother reading aloud from the Bible in the "doleful" best parlor where mourners had once gathered, the boy's been told, for his father's funeral. In one of the novel's present-tense recursions to a past never fully put behind the narrator, there is this: "One Sunday night my mother reads to Peggotty and me in there, how Lazarus was raised up from the dead." Continuing in the present-tense (and presently-felt) enunciation of memory's not wholly shed anxiety: "And I am so frightened that they are afterwards obliged to take me out of bed, and show me the quiet churchyard out of the bedroom window, with the dead all lying in their graves at rest, below the solemn moon." Not just "under" earth but *"below"* a "solemn" cosmic oversight, where, beyond that unvocalized graphic link, the irrelevant etymological nucleus of "sol" for the parent sun, antithetical here, is still within the orbit of the unsaid yet embedded melancholy of the scene. With that richly Bardic "solemn moon" (further remarks at the start of chapter 2 on this "sequestered" legacy from Shakespearean theater and sonnets alike), more than just such a middle space-between eye and ear rhyme-rounds out, in a Dickensian lexical economy, this picture of the moon in its emotional fullness. In Gurney, we would have to endure the eclipsing pictographic equivalent of *slmn mn*. In the Other Dickens, we help produce a ballooning from within of solemnity's objective correlative—or say, the "concertina" spread from syllable to substantive. The fact that growing attuned to such backdrafts and undertones in reading the Other Dickens thrusts one further into the kind of curious graphonic syncopations that make "b/elo/w" seem to the eye a better preposition for "s/ole/mn" than "under" would be is all of a "secret" piece (more soon) with the aural oscillations of everything from "hard-headed, harder-hearted" to "solemn moon." And at this point of syllabic investment, who is to discount the diurnal microdrama by which "moon" may seem released—freed up from lexical eclipse in the phonemics of *sol/mn*, with its ghostly etymological hint of solar impingement—by the doubling and upward pitch of its own inner quasi-hieroglyphic *o*? [...]

Early in the novel, still at the misnamed (because deserted) Rookery of David's first home, shadowed by the prenatal death of his father, the sounding oscillation between inscription and its described scene cues us to the peculiar "burden" (in the musical sense) of "some weatherbeaten ragged old rooks'-nests, burdening their higher branches, swung like wrecks upon a stormy sea." The prose line, in subtending lexical boundaries, has more lilt to it—and more alliterative ring—than mere spelling might seem to actualize. For in the seesaw of syllables, the *w* takes an extra breath when the mention that "some" nests in "higher branches, *swung* like wrecks" is directly evoked by ligature in the prose's own swing-song rhythm. In the process, the "some/ung" oscillation only buoys (by varying) the figured nautical thrust—as if by some free association with crows-nests—across the cresting *rag/wreck/rook* pattern. Again Gurney in reverse: the Other Dickens regurgitating once more those swallowed vowels of pure phonetic reduction in *rg wrk rk*. [...]

In direct contrast to any such links and kinks in the chain reactions of vocalized prose, stenography narrows the field to lexical markers without the music of speech on which its decryption still depends. With the Master exercising his overarching control, the Other Dickens is forever unearthing the tacit concatenation of speech sounds in prose. I spoke early in this chapter of the "openly voweled" effect of such writing. It is the "open" sound of the vowels themselves that this entails. And in being released from the prison house of speed-facilitating code, they open onto each other as well as out, feathering together across the dovetailed pace of script. After the "short writing" of brachygraphy, that is, come the lengthened-out and slowed-down energies of a convergent rather than suppressed phonetic transliteration back into "vocalized" script. In another sense, of course, that is what reading, even silently, accomplishes in the more general case—and what a published novel institutes. [...]

But I can't step away from Gass' claim (above) about literary language "listened to" when "being written," and of David's weekly diary of desperation as instance, without lending audition again to the critic's sense of "spent breath"—and its slyly reinvested expenditure—in that Dickens sentence. Or without, that is, eliciting from its prose cadence, now finally, what I missed in the narrative passage the first time around. Having been, in drafting these very comments on my second Dickens book, powerfully reminded of this example—and in the very week before the first meeting of my undergraduate "Reading Movies for

Prose Writers" course—I put the sentence on a handout, where I shared briefly my sense of a return of the stenographic repressed in Dickensian assonance.

I give again Gass' typifying example from David's forlorn early days, complete with its driven negative anaphora: "From Monday morning until Saturday night, I had no advice, no counsel, no encouragement, no consolation, no assistance, no support, of any kind, from any one." As if this grammar were derived from some ponderous version of a parliamentary lament, it offers an especially good analogy for Dickens' shorthand burdens. So I gave the class an alphabetic simplification (with missing medial vowels) of the "hieroglyphs" of stenography by which the young David, like Dickens before him, would have been both tortured and, in the powers of echo, nurtured over the course of such a heavy parallel grammar: "no advc, __cnsl, __ncrgmnt, __cnsltn, __asstnc, __spprt." Fill in the lexical and phonetic blanks, connect the jotted dots—and articulation is restored. Made even more apparent in this fashion is the consonant bracket linking "counsel" to "consolation" as approximate affective synonyms. But something else too. With no breath of respite offered from Monday morning through Saturday night, this leaves, as I failed to mention in print, an implicit lip-service to the Sabbath and its potential spiritual solace. Then, too, it was only in working up this handout for class—and with the course's overarching movie analog in mind—that the rutted language suddenly came to me as the kind of protocinematic effect entirely typical of Dickens: prose counting off the other days of the week in a no doubt deliberate *sixfold* iteration like some classic time-lapse montage of daily paper headlines, flipping through the calendar in an ironic vicious circle of privation. Yet again actual teaching gets the jump on a critical writing that—but for this anthology project—would have had no immediate chance to append these extra appreciations to my earlier print "pedagogy" on Dickens' exemplary sentence.

And the classroom feedback circuit never stops throwing me for a writerly loop of my own. When later in this same semester course, discussing with students Sergei Eisenstein's famous essay on what Hollywood cinema got from Dickens, I came crashing into a passage I had wholly forgotten: on what Dickens got from being a "parliamentary reporter for a newspaper." Eisenstein's sense of the payoff seems to me rather too direct. He stresses Dickens' early skill at "compressing long-winded discussion" as "shorthand writer," where "he conveyed a word by a stroke, a whole sentence by a few curves and dashes."[2] This, for Eisenstein, led to later writing in which the novelist "invented a kind of shorthand to reality, consisting of little signs instead of lengthy descriptions." One might more likely say, regarding this *wordiest* of writers, that it was the effect of often quite lengthy descriptions full to the brim with many little signs—quirks of face, gesture, voice, décor, atmosphere—that ultimately, for Eisenstein, concentrated the impact of such hyper-alert prose into "a perfectly precise negative" in the manner of photographic vision.

True to one kind of cinematic Dickens though Eisenstein certainly was, he missed the compensatory spooling-out of fully sounded syllabic words and iterative phrases that I was trying to demonstrate as the ultimate backlash from the tedious crampings of brachygraphy. As it happily provided in class, what a fine foil in print that passage from Eisenstein would have been for my alternate claims! And never better than when, in his fullest citation from Dickens' actual prose, he quotes a 600-and-some word sentence of aggregate auditory bombardment on market day, Sikes dragging Oliver Twist across London under sensory assault by thirteen gerund phrases ("the whistling … the bellowing … the bleating … the grunting," etc.), along with a final shift to pounding participial modifiers, all converged in summation, in the phrasing's own intricate "auralterity" and blur, as "the hideous and discordant din." Nice catch, you may agree—if only, yet again, on the back-to-class rebound, where imagining in a thought experiment (on the blackboard) how Dickens would have reverse-engineered this from his hieroglyphic shorthand (in my book's way of coding it: hds & dscrdnt dn) could only help draw out the chiastic flip at "h*id/dis*" and the assonant slant rhyme and dentalized stutter of "*dan(t/d)in.*"

Given a reprieve (reprise) here for descrying them, the milk isn't quite spilled regarding these once-missed syllabic splinterings. And with the stylistic fate of early abridgements (Stewart versus Eisenstein) now under the bridge, it is time to follow out another swerve, for the second time in my writing, from the inexhaustible fund of inference in literary reading to the book objects that, demediated of print efficacy, can still figure (even while effacing) the power of such reading.

> 15 / *Book, Text, Medium: Cross-Sectional Reading for a Digital Age* (Cambridge University Press, 2020) mobilizes codex history, close reading, and language philosophy to assess the transformative arc between medieval "bookes" and today's e-books. It examines what happens to the reading experience in the twenty-first century when the original concept of a book is still held in the mind of a reader, if no longer in the reader's hand. Stewart explores the play of mediation across the transformation into post-print reading—as the concept of the book moves from a manufactured object to simply the language it puts into circulation. Framed by digital poetics, phonorobotics, and the rising popularity of audiobooks, this study sheds fresh light on both the history of reading and, returning to new examples of the sculptural objects catalogued and critically engaged by Stewart in *Bookwork* (2011), on the negation of legible print in conceptualist book art. Its three-part structure—"The Hold of the Codex" / "The Grip of Inscription" / "The Give of Medium"—moves from the figurations of "book as machine" in recent sculptural assemblages through further forays into close textual reading before a return to the ontology of language itself in the philosophy of Giorgio Agamben (as featured prominently in *The Deed of Reading*, 2015; see Phase V / 11) and to a critique of Friedrich Kittler on medium blindness in Romanticism.

15 / Bookhood in Evolution

Book, Text, Medium: Cross-Sectional Reading for a Digital Age (2020)

IN TRIANGULATING THE BOOK OBJECT, its text, and its medium in light of the vanishing codex of electronic reading, I touch again on earlier writing of mine in this line of thought—before reporting in this volume on new gallery experiments in "book sculpture" and, later in the shifted scope of the study, incorporating a wider range of metalinguistic theory. Where the opening chapter, returning to the scene of reading in painting with new evidence, plays on the stroked plane of depiction with its title "Bibliographics," the second rehearses certain premises of *Bookwork* (2011; see Phase IV / 9) by visiting two different exhibitions that mark a certain shift in the conception of "bookhood" across developing responses to our "digital age." This two-stop gallery tour, titled "Platformatics," sets out (its agenda included) as follows:

> Codex in effigy—and often in elegy. Such conceptualist ironies shape many of the most intriguing contemporary works, sculptured or installed, to be found engaging with book culture in galleries rather than libraries. [...] And so we arrive at New Haven in 2015 for the

extensive "Odd Volumes" exhibit at the Yale Art Gallery, drawn from the holdings of New York collector Alan Chassanof. It was a show, curated by book sculptor Doug Beube, that covered the broad panoply of such works in artisanal and appropriated form alike, extravagantly fashioned or found and defaced. Mostly artificial, rather than appropriated and scissored—but with samples aplenty from each end of the conceptualist spectrum—the odd volumes are often even odder than they may sound (as visible on the extensive website). Most of them are to one degree or another radically demediated of textual message, with words absent entirely from their blank, dyed, crumpled, or shredded surfaces.

Or if not absent, swept from recognition: too fast for reading—as illegible in apparition as if their pages had been glued together and buried in another mode of tome as tomb. Amid the mostly sculptural volumes singled out for refashioning, one installation above all breaks with that pattern to enter the time-based precincts of reading, even while eliding the very focal point of language in transit. This is a 1997 piece by John Roach, called *Pageturner* that played in a doubly prescient way between the exacerbation of electronics in surveillance technology and a fading culture of the codex—and this exactly a decade before the launch of the Kindle "reader" (that noun once personal, now mechanical). It is just the distance between human agent and the book instrument that is exaggerated and disabled by Roach's work. An electronic sensor spots any viewers (and potential readers) in their approach to an open suitcase, as if a variant of some Fluxus assemblage, containing in this case a book whose pages are turned arbitrarily by four small electric fans. This mechanically-rendered illegibility of material, but not textual, continuity is transmitted by video cam to a blurry TV image that makes the pages hard to discern even before their being swept past by currents of an air having nothing to do with the breath of phonetic enunciation. Not only a lampoon of "reading machines"—to vary N. Katherine Hayles' term "writing machines"—this assemblage is a parody of the "audiobook" as well, including a small monaural speaker that accompanies the image only with the murmuring whoosh of the fan blades, no articulated text. When the well-chosen book thus denatured is the obsessively phonetic prose and poetry of Edgar Allan Poe, this euphonic loss seems only foregrounded by Roach.

And there is notable avant-garde precedent in regard to this enforced temporality. In his *Encyclopedia Britannica* (1971), conceptual provocateur John Latham thumbed through every two-page spread of this multi-volume work with a stop-action camera—thus, in gallery projection, "assimilating" the amassed bulk of human wisdom at 24 pps rather than fps. Not only does Roach's alienated book encounter look back to Latham's pre-digital irony of auto-reading the *Britannica*, however. It also looks forward to the voluntarily recalibrated settings of the speed-reading technology known as Spritz (its tag line "Reading Reimagined"). This is an Android app that flashes one word after another past the reader, centered on what is known as its ORP, its Optimal Recognition Point, graphic not phonetic: a technique explicitly designed and advertised to impede all "subvocalization" and thus to speed cognition in an override of phonetic production. Everything the viewer was invited to imagine in the body of the reader leaning over her page in the history of art, the phonic intensification of that body as well as its projection outward into imaginative space, is reduced here to the treadmill of paralinguistic efficiency. As much as in Roach's *Pageturner*, what was a cognitive joke in Latham's *Britannica* is now, with Spritz, an electronic exercise machine for the *weakening* of the reader's literary muscles. [...]

Across the gallery at the same "Odd Volumes" exhibit from Roach's *Pageturner* was another bookwork broaching, in an opposite though equally motorized fashion, a tacitly anachronistic figure for the reading process at large. Mary Ziegler's *The Necessity of Friction*, from 1994, is identified by caption as "found copy of Leonard Gross' *How Much is Too Much*, electric motor, steel, magnesium, and sandpaper." Braced spine-up by a cantilevered armature over a kind of mock turntable, the identified hardback text by Gross is pressed against the rotating sandpaper plate, its abraded circular striations resembling nothing so much as the grooves on a quasi-vinyl disk. In this madcap vicious circle, it is as if the codex had become in its own right a bulky stylus wearing thin the mock-phonography of its own satirized "resistant reading" on the wheeling plate it scrapes against. This produces, of course—as the appropriated and entirely silenced volume implies—decidedly too much friction, constituting thereby, in its hyper-material mode, too much a travesty of any inherent textual phono*graphy* to count as reading. Once again the *bibliobjet* offers the repudiation of bookhood in the very service of its consideration, its rethinking as estranged instrumentality.

In the broader vein of conceptual bookwork, such parables are familiar enough: book reading under palpable erosion, the codex itself in planned obsolescence. And in our present context, if this suggests that books have always been phonographic records in some sense, then yet again anachronism can help concretize a media archaeology. This is what I was attempting at the start in conjuring the phonically oriented redubs of the book as phonographic streaming device, graphonic synthesizer, and the like, including a kind of quasi-aural teleprompter. Compare Ziegler's work with another conceptual book, an actual hand-held object in this case, appearing under the punning phonocentric title *Flip Read* (2005) by British artist Heather Weston. This is a traditional precinematic "flip book" whose artificial motion is reduced to photo close-ups of a woman's lips miming in serial pages the question "What would you do with the volume turned off?" It is every book's at-least tacit question—as the next chapters will inhabit at close audial range in the phrasal tenor of script itself. And never made more explicit, before Weston's pantomime codex, than in Toni Morrison's *Jazz* (1992). In this novel openly named for the eponymous phonetic syncopations of its own prose, the personified book speaks to the reader in apostrophe on the last page, and about just such "speech." We audit the very libido of the writing, stoked by textual transference: "Talking to you—and hearing you answer—that's the kick." Again, in codex hardware, the textually engineered silence of pre-technological voice recognition. Colloquial high aside ("that's the kick"), here is the textual *reflex* of reading spelled out. For the talking and the answering are one and the same, simultaneous, phonetically co-engendered. They are part of the closed-circuit auricular (because to begin with, and to coin another conflated—and in its own way cross-sectional—phrase, *aurocular*) economy of silent phonation in bringing the visibility of printed talk to mind—and mind's ear.

In looking back over the array of "odd volumes" at the eponymous Yale Show, each more or less *sui generis*, I've singled out the two that shifted concern from the carved volumetrics of codex space to the implied volume of its processed wording. If the installations by Ziegler as well as Roach, then, were perhaps the most thoroughly conceptual of the pieces exhibited, at least in installed and mobile form, it is perhaps no surprise that a complicated and "motorized" work of hers, specifically directed at the kinetics of page surfaces rather than their wearing away with the volume as a whole, would have been included in a show curated by Roach himself two years later—even though his own work is not on exhibit there in "The Internal Machine" exposition.

This is, by title, the show mounted in late 2017 by the New York Center for Book Arts, in their Chelsea space, with Mary Ziegler's work marking a transition between the two expositions. Now:

Ziegler's metalinguistically titled *Babel* (2017) uses magnets beneath an inverted braille surface, with holes (rather than raised marks), to direct obstructing metallic inserts in the path of a mobile horizontal wire instead of the normal scanning of textual lineation—all to figure reading as an obstacle course for those not in command of a given language. The book's instrumental difficulties are, for this show, quintessential. For it is there in Chelsea that the serial (temporal) engineering of decryption, and sometimes its aberrant imageering, rather than the fate of the codex shape, is uppermost in the ironies of these mechanized *bibliobjets*. The shift appears typifying. Referred away to the digital age in which its screen variants partake, the vestige of book reading under gallery investigation is more likely than ever to stress its temporal mechanics rather than the spatial shape of its mere artifactual instrumentality.

And why not? This is where the utilities of the codex page, one by one, one after another, have computational programs to compete with. In such experimental structures, and in the interlocked terms of our ongoing cross section, *book* form can become the figurative *text* of its own *medium*. Once again, the self-tallied losses of illegibility in the bookwork tend to carve out and reshape their own history. Implicitly at least, they cut across absent text as such, a missing script, to the underlying cultural fact of medial transformation. In so doing, they prepare for the remaining chapters of *Book, Text, Medium*—in which actual literary writing looks both ways from its textured center, splitting the difference between materialities haptic and linguistic while participating in the *feel* of both.

Technomaterialisms of the Page

One can't, of course, judge what decisive re-orientations may be "exhibited" by an evolving art genre from a single artifact, or even from a single exhibition. But from any broad-based gathering of quite recent works, one might well detect, or at least begin to suspect, a trend. On the evidence of a recent sampling of works brought together in the major New York exposition assembled by Roach, book art may be passing from a phase of media crisis regarding the codex to a more open-ended rumination on the technicities of reading itself. Most of a decade had elapsed since I closed my files to begin writing up, for *Bookwork*, what I had been finding, here and abroad, in both the previous decade's Conceptual art of the codex and its own immediate predecessors after the heyday of the more conventional artist's book. This was gallery work executed only implicitly, for the most part, in address to digital encroachments on the legacy—and envisioned future efficacy—of the print codex, some exemplary pieces of which were on view at Yale. Then [...] under Roach's oversight, a show that recapitulates and advances many other of the architectonic and immersive tropes deployed in the kind of codex sculpture I had previously discussed—but returns to such themes now with something of a more dispassionate and speculative tone. In this respect, "The Internal Machine" traces an implicit shift from sculpture directed at the shaped dimensions of the long-canonical reading platform—the autonomous *volume*, as often manifested at the Yale retrospective in the hand-crafted efflorescence of its threatened end—to the *mechanics* of textual transmission per se: a revised focus that may alone speak volumes concerning a new emphasis—and perhaps a new trajectory—in book art.

On what adjusted grounds, exactly? As distinct from the frequent luxuriousness of the artist's book, as even in the most picturesque water-stained ravages of found volumes, no pages in the Chelsea show are seen fanning their obsolescent peacock feathers in strutting the codex's last stand. Nor are these bookworks warped, slivered, or carved away into inutile beauty—or pinioned, clamped shut, in the disposable flourish, or even literal burn-out, of the outmoded. (I review there, in rapid mind's eye, various tendencies—cutting and sealing and searing—in the previous works I had written about, versions of which were represented in the "Odd Volumes" show as well.) As confirmed by the different tone of its accompanying captions and catalogue texts, the works at the Center for Book Art—curated by that least "artisanal," most conceptual, of the exhibitors at Yale—are more analytic than retroactive: neither sponsored by nostalgia nor steeped in either regret or anxiety. They look inward as much as back, to the gearing of optical decipherment—and its silent hearing—in the cognitive engagement with the generative mechanism of text support.

In this potentially refurbished phase of bookwork, and to lift a mixed metaphor from its own precincts, a page may well have been turned—indeed an inner ("internal") leaf—in ruminations upon the original "reading machine." The vantage of the exposition is historical, archival, but not epochal or catastrophist. We are long used, inured even, to what electronics has done to the sanctity (because the *inner* sanctum) of the codex, to its privileged cultural utility—and spatial iconology. This outplayed rule of the book form is manifested by proxy, in Roach's new gallery consideration, not so much as elegized but rather as catalogued in its overlapping facets and functions, understood now *within* a history of technology rather than over against it. So that if a so-called corner has been turned, it is one associated with the inner fold of utility itself in what, including the pivot of facing pages, has always been, since Gutenberg, the engineered space of reading. Rather than reframed, antiquated, in its lost hegemony, the codex, under figuration as "the internal machine," stands exhibited—indeed excavated, autopsied, and alchemized all at once—for what it always was: a feat of mechanics as well as of cultural instrumentation.

But on the latter score, concerning the book's cultural longevity, and in probing the internality of its mechanics in just this regard, there is a notable touchstone worth revisiting—especially in connection with our coming chapters in Part II on the linguistic textuality of the literary codex. I. A. Richards' famous maxim, "A book is a machine to think with," is regularly quoted out of the context of its own compound sentence. The first clause of 1924's *Principles of Literary Criticism* seems a sufficient principle unto itself. By immediate phenomenological engagement as well as by further interpretive work, a book is operated in reading so that we think "along with" it as prompt, but also by means of it ("with it" as tool) in further empowered cogitation. A book is not just an object but an instrument, yes, "but," as Richards wryly adds, "it need not, therefore, usurp the functions either of the bellows or the locomotive." To deliver its goods, it doesn't need to be stentorian or monolithic—and only now do we realize, one sentence in, that Richards is in part specifying the nature of his own miscellany, "this" particular book of brief pieces. The kind of machine in question, for his present volume at least, involves a shuttle—and not in the railroad sense—rather than a stoked engine. "This book might better be compared to a loom," on which the author hopes, in this case, to "re-weave" certain atrophied principles, some "ravelled parts of our civilization": a modest affair, neither polemically driven nor thesis ridden. [...]

Internal Works

[...] Juan Fontanive's contribution to "The Internal Machine" exhibit has built out of Victorian clockworks a rotary reading machine (in an update of the Renaissance wheel of open and cross-checkable volumes). This involves a kinetic rotation in which separate Audubon-style "snapshots," ornithological drawings of individual birds on the wing, are rotated into the apparent animation of one moving composite, so that the viewer receives the cartoon of bird flight traversing separate avian bodies on extracted pages. [...] As the artist himself puts it, about what we might call the mimetic mechanism of his post-codex assemblage, "the wings hinge like paper and the paper cards flap at the rate of the bird's wings" (40). And as the curator adds further, about the whirring of the device as it reaches the ear—not as alphabet text but as the platform of "cited" motion—one is likely to recall in this audible flutter "the satisfying sounds of using your thumb to flip through the backs of a thick book." Exactly the further sound, beyond that of Poe's words, precluded by the extraneous noise of thrumming fans in *Pageturner*. Again, in the material cross sectioning of book/text/medium: the haptic dimension of time-based ocular process. To put it more specifically, a classic Audubon codex has been rewired as a rolodex of internally disjointed cell animation.

In Fontanive's work—be the predisposed audition of the flipped page as it may—any such mobile effect would set itself apart from more prevalent motifs of the exhibit. It would certainly operate in contrast to any tangible whisper of traditional book use that we come upon in those "internal machines" that aggressively transmute—and in this way, trans-figure—the sound associated with the dead metaphors of voice and tone in text, to say nothing of the actual sound of subvocal reading. In Nick Yulman's *Index Quartet*, the very idea of a book's "internal" mechanics is ingeniously equivocated. A series of closed volumes (from a related installation of several more books under the title *Index Organ*) are struck from beneath, rather than read from above, in their suspension on underlying plexiglass supports [...] drummed by the tips of electronic "actuators" whose signals are then fed through synthesizers (in the technological rather than cognitive sense) for a percussive broadcast in the installation space. In the role of viewer/listener, the gallery goer's electronically recognized approach to these volumes, as in Roach's *Pageturner*, activates this process, here in a reductive "sounding" of the book for its strictly material, rather than affective, resonance. The thumping beat begins only when you approximate the status of reader by opening the book before you, thus figuratively touching off a flex sensor installed in the spine. The closed cover amounts in this way, as in effect it always does, to the mute button (here automatically depressed) that would arrest any reading act. Yulman's wry process converts all activated textual energy—the "indexical" trace of a sound made *from* rather than *by* the books—into something like a punning sense of *volume*, ambient rather than merely encased. As elsewhere in this exhibition, logic is repeatedly put backwards to set things straight in the end. Once more, then: the lurking metalinguistics—or call it the plastic troping—of the unheard page. But other works occupy distinctly different positions on the acoustic spectrum of any such readerly reverb.

How different? Or, more pertinently, different how? Less like the externalized harmonics of the machinated book in Yulman's case—and surfacing from within something more like what we might call the line-strung instrument actually "played," or performed, across the word rows of even silent ("internal") reading—is the intricate construct of "secondary orality" in Ranjit Bhatnagar's *Sonnets from the Portuguese*. This is a work named for those "little songs" of Elizabeth Barrett Browning whose evocation by a "collage of words and music" (another name, in a sense, for imprinted verse) is quietly broadcast from embedded microtransmitters. This phonic collage can only, as we say, be *picked up* by the ear from the closed Victorian volume: not by holding open the codex, but by holding up to its embossed antique cover a glass jar fitted with a microphone in its cap. It is like listening through walls in some espionage setting—

or, in another implicit verbalization of textual constraint: like keeping the lid on the secret signals of the "internal machine." Or better yet, to quote another Victorian writer on the phonic space of poetry—namely, John Stuart Mill, from "What is Poetry?"—it is like some quirky illustration of the maxim that, whereas eloquence is "heard," poetry is "overheard," as if eavesdropped upon. And this with the full phonetic implications that our remaining chapters will keep touching down on—and drawing out.

In comparing these two divergent innovations on the "audiobook," Yulman's against Bhatnagar's, it is fair to say that the codex brusquely "tapped" from without, just as the antique volume message-equipped from within by updated electrical vibration, artificially produces in each case, rather than induces, what their texts, if visible, might otherwise bring to ear on the way to mind. Neither work, of course, sounds (out) a straightforward text. Nor does this happen in a *bibliobjet* more immediately concerned, if aberrantly, with words on a once visible page. The subvocal ear of phonemic production is there bypassed altogether, in envisioning the mind's eye of response, in the show's most highly contrived and processual work. This is a complex and time-based installation by Alexander Rosenberg that—rather than invoking the phonic activation of alphabetic text, or even the visible *recognition* of letter forms—disappears each into a radically abstracted, even while still reductively material, *understanding* of mediality per se. This is an understanding well beyond containment by anything resembling the shelved availability of writing in the traditional *bibliotheque*.

Bibliotech (1): Beyond Hypertext

The drastic disappearance on display in Rosenberg's assemblage, exceeding any mere vivisection of the book's "internal machine," is laboriously achieved—laboriously is the only word, given the lab work of its outlandish chemistry—under the title *Hyperpyrexia*. The very letters of text are liquefied—liquidated—in advance, leached away from found books before the viewer has any glimpse of these material signifiers—all in a byzantine closed circuit with reconfigured prose content. As bizarre as it sounds, dissolved text become the refracting medium for the adjusted mind's eye. Any careful *description* of this occulted procedure, in its inevitable drift into figuration, into discourse, would seem to be the work's own point in submitting legible surfaces to something like a negative alchemical process older even than the codex's own invention. In the staging of this experiment, its phases are everything. Beginning at one technological remove, already, from book mechanics by their passage through laser electronics, bound pages concerned with fevers literal and metaphorical are photocopied, with these replicas then sliced up in turn to isolate the passages most explicitly about such somatic and psychological overheating—and then left to ferment in an alcohol-based compound that removes the laser-jetted ink overnight, at which point the muddy blend is gradually heat-distilled and purified until transparent.

Under the onslaught of thermal chemistry, amid a nest of flasks and test-tubing, *Hyperpyrexic* (the technical term for extreme feverish states) thus "burns away" the words from a series of texts evoking just such mentally inflamed conditions. Their own imprint matter, that is, in this ad hoc chemical furnace, is siphoned off from the dissolved page surface into reductive distillates. These are the thick and "essential" oils that—wait for it, as you must (indeed over the run of the whole two-month show)—only gradually fill up the inner chambers of a hollow magnifying glass trained eventually on inverted visual diagrams and other images (etched on more glass) representing the fever states otherwise verbally described in the s/melted books. Trope again, surely: words reduced, filtered, and purified—consumed only in this sense—as the magnifying medium of the virtual intensities they depict.

The parabolic logic advanced by Rosenberg seems unflinchingly clarified (distilled) by the fastidious eccentricity of method. Imagine it this way: in the warmth of engrossed reading, whether or not at fever pitch, the intensity of overheated lives does not remain on the page, but appears to dissolve wording itself in a transparent picture of the febrile said. In their very invisibility as such in this scouring case, discrete word forms have deliquesced into the sheer *flow* of their own focalized designation. So imagine, then, to pin this to specifics, some similar laboratory distillation of Brontë's *Wuthering Heights*, where, in a further meltdown of Cathy's fatal brain fever, its narrative wording becomes nothing but the nondiscursive optic interface—or lens—of its plot's hallucinatory fatality. And think, by contrast, of digital artist Jim Campbell's palimpsestic but self-occluding photograph of the novel *Wuthering Heights* (2001)—not the book but the textual (rather than narrative) through line itself, its sampled pages in overprinted spectral lamination: a codex form read all at once in the thick density of its dark, fateful, and here totally redacted tale. Such an impacted capture of duration appears like a composite shot of Latham's smeared "reading" in the *Britannica* film—or of Roach's video transferred Poe.

More baroque yet, though, Rosenberg's installation of dematerialized word forms offers the *ne plus ultra* of the Chelsea show's conceptual ab-straction—in this case, in the root sense, summarily stealing away the book's letters (demediation by any other name) in order to refigure their function. At which point we *see straight through* the dissolve of text, so to speak, into the schematized ideas portrayed. The phenomenology of reading, with its referential investments, is thus reduced to laboratory travesty—and parable. By such means, the traditional mechanics of book reading, in our standard access to its "internal machine," burns through all physical objecthood to decipherment's parody and apotheosis, passing through the alembic of chemical technology to transfigured conception. Reading, we might see this assemblage as saying (*see*, in the visual magnification of its irony)—reading can seem to lift the words right off the page in the very process of their understanding. And to round out the emblematic inference: it does so by catalyzing their import in the mediating *fluidity* of the reader's every reactive image—the machination gone "internal" again after all. [...] Either in a transcendence of the lettered page or its chemical obliteration, one is in each case still *reading one's way* into the circumstances in question. [...] The process, in Rosenberg's treatment, is as tortuous as the point is simple. Simple, that is, only given the intricate, even when instinctual, gist—the cognitive white magic—of the reading act itself.

If this example marked an extreme form of book disappeared into text—and dissolved in turn into a medial metonymy for resultant melt—it was also within the remit of *Book, Text, Medium* to look further into the medium of language altogether apart from text—and hence into the work of Mexican Canadian artist Rafael Lozano-Hemmer's (b. 1967) arts of the ephemera. In *Volute I: Au Claire de la lune*, the cross-media artist scans electronically and then casts into computer-printed aluminum—in a sculptural demediation not of the booked word but of speech shape itself—the ruffled puffs of expelled breath from the recitation of the song lyric that was the first-ever recording (without plans for playback) on Edison's 1860 phonautograph. Since my first writing about this and other of the artist's transmedial experiments—works I came upon too late for inclusion in *Transmedium* itself, but taking me to the far titular horizon of *Book, Text, Medium*—Lozano-Hemmer has extended further yet his aesthetic of transience into an affecting pictorial mausoleum at the Brooklyn Museum, October 29, 2021–August 7, 2022. Under the title "A Crack in the Hourglass," the gallery's walls are lined with spectral photographs of COVID-19 fatalities in an electronic performance piece at which this retrospective Reader allows me to append my attendance—after a sober encounter in person on a recent research trip.

Lozano-Hemmer's event-work is all but vanishingly interactive: all but. Visitors to this, in effect, self-instigated exhibit send to its central apparatus from their cell phones a captioned image of a loved one lost to the pandemic. This image file is then electronically transferred to a lateral scan of fine sand sifted from a giant hourglass and dusting out a computer-spun facsimile of the memorial image—in pale half-tones—on a glass plate: an unstable transparent backing that, as soon as the complete portrait has been electronically generated, is tilted away to dissipate—as if in an unsaid return of a textualist master trope—a life *writ in sand*. Beyond a likely cross-cultural reference to the ephemeral sand mandala, there is an extra technological subtext. For conjured as well is a transmedial throwback (pre-pixel)—in this array of computer-distributed grit—to the granular nodes of photographic emulsion in traditional (silver gel) photography, where silver halide particles not activated by light in forming the latent image are washed away in development from the exposed paper surface. In Lozano-Hemmer's process, digital printouts of what become, in effect, posthumous portraits are then affixed to the walls by the survivors in an externalized and collective mourning pitted against melancholia.

In contrast, leaving no printout trace, Rosenberg's self-consuming codex liquefactions in the "Internal Machine" exhibit suggest, as previously noted, a yet more radical internalization of the trace, not in the moment of memory but of readerly identification. Opposed to this almost parodic phenomenology of reading as a bonfire of identification—taking at least some of us back to Cathy's fever in *Wuthering Heights* from *Death Sentences* (1984; see Phase I / 2, 63)—stands an insistence on mediation per se. Ignored in the very act of its being refigured in *Hypopyrexic* is any sense of platform not literally *dissolved in projection*. So, later in Book, Text, Medium, it was again time to open some real books—and in relation now to other mechanisms of serial inscription. Part II entails the close reading of assorted literary moments that benefit in turn from a comparison between writing read and the image of verbally marked surfaces in the equally (but differently) time-based medium of film, where (in Michel Chion's stress) decodable text implies an inherent departure from the flow of image. Part III then ups the stakes, or say deepens the question, with an extended rumination on the gap in Giorgio Agamben's metalinguistic reflections opened by conjunction in his very title, "The Sayable and the Idea," which I'd only recently begun teaching. Yet in connection with his thinking, I do now find occasion, in this monograph, to summarize many seminar weeks over the years spent, concerning the media theory of Friedrich Kittler (1943–2011), on his own sense of a vexed interface between the sayable and the meant: between the operating systems of signification and its conjured referents. When addressing his rigorous and far-reaching critique of (German) Romantic verse as medium-blind, assimilated instead to the "discourse network" of post-Enlightenment poetics, I'm at pains below to underscore what strikes me in this as a tendentious exaggeration—one that British Romanticism has its own rich way of resisting. Against Kittler's critique I summon again a sense, one I've held to ever since *Reading Voices: Literature and the Phonotext* (1990; see Phase II / 3), of a pervasive wordplay on the part of Wordsworth and Shelley and Keats. And I bring this back into evidence (entwined, as it happens, with my own writing on the film medium) in rebuttal to Kittler's trope of an ideological stylistics in which Romantic writing aspires to the transparent "film"-like record of natural forces.[3]

In his "Afterword" to the second printing of Discourse Networks, Kittler targets what amounts to a presumed deficit, at once, in book studies, literary studies, and cultural studies, though he levels the charge against "literary criticism" as a broad umbrella term for such zones of oversight (neglect as well as purview): "Traditional literary criticism, probably because it originated in a particular practice of writing, has investigated everything about books except their data processing". This neglect results, for hermeneutic and sociological approaches respectively, from an alternate emphasis now on meaning, now on labor, that diverts attention from the middle ground of writing itself—as "informatic" receptacle, and vehicle. But one pauses, surely, over that overly tentative "probably" in his summary critique, since hundreds of his pages before this have been mounted to trace the occlusion of literary "data" channels back precisely to a falsified view of just such "writing" as extruded inwardness: the myth doubly vouched for by the limited liability partnership of German metaphysics and Romantic philology. This whole line of thought is deeply enmeshed in that ontological conjunction of human being and human language that, in Kittler's earlier demonstrations, rendered writing the work of expression rather than inscription. On his view, certainly the temporal moment of the reading experience allowed, for Romantic theory, no recognition of literature as a time-based *medium*, but merely as a closed interpersonal "network" participating in the lived undulations of natural (and mortal) duration, phonically evoked on the page.

Time-based: easier said than parsed, then, in its implications for print textuality, at least in a long view of linguistic theory. For such implications are ultimately dematerialized in the throes of German idealism—whose epoch and its aftermath, as Kittler reads them, tend to drain mediation of its recognized channeled matter, rob literary discourse of its textured "data base," ignore storage functions, and even the seriality of access, in the name of spiritual immediacy. But this is where Kittler ironically dogs the heels of idealism so closely that his own terms for its mystifications inherit a certain deaf spot in respect to the audial signifier and its operable slipstream. One must go carefully here, but not by sweeping the problem from sight—or audition. When phonetic language is understood in a truly "material" sense, it is always divorced to that extent from ideation (even as serviceably fused with it in referential usage). In this sense one readily locates the drawback in Kittler's sustained wry irony concerning idealism's bias toward voice rather than script. And this, in particular, with regard to the grounding thereby provided for Romantic poetry in aspiring to the internalized rhythms of nature. For Kittler settles too quickly, even on his own distancing terms, for the phenomenological abstractions he renders steadily suspect. The most rigorous of media theorists thus ends up missing, to some strategic extent, the operable mediality, the vacillating data channels, of the period's own poetic evocations at the level of differential vocalization itself—quite apart from any fantasies of natural presence, maternal or environmental, they might be summoned to manifest or authenticate. But in missing this (more generously: underplaying it), he has nevertheless amassed a full panoply of theoretical evidence for it—even with tongue often in silent cheek for his deadpan renderings of the metaphysics that would suppress any such linguistic instrumentality in the name of Muse-inspired effusions.

Under a proto-Romantic aesthetic, as Kittler shows in extensive cullings from late-Enlightenment commentary, poetic measures approximate the time signatures of a nonlinguistic music. They do so not as an interart gesture but as a mode of essentializing the relation of language to the transient rhythms of the natural world. Intoned in this sense, poetic language proceeds not first of all as a train of signification, and not as another thing among the world's material substances—and certainly not just as written glyphs—but as participating immanently in the world's felt duration. This is to say that, for Enlightenment philology, the work of humane *letters* disavows its (their) very basis (the grammatical ambiguity, just there, being quietly definitive in the split between the literate and the lettering that facilitates it). In the case of *belles lettres* especially, fixed graphemes—text markers on the page—are flashed away in their own vanquished letteral form: a materiality denied, evaporated, by the physical soundings they induce rather than produce—and these merely en route to feeling in conveyance. Elicited in Kittler's rendering, and tacit undermining, of Hegelian phenomenology is thus the philosophic idea that poetry does not emit music, but is met by the mind's own internal tonality. Hence, for Romanticism, poetry's ontological force as a temporal *experience* more than a time-based *medium*. In the phonetic regime of "alphabetization" (rather than inscription), poetry annuls its own lettering in the letting loose and slipping away of sounds. But these ripples of enunciation disappear less into the meanings they are barely recognized to signal, via the *techne* of writing, than into the thoughts they seem to educe, the unfolding nature—the naturalness itself—they manifest as inward idea.

Early on in *Discourse Networks*, Kittler draws support from Foucault on how German philosophy at the turn into the 1800s served to shore up German metaphysics by separating language from the material esoterics of script. Direct human expression, as Foucault is borrowed to phrase it, "has acquired a vibratory nature which has separated it from the visible sign and made it more nearly proximate to the note in music." And it is a reprise of this articulation by Foucault that coincides later with Kittler's citations from Hegel on "tone" as "the fulfilment of the expressiveness by which inwardness makes itself known." This phonically inflected inner life, this innerness of life, is manifest in a cognate relation to tonal production as a "determinate being within *time*"—which is to say that it is thus recognized as a "determinate being which disappears in that it has being." Call tone, in this sense, *over*determined: as transience embodied, at once instance of and figure for inward duration—and this in response, as reiterated by Kittler, to the world's no longer quite outer rhythms, whether in reading or in other forms of internalized consciousness. The titular "phenomenology of spirit" in Hegel's masterwork, one might summarize in this case, is that of flux itself—and language its articulation in the same experiential vein: the paradox of ephemerality concretized. Immediacy incarnate.

Sensed vs. Sounded

To convict a leading media theorist like Kittler of skimming just above the avowed subliminal channel of poetic mediation in his materialist literary history is not as unlikely as it sounds—if exoneration is included, which certainly it is here, for his having brought us closer to this level of perception than most previous writing on literature. His psychosociology of the phoneme (one tempting way to characterize it) bites right to the core of textual enunciation as practiced in the laboratory of poetics—but not, there, by excluding medium from the naturalized work of the literary book, as he would claim, but by energizing its latent features apart from any maternal ideology of naturally sourced word sounds in a Romantic aesthetic. The scope of the book/text/medium nexus—as a continuum—is not thereby dismantled in the resistance exposed by Kittler, in contemporaneous late-Enlightenment philology, to both the constituent letter and the lexical unit under the auspices of auditory flow. Identifying and parsing the ideology behind this linguistic negligence—and here my departure from Kittler—isn't necessarily to follow the discourse network's own 1800 creed, its philosophy of spirit speech, in charging Romanticism at large with an implicit denial of technical mediation, of "data processing," in the intuitive pulse of a natural enunciation. Poetry, even at the time, may have known better than philosophy. To repeat Kittler's critique (from our citation of this summary remark in chapter 4): "In 1800 linguisitic analysis was not allowed to approach the two forbidden borders of the word and the letter." It was concerned instead only with whole words and their naturalized familial roots. Synchrony was bypassed by diachronic backfill; etymology trumped structure. Yet literary wording, one wishes to insist, beat back this veto on the lexical incre*mentality* of reading. Between the upper and lower limits of word and letter, even if granted in the rigidity of their exclusion by Enlightenment thought, and even if for English as well as German philology, the phoneme could still, as we've noted, bring the syllable to life as a writing effect. That would be one aspect of poetry's operational backlash, even if not deliberately counter-ideological, against the linguistic science of its day.

How sayable some ideas may be, of course, remains an open question—and to what degree wording may exceed all direct saying. The premises of ideation can, in fact, turn back on themselves quite forthrightly—and in forceful phonetic terms, where alphabetized graphemes do more than effortlessly disappear into a presencing of thought and its rhythmic perceptions. So that a longer view of technical mediation is of use here—and not least Kittler's own. We know, from his later work, how film constitutes for him a fulfilment of the imaginary rather the symbolic order (in Lacanian terms), and we can further see, in Julian Murphet's related approach to multi-mediation in its cross-over aesthetics from poetry to film, how a later century's new medium of mechanical reproduction, recognized as such, thus arrives as, in its own way, the technological naturalization of a Romantic myth. The world can suddenly be made present (visually rather than just spiritually so) by the virtuality of art. It is in contrast to this, as we've noted, that Kittler understands the invention of phonography as a capture of the "real" (rather than the imaginary or the symbolic). This is exactly *not* the material reality to which subvocalization is said to aspire in the Romantic verse circuit, where all such physiological vibrations (ultimately Muse-derived via maternal rather than material phonics) are ultimately deferred away to the ruse of referential access and pure conception. Phonography comes later, in a different relation to writing and the mind's eye. The earlier results of oral pedagogy are imagined to feed achieved poetic speech directly into the flow of the world's duration.

When insisting, early in the Romantic trajectory of *Discourse Networks*, that it is only by means of such dematerialization—in the tonal dissipation of the word's mere signifying function—that (again) "Poetry could let its film roll," Kittler is thereby conjuring the hallucinatory override of symbolic language as if pure enunciated thoughts and images were spooling past on the invisible sprocket catches of the graphemes and their fleeting phonemic clicks. If writing were only that easy; facility, that much of a sheer flow. Unlike the traditional stress in phenomenological film theory on the world "becoming-image" before our gaze, the myth here is an equally "lifelike" *vanishing* of alphabetic operation that evanesces literary tonality into mental image. So that the taboo imposed by an audiphiliac philosophy of expressive spirit on the too-obviously *structural*, rather than natural, facets of literary speech, letter and word, is often lifted by the word/s/play (cross sectioning degree zero) of the period's own verse. And it is precisely for this reason—in the syllable's quiet (murmured) collusion with, rather than exclusion of, both lexeme and contributory letter—that I have wanted, here and elsewhere, some shared focus on the filmic photogram and the literary phonogram. About literary writing, however, there is a further way to rephrase and engage the premise of incrementality against the presumption of Kittler's "forbidden borders." If modern poetics began in thrall to an ideology of an entirely natural rhythm of ephemera rather than of built phrase, poetry itself, literature in general, has a way of answering to this dematerializing specter. It speaks back in the only terms available to it: speech form itself, wording in process, the nexus of syllabification in precisely the bridge between letter and word.

Literature a time-based function, yes—but not, as we're seeing, to be taken lightly or at face value as such. Here media archaeology can reward any attempt to understand text production in its slippery graphonic terms. It's not a matter (material or otherwise) of the time it takes to read a sentence or a page. Paintings take time to "process" as well. It is not the overall duration of semantic comprehension that is at stake in the temporality of reading, but the pace of reading's own serial linguistic process: the time a word's formative elements must take to fade—or say flicker—into meaning; not just to disappear as language into grasped sense all told, like wind on a purling stream, but to slip away into sense-making succession. [...] Kittler again cites a key phrase from his earlier recourse to Foucault, stressing once more the syllabic increment as a "pure poetic flash that disappears without a trace, leaving behind it but a vibration suspended in the air for one brief moment." Not unlike, say, all that wind through the trees (not to mention through Aeolian harps) that the maximization of tone in Romantic verse made reading so uncannily connatural with.

Hence—no argument here—the *ideology* of such verse. But the Romantic period's enacted *poetics* may operate otherwise, aslant to its ideology, with a resistant syllabic granularity inherent to linguistic flux but not detached from inbuilt graphic tensions and their own ineradicable mediality: tensions whose small-scale velocities, within a time-based continuum, remain all the while variable, recursive, sometimes concussive. In moving to English-language examples in Romantic verse, who can think that Keats' projection onto the figured pipes of his fabled Grecian urn—in imagining certain harmonies "more endeared" than actually audible (to the "sensual ear")—has not generated an interlinked and embedded phrasing inviting us to linger over its own linguistic play on internalization? How to ignore, in the counter-syllabics of "end*eared*," such an exemplary instance of densened phonetic sensation—rather than simply thinking of it (thinking it) dissolved into a described and strictly idealized fantasy of mental audition?

Kittler's provocative sense of phonic evanescence in poetry's nearly hallucinatory spool of rhythmic imaging might be enough in itself to invite my return (if I hadn't been working on the two books concurrently)—and your return here, I hope—to the medial status of actual cinematic technology, filmic and digital, taken up next again (after Phases III / 5, III / 7, IV / 10, and more intermittently Phase V / 12) in *Cinemachines* (2020; see Phase VII / 16), where it is shown once more, with diverse new evidence, to be inextricable from the aura of its affect, just as the graphic nexus of writing is from lyric evocation.

But besides looking past Kittler's metaphor of film rolling in the mind's eye of Romantic reading, beyond that to the rise and eclipse of an actual medium's plastic apparatus, we can look back more immediately on the late media theorist's influence, even prescience: both his assumptions and their intended affront to the status quo. What was so bracing once, for so many, in the antihumanist shedding of all sentiment regarding "internal" consciousness, with the human mind rethought instead as a mere receptor and switch point in a discourse circuit, has lost some of its skeptical charm in being overtaken by actual network affordances. It is a case of theory put not just to the test but to the knife by practice. Writing machines and reading machines are no longer controversial tropes for human consciousness. They are its pending usurpation as well as its latest tools. I don't mean to be alarmist; just, like Kittler, allegorical. From the perspective of incidental pedagogy, my babysitter taking turns with my mother in reading me Dickens (see Phase VI / 14 above) would be out of a job today (at least one part of its job description), and not just because of phonorobotics and the audiobook. What we call machine learning is rapidly replacing, in Kittler's satirized hegemony, the aura—indeed the deep hard-wiring—of the Mother's Mouth in subject formation. And with it all the anchoring aurality that such a naturalization is meant to figure. The tub is emptied not just of some tepid conceptual backwater but of the babies themselves awaiting immersion (*infans*, without speech). That many of them should grow into student readers deaf to the variable phonic ripple of on-screen lettering is little surprise.

And our higher pedagogy follows suit, with the Digital Humanities, though entirely straight-faced, catching up with Kittler's machinic humanity in all the wry siren calls of his cool irony and skepticism. Which is just where the concerns of *Book, Text, Medium* send me back to the grounding question, six books earlier, of *Bookwork* (2011, see Phase IV / 9). In the likes of corpus stylistics and computerized reading more broadly, where big data replace phrasing, where distant reading might as well be called big reading, skimming is carried to new heights. Not just pages, but books themselves, whole libraries, whole epochs, are flyover country of late, no covers needing to be opened for what counts as discovery. And even as machines do our scholarly reading for us, they can now do our literary writing: Shakespeare or Dickens or Woolf by the (algorithmic) numbers. That's why, in all its transformations over the decades, the counter-genre of the *bibliobjet* remains still so timely as a litmus test of culture's shifting literacies. What began partly in nostalgia for legible paper has developed into a last enclave of reading itself: the aching, or at least nagging, lack of words in a confronted codex shape forcing attention onto, into, the reading of what's left: the material residue on deposit once, as we increasingly suspect by inference, the actual work of optical character recognition, to name names, has been farmed out to data harvesting. The least one can do about all this, if sometimes the most, is remain ironic about it in turn.

Notes

1. Hugo Bowles, *Dickens and the Stenographic Mind* (Oxford: Oxford University Press, 2019).
2. Sergei Eisenstein, "Dickens, Griffith, and the Film Today," in *Film Form: Essays in Film Theory*, ed. and trans. Jay Leyda (New York: Harcourt, 1949), 210.
3. Friedrich Kittler, *Discourse Networks, 1800/1900*, trans. Michael Metteer (Stanford: Stanford University Press, 1990). Originally published as *Aufschreibesysteme 1800/1900* (Munich: W. Fink, 1985).

VII.

KINETIC TEXTUALITY

16 / *Cinemachines: An Essay on Media and Method* (University of Chicago Press, 2020), Stewart's fourth monograph on film, renews his analysis of its medium conditions by revisiting the theory and practice of Jean Epstein to see a "machine intelligence" in operation across a wide range of genres, including comedy and science fiction. What Stewart recovers as "apparatus reading" from the vestiges of ideological "apparatus theory" thus helps, along with Stanley Cavell's notion of "assertions in technique," to make legible the intentional inferences of medial disclosure in many of the narrative screen's most searchingly reflexive moments. Stewart returns to landmark essays in both the ontology and the technology of the filmic medium for revisionary engagement, especially the theory of "trick effects" by semiotician Christian Metz.

16 / Cinemachination and the Legible Apparatus

Cinemachines: An Essay on Media and Method (2020)

IF *FRAMED TIME* (2007) WAS MY "DELEUZE BOOK," this subsequent treatment of inferential technics, beginning with the filmmaker's own experimental silent narratives, is my "Epstein book." The recent translation of Jean Epstein's 1946 *The Intelligence of a Machine* sets many of the terms pursued in my roster of reexamined film narratives.[1] Early on in this "essay on medium and method," I put it this way—with a deliberate anticipation of the last two chapters on VFX in the overt "machinations" of the now-digital machine:

> Record, editing, and projection require geared mechanisms—the founding *cinématographe* performing all three functions at once—even as the resulting spectacle may emerge in turn as an engine of human desire, identification, and its potentially blinkering cultural stereotypes. If the times have left apparatus theory behind, with its claims for cinema's bourgeois constructions of the passive viewer,

why would that seem to require any deliberate overlooking of the machine itself—or its descendants in digital electronics, on private as well as public screens? What reasonable objections can be raised, or resulting constraints imposed, to discourage *apparatus reading*, rather than a once entrenched, now discredited, apparatus theory—at least when the technology of a given film openly declares itself, if only by optical allusion? Which is really to ask: how can we fruitfully be denied the evidence, the informed evidence, of our senses? When really looking at a film, and thereby into its material as well as thematic structure, we can't. And when the normally invisible cinemachine seems to demand attention in its own right, whether by misfirings or other signs, one has already begun looking under the hood.

Let me anticipate how this might go by jumping ahead to my penultimate screen example first, the unexpected 2016 hit *Arrival* (Denis Villeneuve)—with a fuller discussion of this film eventually closing out the "Technopoetics" of chapter 7, as followed in the "Postscript" by the tracing out of certain further inferences of digital legerdemain from the director's next film, *Blade Runner 2049* (2019). In a lower-profile mode, *Arrival* is a sci-fi narrative that, as screen realization, raises (and concentrates) almost every question to come in this essay about medial immanence in screen response—and does so, at one climactic point, from within the entrenched "special effects" context of its own genre. For there—in the specificity of these effects, within an underexplored tradition of film theory that sees all cinema as a "tricking" of vision—rests a typifying instance of this essay's recurrent evidence. Given that *Arrival*'s alien visitation plot brandishes no high-tech forms of mediation on the part of the invasive and levitating mother ships, but finds them baffling earth's scientific community with the lack of intercommunicative circuits kept open among these separate hovering vessels, their dozenfold benign flotilla—delivering a collective wake-up call from the future—emerges from the intricacies of plot (as if by default parable) as a collective interstellar medium in itself: a signal channel from the future, needing no second-order modes of coordinated transmission. Our guess at this emblematic function is only enhanced by the homebound "return" of the ships at the end: a return—by way of sheer optical reversion—to their conveyed status as an urgency millennially pending, whose time has not yet come. They go into astral hibernation before our eyes.

But how do we actually *see* in order to realize this—especially with so little valedictory *show* entailed? And how, in media-archaeological terms, can the mere fade-away of one vast craft after another in a puff of its own dematerialization rather than flight (its apotheosis, in effect, as temporal rather than spatial vehicle: again, as pure medium, more transmit than transport) manage to evoke a definitive lineage of technological film history as well as a cosmic future within the far horizons of the story's premise? How, that is, can *Arrival* microtool such departures by a sheer "atmospheric" (both nebulous and in fact sheer) digital version of the rudimentary lap dissolve in the conversion of vehicle to vapor? Technical specifications for this imaging by the VFX (visual special effects) designer, as we'll later see, can only enrich its mystery—and the depth of its evoked media-historical backstory. Dated (say archaic) in optical evacuation, the return to millennial latency of the giant ships is rendered in a time-loop irony medial as well as thematic. Reverting to the earliest special effects of the cinematographic medium, here is the *arche*-trick of filmic cinema: the laboratory cross-fade of both ghostly materialization and phantasmal erasure. Moreover, within the fading ellipse of one giant lozenge-like ship after another, how, beyond this throwback technical allusion, might we find summoned to mind's eye the shifting optic valence by which, in film history, such a dissolve—though once a spectral effect within the scene—soon became (in the other sense of elliptical) a gesture of syntactic elision (...) in the maturing function of screen grammar? How, that is, might we intuit such a dual (and, so to say, metamedial) function—the conversion of ghostly machination to technical styleme—as reprised in the very grain of this later diaphanous trope for the once (and still coming) epiphany of an alien future?

Or to put the question more programmatically in the present essay's terms: how does a viewer's instinctive reaction to the hazy, phased-out texture of such a special effect—a digital evocation of a predecessor filmic technique—draw at least part of its power from the cinemechanics (the asserted apparatus function) it exploits, transfigures, and re-historicizes? We can, I promise, get closer to answers when, after intervening arguments, this screen narrative comes round again for a more extended interpretive discussion. I've introduced Villeneuve's film as an anticipatory "example," but in fact the methodological stakes of its consideration, here and later, render it less an instance of a device than an *exercise* in particular medial options or tendencies. Such moments, in current as well as classic films, register a *performance* of the apparatus rather than the simple proof of it. More than ever, perhaps, given the way VFX designers are to be numbered among the true *auteurs* of recent cinema, such effects thereby deliver up, and precisely from affect to interpretation, the legible (the "authored" and readable) as well as the merely visible. And often do so in the fashion of a rear-view mirror, as well, on the historical vicissitudes of the apparatus.

Two chapters at the end of this "essay" (this synoptic *attempt*) called *Cinemachines* make a return to such special effects in their updated digital proliferation, with the issue also coming up two books later (and sampled again for the present anthology) in *The Metanarrative Hall of Mirrors* (2022, see Phase VIII / 19). But in *Cinemachines* I wanted to note a backdating of the question, and its "thinking," to the metafilmic ironies of silent screen comedy and its postwar legacy. The task was to develop a model for the intrinsic "comedial" in-joke about film's own apparatus, under the allusive rubric (Scorsese's later and technically unrelated film in mind) "Kinks of Comedy." Connection is made as well with my literary work when Jean Epstein leads us sideways into Henri Bergson's theories of verbal comedy—so instructively correlated in that philosopher's work with the physical ironies of silent slapstick.

> What philosopher of time Henri Bergson resisted—found, we may idiomatically presume, *laughably sad*—about the turn-of-the century cinematograph does not stop there. This is because film's way of spewing forth, for screen display, what one now calls a time-based medium—to Bergson's eye, merely an optic sputter of mis-represented duration—can take us straight to his influential essay "Laughter." And from there to the effects I would identify as the *comedial* disruptions of mechanized motion in certain filmic turns: the machinic kinks of their risible hijinks. All too selectively screened, of course, in this rerun theater of investigation, certain exemplary cases nonetheless default to *cinemechanics* in numerous and instructive ways. And therefore connect directly with Epstein's template for engineered sequence—operating still-by-still in a frame-advance rhythm clarified by the very possibility of its own altered tempos. This is for him the undeniable core of cinema's world-historical advance in both visual imaging and its poetry, to say nothing of its implied philosophy of an intertwined time and space.
>
> In the opening chapter on "Signs" in *The Intelligence of a Machine*, which begins with a section revealingly called "Bewitched Wheels," Epstein's subsequent treatment of "The Reversability of Time" stresses the link between "avant-garde film" and "burlesque comedy" (thinking of a single unnamed instance of both together) in their shared instinct—because their technical potential—for reversing the "vectors" of time and thereby moving back from "effect to cause." What the "cinematograph" thus "describes, with clear precision" ("describes" as if in the sense of inscribes or sketches as well as more neutrally depicts)—and here, the crux of Epstein's whole

counterintuitive argument about the thinking machine—is therefore a conception of temporality that "humanity could scarcely represent to itself." Backward time has to be thought for us in machinic images. And from that previous formulation of Epstein's, a broader suggestion yet. The intelligence of cinema—though described always by its mechanical status as "cinematograph" as well as its screen result in motion picturing—may serve ultimately to posit the very idea of thought, of human cognition, as a "representation to itself." [...] Even aside from any such implied definition of consciousness-as-image in its own discontinuous segmental generation, however, we could be content at this stage simply to settle such questions, for cinema in particular, as raised by Epstein in his passing link between the quintessential and the burlesque. What is it that aligns cases where the apparatus is pressed to its aesthetic limits, on the one hand, with, on the other, the accidents of slapstick? What links emerge between programmatic intensities and zany contingencies? Between the probing avant-garde gesture and the goof? Each, of course, has its genius. And both depend on conditions only implicitly visible on the image surface.

Even broader terms of comparison, however, come into play at this juncture. Apart from the slapstick of pantomime, its mugging, pratfalls, and the rest, there is often something verging on the seriocomic in the deadpan unearthing of cause from the superficial ground of effect, of technicity from opticality, even in noncomic film: an irruption so complete that its double-take can seem almost giddy, even when not a punch line in itself. This is all the more likely to be the case, then, in explicit comedies near to the founding moment of cinema—not least those by directors arriving from stage careers to film's fresh possibilities (Chaplin, Keaton). For these are artists in whose work such instances of machinic upset often seem fixated with keen delight on the disparity between tool and illusion in the not wholly familiarized new medium. [...]

So, with Keaton on hold, we start with a famous episode about modern industrial technology comprising the first third of Chaplin's feature-length *Modern Times* (1936), whose factory setting grows inseparable, if not quite indistinguishable, from the workings of film's own industrial production and, in the case of voice recording, its suspect innovations. [...] *Modern Times* includes, first and foremost among its apparatus ironies, the fact that it is "a talkie" merely by proxy. Voice is carried only through the vinyl whine of a recorded sales pitch or, in present emission, through the raspy aggression of the corporate President in closed-circuit and one-way broadcast to the factory floor—and from there to the invaded privacy of the time-clocked privy, where the voice of authority further demands more speed and efficiency. When Chaplin's own voice is finally heard in the last scene, it is only a sing-song gibberish: music, not speech. Across the main factory episode that begins the film, certainly, Chaplin sustains his international essence as the seen but not heard—and does so against blatant alternatives in audial technique.

As restricted at first to an entirely inimical optic field, these include the factory President's coercive one-way telescreen (and near screech) of authority appearing alongside Charlie [the figure usually named the Tramp] without ever containing him in its reproduced field of vision–all noise limited to *its* hectoring voice, never our hero's. Building on this double-pronged satire of corporate *command* and *oversight*, once Charlie has gone "nuts" by being expected to tighten a countless series of them at high speed on the assembly line's conveyer belt, he is sucked into the bowels of the factory apparatus as if it were a composite of gargantuan film spools rather than turbine wheels. In default of any mediated surveillance relay from the President's POV, we have until now seen only the hero full-screen, not his secondary image. We have watched Charlie only as our star, that is, not in power's line of sight as a managerial pawn. And now, one literalized level down, we see *how*. As the film cuts from the factory floor to a medium shot of those mechanical innards—this previously off-frame (and sub-frame) space—we encounter one of the great iconic sets in the history of film. It is as if it were the *inset* stage, one stratum beneath the President's screens-within-the-screen, for laying bare a sophisticated engineering equivalent to that which makes the whole film possible. Round and round goes the serially-propelled human figure, his wrenches flailing as he goes, bolting himself as character to his own laborious round, servicing his own mechanism, ultimately cause to his own star effect.

But with a resistant difference, even so—since Chaplin is still fending off the "talking picture" and its two-track rotary mechanics, still holding out for the purism of the soundless moving body choreographed in its usual comic dips and slips—many of them quasi-mechanistic themselves, of course, for all their antic dance of gesture. By this point in film history, Chaplin's silence has become deafening—and obliquely alluded to here in association with the dehumanized phonographic sales pitch and the grating address of the industrial overlord. With Charlie submitted at bodily (rather than aesthetic) risk, headfirst, to the spinning motors of corporate production, this exposure of the works is no doubt also to be correlated, at least in part, with the new burdens of synchronization brought on by sound technology. [...]

This gets us to what accounts, via the exquisite precision of its famous set, for the true probative brilliance of this "underworld" episode in the context of the film's layered techno-critique. For when the gears go into reverse, and spew their victim back out of their churning innards onto the factory floor again, the process is achieved by an all but indistinguishable trick of plastic and material resource: a strictly optical, rather than embodied, *rewind*. All the director needed to do—in lab rather than factory, and as if coached by Epstein in his early allegiance to cinema's unique properties in the picturing (and refiguring) of motion—is reverse the photo strip that has produced the image in the first place, while leaving the ironic calliope music on the sound track for its contrapuntal comedy in association with this mirthless merry-go-round. Isolated here is exactly the machinic option that, as it happens, the one-way nature of sound recording could never tolerate. It isn't that Chaplin the director has troubled to have the giant wh/r/eels of the set geared so that they could reverse direction, with Charlie lifted improbably up and back into the initial aperture through which he initially slid face-first and straight down. Any Hollywood-factory cost efficiency would rule that out. [...] A full decade before Epstein made his suggestive link between burlesque and the avant-garde, between slapstick and the tricks of the medium per se, between screen lyricism and filmic "special effects"—and this on the very score of the reverse action that is only made possible by the nature of film's serial increments—Chaplin has rendered up a comparable disclosure of the medium's calibrated micro-linkages in a parable of the apparatus as serial gearbox.

The plasticity of the image, the Epsteinian modulation of the photogram's separate fixed-frame molds, couldn't be more succinctly rehearsed. In ways hard for the naked eye to perceive in the grips of spectacle, we thus come upon what, fusing Epstein with Metz, one might call illusionism squared: the metafilmic specification of an inherent special effect. Motoring this reversal of time's curved arrow via the rotary vectors of industrial machination, that is, we apprehend here, at least under repeated scrutiny, the simple reverse enchainment of the photogram sequence—for which the rotarized Charlie, Chaplin's screen double, is both emblem and scapegoat at once, international poster boy and celluloid figment. Burst on-screen from the realm of the constitutively off-limits, there can't have been many greater tropes of motion picturing in the whole history of cinema—and certainly not in so knowing a reflex of its medium as a cinemachine.

Body/Language: "Reciprocal Interference of Series"

In plot-long fantasy rather than local trope, the question of such technological doubling has been raised more explicitly, by dream parable, in Keaton's *Sherlock Jr.* a dozen years before (1924)—and in ways equally available for illustrating Bergson's theory of "laughter" as the rendering mechanistic of human action. In his broad category of "transposition," such is comedy's signal displacement from norm to deviance, whether the comedy is physical or linguistic, cinematic or verbal. Like the human form, human speech becomes, in wordplay, when saying other than it seems, a mechanical as much as a discursive function—and thus matches the routines of slapstick in taking on a life of its own, radically linguistic rather than technological. As a putative human tool, that is, speech is suddenly acting on its own behalf, acting *up*. Mechanical, this backfire of wording, because something in the nature, or rather the works, of language itself has taken over from the locus of expressive intent. As Bergson sees it, language is operating on its own behalf, taking charge, taking liberties. No episode, even in the jaw-dropping acrobatics of Keaton's comedy, could more readily distill Bergson's sense of mechanization than Chaplin spun on the revolving rack of his own medium. But Keaton's greater reliance on silent intertitles, and his readier way with verbal and ocular puns, makes clearer than ever the link between Bergson's theory of verbal as well as visual comedy and his rejection on similar grounds (a rarely noted bridge between phases of his thought) of film's own "mechanization" of the human, its engineering rather than inhabitation of *durée*.

With the category of mechanical "transposition" broken down by examples in Bergson's "Laughter," the three hallmarks of verbal as well as physical comedy are repetition, inversion, and interference. We might think of them, respectively, as the rut, the upending, and the static disruption of natural motion—or communication. The last disturbance is more fully characterized by Bergson as "reciprocal interference of series," when one train of association is double-crossed by an alternative through a "transposition" from one received register to its anomalous alternative. And there is a further mechanistic reciprocity as well, for it is by way of response, by our own reactions in the automatic belly laugh, that we too are mechanized. […]

In moving from Chaplin back to Keaton in *Cinemachines* I was in fact returning across four decades to my first two essay-length pieces on film from the late 1970s (for *Critical Inquiry* and *The Georgia Review*, respectively) to do fuller justice to medial ironies discerned in teaching the films since. And something more as well, by way of retrospect. What follows marks, no doubt, the most direct intersection of my interest in literary stylistics (syllepsis again, in particular) with screen syntax. Only in the thick of this career review did I register the full redux function provided in *Cinemachines* by my Bergsonian comparison—across media so explicitly—between such time-release encapsulations of discrepancy in (a)wry overlap:

When the comic rudiment of staggered "repetition" extends, in the case of an "equivocal" linguistic "situation," to verbal "puns" and other dualisms, this is part of exactly what Bergson means by that specialized subset of "transposition" known as a "reciprocal interference of series." [...] A ready example comes to hand in the form of a full compound predicate, not just a prepositional pairing (as *with* a and b). It happens that the first instance of such a sylleptic trope in Dickens' own first novel, *Pickwick Papers*, appears in a compound (if elliptical) verb phrase that double-tracks Mr. Pickwick as he "fell into the barrow and fast asleep, simultaneously" (ch. 19). This discrepant effect matches the stiff grammatical linkage in a stilted inversion given by Eisenstein, apart from his focus on Dickens, as the verbal equivalent of a forced and flaccid montage: "Came the rain and two students." In prose rather than edited image, such an internal montage of actions—rendered in nonparallel grammar, but "simultaneously"—is Dickens' own version of something between a jump cut and a match cut, straining at the continuity that its own "and" posits. Neither strictly repetitive (the difference marked by *and* prevents that) nor inverted (since a commonality rather than a flipped sense is posited), "reciprocal interference of series" seems indeed, in this case, name for the tempered jarring of this cut on action.

Just this kind of *syntactic* pun finds its redoubtable screen update when Groucho Marx, in dismissing Mrs. Teasedale in *Duck Soup* (1933, dir. Leo McCarey), plays between three (not just two) divergent senses of the preposition "in," regarding both mood and mode of exit, for a sylleptic brush-off capped by a homophonic pun on *huff* for *half*: "If you can't get a taxi you can leave in a huff. If that's too soon, you can leave in a minute and a huff." More than one colloquial series, to be sure, is "interfered" with in those dovetailed alternatives. As is the case in Howard Hawks' film *His Girl Friday*, in a grammatical quick-cut not there in the theatrical source (the 1928 play *The Front Page*). Its transposed seriality is as fast in syntactic overrun as is the ricochet of reverse shots in this same newsroom sequence. This is the moment when the exclamatory grammar of confirmation (in an announced proper noun) turns adjectival on the spot to somatize nomenclature into anatomical euphemism. "What was the name of the mayor's first wife?" / "The one with the wart on her?" / "Right." / "Fanny." Again Bergson: two lines of apperception intercepting and almost discommoding each other, here in a *verbal* prat-fall regarding the phantom blemish of a derrière.

This fillip of overlapping dialogue, this match-cut superimposition of separate semantic streams—choose your preferred cinematic metaphor—manifests another version of the Bergsonian "reciprocal interference" that buckles convergent sequences out of shape,

> foiling serial continuity along its own dialogue channels. However felt or analogized, such a mechanical hiccup in sense renders obtrusive the comic equivalent of those overridden breaches in the forced rather than organic continuum, according to Bergson, that make the cinematographic effect a mockery of lived duration. Low comedy thus waxes philosophical by default, from within its own nonsensical, if punningly recuperated, fault lines. In the rapidly elided dead space between preposition and its object (turned subject) in this Hawksian banter—"on her ... Fanny"—flickers, that is, the grammatical equivalent of some jammed frame-advance giving the lie to all sense of the seamless on screen: here in an open disjunctive counterpoint across the slipstream of syntax itself.
>
> Certainly the kind of verbal dexterity, sampled from Dickens through Groucho to Howard Hawks, models the investigative slippage that makes visual slapstick tick—and stick: a conceptual traction behind the manifest frolic. [...]

And it is in this spirit that I turn later, in sound film, to the metafilmic farce of 1941's *Helzapoppin'* (Ole Olson and Chic Johnson)—including a sense in which characters get caught between frames of their own apparatus like victims stuck in a stalled elevator in arrested vertical progress. Given that this film was, in my preteen years, a high-ranking favorite, eagerly awaited on afternoon TV when it appeared wedged between *Three Stooges* starrers, it must have been my first screen encounter with the meta.

> Analysis is thus able to move rather directly from Dickensian sylleptic comedy to the comparable optic splits and forkings in Keaton. If one takes the Bergsonian format of a "reciprocal interference of series" in a spatial rather than temporal sense for screen gags, especially if the series lays itself out along an actual visible axis traversed by narrative action, then one model for the comedy in the central dream sequence of Keaton's 1924 masterwork, *Sherlock Jr.*, is prepared in the waking time plot of *Our Hospitality* the year before: and not just via the deft costume shifts across gender (and species!) in that earlier film, but in regard (optical regard) to the camera-managed sight lines that facilitate them. Indeed, much of Keaton's double-take humor turns on the difference, in metafilmic comedy, within the turn—or wrench—between an orthogonal axis of spectation, as channeled further by point of view within frame, and the alternate vectors of lateral action. Such, within the diegesis, is Keaton's deep instinct for thematizing precisely the difference between screen plane and the vectored gestures it isolates and frames. Sight gags in his films turn with striking frequency on the ironic twist of sight lines, which is one of the main ways in Keaton that the comic is rendered

reflexive, *comedial*. In the mode of apparatus reading invited here, the work of the *dispositif* can thus tacitly be read as its own kind of wry "frame-up," bracketing actions that redraw their own lines of sight, and alike of motion, before our eyes. [...]

When the photogram chain is interrupted in *Hellzapoppin'*, the characters try taking action themselves, by pulling down the particularly bulky frame line—or pulling themselves up to another sprocket-aligned rectangle—giving a special vertical emphasis to any more general theory of off-frame space. The move is as ingenious as it is ludicrous—and useless. There is no edge to grab in that sense. These characters, as if we didn't know it by now, are the epiphenomena of the machine, not its masters. The next effort to recover the norm is the projectionist's, but he ends up putting the film in upside down, again reminding us—in full-screen inversion—of its photogrammic materiality and verticality alike when operating, right side up or not, at right angles to the arc-light's beam. Even more illogically, when he switches reels again, the film-within-the film becomes a kind of punning *double picture* where a shoot-em-up Western has overlain (from behind) not just its image but its whole threatening diegesis upon the main characters, resulting in an actual gunshot from—and in—the rear. This happens when the frame ratio changes from an ominous close-up of the vengeful Indian to a medium shot (pun no doubt intended) that allows the rifle itself the focal length it needs [...].

It again grieves me to say (quite parenthetically here, where the point is short on excerpted evidence) that I nodded again over a pattern it would have been illuminating to draw out in the book. Given (from the fully detailed roster of episodes in this comedy chapter) the famous trick in *Sherlock Jr.* where Buster dives into the apparent abdomen of a woman and emerges ass-backwards, or the joke on the besmocked horse's ass earlier in *Our Hospitality*, or (unmentioned) Chaplin's Tramp distracted in his madness on the factory floor by the blond secretary passing with six large visually punning buttons at the back of her skirted buttocks, our hero chasing after them with flailing wrenches in hand, and on past the warted "Fanny" of *His Girl Friday* to that latest send-up of *rear-projection* in the *Hellzapoppin'* shoot-out, one can stop short of a full Freudian reading while still noting that in the carnal unconscious of slapstick there are more prats than actually take a fall.[2] But it is the laminated double-feature in *Hellzapoppin'* that remains the most baldly *comedial*.

The collapse of the cinemachine could scarcely be more complete. Misalignment versus inversion versus superposition: jammed adjacent frames now popping us from the plot to its obtruded apparatus; flipped reel now turning the whole thing upside down;

overlaid frames now inducing a crossfire of both plot—and sight-lines. This threefold optic farce is in a very particular way *definitive*. Instead of being jinxed by such disjunctures, of course, screen comedy turns them to optical puns, one image for the plot, one for the razzed if not downright unraveled medium. [...]

Comedial—or, if you prefer, in an alternative imbrication of the comedic with its own means: comediatic. The deep-seated belly laugh (Bergson)—in somatic response not just to bodies in risible distress but to the unnerved materiality of the image track itself: that's what makes otherwise self-estranged bedfellows of burlesque turns and avant-garde ventures (Epstein), shtick and considered estrangement.

The theoretical apertures operate differently in *Cinemachines* as a whole, by variably opening upon larger technical and thematic concepts before closing in again on-screen readings. Here, though, in reverse order, I'll try digesting next, as briefly as feasible from earlier in the book, the impact for me (and for my return to Chaplin and Keaton as reflexive exemplars) of Epstein's book on *The Intelligence of a Machine*—and in particular how it connected with a trajectory in my thinking that had long been indebted to the work of Christian Metz on the metafilmic valence of "trucage" (from which the final two chapters of *Cinemachines*, on digital VFX, derive). In all this, Epstein's radical paradigm has served to help graduate students to a firmer grip on the place of film, for Cavell, in a recoil from skepticism—as signaled by epistemological relaxation in the very title of *The World Viewed*. It was in fact the convergence of Epstein with Metz, around the differently spelled word in French for trick, that precipitated, after a good deal of preliminary discussion, what I offered in the first chapter as belated epigraphs (immediately below) for the whole volume.[3] And what ensues after the second subhead in this following excerpt is an attempt to separate Epstein's theory of probative mechanics from any partisan reliance on preternatural technique in his own film of Poe's "Fall of the House of Usher."[4]

> The cinematograph merely possesses the mandatory faculty to realize—to render real—the combination of space and time, providing the product of space and time variables, which means that cinematographic reality is therefore essentially the idea of a complete mode of location. Yet it is only an idea, an artificial idea, of which we can only affirm an ideological and artificial existence—*a kind of trick or special effect*. Nonetheless, this trick [*truquage*] is extremely close to the process by which the human mind itself conjures up an ideal reality for itself.
> —Jean Epstein, *The Intelligence of a Machine* [emphasis added]

> Montage itself, at the base of all cinema, is already a perpetual *trucage*, without being reduced to the *false* in usual cases.
> —Christian Metz, "*Trucage* and the Film"

Two embedded epigraphs, that is, on the "world" of moving pictures as sheer illusion: including in the first case, by analogy, the exterior world of pictured motion itself as its own merely "idealized" real; and in the second, a distinction between overt deception and a general fabrication. Within the sphere of cinema per se, two variant French spellings of *truc/qu/age*, one striking idea: that any local "trick" is a synecdoche for the medium all told. The Epstein translation renders the single phrase "trick" ("of a sort") by adding for clarification its more common English sense in "a kind of trick *or special effect*"—in any case, a faking of the real. The liberty of amplification is entirely apt, given Epstein's broad argument. Identified there is an inherent rigging of vision—and not just as regards the screen world, but, more striking yet in Epstein, the world's own cognitive screening: namely, the sensorial interface that always operates, well outside the movie theater, between us and those perceptions we accumulate in order to derive our sense of placedness—of space-time "location," here in the now. Epstein's radical point: we are only in the know about our whereabouts through mediation, necessary for the mind in "conjuring" a running image of what lies beyond it. Just as film is necessary for the screening of *its* world, or digitization since, so must the brain's electric medium override intermittence in order to picture the continuum of ours.

The point is, in short, as much epistemological as cinematographic. For consciousness involves a sense of embodied locus that is, in Epstein's view, as "artificial" as focalized continuity in the screen image: an experience of presence mentally constituted, indeed constructed, rather than directly received—in his terms "ideological" (idealized) rather than ontological. We are always taking the virtual for the actual. This is because only neural *constructs* make possible our access to any outside source of sensation. Movies replay this distance from immediacy at one further and absolute remove. In this sense, what filmic cinema tricks out on screen, by way of dissembled motion from its own celluloid movement, offers a screening of dubiety itself—and then, of course, its immersive undoing. This is a measure of the "intelligence" (in Epstein's title) that the celluloid cinemachine imparts as well as embodies. [...]

Tricked Out/Space Doubt

[...] According to just this epistemic premise in the passage on "truquage" above—arriving in the second-to-last paragraph of Epstein's final chapter, titled "Irrealism"—we find lodged a central concession about the "special effect" of recorded reality when manifested on theater screens. Duping is constitutive. The point bears repeating, since it is just this tricking of world coherence that can instruct us in "those processes by which the human mind itself conjures up an ideal reality for itself." Indeed, to pick up on Epstein's heavy iteration there, this is how consciousness fashions its "irreal" (its virtual) notions of the "itself" per se. [...]

By the tenets of "irrealism," all is never more than intermittence and probability. In this light, "the cinematograph brings us back to Pythagorean and Platonic poetry: reality is but the harmony of Ideas and Numbers." Nor does Epstein stop there with his backcast to a mathematical idealism at the basis of physical science and screen mechanics alike. Written on the postwar eve of the computer revolution, his book's closing note seems sounded in full theoretical anticipation of virtual reality—a terminology, for him, quite the opposite of paradoxical. Since physics admits that it "can only know reality" in "the form of numerical rules prescribing the conditions under which reality is ultimately allowed to produce itself," then it is only these formulas that "create a specific and fictive zone in space that is the locus of this extreme reality—and no one knows how to get any closer to it." The real is always, we may say, *screened from us* by probabilities rather than met with present confirmation.

Film looms large here as a new cognitive model. The "artificial" continuities and coordinates thrown up by celluloid projection might thus be construed as a mode of recognizing—and reckoning with, not numerically but imaginatively—the fact of our epistemological remove from the world. Such is a mode of thinking—with and through, and finally beyond—the automatized intellection of *une machine*. Rather than merely represented by projection, the world's ingrained virtuality is revealed in synchromesh with it. Arriving decades later in screen production, the algorithmic basis of the computer image offers the same potential analog for perception (or, in pixel breakup, its travesty) but gets us no closer, in Epstein's sense, to the receding abstraction of the real—just, perhaps, more algebraically (if invisibly) attuned to the world's infinitesimally flickering field of intermittence. When Deleuze ended his career wondering whether the coming "numeric" basis of cinema would change everything in our conception of the time-image, Epstein's proleptic answer might well have been: not "really."

Machination: Between Axioms and Praxis

Epstein: arguably the greatest theorist-practitioner of the cinema after Eisenstein. [...] His pervasive claims for cinema as the dissolution and remolding of the recorded world and its mobile agents—a world whose own optical fungibility and intermittent signaling is only answered by the manipulable frames of celluloid itself—needn't appear selective and tactical, driven by agenda rather than genuine medial apprehension. Yet the claims bear interrogation, to be sure. This is the case, most famously, with variable speed, as distilled in the *Usher* film by a distended loop of the sister's decelerated physical collapse, in slower and slower descent: her falling body perceived as if from inside her own lost grip on consciousness. How can this anomaly be constitutive? Or ask: what are its tacitly obtruded mechanics meant to be thinking out, thinking through, for us in this event of mechanized "intelligence"?

Considering Epstein's stress on cinema's distinctive features, we may wonder just how montage and the close-up (those definitive elements traced back through Griffith to Dickens by Eisenstein) wouldn't be more definitive, as ingredient features of cinema, than the anomalies of slowed or accelerated motion. What in the case of Madeleine Usher's fall, for instance, makes retardation quintessential, its effect an *intrinsic* trick? The answer is implicitly approached by Epstein only through interrogating the celluloid medium (or means) in particular, not the screen experience as normally managed by shot and montage. Slow motion is a second-order function of serial arrest on the strip. If the lock-step chain of photograms can be routinely overcome by split-second pauses matched to flickering disappearances—so as to produce the looks of a hug, a lunge, a gallop, you name it—it is through just that staggered seriality, by further internal duplication and thus prolongation, that the image can be slowed, say, to a float in descent. Or by sheer iteration stopped dead in its track(s)—so that the micro-pause that alone permits a resolution of the image on screen (rather than just a spooling blur) is recapitulated at the scale of the action itself in arrest.

Cinema, *because it is first of all film* (its image units discrete, variable, plastic), can thereby study, whether by stalling or skimming, the effects it produces. So far, Epstein. Only film can *think* this for us, imagine what it would look like to hover in freefall—as well as to commute instantaneously between places, or for the eye to zoom-in upon the speaking countenance. Only film has this quality with regard to the quantifications of time—or revise that, historically: only film and, in the conjoint perspective of this essay, its evolved substrate in digital imaging as well (its units discrete, variable, electronic). Whatever intelligence accrues to the motion picture's optic mechanism can be found inherited, via sometimes extreme genetic modification, by the systems of electronic imaging—TV broadcast, portable disk playback, on-line streaming, etc. After Epstein, cinemachines proliferate—and within a lineage not just worth tracing but often delineated by given films. [...]

Here is his most straightforward assertion to this (defining) effect: "Outside the viewing subject there is no movement, no flux, no life in the mosaics of light and shadow that the screen always displays as stills"—"stills" that, of course, appear to us only as they are vanished into action, their separate image cells sprocketed past the aperture. If Münsterberg's psychopoetics of cinema sees the field of projection operating like the mind in working over the world both present to it and past, Epstein's more unflinching subjectivism understands film operating like the world per se (as much itself on screen as it can ever appear to us): the world in its being worked up by the mind, its coherence and continuity lent only by the human sensorium. [...] Any localized "special effect" thus helps keep honest this tricking of the screen all told—even while addressing by association the "idealizing" mind in the flow of phenomena. In *Usher*, all those lyric waverings, overlays, and slowings tend to circle round on their own basis to testify more directly than usual, in their very abuse of the (recently established) cinematic norm, to the segmental nature of the filmic spool, becoming a descriptive poetry of the photo-chronic transcript.

On this score, Epstein minces no words from the start about the chopped-up nature of the substrate, for the most "striking wonder" of the new machine is that it "transforms a discontinuity into a continuity," each virtual snapshot snapped past fast enough to smooth out this illusion. It is then that the trace of photochemical exposure-time is pulled into a different time frame altogether as the serial lurch of gesture and motion, rendered in parable by Usher at work on his sister's portrait. At which point it is clear, if typically invisible—or, in other words, *thought* for us by the machine—that time is merely an abstraction from succession, just as space is abstracted from the contiguity of objects. In this respect, cinema's function as an "annex" of the "brain" in its role as "the alleged center of intelligence" is the wising-up of perception: a model for acknowledging the relativity and interdependence of supposedly separate a priori conditions. Here is how film images "bear a subtle venom" that Epstein insists has been given "little attention" in regard to its "corrupting" force, which is— in precisely the medium's "philosophical" use—to poison reality's facile assumptions for us. Thus, "having taught us the unreality of both continuity and discontinuity, the cinematograph rather abruptly ushers us into the unreality of space-time"—when any such localized temporality is in fact merely a function of discrete images in their timed spacings. Effect to this cause, mirage of this machination, all cinema—like all supposed reality—is, again, a "special effect" of perception.

Discussion in *Cinemachines* connects at this point with the book's opening critique of "cinematic body theory"—and its debatable mix of phenomenology with an epidermal view of the screen surface as a somatic interface. Such strike me as exactly (or inexactly is more like it) the too-metaphoric claims about the screen's imagistic tissue that are meant to be corrected by a strip—or pixel-based—"apparatus reading."

> Epstein's sense of cinema's own processual fabrication of screen movement from mobilized photographs should make that obvious. These are not bodily tissues in their rotated transparencies, nor, it bears repeating, are they palpably embodied when their shadows hit the screen. No need for a sweeping haptic metaphor for the way their induced affect embraces us as more-than-mere-viewers in our nerved and braced seats. Epstein's work in *The Intelligence* depends on a more strenuous epistemology, as we've begun to appreciate, than any such somatography of viewing might suggest. By his reasoning, weighted bodies in action, apart from the foursquare space of projection, are in fact comparable, as atomistic congeries, to the piecemeal chain of photo imprints that propel their equivalent on-screen representations. Epstein is thus instructively positioned between Bergson and Deleuze in regard to the latter's one foundational demurral from the former (and much earlier) French philosopher's disdain for cinema. For Bergson, notoriously, any sense of *durée*, of temporal continuity, was dubiously simulated, rather than captured and reproduced, by the new medium he rejected. Where time is a function of motion in Deleuze's sense of the movement image on screen, Bergson saw the ersatz continuum of screen event as a misleading fabrication. What Deleuze thought Bergson missed, however, was that the intermittence of the strip does nonetheless produce, in projection, images we can accept as cross-sections of real temporality. [...]
>
> Epstein's claims for a machine-spurred thought on this score would [...] intervene by insisting that embodied duration itself is only a stitched-together fiction not just in screen recognition but in everyday cognition: the product (because never other than a process) of molecular and even subatomic instabilities, psychic intermittences, and so forth. Even supposedly fixed bodies are only constellations of invisible motion, while their duration, in movement or not, is constituted only by what we might call the invisible or cognitively blurred gaps, the perpetual interruptions, overleapt by the fiction of presence in three-dimensional space. This is as much the case, there, as in the two-dimensional screen field—and in either case virtual through and through. Film itself, one level down

from its imaged representations, is thus culture's ultimate mirror held up to nature. [...]

This takes a minute to compass in its full historical sweep. Descended both from the optical toys of intermittence (the alternating flip of the thaumatrope, the spun slatted glimpses of the zoetrope) and from the subsequent micro-staging of motion in chronophotography, the subsequent genealogical shift from the double tracking of image and sound on the modern screen to the bit-map transformations of digital image and editing only helps italicize how the history of the medium is the evolution of gaps, elisions, ellipses, compressions—all the way from backlit gram to LED-ignited granule, from cellular unit to digital fragment, picture cell to pixel (pic[ture] el[ement]) [...] Epstein may have in fact conjured for us a trajectory he never fully charts. Under his conceptual impetus, we may end up seeing the whole history of temporal media (or time-approximating plastic and now computerized art) as, in its truest shape, the history of compression per se: again, the generative illusion at the base of a "continuity" that is, in fact, intermittent and elliptical. [...]

The convergent inferences of Epstein and Metz with those of Cavell are ones I would ultimately summon back in that later chapter on comedial screen disclosures. Such are the theoretical confluences that also fuel my crossover graduate teaching—and again under this one monograph's subtitled sign of "media and method." Designed to sponsor a theoretical confidence on the part of students, such triangulated dialogue among these major critical voices would help chart a path for those concerned less with auteurism or national cinemas, festival venues or technicians' unions, distribution practices or videogame tie-ins, than with the wider hyphenated field of film-philosophy (with a journal to its name) that will, in helping to frame medium-deep approaches, equip these students for at least some of their own undergraduate teaching as well as their critical writing. In view of *Cinemachines*' later consideration of Epstein's use in engaging with a Bergsonian view of apparatus comedy, it should help to recover this brief flavor, for want of further space, of its Cavellian overtones:

> Through such kinks in the "thread" (Cavell) of reeled celluloid, filmic (rather than just film) comedy backflips to a wild realization of its own underlay. Bergson: repetition, inversion, reciprocal interference of series. Olson and Johnson: snagged differential iteration, upside-down spools, and the collisional nonsense of interfering projected worlds—with one transposed upon, sneaking up upon, the other from behind. Beyond any narratively assimilable "assertions in technique" (Cavell)—beyond any unique power of the photogram

chain, like pause or acceleration, that might affiliate the hijinks of machinic comedy with the ingenuities of the avant garde (Epstein)—here is the apparatus not appropriated for rhetoric but dismantled as coherent image.

Antics/Mechanics/Ethics

A tempting plateau opens at this point on the very ground of theoretical reorientation. For we can retrack two of our previous film-philosophy intersections across some further and intriguing cross-mapped terrain. Cavell, for whom cinema is, uncontroversially, and throughout *The World Viewed*, an "automatism," coins his own far more deliberately alienating term—in his major philosophical work, *The Claim of Reason*—for one's doubt of the Other as availably human: a suspicion, under skepticism, of "automatonity." In that withering mood of mind, disengaged from any interpersonal ethics, everything and everyone seems alien to humanizing recognition, to intimate acknowledgment: ultimately a false front, an artificial intelligence, emptied, robotic. Which invites us, or might, to triangulate the basic automatism of cinema with, on the one side, the particular automata to which slapstick screen figures are sometimes (emblematically?) reduced, those ricocheting bodies of comic agency, and, on the other, the larger paradigm of skepticism's distancing of the world through a dubious response to its inhabitants as virtual automata: a universe merely *going through the motions* as real. Not immediately obvious, this triangulation, its effort can benefit from other theoretical conjunctures already on tap in these annotations.

In particular, a repeated touchstone of Cavell's thought centers on the way movies can offer a kind of screened-off test of one's credence in the world—as if to say, those endearing or enduring figures, those human shapes, are of course only "automatic ... projections," but we can feel for them anyway, acknowledge them as enough like us to care about their travails. To paraphrase the logic, in this overt a way, helps bring Cavell's frame of reference into relation with Bergson around a curious reversal from which, as Cavell himself suggestively says, "further paths beckon." For us, it is equally the case that earlier routes are harked back to and retraced. Cavell: "Picking up Bergson's idea of the comic as the encrusting or the obtruding of the mechanical or material onto or out of the living, we might conceive of laughter as the natural response to automatonity when we know the other to be human." Skepticism is, then, the reverse: "In that case it would follow from the absence of our laughter in the face of the impression or imagination of automatonity in others that we do not know others to be human." This is to say that Bergson's sense of laughter, as inducing an almost mechanical reaction to an already degraded human fullness, is symmetrically matched by skepticism's eroded confidence in the lived world.

But the question still hangs in the rarefied air between ontology and ethics: how does this reversal overlap with our separate effort to align Bergson on the rejected material discontinuity of film and Bergson on the mechanical reductiveness of comedy (the denaturalizing joke on page and stage well before screen)? And how might this alignment be enhanced by putting Cavell on the dubieties of skepticism (and its automatonization of the other) together with Cavell on the undenied machinic basis of film? Only examples can, in the long run, negotiate. And an enforced if staggered continuity is often the weft of their sequencing. Chaplin in *Modern Times* is explicitly engorged by the industrial apparatus, to become not a cog in its wheeling engines, nor just grit in its machine, but spasmodic grist for the mill of its productive slapstick visualization. Keaton in *Sherlock Jr.* converts random things of the outer world to tools for his extravagant use, even while becoming a kind of instrumental body himself, a mere link in the mechanics of transit. Split from within screen manifestation like one of their own blatant verbal puns, together Olson and Johnson in *Hellzapoppin'* get caught between frames not as people, with any credible agency to correct the automatism, but as photogrammic snags in its serial aggregation.

My subsequent study, *Cinesthesia* (2021), is certainly no stranger to these defamiliarizing views of the human body on screen in later avant-garde video, where the tone shifts from comic travesty to an often deadpan medial investigation.

> 17 / In *Cinesthesia: Museum Cinema and the Curated Screen* (caboose, 2020, distributed as Kindle text by Indiana University Press), Stewart studies the effects of the moving image as it enters the art-historical context of museum display. His first e-book publication allows for dozens of color images to complement an account of "curated" screen artifacts over the last six decades, from 16mm loops to CCTV montage. Placing individual works under close formal and cultural analysis, and in steady dialogue with each other, Stewart "reads" this aggregate gallery not just as a set of intrinsic experimental ventures but as medial challenges both to their parent forms and genres (theatrical film, broadcast TV) and to the contemplative aesthetic of museum *looking* (rather than viewing). Exemplified by nearly thirty artists, including Christian Marclay, Tacita Dean, John Akomfrah, Rodney Graham, John Stezaker, Alfredo Jaar, and Matej Krén, the kinetics of watching are found in this way, repeatedly and often ironically, to reroute or even derange—and ultimately to reform—the apprehending gaze.

17 / Museum Screens

Cinesthesia: Museum Cinema and the Curated Screen (2021)

In this (my first) e-book, with the adjustable scale of its illustrations, I was able to do far more justice to visual quality—and with many more images—than ever before. The title was, of course, more than a homophonic double of sensorial transfusions in literary language, instead putting implied pressure on the root of syn/cine-*esthesia*. Per the dictionary, but understood here on something of a sliding scale: "a capacity for sensation or feeling; sensitivity." When the organs of perception brought to ordinary museum experience are differently recruited by time-based imaging, with or without the further continuum of sound, one is newly primed for a "sensitivity" to "sensation" itself. Then, too, the *syn*esthetic regularly maps with the *cine*matic when we are prone to feel "through" different senses—responding to a grating backlight, a spacious chord change, a thunderous zoom, a heartrate-elevating "static" long shot. This syn/cine sensation was an emphasis incidentally redoubled for its author, in turn, in the full esthesis of optic perception, as I was working for the first time with exclusively electronic exemplification—even with artifacts not necessarily born digital—involving a newly varied sensorium of adjustable frame and resolution in the Kindle format.

And yet by the nature of these often experimental—and densely conceptualist— works, as much elucidation was incumbent on my pages as on museum plaques next to the works themselves. I'll give one illustration here, the book's first, of such motion-picturing under noncommercial auspices—a composite video by Christian Marclay (b. 1955). Its typical need for an explanatory paratext in the "advertising" of its intent will then send me back—in this last snippet of allegorized autobiography—to my own early days in the hand-set promotion of the commercial screen image, this as high school arranger of weekly marquees at my local theater. I approach that subheaded flashback with the self-partitioning TWO | PLIED graphics used throughout *Cinesthesia*—and precisely by association with an intrinsic interplay in (again) the "transmediation" at stake in so many of the pieces I catalogue and gloss. In this excerpt I'm first comparing Marclay's *The Clock* (2010) to Douglas Gordon's (b. 1966) famously decelerated *24 Hour Psycho* (1993).

> **TIME | PIECES** [...] More popular yet with museum goers than this retardation of Hitchcock, such "viewers" become actual mesmerized "audiences" in attendance at Marclay's *The Clock* (2010)—also running continuously for the same 24 hours as Gordon's *Psycho*, though often with controlled admission to spaces with limited seating. Marclay's work inverts the granular analytic of Gordon's film to a hypermontage instead. It does so, across a vast narrative data bank, by cutting from one film to the next whenever a piece of dialogue or a wristwatch glimpsed within the narrative space, and more commonly desk or wall clock, registers the numeric index of real extra-narrative time (the coterminous time of gallery display), with shots so carefully synchronized that they often jump cut on the abrupt advance of the minute hand. As with Gordon's *Psycho*, Marclay's reduction of narrative to mere temporal process serves to implode the distinction, famously promulgated by philosopher Gilles Deleuze, between the movement-image and the time-image, with motion in *The Clock* narrowed to mere temporal calibration. In this way, under the titular spell of Marclay's grammatically singular assemblage, separate instances of each clockwork mechanism within the screen frame offer a synecdochic comment on the film itself as an eponymous machine of raw synchronicity, where narrative duration is splintered and respliced, inverted in its usual dominance over screening time, leveled to equivalence with an exorbitant, round-the-clock display.
>
> **OVER | KILL** [...] Nearly a decade later, an arresting gallery venture by Marclay offers an inversion of this inversion. Where he had once intercut, as if on an accelerated treadmill, a corpus of work, including many Hitchcock thrillers, one of which Gordon had slowed to a snail's pace, Marclay has since reversed emphasis and let the normal screening time of narrative operate its own effacement of plot. In his latest impacted composition, the constraint aesthetic of the pastiche has given way to a quite differently constrained palimpsest, occluding the very images it accumulates. In this 2019 work premiered at the Venice Biennale, *48 War Movies* produces a vertigo effect: a kind

of stabilized track-zoom gestalt, though with no supervening camera movement outside the overlain commercial narratives. The full screen version of one arbitrarily chosen war film, once overprinted with the slightly smaller dimensions (though identical format) of the next, and so on, all in color Blu-ray release in the same aspect ratio, develops a nested layering that seems ultimately to recess rather than accrete the last of the laminates. That final kinetic rectangle—smallest in scale, and thus dropping away from its otherwise foregrounded claims on the eye—is the only full-frame war film we glimpse, yet it is functionally invisible in its tiny lozenge of blur.

In one of the myriad if-onlys that have laced my way through this re/view of irrevocably printed work, I do wish I had stressed here—in Deleuzian terms perhaps, but one way or the other—how anything like the "action-image" in these war films, these "action thrillers," is blocked by the fact that the cramped stack of video feeds, apex forward (what I meant by the subtitle OVER | KILL), makes nothing visible, nothing legible at all, except a thin rectangular border of kinetic fuss around the dropped-back edges. It's my thinking about this jammed file of digital movie files, in the political irony of their repetition, that leads discussion back to the long parade of films I (over)saw—in their scheduled recurrence befitting the movie house business model—as a teen theater employee.

> The result is a *mise-en-abyme* of choreographed violence, with all diegetically rendered motion discernible only in rectangular bands around the edges of the next enframed (superimposed) scene, terraced in an abyss of iteration like the eternal recurrence of war itself. Here clustered popular entertainments in the spectacle of violence, culled from the archive of theatrical exhibition, enter the gallery not one at a time, but all at once. Thus bombarding each other's optical planes, Marclay's war movies capture only the ambient noise and threatening motility of the mayhem their genre is named for, not its individual motives, plot agents, or dramatic vistas. In the process— and chaos—of recession, each of the four dozen titles plays itself out at different lengths, the palimpsest thus disintegrating, fraying in layers, near the end of its formulaic second hour.
>   All told, and with no separate tales visible, the very category of "war film," reduced to image trace rather than tracked narrative, suffers abject defeat at the hands of its own collective status. Its instances manifested as four dozen screen treatments in mutual eradication, the resulting cacophony of image is a kind of genrecide. Vying for distinction, the individual screen narratives lose their power in the impacted and cramped visual field. Video overprinting undermines any dramatic representation. All sound and fury without focus or direction, the thick of battle emerges—or is submerged—as merely

a dense laminate of image. The very "theater of war" is rendered dysfunctional. Such is, of course, the optical rewrite so common in the museum reuse of big screen spectacle, where some tacit antithesis feels lifted to view: here the distinction between widescreen breadth of image plane and something like a flattened ethic of depth. It may look, at first glance, like imagery has penetrated to some elusive core—when it is only slapping on more of the same at gradually reduced scale, more of its proliferating war pic representations. The 3-D illusionism of Renaissance perspectival formats so directly inherited by cinema (with their own incidental debts to ballistic geometry)—whereby the optical vanishing point drops away behind the image, whose angles converge to turn planes into space—may be thought radically reversed here. What results is a *trompe l'oeil* telescoping of overlain rectangles into a stair-stepped illegible access to some putative—yet punningly "superficial"—stratum beneath. Beyond the optical violence and disorientation provoked in this way, all the while making war on the motorized panoramas of violence itself, few ingenuities of conceptual video, apart from their immediate thematic charge, could point up more dramatically the serial consumption of commercial cinema by contrast with this travestied gallery "digest." File, alternately, under WARRING | PICTURES.

Further, for all of Marclay's conceptual originality and technical finesse in this "single-channel video," battles not dissimilar are waged across many of the works to come, pivoted around inferred binary options either abrogated or exacerbated. And not always obvious to sheer visual response. What you see isn't all you get. Percept again requires conceptual discourse in order to "get the picture." Almost literalized by overlay in Marclay, opacity is regularly a sales pitch for the catalogue essay. Or at least a call for paragraphs of exegesis—where explication is by nature complication—*in pages like this*. But we should first back up for a wider (and longer) view before zeroing in again on contemporaneous installations. One way to be "ushered" into the contest of modalities within time-based media is through the coming foyer of exhibition history in the dissemination of commercial screen narrative—including my own teenage labors in the cinematic service industry when read into evidence as a routine (which is the whole point) example. [...]

"Ushered" into the museum by such preliminaries, did I say? The metaphor is indeed drawn from my own, at the time, unwitting backstory as image critic: namely, my high-school night job as just such an usher in a one-screen local theater [the aging movie House of this beleaguered but surviving Usher]. I dwell on this long-established dwelling place for the moving image to make clear how the difference between going to the movies, as I grew up with them, and experiencing moving-image objects, as gallery culture grew into them, is the difference between night and day. Not just between full darkness and the typical gallery blend of natural and track light, but between traditional times of exhibition: the evening screening at local theaters and, opening hours variable, the daytime gallery notice of one or another wall screen next to the Pop lithograph or Dada collage. There is, of course, given the digital outmoding of hands-on celluloid projection and its reel changes, an escalation and increasing overlap of screening times at the multiplex itself, movies often available all day—from late morning till after midnight. You can now catch a feature film before some museums have even opened their doors. Yet the scheduled temporality of the movies as popular entertainment, as narrative vehicle, has retained its distinction from continuously available gallery images.

Night and day, too, the difference in perceptual encounter. As you take it in, mainstream film is made to take you in as well. By scale alone, it is engrossing—and has labored to be more and more so with the passing decades. I can retrace first-hand, given my own early fascination with "image quality," most of the major changes in postwar projection, including the closing of the grand movie palaces—and vast screens—familiar from my early metropolitan childhood, before outposting to a one-theater town. Including, too, in terms of technique, the fading away of a postwar aesthetic of deep-focus in the gripping chiaroscuro of black and white, the gradual dominance of color in its various palettes and saturations from one process to another, as well as the screen's widening (Cinemascope) and subdividing (Cinerama) and curving (anamorphic Todd-AO), all with the motive of engulfment in the accompanying resolution race leading from the latter's 65 mm through the sideways expansion of the 70 mm frame for IMAX all the way down to, long since the advent of digital rather than celluloid projection, the dawn of a sporadic (still rarely available) 4K 3D process (120 fps rather than 24 fps) in, for instance, Ang Lee's latest experiments [see *Billy Lynn's Long Halftime Walk*, 2016].

INDUSTRY | SERVICE [...] In such a retraced evolution of the commercial medium, my memory can't help but also traverse the actual theater aisles of my first early employment. It's important, at least for me, to remember that dedicated topography, amid a standardized architecture of display, in thinking ahead—and instead (against its archetype)—about moving images attended to in passing (rather than movies attended) along the walls of gallery space. The fact that my unskilled service work was serving an industry I was also coming to think of, striving to think about, and would years later begin to write about, as engineering an art form: this certainly reflects (upon) one aspect of the museum film in its theatrical prehistory. At the formative stage of my high school viewing life, long before I had ever encountered museum video, I lived and breathed commercial cinema—breathed its electrified diegetic air, to be sure, but also its industrial room fresheners. I was caught up equally in the general crowd appeal of popular cinemas as well as in the testy special pleading of its actual customers, night after night—all this as so-called usher and refreshment-stand flunky at the lone beachside theater in the Southern California hometown of my uprooted teen years. While farther up the coast, Hollywood was turning out the features, I, a cog in the wheel, was employed in turning them over, week by week, if always a few weeks behind the buzz, and at the pace of a mere two shows per night, max, depending on length. Much of what this book, *Cinesthesia*, is about, concerning the coming of the curated rather than the marketed image, comes clear to me in remembering the contours, emotional as well as spatial, of that auditorium (as distinct from film-historical) experience. Too seldom was there enough free time, even after the concession stand closed, what with windexing and sweep-ups, to do more than sneak my head in to catch a favorite scene in a film I may already have elected to enjoy in its entirety on a night off. But it was the nature of that "in" that I'm out to remember now, not so much the on-screen as the in-house ambience that is so radically overthrown, and sometime so trenchantly rethought, by gallery film.

Except for morning janitorial services, such as they were, left to a crew I never met, I was expected to take up much of the other slack with a rotating (often rapidly alternating) set of chores. There were my flashlight-armed duties in the aisles and my alternating expertise at the popcorn machine (a misnomer, since the less than burstingly fresh offering came pre-packaged in giant brown-paper bags of the sort now familiar from yard-waste disposal, to be dumped on the sly beneath the broken popper in the familiar glass cabinet). Beyond these originally contracted obligations, I gradually, without official promotion or pay raise, became a jack-of-even-more-trades, not just ticket-taker but box-office vendor from its sidewalk booth, the firm paper tickets then resembling, in the days before credit cards and digital receipts, the perforated rolls at a state fair carnival, or to those predisposed, to frames of a cinematic reel—but requiring only one per film, no matter how popular the ride. As soon as customers had paid up, there always seemed two things to do at once—and I was expected to be cordially busy at everything, ludicrously suited in black with matching tie—everything except for counting the days' receipts, either from seats or treats. This was left to the surly manager, whose mood swings had the flavor of one-too-many from his not always discreet hip flask, and who was later removed by the owners for serial embezzlement. Yes, the movies were certainly a business, subject to frauds other than aesthetic only, but—my main point here—they were also a complex and entirely "manned" exhibition practice, enlisting, beyond the union-waged expert projectionist, an infrastructure of menials (and moving sentinels) to purvey and patrol their serial offerings at communal outlets.

Looking back now, I see that what was gainful in my earliest employment had little to do with the pittance dribbling out week-by-week in under-age wages. Profit was instead banked for such future professional labors as those of a cinema theorist concentrating on the epochal shift from plastic to electronic projection in the move from filmic to digital cinema. And other deferred gains are here cashed out in assessing a contrastive mode of exhibition practice in the urban gallery, one that emphasizes the specular per se over any narrative spectacle. My on-the-job training was, in this sense, of a different order altogether—and currency—than I realized at the time. In view of the present gallery investigation, as well as my previous books on cinema, I was an apprentice back then, not just a part-time employee. Hard won by light labor was the rooted sense of a commercial prototype for cinematic projection—technical, temporal, and spatial alike—precisely as a model to be obliquely veered from, or openly violated, by the kind of experimental video and other time-based conceptual art that, decades later, came to interest me. So that opening with a walk down memory lane, in its form as a theater aisle, is meant only to map the terrain of a former institutional given. Certainly, the anecdotal facets of this throwback episode are called up less in the mode of nostalgia than of screen historiography—even allegory. It is in this vein that my earliest work and my latest, my long-separated jobs as mercantile cinematic functionary and contemporary art commentator, interpret each other. They do so around a scenario, almost a parable, of production, distribution, publicity (and such paratexts as marquee lettering and lobby cards)—as well as around, and within, the architectonics of an exhibition space soon to be restructured in various ways, and electronically reengineered, quite apart from the importation of film and video into anthologized gallery offerings.

PALACE | PLACE [...] If you've never "been there," it may be a bit hard to picture the collective nature of the old-fashioned, narrow-seated, down-at-the heels local movie theater in the pre-mall era. And there is a sliding scale between "renovations" in this regard and innovations in the screen picture. Postwar Hollywood was operating for years in competition with the "small screen" of TV broadcast, of course, even as the latter's screens got larger over time. And as the formats of theatrical projection have been continually scaled up, wider and higher, so in fact have theater seats—so that, even if not fully reclining, or affording the latest "dine-in" options, they have become increasingly private pleasure pods in multiple time slots more-or-less niche-marketed and demographically marked, including expanded afternoon viewing times that favor the retired crowd. In the "old days," age and youth gathered together in the evening, with less to choose from, less to segregate them, and in this earlier puritanical moment, with less tolerance on the part of adult customers for undue intimacies right in their line of sight on low-backed, unraked, pre-stadium seats. Hence my inglorious job mandate: to keep things at least as minimally clean as the janitors did. That's why I incline to put scare quotes around my job description as "usher." True, with the rare big hit, I did sometimes need to help an adult couple find a vanishingly available pair of seats down front, or light the way for a wobbly patron returning from a restroom break. But mostly, flashlight in hand as optical cudgel, I was assigned to hush, chasten, or occasionally usher out kids of approximately my age who were either making noise or making out too demonstrably, whether the interruption was spoiling a technicolor exchange between Doris Day and Rock Hudson flirting on the telephone across split screens in *Lover Come Back* (1961) or the black-and-white harangue of Angela Lansbury plotting the communist overthrow of the US government in *The Manchurian Candidate* (1962). Needless to say, I patrolled the statistically younger crowd in the balcony less than expected by my boss, to preserve what was left of my teen dignity. But I *don't* digress: for beyond the pathetic nature of this disciplinary chore, there is the cinesthetic model at its core: the ready assumption of the private-in-public of theatrical immersion. No museum goers need crane their necks past necking couples on the sparse gallery benches of a black-box installation. The only making-out invited is to grope for orientation in the frequently oblique torrent of images—or their dilatory fixation.

Visually rather than morally, I was enough of a teenage purist, more than enough, to regret even momentarily distracting from the thrown light on screen with my flashlight beam, whether elucidating or punitive, enabling or castrating. My active intrusion upon "cinematic space" was even worse, certainly, than the passive embarrassment I always felt at that little shock of naked light bulb behind the fractured red plastic of the EXIT sign screen right, whose glare ate away, to my perfectionist eye, at the sheen of the screen prints, which, by the time the films reached us, were never exactly in mint condition anyway. And there's another factor of imperfect viewing hard to reconstruct for the digital generation. With the odd flecks, scratches, or splices (the lost poignant vulnerability of celluloid!), nothing was ever mint crisp. Maybe that's why the manager never responded to my suggestions about fixing the exit sign. Who cares? It's all of a damaged piece. And broken plastic was the bane of my existence on another front as well—out front on the pre-LED-lit grooved slots of the do-it-yourself marquee, where the red and black oversized alphabet I had to work with had seen decidedly better days. Yet these marquee adverts were the main commercial interface between second-run bookings and audience alert. And this, too, in hindsight, has a curious way of pointing forward, from brick-and-mortar theaters to the smaller chambers of gallery exhibition. [...]

I recall the marquee work, in particular, for the way its minimalist "discourse" comes into tacit contrast with the annotation space assigned for gallery video, with full interpretive abstracts so often affixed alongside the inset image surface, the wall text covering more square inches at times than the DVD-transferred screen plane. "Descriptive" chores, for me then, were certainly more straightforward—however technically impaired by alphabetic shortfall—than are any of the supplemental analyses I'm taking upon myself to offer here in the case of gallery screens. The equivalent of the rarely settled-for artist and title these days, just two kinds of names were enough back then: star and title did the trick. Come rain (rare) or come shine (most days), on early afternoons before the new week's change-over, Wednesday in those years, out came the shaky ladder I'd climb to snap into place the letters, after having scrabbled together a credible subset from the damaged and shrinking stock, always seemingly short of the one character or two I wanted. Often in a hurry as I was, I would probably have settled, with some degree of fan's chagrin, for the likes of R. RUSSELL IN GYPSY so as not to squander too soon, on "Rosalind," the needed third "S" or second "L." It took a while, I'm sure, to find, later in 1962, a third intact G and K for the two-line blazoning of GREGORY PECK/TO KILL A MOCKINGBIRD, any association with nibbling beaks to be avoided by the requisite (if inconveniently trisyllabic) first name. And looking back now on this same busy Hollywood year, I wonder: could the lamentable Jeff Chandler "starrer" MERRILL'S MARAUDERS (with its own challenge to the stash of marquee R's), be one of those now-on-Blu-ray (surprisingly) color films indiscriminately included, for resolution and aspect ratio alone, in Marclay's unidentified *48 War Films*?

Proleptic happenstance aside, it was, in general, only the marquee's minimal up-front signage, the more red letters the better, that rolled out what was left of the proverbial red carpet at our second-run venue. Snap, slide, space—and by that evening, lights, camerawork, action. Any film's reputation having well preceded it, via national press in the wait for our local opening, my marquee chore was simply to announce the advent, in as few words as possible, of the movie I would eventually have to police. More to the point, then: lights down, action up—on the screen, if too often in front of it as well. But with no unnecessary fanfare, that switch-over of lighting before the screen came to life, that initial dimming before the onset of glow. Our theater did have a curtain, careworn red velvet, heavy and dank, but it was jammed—jammed open, luckily, and left that way, year after year, just a little sad plush still visible flanking the screen—as if our second-tier venue nodded to ceremony, at least in the form of faded glory, without expecting its clientele to be falsely wowed by the event factor of a screening reaching us only weeks after the LA first-run. The only modest foot put forward, besides the production stills in the glass display case street-side, were the posters on our lobby sandwich board, mutedly trumpeting next week's billing. Decades before internet had taken up that publicity burden along with the proliferating in-theater "trailers" whose on-line version the websites also link to (then called "coming attractions," or "previews" for short, and with far fewer of them front-loaded in those days), the marquee and the movie poster (the infamous grammatical violence of "The Birds is Coming" during my last summer on the job) shouldered the responsibility of advance word(s).

ATTRACTIONS | COMING [...] Things have certainly changed, venues included, and the discourse with them—and not least when images move before our eyes in spaces where traditionally it was only us moving past them. Once you take the kinetic image out of the neighborhood cavern, and social haven, of the single-auditorium movie house—or detach it from a later escalation beyond duplex to multiplex, where digital projection has been kept pace with by computer bloggers opining on every screen effect—and deliver it over to the dispersed circulatory system of gallery display, often truncating or looping it in the process, and leaving the vestigial theatrical curtain far behind (replaced by the darkening drapes that often block off a black-box projection space), the terms of presentation are decisively rewritten. All of a sudden, the wall placard becomes the ever-expanding equivalent of the marquee and press release at once, with curatorial data swelling exponentially in proportion to the more and more arcane conceptual inferences of the counterintuitive moving image. Or one may think of it (often forced to think hard about it) in a related way. It is as if movies, as resident aliens in the museum, have immediately become "foreign film," needing translation, with adjacent captions replacing superimposed subtitles. Viewers may often feel they are doing as much reading as looking in the contemporary gallery exhibition.

My own nightly roles as menial ticket taker up front and erotic sentinel inside, and then outdoors as minimal weekly publicist, bear scant relation to the museum docent or even gallery security guard, still less to the informed curatorial scribe of explanatory wall text. My services mark not a transition so much as a former dispensation, wholly overthrown on museal terms. Having traversed the historical and cultural distance between nightly showtimes and daily displays, from film as commercial product to a gallery-sanctioned aesthetics of its pictured motion, with numerous figures to illustrate the latter, in my next book, *The Ways of the Word* (2022), I move further away from theater screens to the kinetics of prose, yet concentrating there in considerable part on the paracinematic oscillations and overlaps of narrative writing.

> 18 / In ***The Ways of the Word: Episodes in Verbal Attention*** (Cornell University Press, 2021), Stewart departs from his sustained attachment to the rigors of literary and media theory to focus on the sheer pleasure of attentive reading, including the excitement of recognizing the play of syllables and words upon which much of the best literary writing is founded. Emerging out of a turn to teaching creative writing—in a broader effort to convene writers and critics—Stewart's "episodes in verbal attention" track the means to meaning through the byways of literary wording. Through close engagement with literary passages and poetic instances whose imaginative demands are their own reward, Stewart gathers exhibits from dozens of authors: from Dickens, Dickinson, and DeLillo to Whitman, Woolf, and Colson Whitehead. In the process, idiom, tense, etymology, and other elements of expressive language and their phonetic wordplay are estranged and heard anew. Though less embedded in theoretic debate than most of Stewart's monographs, this predominantly literary analysis makes perhaps an unexpected connection with his film scholarship in two final chapters devoted to the stylistics of "cinematographic" prose.

18 / Toward a Cinematographic Sentence

The Ways of the Word: Episodes in Verbal Attention (2022)

IN MY FOLLOWING OUT, BY TITLE, the asserted *Ways of the Word*, a return to George Orwell's classic diatribe against slack phrasing—ethically hijacked by clichés (like politics by unexamined ideology)—sends analysis forward to Colson Whitehead's satire of marketing diction, with all its portmanteau contrivances. His anonymous African American narrator in *Apex Hides the Hurt* (2006), a Madison Avenue hotshot, is called in as "nomenclature expert" to rebrand a modest township that was once founded by freed slaves.[5] His gradual facing up to this history thrusts his wording into a salient anticipation of Toni Morrison's at a similar climactic moment—each giving a new miniscule spin to Orwell's conjuncture of "Politics and the English Language." I pick up the argument at the point where it recalls yet again the transegmental syllabic ironies of *Reading Voices* (1990) and *The Deed of Reading* (2015), about which, see respectively above Phases II / 3 and V / 11.

> The novel's wordplay so closely anticipates the climax of Toni Morrison's *A Mercy* (2008), two years later, that Whitehead's verbal move shimmers as intertext. Morrison's 17th-century historical fiction about the Portuguese trafficking in human labor for the New World, before the American institutionalization of so-called "slavery," never

deploys that abstract noun for such bondage—except in its final defiance by cross-word phonetic irony. In the heroine's climactic speech, trying to break free with her own abrupt end-stops: "Slave. Free. I'll last." In Whitehead's millennial novel, set long since official emancipation, the portmanteau collapse—quite apart from any of his marketable ingenuities—runs (together) like this: "Before coloured, slave. Before sla*ve, free,*" the inescapable sounding of the *slavery* to come. Even for narrative discourse itself, it would seem hard to recover a memory free from the shadow (phonetic, ethical) of that curse, any "before" kept clear of its encroachment.

After this chapter on "Lexical Timelines, Phrasal Timings," I turn over discussion to the ironies of grammatical tense in narrative structure, from George Eliot to Kingsley Amis, followed by a chapter on the revelatory reading aloud of F. Scott Fitzgerald's prose in the off-Broadway play *Gatz* (2010). I move then, from stage to screen, in the following excerpts from a classroom-geared argument for the possibility of a "cinematic" prose, developing a scalar paradigm of "Fframe-advance" in comparing the narrative dynamism of the two media. Below I share details of the word's design as here proffered, but I want to note—as an invitation to further reflection—how the "Ff" signals two scales of frame-advance "action" occurring simultaneously. In the process of laying out this argument at the manuscript stage, I was asked by a referee at the press to address an obvious limit to this comparison, making clear that a sentence can be "reread" even in progress, whereas film is reeled past inexorably in its normal conditions of screening. I took up this suggestion with the following proviso when the topic was first introduced in the second chapter:

> In literature as well as film, parts are as serially determined as the whole. In making our way along the cognitive chain of meaning, phonetic lettering flashes past into gathering word forms even as these so-called parts of speech, one after another, cede syntactic space to a sometimes unexpected next-in line across the resting spots and run-ons of adjusted sense. This is the *drama* of writing— and its kinetic art: the never-stabilized ways of the word whose temporality cannot therefore be dissociated from the flicker effects of screen motion. The fact that the emergent screen image, the photogram-impacted gesture, can never be returned—in unaided ocular experience—to the file of cellular frames that induces it, whereas in prose a suspected syllabic echo in segue, or an ironic slippage between script and phonetic enunciation, can always be double-checked before spooling forward: this fact does not disable the transmedial comparison; rather, it can only help sharpen our sense of prose resources in in their cinematographic ambition.

Here, then, is a cut through the fuller discussion concerning the specifically cinematic *Ways of the Word*, bridging the closing two chapters—and including the undergraduate catalogue description that began it all (indented below under the "Not the Same Difference" subhead):

> At the dawn of the film medium, the cinematograph was a device for both record and retrieval in a single mechanism. Before the lens: light, camera, action, matched behind the aperture by their intermittent trace. Later, on the reverse s/trip to the screen within the same apparatus: spool, beam, projected motion. Any imagined cinematography of the sentence is a comparable recording of segmental sequences for the purposes of their own playback. On the page: letters, lexemes, sentences. In reading: phonemes, syllabic patterning, the syntax of sense. Centuries before film, at the dawn of the codex, the mechanics of vertical scrolling gave way, page by turned page instead, to the lateral unrolling of syntax alone, with no mechanical spooling. But celluloid cinema involves—is revolved as—its own kind of coiled scroll. And even after the digital revolution, post-filmic cinema depends at base on binary triggers driven by an algorithmic rather than alphabetic code—whose oscillating differentials have their counterparts, as with the filmic photogram, in the unfurling of lexical succession. Distant counterparts in each case, granted, even beyond the very different "visualization" involved in literature and cinema. And a distance not to be forgotten—since screen image is automatic (whether mechanical or electronic) and normally irreversible, whereas prose on the page is always individually paced in reception, forward and often back. But at the many ways this difference licenses such a comparison between movies and prose motion, rather than silencing it, these next two chapters are aimed.
>
> Their goal in moving between media is to find mobilized in verbal style the prose counterpart of cinema's twin frames: the big Frame of the moving screen picture together (always together) with the little frame of its composite photographic imprints, as those are subject to the traditional understanding of "frame-advance" in the spinning past of the celluloid reel in projection. Movies derive at base from the instantaneous replacement of these so-called photograms (and their pixel equivalents since) in generating the actual motion on which pictured movement depends. As with syllabic sequence in syntactic perception, within and across phrases and whole sentences, the two scales of "action" are in fact all but simultaneous—and functionally inseparable. Hence my heuristic typography for the momentum at play and at stake in each "time-based" medium: Fframe-advance. [...]
>
> When one entertains it, the literary equivalent of this overall narrative field is the discursive *frame of reference* in any one textual

passage, mounted of course on the internal struts and frets of the prose *framework*. In my composite coinage, such, again, is the structuring Fframe-advance in literary as well as screen fiction. In process, in procession, it is in just this sense that the projected rectangular image or shot (F) subsumes its optic increments on the strip, its photogram frames (f), the way a syntactic span (S) does the amassing syllabic units (s) of its grammar, one lexical unit advanced after another. [...] Subsuming the spooled band of a celluloid image track to the perceptual thread of action on screen, what could otherwise be designated as the F/film distinction—with the moving image riding on, overriding, the individual filmic cell—can be productively correlated with a similar tiered process in the act of narrative writing. And its reading. Alphabetic characters disappear into phonemes into syllables into words in the phrasing of characterization or plot.

Beyond this generalization, in conjuring with the idea of a *particularly* cinematic sentence, or with its possibility at least, no priority need be given to authors who have made film's "universal language" a signature feature of their style, beginning famously with the montage aesthetic of post-Cubist modernism in a writer like John Dos Passos, or in a different way, penetrating to the skids of word-formation itself, in James Joyce or Gertrude Stein, including verbal channels of jagged seriality in everything from alphabetic flicker effects to jump-cut clauses. Given the punctual linkage of word forms under sudden duress in such writing, strange surprises are pried loose from conflicted lexical junctures. These impacted syllabic segues or cross-fades flare into observation by analogy with precisely the variable tracks of that defining cinematic Fframe-advance. [...]

Freeze-Fframe for a moment in this retrospect, if I may: may pause for yet another such postmortem, that is, and may put it just this eccentric way once more. The actual stop-action image in celluloid cinema would in fact best be rendered, in my typography, as a Fffffffffreeze: the screen frame holding tight as the photograms iterate into simulated fixity. Which brings me to something like an opposite understanding—though equally relevant—of my chosen term and its alphabetic emblem. The press reader wanting me to spell out the different temporalities of the cinematic continuum over against the available backtracks of prose sequence didn't go on to query the double fricative of my spelling, but I've been asked since if I meant by it—which I didn't, or hadn't until then—an actually *pronounced* rather than elided alphabetic doubling, as if by loose analogy with the familiar "F/X" rebus, namely, the enactive frictional stutter of "EFF-frame," an evinced flicker effect in its own over-enunciated right. Now, many of my meditated addenda in this volume do amount to corrective adden-duhs, belated if-onlys when not downright my-bads. But in this case I all along wanted to make a quite different point: about the little frame imperceptibly (say silently) subordinated by multiplication to the big, an indistinguishable continuum. But that doesn't keep me from wishing I had raised the alternative reading, which frankly never occurred to me, not to rule it out but to install it—since it could well come to the mind of others—as the flip side of the same perceptual gestalt, its complement and confirmation.

Not the Same Difference

In tracking, comparatively, the reigning time-based media of modern narrative production, there is no ignoring their divergent modes of timing per se—automatized on screen, voluntary for the prose reader. For just this difference (in their differential pulse) is the reason, in a book like this, for the comparison in the first place: the better to know the powers of the latter in regard to the former, prose sensed anew in the equally discontinuous light—but mechanized and irreversible stride—of motion picturing. [...] On the score of such ingrained narrative momentum, the point isn't that one reads the increments of prose the way one watches the flux of cinema, even when the latter is facilitated at the elective pace—and pause—of home video. Beyond the everyday nature of skimming and skipping in the waywardness—or tactical willfulness—of the reading eye, including its quick recuperative returns to the flow of sentence and sense, prose invites its quite distinct forms of doubling back: through echoes, second thoughts, mental addenda, disruptive undertones, what have you. It does all this in a very different way from the cognitive hiccups or segues—call them the disjunct visual tissue—sent to the screen by the motored pulsations of montage.

On this generalized model of translation (or, better, transposition) from one medium to another, any notion of functional exchange—for the experimenting student writer, for instance, as in examples to follow, testing out some movie-like moves in wording—begins in a distinct mode of analysis whose intensity *is itself transferable*. When approximating the cinematic in narrative sentencing—say, the observant seriality of the tracking shot, the magnified emphases of the close-up, the iterative fixation of the freeze-frame, the variably timed cadenza of the fadeout, or the doubling overlay (and potential ambiguity) of superimposition—the point, far from exact equivalence, is that any effort at devising approximate ingenuities in prose would serve to disclose, and maximize in action, their own intrinsic medial grain. And this is vividly the case in the creative reading of prose as well as its creative writing. Ranging, under close enough attention, anywhere from the scale of a "jump cut" between paragraphs to a recursive "loop effect" of anaphoric syntax, the act of *thinking cinematically* about prose fiction becomes its own unique method of *verbal* close looking. So that, at the narrowest scope in the phasing of sequence, even a flickering surprise of phonetic juncture—whether or not elicited on the page by visible alphabetic cross-over, or just summoned by silent enunciation—can, under scrutiny, or just simply underway, ring not merely reverberant but narratively true. And, in so doing, can achieve its productive cognitive skid at roughly the same relative scale—minimal, constitutive, primal—as effects deriving from the jammed or accelerated frame advances of the optic strip. [...]

None of this has anything to do with writing for the movies, nor (or at least not much) with imitating their narrative materials in story form, but rather with seeing filmic sequence as itself a mode of inscription that may harbor lessons for prose composition. Film is a "writing with movement," it has been famously said (by philosopher Jean-François Lyotard)—or elsewhere a mode of *camera stylo* (by film theorist Alexandre Astruc): inscriptive, authorial. Conversely, but still comparatively, style in literature can be characterized as a *movement in writing*, where words are released or throttled, shoved ahead or bent back on themselves, in the momentum of sentencing. How does one respond to this in appreciative reading, test for its lessons, attend the inner energy of its kineto-graphic force? To ask this is only provisionally to demarcate one minor facet of literary response, to be sure, but one which may have an unexpected medial yield in any writer's (or reader's) striven-for acclimation to the intricacies and grip, the sweep and flash, of prose disclosure. [...]

Parallels in this zone of transmedial comparison need a good degree of latitude, though not laxity, to be useful. Or put it the other way round—in the form of nagging uncertainties regarding a contemplated or boldly posited filmic equivalent for a given linguistic effect: Is that verbal maneuver really more like a match cut than a cross-fade? Doesn't that grammatical disruption or impasse, that choked-off rhythm, still feel more like rapid fade-out than stop-action? These hesitations locate the very point. The fact that there are no strict counterparts between medial devices is what most suggestively tests—along an always tentative, and instructively restless, axis of comparison—the uniqueness of the language event. Such is always the generative drama of wording in making (its way to) meaning—whether in the looping or jam-up of syllables, the parallelism of phrasing, the junctures of punctuated syntax, let alone the lexical cast of "image" in the literary mode of figuration. And here again the closely related caveat. In regard to the healthy looseness of alignment between phonics, diction, and syntax, on the one hand, cinematic engineering on the other, it is crucial to insist—for this mode of stylistic rather that contextual analysis—that the writers taken up for study don't have to have seen movies, or even to have written in an age when that would have been possible. [...]

How would this stance, though, help teach not stories, but "writing" itself, inscription, across media? And why? Why, that is, take this line of approach? In my case—full disclosure—it was and is partly, and tactically, because my university's English department had mounted a new Creative Writing major, limiting the number of elective courses in "literature and culture" that could be offered by a dwindling faculty. In order to teach cinematic analysis on a par with literary study as part of a culture of narrative expectations and medial formats, as I had repeatedly done, but in a way that would help meet and staff our new course demands, it occurred to me that I could float such lessons in a way that might directly appeal to apprentice writers in an age of dominant visual literacy. So here is the description that went up on the department website under that loaded lectographic title "Reading Movies for Prose Writers":

> This class will concentrate on the rhetorical and structural strategies, and nuances, of narrative cinema, both filmic and digital, as they might be productively mapped onto student ventures in narrative writing. Direct address and other ironies of "the fourth wall"; the syntax of parallel montage, ellipsis, jump cuts, matches on action, dissolves, cross-fades, and superimpositions; flashbacks and flash-forwards; the closural grammar of freeze-frame and iris-out; plus the broader management of frame tales, depth of field, objective and subjective POV, other varieties of focalization and the optic equivalents of free indirect discourse—all this, as well as the potential yield of metatextual reflexes in the mode of self-commenting narration, will guide our investigations into established film techniques (always with ears to the ground for their verbal equivalents). Screen examples will range, in a variety of clips and full screenings, from silent screen comedy through the classic genres of detective noir and sci-fi to the genre-bending experiments of European high modernism and its influence on the so-called New American Cinema, including the latter's aftermath in the offbeat narrative strategies of certain indie productions and the recent trend in hypermediated laptop and Facebook narration, where silent film intertitles may be thought to resurface in formats related to electronic text messaging. The main focus will be on mastering the structure of screen storytelling—as a "reading competence" in its own right. But examples of cinematographic borrowings or parallels in major literary fiction, as well as essays commenting on them, will also be discussed in conjunction with frequent brief writing assignments meant to experiment with—from scratch or in revision of students' previous work—the potential dynamic advantages of a cinematic prose.

"A cinematic prose": whatever that is. In the first iteration of the course, I leave it for the enrolled students to ask, or to find out for themselves, slowly but—with luck—surely. Apparent from the start, though, whatever such prose might amount to, any viable sense of a kinetic writing would have to do with how word order—within the whole order of words—moves us to mold and pace our literary response from one unit of perception or conception to the next, spurs our cognitive production of the described scene in its unfolding phases, often involving their own irregular intervals of grammatical reaction time. Though far removed from any professional goal of writing for the movies, the point is to see how writing moves. [...] Such, then, where and when one comes upon—or construes—it, is none other than the cinematographic sentence. It is a unit of assumed (say provisional) authorial intent brought to the uncurtained display of its time-based content from the private theater balcony—and strategic mental vantage point—of sequenced audiovisual response: the perch of appreciative purchase in the headspace of materialization, of visualization, of temporal immersion. So, it can't hurt to say again that none of this has anything to do with writing screenplays, only with the play of images on screen: moving pictures in their relation to grammatical momentum, an energy inherent to prose in any period, from the hand of writers as different as Dickens, who knew no movies, and Faulkner, who wrote for them. Such is the spectrum of my in-class examples—and here in this chapter as well. Analysis moves deliberately between committedly cinéaste authors and earlier stylists with no plausible thought to automated image projection in the motions their prose inscribes even while describing.

Having illustrated the cinematic in a novelist like Thomas Hardy, writing for much of his career before the invention of cinema, the chapter then steps ahead to the mid-century—and beyond, into illustrations from the recent work of Jonathan Franzen—before returning to the pre-screen cinematographics of Herman Melville.

Syntactic Time-Lapse

If nothing privileges twentieth-century writers in claims for a cinematographic style, certainly nothing should argue against recognizing such effects when they happen to seem spilling over by lexical or syntactic association from explicit cinematic allusions, let alone when recruited to describe the medium itself in operation. Certainly, with few consequences for the actual technique of prose, many a novel may call up cinema as its cultural context or backstory. But sometimes the rubber of allusion hits the road of representation with an unexpected traction. In Vladimir Nabokov's deliberate prosecution of cinema among the pop cultural subtexts for *Lolita*, some devices of rhetorical irony are explicitly lifted from film, or interpolated into the text as cinematic asides. When Lolita happens to pause in front of a "rogues' gallery" of wanted posters in her narrator's pedophile road trip with her across the American landscape, Humbert's *projected* identification is unmistakable: "If you want to make a movie out of my book," he says to an anonymous reader in breaking the fourth wall that prose fiction in fact shares with film, "have one of these faces gently melt into my own, while I look." The fluid internal variables of syllabification in that effortless adverbial transition, in the modest assonance of "gently melt" and its equally fluid chiasm (*tl/lt*), hardly constitute, even as they contribute to, the blurred superimposition otherwise evoked: a histrionic lap dissolve that—to speak anachronistically—would *morph*, or say transmute, Humbert into the spitting image of a criminal deviant. And in his own as well as Lolita's eyes—and given the author's or narrator's proposed cross-dissolved cinematic manifestation, ours too. But sometimes the imitative filmic syntax waxes more dramatic than in the spectral delicacy of "gently melt." Sometimes—make that often—and even elsewhere in this one novel.

    The explicit filmic touch of dissolving face recognition, as it were, in those wanted posters has recently been compared to another, less explicit, cinematic nod in this same novel—but with no further comment on the technics of prose that convey it. Amid the narrator's many overt allusions to star cults, Hollywood screen images, genres, and camera movements, this later and more specifically *filmic* call out—also guilt-driven, and ridden all the way to parody as such—involves Humbert's mordant take on the unmentioned mechanism, not of screen editing in general, but of the inset "montage" compendium of classic narrative film. The borrowed device is tacitly deployed in an accelerated distillation of an unachieved future in the star-is-born mode. Humbert realizes that, without his damaging presence, Lolita, with her fine tennis form, might well "have become a real girl champion." The internal filmic montage in question: "Dolores, with two rackets under her arm, in Wimbledon. Dolores endorsing a Dromedary. Dolores turning professional. Dolores acting a girl champion in a movie." Such juxtaposed images of Humbert's imaginary flash-forward are serial, exponential, and in every case mediated by the publicity "vehicle" of screen dissemination in quick-cut biographical acceleration. If this isn't a close technical approximation of classic time-lapse, in its preternatural speeding-up of the frame rate itself, it certainly does leaf through the frames of a life-not-lived—and does so in a manner derived from the precinematic flip-book so often rehearsed in elliptical screen narratives of this sort. Each "period," each punctuated epoch, marks a counterfactual narrative phase in itself, spanning between episodes of celebrity ascent—and resembling in turn a kind of newspaper montage of captioned photos tracing the juggernaut of fame. In this brand of condensation, fragmentation argues the forged continuity of the unstoppable.

With the mass-media paradigm perfectly understated—and understood—in its stylistic blatancy, no reader could process this without sensing the editorial work extruded by the prose itself. But to further the transmedial *sensibility* to which such recognition might lead in a student's rhetorical arsenal, some closer parsing of this *Lolita* passage is advised. Disjoint syntactic cameos are set in motion at first by a mere noun phrase ("Dolores ... at Wimbledon"), its modification set off by commas, but then further animated from this snapshot logic to something more, beyond implied newspaper coverage, like the sweep and shuffle of newsreel footage—entirely unspoken but syntactically phrased—on the way to an actual fiction film ("a girl champion in a movie"). Hollywood is both the model of the prose and its incarnate destiny. In each of these later moving-image glimpses, the action is conveyed by participial progression in what amounts to a "reframed" absolute construction (a grammarian's category for the collocation of noun and verb but with no predicated tense structure, as in "Dolores endorsing ... Dolores turning ... Dolores acting"), all in this case part of the onward spread and fallout of fame. The cross-sectioned slices of this snowballing celebrity come to rest only with the break from the participial cinematics of those progressive absolutes, those autonomous serial film clips in mass audience release, when reverting to the slack compound grammar of another snapshot-like fixed frame—and eliciting there a final alliterative fantasy of sports star and her legalized marital trainer: "Dolores and her gray, humble, hushed husband-coach, old Humbert." The very salience of that iterative syllabic wording, with exactly the kind of palpable phonetic drift (and deflation) unavailable to film optics, is symptomatic. The montage aesthetic is caught ceding deliberate ground again not just to the fixed-frame two-shot but to a huffing phonetic excess that—hard on the heels of those jump-cuts into eventualities unachieved—reaches through, reaches back and down, to the insinuated undersong of prose itself. Dolorous in all its lost possibilities. To summarize otherwise: the planar negotiation of tense is exactly the malleable stratum of representation that is both maximized and collapsed in the cinematics of temporal condensation, even without an actual fast-forward time-lapse.

In the relation of prose to the edited and projected film image, or its video derivatives, imitation may be one form of flattery, but it need be no more sincere than it seems in certain satiric treatments—as there in Nabokov's black-comic send-up of media notoriety in headlined, or otherwise visually newsworthy, escalation. Catching the tone of such writing, along with the technical allusion, is crucial. A recent scholarly book on America's dream of literary "immediacy" in writing's contest with emerging media, from photography to video, makes note of the way Robert Coover's account of precipitously dashed hopes, in his famous story "The Babysitter" [1969], explicitly travesties—and in ways worth examining more closely—the happily-ever-after montage of a movie broadcast or its derivative in Hollywood-trained TV editing. Watch it wash past, as the babysitter does, if only out of the corner of her eye, when noticing "a man ... singing a love song on the TV": "He loves her. She loves him. They whirl airily, stirring a light breeze." In its quick-cut, then perhaps cross-fade, logic, think of these short sentences from Coover as beginning with a shot/reverse shot treatment of some screen couple's loving gazes, yielding place to dreamy two-shots of their ongoing bond. But in that romantic twirl, whether in small-screen movie replay or directly pillaged technique, more is spun round than their magnetized bodies: "They whirl airily, stirring a light breeze," where even that whoosh of internal rhyme (*irl / airil / irr*) impels, with an extra giddy flurry, the remaining images. The montage goes so far—from all credibility—as to close with the noun "wisp" transfigured to an ersatz, kitschy, and illicit verb form, as fake as its evoked effect amid this kinesis of embodied romance in "a landscape of rose and emerald and deep blue"—where "her light brown hair coils and *wisps* softly in the breeze." No such verb, no such believable event. In contrast, for the woman employing the babysitter, an ensuing fast-forward replay of her own life shatters the sedate grammar of uplift into fragments (or fast-forwards) of erosive decline: "He loves her. She loves him. And then the babies come. And dirty diapers and one goddamn meal after another. Dishes. Noise. Clutter. And fat." The discrepant teleology of "fat" added as temporal effect to the ongoing pressure of mealtime chores answers to the capstone artifice of the preceding screen musical, a sylleptic phrasing that immerses the hero "in" his own outflow across the separately ironized manifestation of something like "vocal sincerity" when, instead, in forked phrasing, "He smiles in a gushing crescendo of sincerity and song." I had said above, regarding Nabokov's syntactic irony and its montage "condensation," that "fragmentation" of that sort "argues the forged continuity of the unstoppable." As of course it does, too, in the swifter precipitation of Coover's second, antithetical montage of biographical decline.

Across these contrasted passages in Coover, paradigm and parody are slammed together in an unmistakable node of debunked media clichés shared by film and TV.

This is the same Coover who, a decade and a half after this landmark story, will turn to more explicit versions of "montage" manipulation, and to even subtler, less explicit equivalents in their prose conjuration, for the opening chapter of *A Night at the Movies*. Called "The Phantom of the Movie Palace," this tour de force passage unfurls one absurdist gesture after another in ways that double, quite incidentally, for a useful classroom checklist of cinematic techniques—and in some cases their mimetic phrasal equivalents. There, a lone projectionist in an abandoned theater mixes reels and projectors, "creating his own split-screen effects, montages, superimpositions," with that unpunctuated series netting something of the disjunction and overlap it rushes to sum up. Similarly: "Or he uses multiple projectors to produce a flow of improbable dissolves, startling sequences of abrupt cuts and freeze-frames like the stopping of a heart, disturbing juxtapositions of slow and fast speeds, fades in and out ...," where that last pair of technical terms is, one might say, superimposed upon (almost mimetically) with a fleeting present-tense sense of the compound phrasal verb *to fade in and out*. Sometimes "thick collages" show car crashes and battling soldiers, cowboys, gangsters and "mating lovers" all, in the narrator's sexual pun, "banging away in unison." And sometimes it is only sound collage that the projectionist attempts, when he "leaves the projector lamps off altogether and just listens"—as we do to his own phonic recurrences, verging on the onomatopoeia of plop and shriek, in "the sounds of bl*obs* and ghouls, ro*bots*, gall*op*ing hooves and s*cree*ching tires, c*reak*ing doors, s*creams* ...." And in a further test of our eared attention, there is a final paced run of ellipses—"fists hitting faces and bodies pavements, arrows targets, rockets moons"—that seems again to volatilize noun forms ("targets," "rockets") toward the flash of inoperable phantom verbs.

After analyses of writers from Willa Cather and William Faulkner down through my increasing focus on contemporary American fiction, from Coover and Don DeLillo to Richard Powers, I come to a remarkably cinematic moment in Jonathan Franzen's 2015 novel *Purity* that is found, in action, circling back to the early taxonomy of extinction's several narrative displacements in *Death Sentences* (1984; see Phase I / 2).[6] In what thus amounts to a concentrated "narratographic" fashion, it is a moment in prose so cinematic that it is also grippingly linguistic. For, as I might have said below, the pivotal phasing at issue ("before it was over and pure nothing")—tapping a grammatical irony that has fascinated me from Shakespeare to Pope, Austen and Dickens forward—turns once more, and yet again even in these pages, on what amounts to a terse and morbid syllepsis. How could I have left that unspecified? Overriding this as a mere rhetorical question, let me rise to the delayed occasion by asserting how the very lack of terminology proves its own point about a linguistic effect always arrestingly cleft but still often elusive, however you decide to bookmark or tag it.

A more widely heroized version of Julian Assange in Franzen's plot, the brilliant German hacker guru and political leaker Andreas Wolf, holed up at his mountain-rimmed compound in Bolivia, is consumed—in the penultimate volume of the novel, called "The Killer"—by the memory of an earlier brutal murder committed by him during his time in the former East Berlin, with the killer instinct now overmastering his personality to the point of a recognized suicidal drive. Eavesdropping on the world until this point, in an unchecked tech network of intercepted voices and their texts, finally he realizes that he's never really been listening to others after all, except as functions of his notoriety—has always been emotionally severed from the web of community. The man facing him now on the edge of a cliff face, one of the few who know his homicidal secret, and once his only friend in the world, refuses to shove him off the symbolic "pinnacle" where he has hoped to stage his relief from torment, and so Andreas must take the leap in full admission that the killer *within* has won. Three aspects of the literary death scene I once, long before Franzen's novel, anatomized under the headings of displacement, transposition, and epitome—the death that projects consciousness onto an outside force, transposes realist representation into metaphor at death's epistemological limit, and figuratively sums up a life in the process of expunging it—all operate in close coordination here. The Killer has become someone other to himself entirely, who can no longer hear an actual human plea (the silent scream of his antagonist)—only nature's ambient, impersonal noise instead, which is transfigured at the last moment into a synesthetic rush of distant vegetal thrashing registered as sonic force. All this goes to suggest—in its narcissistic distillation of death by epitome—that Andreas Wolf dies in the burst bubble of an isolation lethally true to form, a kind of death to others all along.

Before quite unmistakable cinematic effects are engaged, the scene builds by its own brand of schizoid dialogue, summed up in Andreas' advice to his alienated friend Tom: "If I were you, I'd kill me," which captures the canonical death scene's frequent psychic displacement, here in a crisis of grammatical shifters. When the suicidal protagonist is instead collared by his betrayed friend, Andreas no longer seems his own agent, but a second self looking on from the recesses of internal monologue: "Tom tightened his grip on the collar.

18 / Toward a Cinematographic Sentence 235

Someone took hold of his wrists" (italics added). That "someone" is the Killer, now the would-be self-slayer, cogently suggesting that it would be less incriminating for Tom to shove him off the cliff than to strangle him. And again the displaced agency: "Someone went close to the edge of the pinnacle," asking to be pushed. Self-destruction is already transferred to a kind of out-of-body option, the fate of some doomed other. Accused of wanting to do it in a further desperate exchange, Tom refuses, until the diagnosis forced from him at this point of no return, explicitly delivered by in the novel for the first time, delivers the split in Andreas' consciousness as a death trigger: "No. You're psychotic, and you can't see it because you're psychotic. You need to—" But the paragraph is over. No more room for the infinitive mood of posited counteraction. All is finite now—and fatal.

Immediately: "The sound of Tom's voice stopped .... Tom's mouth was still moving, and there was still the distant rush of water, the screeching of parakeets. Only human speech had ceased to be audible." Silent human cinema obtrudes within a technicolor cacophony. The final epitomizing thought looms in a cornered version of free indirect: "Had the Killer always been deaf to speech?" In this "mysterious selective silence," transposed from psyche to scene, even though a dimly echoic "sc*rabble* of feet on the g*ravel*" is heard in Tom's lurch to prevent "someone's fall," the latter's panicked gestures come with no words. And now, in Andreas' toppling forward, the scene's panoramic lens enters upon an exponential traveling shot in POV, naming no action but the space of a rapidly evacuated cognition. The only human sounds are those of the prose's own mordant assonance: "He turned back to the precipice and looked down at the *trop*ical tree*tops*, the la*r*ge sha*r*ds of fallen *r*ock," with "the green surf of undergrowth crashing against them"—the last some hallucinatory metonymy for the sound of distant, unseen waterfalls, so that implicit *waves* of foliage heave up an unwritten "turf" into a sound-drowning "surf." The only immediate physical "crash" is still pending.

From here on, vanishing distance is measured in the adverbs of intimacy rather than height (these topographic details, trees, rocks, undergrowth, moving "closer" rather than "upwards"), so that the accelerating Newtonian onset of obliteration arrives along the descending cadence of a single sentence: "When they began to drift slowly closer, and then moved rapidly closer, and more rapidly yet, he kept his eyes open wide, because he was honest with himself." Because indeed he himself was, is, the Killer: the now dominant "someone" within. And because this fall must sustain its hold on the aperture of a wide-eyed objective shot: nothing subjective about this POV, in a vertical tracking turned zoom, except for the subjectivity it is momentarily to eradicate. The rapidly telescoped long-shot has lasted only until the next and last sentence of the paragraph, chapter, and volume alike, closing on a parodic apocalypse of global telecommunication for this morally deaf hackmeister—and preceded by an unnerving, disjunctive syllepsis collapsing space and time together: "In the instant before it was over and pure nothing, he heard all the human voices in the world." No remission implied in this received universal transmission, this final effacing noise.

But what about the adverbial temporality of the wording per se—even beyond the internal phonic undertone and hinge of "be*fore* it was *over*"? The equivalent of a mediated "over and out"? At once "over and nothing"? Deliberately awkward? Brutally abrupt? Radically precipitous? At this instantaneously truncated mortal vanishing point, any syntactic characterization sounds stupidly euphemistic. In the harrowing Fframe-advance of this plummet, the narrowing of vision operates the differential calculus of extirpated consciousness. With the surveillance genius infinitely plugged-in at the instant of going off-line forever, there is no time for a grammar like "before it was over and there was then pure nothing," with its rational parallelism. Cut loose from any antecedent, the "it" (life, the moment, anything, everything) is effaced even as mentioned. The syntax at this climactic turn of *Purity* thus divides, or more like implodes, across a subordinate clause ("before it was over ...") and some version of a perverse title image in an elided phrase: any beforeness—effaced too fast for grammar by speed itself—now simultaneous with an arrived "*pure* nothing." The instant no sooner come than gone. After the dilated iris view (the eye's rather than camera's) of face-down (and faced-up-to) annihilation, the passage's heavily cinematic cancellation comes with that final implicit synesthesia of universal audition: the blinding blood roar of brain death. In wording's comparable terms, cut (not fade) to black.

And not only is this perhaps the most undebatably cinematic "shot" in our prose samplings so far, but its grammatical apparatus can help round out—even as the exception that proves the rule—the admittedly unstable homologies between screen sequencing and prose sentences with regard to their time-based mediations. For no matter how often we might slow down and reread (as I have done with the Franzen many more times even than the preceding analysis would serve to re-enact)—and, in rereading, have worked to slow that weirdly elliptical phrasing ("before it was over and pure nothing") to the remote control of virtual frame-advance, one lexeme at a time—the effect of its portrayed fatality is always just as inextricably fast and final in any coherent reading as its film version could ever be. Such is this prose's semantic shock effect before silence slams it shut. Without the reflections of these last two chapters behind it, that phrasing might seem to offer a misleadingly rare point of convergence between imagined viewing time and actual reading time.

And finally, in closing *The Ways of the Word*, I circle back to a famous threefold distinction in Ezra Pound's *How to Read* (1931) explored early in the book—and applied now to Melville: an author taken up again for his own Fframe-advance grammar in *Moby-Dick* (1851), here with a striking pre-filmic example of cinematographic prose:[7]

> As with the present book, Melville's too has an epilogue, one begun in his case of aftermath by its own epigraph from Job, with its oddly jogged, adverbially overloaded, and ultimately ambiguous phrasing: "And I *only* am escaped *alone* to tell thee." Two exclusivities converge on our privilege in listening. "Call me Ishmael," the now surviving narrator had opened the novel, and again, at the end, he has "paged" the reader, by citational displacement, as the "thee" of what we can only think of as a discourse-rescuing sequel, however brief. This call comes via a grammar that, across the seemingly redundant indication of Job's singularity, has its own way of suggesting that "I, solely, am escaped—and for the lone, the only and single, purpose of telling this tale." By Biblical precedent, verbal witness is the all or nothing of literary form.
>
> And this afterpiece by Melville has its own signature aftertones, as fluid as the nautical closure they inflect. Our narrator, about whose imperiled person we'd almost forgotten in the phrasal histrionics of the sinking ship, had been left on the periphery of the narrative with the rest of surviving crew in the passage previously examined—only now remarking, in retrospect, that he was there "floating on the margin of the ensuing scene, and in full sight of it." Even from that distance, however, when "the halfspent suction of the sunk ship reached me, I was then, but slowly, drawn towards the closing vortex." He speaks from the "margin" like the drama's own gloss. Coasting in on the sibilant alliteration of that "en*s*uing *s*cene, and in full *s*ight of it," the tongue-twister "halfspent suction of the sunk ship"—the first noun turning on the German origin of an Indo-European imitative root related to "soak"—has produced a broader scope of imitative syntax propelled by "halfspent" breath (the epithet itself rushed forward, hyphenless). In an ironic emphasis sprung by the very proximity of "suction" and "sunk," we encounter the etymological deep time of the word per se—and this in its extra anagrammatic reduction of *suc/n* into *sunk*, again cause to effect, on the thickened tongue of enunciation. With the narrator spiraling inward all the while, the inverted syntax spins on and out: "Round and round, then, and ever contracting towards the button-like black bubble at the axis of that slowly wheeling circle, like another Ixion I did revolve." Not only does

that delayed predicate in "revolve" further imitate the cause-to-effect suction of the vortex and its resulting gravitational pull, but the openly onomatopoetic burbling ("the *bu*tton-like *b*lack *bubb*le") is part of a causality so fateful that—perpendicular to the narrowing diameter of the whirling circle—the downward vertical "axis" seems declaring its death spiral under the coming phonetic spell of the "Ixion" archetype and its own first syllable.

On, down, and up again the narrator has gone. The plosive density of "black bubble" is only fully unleashed, next, when "gaining that vital centre, the black bubble upward burst" (even up-word, by inversion in the phantom wake of "bubble up—d")—"and now, liberated by reason of its cunning spring, and, owing to its great buoyancy, rising with great force, the coffin life-buoy shot lengthwise from the sea, fell over, and floated by my side." Enhancing the underlay of personification in "by reason of … its cunning," the etymological relation of "buoy" to "buoyancy" is no sooner capitalized on than the nouns are turned verbal in the past-participial precondition of rescue, with no attempt at lexical variation for a material fact upon which the narrator's whole salvation rests—and is, as a result, verbally suspended: "Buoyed up by that for almost one whole day and night, I floated on a soft and dirgelike main"—dirge rather than surge, in concert with that previous "shroud." And in this case the placid if grave surface is marked as such by immediate assonance in the notation of suspended threat. "The unh*a*rming sh*a*rks, they glided by"—in idiometric deflection, we may well think, of "un*a*rmed"—"glided by," that is, "as if with padlocks on their mouths; the savage s*ea*-hawks sailed with sh*ea*thed b*ea*ks." Alliteration in its own right would seem part of the sheathing in which these tamed beaks are encased.

With the saving advent first spotted in the arriving next sentence, the aquatic analogy (dead metaphor) for aerial flight ("sailed") is turned to an actual nautical object, as focalized through the narrator's adrift vision: "On the second day, a *sail* drew near, nearer, and picked me up at last." After a paragraph of potent syntactic and syllabic enactment at the full reach of Melville's opulent rhetorical coloration, here instead, in a colloquial and mostly monosyllabic simplicity, is perhaps the most imitative wording of all: the tension of an ongoing tense in an elided—or, better, telescoped—concision of phrase. The narrator living to tell the tale, he has told it so much from the inside out that the POV of his prose has not simply fixated on "sail" as functional synecdoche for the potential rescuing vessel. Further, in this condensed suspense, prose has enacted the very hope of rescue in the step-time Fframe-advance of this telephoto shot. It has done so across the swift rippling melodrama of a mere comma splice in the breathless "near, nearer"—nothing less than the incremental time compression of the unspelled but simultaneously enunciated "near'n' nearer": normalized synonymous aftertone of the elision as written.

I like ending with the most famous prose passage in this entire book, returning to those last paragraphs of Melville's novel as one does, and must, with new ears always: aware of its "style" to begin with, of course, and scarcely exhausting its nuances under further episodes of attention: never in danger, that is, of over-reading it in reading it over again. In the splendor of Melville's dedicated lexicon and syntax, stretched over the passage's own conjured abyss from turmoil to subsidence, the echoism and onomatopoeia are (Pound one last time) melopoetic, certainly; the evoked suctional vortex and the sprung coffin dramatically phanopoetic as well. Both registers of the poetic, aural and visual, are then further instanced under compression in the phrasal zoom (or time-lapse) of that phonetically elongated second *n* of "near, nearer." But there too, as in the passage as a whole, a logopoetics is quite directly engaged: a prose poetics of phonemic juncture here, as before of etymology, of grammatical inversion, of syllabic insistence, and the rest. In all this *the ways of the word* invite access along the trail—and trailings—of undertow and aftertone at one level or another.

Notes

1. Jean Epstein, *The Intelligence of a Machine*, trans. Christopher Wall-Romana (Minneapolis: Univocal, 2014). Originally published as *L'intelligence d'une machine* (Paris: Éditions Jacques Melot, 1946).
2. *Sherlock Jr.*, directed by Buster Keaton (Buster Keaton Productions, 1924); *Our Hospitality*, directed by John G. Blystone and Buster Keaton (Joseph M. Schenck Productions and Polyphony Digital, 1923); *His Girl Friday*, directed by Howard Hawks (Columbia Pictures, 1940); *Hellzapoppin'*, directed by H. C. Potter (Mayfair Productions and Universal Pictures, 1941).
3. Epstein, *The Intelligence of a Machine*; Christian Metz, "*Trucage* and the Film," trans. Françoise Meltzer, *Critical Inquiry*, vol. 3, no. 4 (1977): 657–75.
4. *The Fall of the House of Usher*, directed by Jean Epstein (Films Jean Epstein, 1928).
5. Colson Whitehead, *Apex Hides the Hurt* (New York: Doubleday, 2006).
6. Jonathan Franzen, *Purity* (London: Fourth Estate, 2015).
7. Ezra Pound, *How to Read* (London: Desmond Harmsworth, 1931); Herman Melville, *Moby-Dick* (New York: Harper & Brothers, 1851).

VIII.

AUDIOVISUAL MIRRORS: SCREENING TEXT AND VOICE

19 / *The Metanarrative Hall of Mirrors: Reflex Action in Fiction and Film* (Bloomsbury, 2022) is the first comparative study of how image patterns, tracked differently in prose and fiction, still share certain common features in the reflex recognitions of their media across the reading and viewing act. In film examples ranging from *Citizen Kane* (1941, dir. Orson Welles) through *Apocalypse Now* (1979, dir. Francis Ford Coppola) to *Blade Runner 2049* (2017, dir. Denis Villeneuve), then on to Christopher Nolan's 2020 *Tenet*, Stewart develops a varying template for the "beveled mirroring" by which some arresting moment in the narrative text slants back to its structuring function or outward to some inferential context beyond plot. In again following out the shift from celluloid to digital cinema through various narrative manifestations of the image, from freeze-frames to computer-generated special effects, his technique\text/context model is put to varied and revealing use. By bringing cinema alongside literature—not just set in parallel but somehow held up to the light together—Stewart discovers a common tendency in contemporary storytelling, in both prose and visual narrative, from the ongoing trend of "mind-game" films (again, with Nolan being a chief progenitor) to the often puzzling narrative eccentricities of such different writers as Nicholson Baker and especially Richard Powers, with three chapters exploring the encyclopedic wit and intricate phrasal surprise of the latter's fiction, down through *The Overstory* (2018) and *Bewilderment* (2021). For further remarks on Powers, see also "A Dialogue on Critical Conversation" below.

19 / Reflex Reading

The Metanarrative Hall of Mirrors: Reflex Action in Fiction and Film (2022)

AS A LINK BACK TO *Cinemachines* (2020; see Phase VII / 16), one of *The Metanarrative Hall of Mirrors*' early examples of "reflex action" returns to the issue of technical "assertions" in Stanley Cavell that feature, so prominently, the freeze-frame—illustrated further in this subsequent study by its anomalous use in the habitually long-take structure of Stanley Kubrick's narrative cinema:

> In the freeze's definitive celluloid phase, with its function electric rather than electronic, the stop-action jolt serves to call up film's motorized two-dimensional plasticity in the midst of its projection of seemingly inhabited space. It amounts to the disclosure of motion picturing, frame after frame, from the very clutch—or teeth and sprocket holes—of negated movement. And is, yes, always latently metanarrative in operation. Besides textbook examples in such European modernist films by François Truffaut as *The 400 Blows* (1959) or *Jules and Jim* (1962), there is an unexpected deployment of the freeze in a very different auteurist aesthetic—hence even more instructive by its anomaly. Amid the staid and patient long takes (and blunt surgical cuts) in the torpidly populated social ambience of Stanley Kubrick's literary adaptation of William Makepeace Thackeray's novel under the shortened title *Barry Lyndon* (1975), a narrative halt is called—and optically called out. Following long after early battlefield footage, with the lockstep rank and file of dated slaughter answered by the stark implacability of the fixed-frame camera, comes a surprise freeze that pries wide the jammed flow of photograms into a kind of gaping narrative wound to match the hero's own amputation after a gun duel. To whose optical impact, in practice, we come—after a thumbnail sketch of its theory: the most immediate film-historical context for its textual deployment as technique.
>
> Such a freeze-frame is loosely comparable to a syntactic trope in verbal style, a piece of iterative or stalled grammar—as, for instance, a pileup of appositive noun phrases going nowhere, an impasse, stalemate, deadlock, lockdown. But, on screen, its interest is entirely cinematic at base. In his philosophical treatise, *The World Viewed: Reflections on the Ontology of Film*, written early in the 1970s on the cusp between two decades of celluloid modernism, this stop-action image is the most prominent—and markedly ontological—of Stanley Cavell's "assertions in technique" for acknowledging "the fact of film": assertions not just in or through, but *in regard to*, technique, and thus openly metafilmic. What is asserted by such devices is inseparable from the narrative text they serve. For classic cinema as

an imprint mode of projection, one may say that a stylistic "assertion in" the materiality of film—on such a technique\text cusp (familiar from its fuller form as technique\text/context)—edges directly into the *meta* by its assertion *of* the filmic. In the very rupture of its temporal asseveration, the freeze is a canonical effect of reflex-action paralysis during a technological era of cinemachination when this device (faded in aesthetic prominence with the digital) felt directly geared to the fundament of the medial process: one picture showing through after another, though in this case each the same in iteration.

It seems fair to say that the effect is seldom more assertive or serviceable than in its lone instance, rare anyway in Kubrick's oeuvre, at the studied anti-climax of his one historical drama, *Barry Lyndon*. As follows—with nothing then following in the account of Barry's personal adventures. Even though all stretches of exposition in the director's own script for this adaptation of the Thackeray novel have been dispatched in mordant flat voiceover, its dismissive tone works with particular blunt emphasis in the last we see (or hear) of the protagonist, one leg surgically amputated after a duel with his brutally mistreated and vengeful stepson Lord Bullingdon, leaving Barry now grappling his way on crutches up to the door of a coach that will take him into bribed exile on a modest stipend if he never returns to England. The acoustic overlay pulls plot itself up short, just before the optic freeze: "Sometime later he returned to the Continent. His life there we have not the means of following accurately"—with these last words ironically concluding a tracking shot that has already been "following," from behind, his one-legged progress toward the waiting coach. A servant, taking his crutches from behind to ease him into the carriage, thus sees him out of the plot altogether. In the last moment of his cinematic "appearance," narrative disclaimer indulges in this useful loophole: "But he appears to have resumed his former profession as a gambler without his former success." Dead end. Begun with the words "He never saw Lady Lyndon again," all motion *in* or *of* the image is just then suspended, the film going into sudden seize-up—with the maimed body still stationed (and stationed still) on the carriage threshold—in a momentarily fixed tableau of abjection, dependency, exile, and truncation: a biographical and ultimately narrative amputation.

Before pausing over this obvious obtrusion of the apparatus from beneath the plot, my own *Metanarrative Hall of Mirrors* opens with a famous emblematic instance of a mirrored corridor (from Orson Welles' *Citizen Kane*, the eponymous image-maker's multiplied image in the hallway at Xanadu)—and moves to an equally famous later case of optical refraction, via shattered mirrors, in Welles' *The Lady from Shanghai* (1947, dir. Orson Welles)—as called up by a digressive digitized allusion to it, by exaggerated optical fracture, in the Marvel franchise *Spider-Man: Far From Home* (2019, dir. Jon Watts). That last is a film, in many similar scenes as well, in which the unrestrained proliferation of computerized "trucage" (Metz) has reached its apogee and travesty at once. If the discussion of Metz and Epstein in *Cinemachines* was there to sample in part the kind of graduate mentoring that seeks, over time in the seminar room, some comprehensive view of ontological (over against phenomenological) film theory—say, material rather than corporeal in the latest round of debate—the coming excerpt from *The Metanarrative Hall of Mirrors* marks a curricular shift to a larger undergraduate classroom. The analysis brought forward in this excerpt represents a level of attention geared to a more intuitive kind of instruction (that is, with a film whose contemporary vintage and superhero franchise provides a proximate frame of reference), leading students to think harder about a given popular release through the lens of their mostly quite well-developed (if not yet fully schooled) visual literacy. Certainly, it is not hard to get discussion going about a film so completely saturated with contemporary issues of political hucksterism vis-à-vis climate catastrophe. In *The Metanarrative Hall of Mirrors*, I therefore instance at some length this mainstream blockbuster, *Spider-Man: Far from Home*, partly in connection with the recent spate of so-called mind-game films, often more cerebral in their assumptions and demands—to illustrate the technique\text/context template (cited in the first paragraph below) of this book's ongoing reflexive pattern. And I should gratefully add that the first opportunity to test out this model was provided by my then, as well as current, editor, David LaRocca, in a contribution ("A Metacinematic Spectrum: Technique through Text to Context") to his 2021 volume *Metacinema: The Form and Content of Filmic Reference and Reflexivity*.

> Reflecting the escalating CGI (computer-generated imagery) aesthetic of the Hollywood action film over the last two decades, here is a movie—*Spider-Man: Far From Home*—that comes down to the wire of this present media-reflexive commentary almost by being cornered on the ropes of its own technical expertise, slapped all but silly in the ricochet of the special-effects ironies it unleashes. And it can best be comprehended in this framework under one final rephrasing of the sliding scale of such reflexive functioning—with technique\text/context translated on the spot to apparatus\plot/production, each of these zones of response being shot through—as a further zone of contextual reverb—with intertextual links to the epidemic of mass manipulation in contemporary politics. This outer range of contextual reference is secured only once a midpoint reveal has reset our terms of engagement with the film: namely, that in regard to (1) the digital bravura on display so far, we've been watching the medium's computer apparatus generate, as in the normal operation of VFX, a cataclysmic series of trick effects to materialize (2) narrative threats

that are in fact, diegetically, just that: deceptive effects, tricks—or, in other words, (3) explicitly projected illusions of Hollywood-style industrial technique, as well-funded but unreal as the self-styled superhero who vanquishes (vanishes) them.

The overriding trick of the plot, then, in this attenuated and soon-truncated mind-game mold, can only be to banish the risk of tech disaffection by a metaphorics of damage control within a familiar genre pattern of unrest and restoration. To summarize this way, however, is to recognize that the particular slant or bevel given to medial inference in the outward double learning of the apparatus\ plot/production model is pointedly rooted in the hermeneutics of recognition: namely, in what reading for the plot can still help us to read about narrative constitution both before and beyond it, now reverting to generative machination, now adverting to cultural impact. This matter of perspective is an important proviso. For it is equally, or reciprocally, the case—if understood as picturing in formative terms what puts pressure on narrative material in giving it shape—that our template could be installed instead as the inward slanted technique/text\context. In that form it would schematize the way story's manifestation is determined by, as well as reflective of, pressures now behind, now beyond it, now technological, now sociological.

Optical Allusion: Causes and F/X

One rule of action genres—western, detective, and sci-fi especially—is that they melodramatize broader cultural anxieties before laying them to artificial rest through some variety of heroic intervention or sacrifice. Franchises, a kind of subgenre all their own, work somewhat differently. In this they resemble serial TV. With the "tag scenes" familiar from the final credit rosters of the Marvel series, these loose ends—despite intermittent narrative plateaus of resolution in a single film plot—keep refueling the cycle from within its own peripheral flexibility. It is all the more likely, then, that broader cultural parameters of intended audience response—rebooted with each new wrinkle of geopolitical anxiety—will coincide with narrative and technological reflexivity in a franchise devoted almost exclusively to digital "marvels" at the cutting edge of technological empowerment—or its revenge upon us.

Certainly this is the case with the latest *Spider-Man*, including its implicit critique of Trump-era demagoguery linked directly to global technological deception (think Russian hacking) in a plot of nefarious VFX technique. The distinction this chapter began with, between cinema as mediatized spectacle (once filmic, now digital) and cinema as designated site of exhibition, has perhaps never been more reductively addressed than in this film's plot about Hollywood-style illusionism in its strategically remote deployment. Plot, did I say? Intertwined with a thin rom-com story about a high school trip through European tourist sites—attended, among the usual typecast suspects, by our secret spider-boy, a goofy nerd sidekick or two, and a would-be girlfriend—is the frail narrative thread of the story's thriller premise. According to which: a maestro of technological illusions generates and projects the CGI mirage of monstrous urban catastrophes (Venice, Prague, London) that only he can fend off, becoming in the process a global hero. The unleashed Spider-Man, with all his teen powers on offer, is recruited to the villain's assistance before the former, our true hero, discovers the ruse. Reduced to the simplest logic of genre showdown, and to near pun on the prosthetic efficacy of the eponymous hero (his *web*-spinning miracles included)—as well as backed in turn by much repeatedly loaded dialogue to this end—the auto-allegory of *trucage* (what Christian Metz saw as the "special effect" that is cinema all told) is impossible to miss. The panic fostered by high-tech "propaganda" (in this case the illusory images of elemental forces out to destroy the world as we know it)—a paranoia to which a self-styled fascistic superman and avenging scourge is the fake antidote—can in the long run be bested rather than abetted, in its campaign of big-budget illusory disinformation, only by the spidery net of our webmaster hero.

Anything we might call the apparatus disclosures of the metacinematic spectrum in all this are so surfeited and manic, almost comic, in their Hollywood overtones that one feels compelled to work backwards from (3) the production end of the sliding scale we've been contemplating toward (2) the plot-transacted sense of its own (1) generative electronics. [...] This latest *Spider-Man* enterprise wallows in an almost uncontainable level of digital reflexivity. Computerized technique has swallowed all action. Which is just where the overarching paranoia plot must kick in, displaced from its own comic book source, so that now the updated glancing barbs at fear mongering and fake news never let up for long. When the wunderkind Spider-Man—fostering in his own right a false cover story to keep one of his heroic interventions under wraps so as to protect his empowering anonymity—suggests that people should always believe what they see on the news, the audience's mild sniggering is merely *de rigueur*. In the age of "post-truth," the plot's whole premise, including a villain pretending to hail from a supposed parallel universe within a wide array of "multidimensional worlds," feels pitched at the idea of Trump-era alternate realities—and not just when this fake superman is anointed as patron saint of terrestrial *border defense* in coming to society's collective rescue. Duping the news outlets with his announced arrival from another version of Earth, where Elementals have slain the populace, the con artist Mysterio is the embodiment of group-think mystification. And what he promises, one simulated alien invasion after another, is only a protective ballistic scrim, exposed eventually as a mere CGI interface, between the spectacle of encroaching horrors and its riveted but vulnerable public audience.

With climate change unsaid but inescapably pressing in the allegory, the world-wide elemental disasters—explicitly subdivided as those of air (emissions), earth (quakes), water (floods), and fire (exponential heat)—all "have a face" in Mysterio's artificial mobilization of their threats. All are incarnate as oversized demons. But here, as so often, is where sci-fi dystopias can get caught up in inverted transpositions of the anxieties they are manifestly extrapolating from. Paranoia is a double-edged sword. The enormity of Mysterio's trumped-up threat is rendered with an enormous and vaguely humanoid form, that is, not because rampant cataclysmic forces are the embodiment of human-induced meteorological disaster, but rather because in this case (phew!) they are all fake: staged flashpoints in a climate of fear itself, stoked with advanced electronic enhancements by the wannabe Avenger. In a no doubt accidental facet—and fallout—of a typically lightweight political parable, climate deniers may thus take some cold comfort even from within the denigration of their parodied hero. "I control the truth," boasts Mysterio (a.k.a. Beck, who thinks he has the world at his beck and call, beckoning them to submission). "It's easy to fool people when they're already kidding themselves." Finally overmastered by the "web"-adept Spider-Man once the latter wins back his billion-dollar experimental upgrade of Google Glass, it is up to Mysterio to repeat one more time, with his dying words, his earlier confidence in mass gullibility. "People need to believe," says this vicious genius of a computer-boosted confidence game, and "nowadays they'll believe anything."

Especially their own eyes. What tucks all this limply scripted topicality back into the coils of cinematic self-reference in the cognitive force field of the postfilmic screen apparatus is that Mysterio is, in fact, a maestro of what one of the teen heroes calls, in knowing industry lingo, "illusion tech." So designated is the whole panoply of marauding demons and heroic resistance that gets staged—make that virtually screened—before gullible mass crowds in Mysterio's digital enactment of his own image as savior. He accomplishes this sci-fi feat by manipulating, from a remote electronic hub, a collaboration of weaponized drones (military-industrial anxiety *du jour*) and gargantuan laser holograms. These we see him testing out under laboratory conditions in the CGI rendering room—and then implementing in real-world capitols by the remote voice-activation of such Hollywood argot as "cue the lightning" (with a genre precedent taken up in the next chapter in connection with rudimentary "mind-game" plotting of *Groundhog Day* [1993], exactly a quarter century before).

Beyond narcissistic megalomania, Mysterio's particular vendetta stems from a festering resentment against his ousting by onetime boss Iron Man. This detail marks the film's most obvious strategic dodge, at the plot level, in avoiding what would have been too explicit a corporate reflex if drawn from the villain's actual backstory in the Marvel comic source. In his original paper incarnation, Mysterio's perverse illusionist credentials are more, so to say, medium-specific in their visual deceits than the film would be likely to withstand without toppling into satire or black comedy. In the original serial pages, Mysterio is an unlikely double-threat as maverick agent: having lost his Hollywood jobs as at once a top F/X engineer *and* a valued stunt man (combining Christian Metz's separate categories of visual and invisible tricks: the fantastic illusions you do see, and the substitutions you don't). In that original comix premise, Beck's deceptive tech becomes the incarnate revenge of the system against its own benign commercial spectacles, turning them to a new kind of conviction and notoriety as global terrors. But the movie doesn't offer up such Hollywood employment practices to be sacrificed on the altar of plot, just its hallowed VFX technology to be implicitly borrowed from—and, of course, signally misused. In his filmed version as anti-hero, Mysterio's CGI stunts, both physical and pyrotechnical, are nonetheless studio signatures: feats of motion capture, green screen, CGI infill, and the rest. Incautiously enough, in this version of the Marvel Universe, everything keeps reverting to a reflex of its own electronic marvelous. So it is that form and content implode upon each other, with any clean delineations in the matter of social or political critique being the first victims of this collapse. Unlike in the film version, Mysterio in the comic version feels guilty, and, staring into an ornate mirror of introspection, thinks he should maybe just make a "short film" and then retire.

Even the immediate narrative backstory (rather than comic-book genealogy) of the franchise confirms such metacinematics—and does so explicitly at the border between technological and corporate contrivance, CGI and the casting department. Explicitly rehearsed, early in this *Spider-Man* plot, is its position in the wake of *The Avengers: Infinity Wars* (2017), where superpower heroes suffer pixelated dissolution along with half of the human race. Five years later in narrative time, though only one year in the fast turnaround of the lucrative franchise, we learn of a remission in this galactic "Blip." The chronological mismatch is itself, one suspects, part of the metanarrative inference. The fact that many other victims of the Blip have been restored (after this half-decade hiatus) to their former stations, their bodies unaged, and thus lagging behind their cohorts, is a kind of industry in-joke. It doesn't take much to see this as a reflection of such franchise filmmaking at large, which can only keep rebooting itself (the James Bond cycle being quintessential and exemplary) if it replaces plot agents every few years with younger actors in comparable roles.

The film wants us to remember the special effect itself of this cosmic devastation as it fills in this backstory. A simulated video newscast by amateurish student anchors in the film's second scene—begun in elegy for the disappeared Avengers, and broadcast on video screens to a high school audience—is the film's genre link to the previous year's *Avengers* installment, where we are reminded of the way the superpower heroes are summarily "retired" from the franchise by seeing, through cell-phone images, the pixelated evisceration of students and athletes vaporized from the school gym. These vanishing ash-gray digital variants of a dust-to-dust paradigm in mortal disintegration remind us, of course, that the splintered, then obliterated, heroes in the *Avengers* saga have in fact been constituted, in their flashiest exploits, by piecemeal CGI simulation to begin with (i.e., pixelated, de-pixelated, re-pixelated—the new cycle of "life"). So that the dissipated victims here anticipate the consolidating splintered nemesis of London at the end.

Moreover, what turns out to be the ultimate threat to Mysterio's computerized disinformation campaign is also part of the closely calibrated Hollywood metatext, around which the last phase of the plot revolves. The closest friends of Spider-Man have come to learn, along with him, that the humungous Elemental predators are just digital simulations beamed by what they guess, when finding one detached from a downed drone, is a "very advanced projector," whose results are "real, very real." At this point the film cuts abruptly, clumsily, to an explanatory episode of Beck in the computer rendering studio, assessing the holographic files of his derring-do at several yards remove from his own image, with the illusion-backing drones next seen hovering behind the optical data banks that are transferring these illusions to the magic upgrade of Google Glass spectacles. In the final siege of London, however, by a kind of trivialized avant-garde "glitch aesthetic" built into the thriller plot, Mysterio learns by remote warning that his looming CGI hallucination is "coming apart" by explicit pixel break-up at the very seams of its interlace—and thus confirming, for all to see, its basis in mere optical trickery.

But there is more Hollywood reflex action yet. Before the spectacle quite literally decimates into bitmap graphics, the teens in the know need to be kept from spilling the beans. As agents of a potential debunking—in a kind of tacit generational parable—they serve to concentrate the audience demographic whose aggressive doubts (as opposed to merely suspended disbelief) would demolish the electronic fabric of the whole Marvel Universe, let alone the thrills, however deceptive, of this one plot. If these kids don't fall for the spectacle, who will? They are in this regard, aptly enough, the intended victims of Mysterio's final lethal retaliation (and in the logic of Marvel drama, its inherent saviors): in this weaponized illusionism, and in an unsaid but deeply organizing metaphor, the once target audience as now renegade target. And as if to make this inference unmistakable, there is the final turning point in the action plot when a lone drone, stripped of its trappings as part of the murky pixelated illusion ravishing London—tracks those-who-know-too-much into the Crown Jewels vault, the remote technology reverting here to its standard operating procedure as surveillance and lethal take-out. It is at this point, given the angst of dialogue, that mind-game reflexivity has unmistakably turned the corner into a gamer-mind logic. Cornered in this way, one of the kids about to die whines in regret that he's wasted his life playing video games, another that he's posted stupid videos to get people's attention. But ludic interactivity and amateur production are now both redeemed, in this era of corporate tie-ins, with the assurance from Spider-Man's handler (former head of Stark security) that this is all that might still manage to save them—a way for the hero to have tracked a digital footprint to their present location. Ah, yes, the nonparanoid upside of involuntary GPS, won back for universal computerization—and by explicit association with gameplay. Spider-Man's Web to the rescue after all.

Again, in the variable interchange of this chapter's threefold template, we find the corporate logic (video adjuncts and tie-ins included) enfolding (3) the political intertext of fake territorial invasions and their self-appointed superman of nativist resistance. And from there the inferences of plot circle back via (1) the CGI screen's own technical apparatus when "read"—that is, when figured or troped in the plot, or say allegorized—toward (2) a textual reflex, at the narrative level, of aggressive computer manipulation (not just on Facebook or in the voting booth, but as the very *specter* of mass paranoia). At the plot level, of course, redemption is pure Hollywood celebration in the formulaic happy ending—yet, in this extreme case, wrung from within the surprise vilification of its own industrial selling point in compelling special effects.

In my earliest writing on cinema, I had occasion more than once, in identifying the reflexive escalation of visual technology in the sci-fi genre, to observe that "movies about the future tend to be about the future of movies." If one were tempted to update this for the transition from the hologram in 1956's *Forbidden Planet* to Mysterio's digital demons, in positing that "vfx cinema is about the future of illusions," the question would remain, in the face of a present dead end, what future? In the normal run of cgi spectacle, we in the audience, like a credulous public at large, will believe anything too, as long as it's expensively enough generated on screen—and not least, in the closed circuit of the fan appreciation sublimated here, when it parades itself as such. In the digital poetics of the Marvel franchise in general, cinema loses nothing in brand loyalty by adverting to the artifice of its own signature effects. But the risk exposed by an unavoidable "apparatus reading" of the pixel substrate in this hypertrophic case has been, if almost too obvious to mention, all the more serious for that. Where can sci-fi screen invention possibly go from here—in bringing vfx along in motivated genre tow—when plot has become all apparatus?

In my effort in *The Metanarrative Hall of Mirrors* to tether discussion with a loose disciplinary leash, that brash and exacerbated case of self-mirroring technology in the digital burlesque of *Spider-Man* is next brought into comparison with one of contemporary literature's most cerebral writers, Richard Powers (b. 1957). The *Metanarrative Hall of Mirrors* thus draws on my developing fascination with the erudition and wit, including the eerily crisp and distinctive style, of this exuberant narrative talent and polymath, including the media-savvy technofuturism of certain key novels: a fascination, enhanced by student uptake at the undergraduate level, that had begun, for me, with analyses of his prose in *The Ways of the Word* (2021; see also Phase VII / 18). Here, in the *Metanarrative* book, Powers gets deserved prominence in three full chapters, long after a launching epigraph from him (in its definitive metalingual punning) for the entire volume: "And yet, a man's speech should exceed his lapse, else what's a meta for?" A glance at his early published sense of "constructivist novels about fiction" helps introduce the much subtler reflexive cast of his own ingenious fictions, which are then contrasted with the pornographic send-up of inflamed reader response in the very different "reflex action" of the comparably gifted wordsmith Nicholson Baker (like Powers, born in 1957). One effort is to distinguish the prose intricacy of these writers from the previous generation, Thomas Pynchon to Don DeLillo, of postmodernist metafiction—and this in light of equivalent tendencies in contemporary cinema, whose irruptions of digital technology in their spur to audience recognition constitute a very different thing from the high modernist "metafilm." The cross-medium scales of attention this book sets out to inculcate is summed up as follows near the start:

> The grounds of comparison between viewing and reading are in this case more closely mapped and site-specific, since ultimately this is not so much a comparative media study as it is a cross-sectional

approach to the reading of mediation itself in the quite different texts it generates. The issue is not the avowed metafiction but the discernible turn within the execution of any plotted text when fictional inscription, optical or verbal, goes, however momentarily, metanarrative. Those last five syllables are thus more useful here as an adjective than a noun. In this call-and-response of story's mirroring surfaces, it is a double sense of *reflection*, then, material and mental, that identifies both what text seems picturing back to you of your own coached response and, in the very process, the work you do in making this out.

Typical of this reflective process (twice over) are the arcane phrasal and syllabic economies in what I term the structuring "echology" of Powers' Pulitzer Prize-winning *The Overstory* (2018), a book about the convergent biographical destinies of anti-deforestation activists turning violent in defense of their beloved redwoods.[1] I explore that novel's organicist sense of a systemic planetary connection—or, in other words, its feel for trans-sentient nature's intricately rooted signal systems—as modeled by the network of the book's own prose. In doing so, I close the chapter with certain phonetic rather than vegetal stem-grafts from the arcanum of Powers' recurrent syllabic play:

> Two discrete instances of such audition near the end of the novel are found to arc within or between single words in sparking verbal microplots that immediately scale up into alignment with the whole curve of the Overplot. First, there is a punning flashpoint in the story of Ray Brinkman, the Minneapolis lawyer (horrified at one point by broadcast images of police brutality against the West Coast tree activists), now a movingly bedridden stroke victim who can barely grunt out his desire to play "Crss ... wds" with his wife, as in their former marital routine. He is convulsed in frustration by not being able to articulate his solution to their attempted puzzle except in scrawling out the alphabetic tendrils of a barely legible—but relieving—cross-syllabic "Releaf" (represented graphically rather than typographically on the page) in response to the original newspaper prompt: "starts with an *R. Bud's comforting comeback*." Yet again, the pun can be laid at other than our author's door. Yet Ray's twisted, snagged script bears immediate comparison with a distant motif in the novel—and with the climax coming: namely, Nick's habitual way of "writing nature." The hard-edged san serif caps that always represent, on the page, the content rather than form of Nick's arboreal word art, even long before the climactic "STILL," force us to imagine for ourselves—in contrast, again, to the illuminated decoration with which they are compared—the leafy untrimmed look of his lettering, whose "borders teem," as mentioned, "with fronds and flowers form the margins of

a medieval manuscript." In Ray's case, however, the impaired, pained venting in letters of the homophonic pun on "Releaf" has recruited modern digital reproduction to simulate the spastic scribal flourish of the damaged hand's involuntary squiggles and volutes: a paralytic scrawl more leafy than readily legible. The filigrees and flourishes we associate with Nick's ecological calligrams, his scraggly fronds of script, have thus been deflected, with hypertrophic visibility, onto the more cryptic, crippled scrawl of never explicitly parsed (and indeed cross-worded) pun awaiting Ray's recognition, dug deep from the undersoil of the novel: a novel where the only *relief* for arboreal devastation is precisely its *re-leafing*, "already" inchoate in those recuperative iterative lap-dissolves we've noted on the novel's last page.

The second and far more covert node of epiphany, or echological *epiphony*, is associated with a last venture of tree art that precedes the closing "STILL" life. Years after his arboreal heroics, with Nick also now on the run from the law, we find him reduced, by way of gainful employment, to "scanning bar codes" on boxed books—the doubly pulped fate (unsaid) of the arboreal—at the "enormous Fulfillment Center" of an (equally unsaid) Amazon of deforestation. The "product" there is "not so much books" as—so the sentence lisps out lazily in its own *crss-wrd* hiss—"convenien*ce*. *Ease* is the di*sease* and Nick is its vector." Worlds apart from the "booklike bark" and "arborglyphs" of botanical inscription and its devoted legibilities early in the plot, phonetic diagnosis names at this point an opposite syndrome, as national ailment, even before the noun of malady, the restless "disease," fully arrives in syntactic delivery. But that is an incidental slippage—a minor ironic sabotage by lexical contagion—compared to what we discover on the next page. In secret provocations apart from his day job, Nick's polemic vandalism is still bent on defacing public as well as private property with outsize tree paintings, whose "furrows of bark"—when *read*, as it were, up close—are said in this most recent case, with their dark irregular striations, to resemble a "two-foot wide UPC bar code." With a pun neither explicit nor funny, opening only between and across lexical ridges, it's the inward turned, blurred "furrow" of this phrasing that claims attention: the double decryption of this *bark code* as undersong culmination to a novel-long *bark ode*. Lexical ridges, yes—scraped past in this ultimate "reflex action" of understoried registration. [...]

An "echological" reading of Powers' novel will, of course, not only pick up the rebound of phrases across the text, articulating its own subsystem in answer to that of the secret forest's. It will attune itself as well, in reflexive notice, to re-soundings that reach beyond—back into the literary "network"—for a new interplay with its previous "actors," near and far. Tree-Patty is at first mocked among academic botanists for the very claim that later makes for her scholarly and popular renown: exactly the confidence that trees communicate, sign themselves, as above, in "semaphores" rather than just in the trace(d) presence of spores and seeds. Short of an intuitive uprush of audition like Mimi's in the park, the work of discerning the trees' secret code is, in effect, that of a fine-tuned disciplinary stethoscope, as if eavesdropping on the leaves themselves. Their impulses are transferred to our ears by a phonically keyed (indeed, as we know from Powers' advice to writers, voice-activated) prose set in train, at times, even by more or less esoteric cross-word effects. And, as part of the literary system, by implicit intertexts. Famously in *Middlemarch* [1871], George Eliot analogizes an impossibly totalized human sympathy to the aberration of "hearing the grass grow," whose preternatural overload would mean that "we should die of that roar which lives on the other side of silence"—a sonic fate quite minimally approached, as it happens, on the keyboard of her own chiastically launched assonance (*die*/s*ide*/s*i*). Powers' gambit stops short of this contemplated fatality. Rather than risking obliteration by audition, he implies that an ear tuned to the inner hives and havens of a forest vernacular—with its parallels in involute or even recondite lexical play—might instead revitalize our senses. With it we might hear what lies on the *inside* of silence, whether in paged words or in the mute *barchives* that prose, in this novel, so vividly transliterates.

But there is more to note in apprehending that twitch-is-which oscillation of "bar code" as a narratographic reflex rather than just a lexigraphic slippage. That more is the context of narrative as a whole in *The Overstory*. Yet again the echocentric is redoubled upon itself, yet here in a single span of words. As a homophonic cross-word pun, the effect of this unbarred crisis of code is in one sense undoubtedly extreme. We might miss it—or not; or in making it out, think we were making it up. Which is the (reflexive) point, but here in a fiction premised on the mystery of signage itself, of nonhuman messaging, on the signal system of trunk, pith, root, and leaves. The stakes of reading are at a unique premium in this novel, and the codes, bark and otherwise, thrown into dizzying recess by comparison itself. The yoked monosyllabic integers in English that capture—in their own double articulation (c/k)—the double vision of painted cellulose striations and imprinted computerized hash marks encrypt more than they say. They serve to conjure in this occulted way the inaccessible coding of tree life as surely as the commercialized graphic jotting depends unavailability on the triggered algorithmic script set in instantaneous laser motion by the pattern's "legible" (optical) differentiations.

As a novelistic irony, prose's reflex action at this point is the very recognition of this regress. Or put it that one graphic opacity (in a painted sheath of wood) translates the other (on cardboard labelling) into a reciprocal cryptic pictogram of silent intent, only to be sounded out by subvocal linguistic equivocation in a fast-scanned pun. Call this crunch of phonetic code, by narrative association, the underwriting of any overstory. Being there reading is our way of affirming there being reading—even if never more than latent and always in translation. What more can a novel ask of us in recognition?

Erratum: Bewilderment *Revisited*

The spirit of self-revision has been optional and extemporaneous until now in these retrospective pages, occasioned only by the minor squirms to which incomplete analysis is prey in an attentive rereading. There is worse coming. This anthology's willingness for second thoughts, even interpretive regrets, reaches here a pinnacle of potential chagrin in acknowledgment of a flat-out "clerical error." Standing accused is a node of sloppiness leading to textual misrepresentation in an overelaborate reading: the method sabotaged just where it lives. For which I have no one to blame but myself, certainly not the generosity of others. And yet I think readers should be able to forgive me once I explain. Taking me back to my earliest bookshop adventures in Laguna Beach (see Phases V / 11 and VII / 17), this time the good offices of the renowned Prairie Lights bookstore in Iowa City had unwittingly made the gaffe possible: with a gratefully received pre-publication copy of Powers' latest novel, *Bewilderment* (2021),[2] but one rendering me vulnerable to a true flub. One I've been bent on rectifying ever since I rushed into print with this latest (wrong) word on the novelist. And am repairing now by way of *erratum* and *mea culpa*.

For the record, a record it's none too soon to fix wherever possible, I've also revised the inaccuracy in publishing on *Bewilderment* as part of a larger argument about inter-art evolution from magic lanterns to virtual reality. This latest of my essays was commissioned for a Cambridge Handbook on *Literature and the Digital*, edited by Adam Hammond: another "occasional essay" in a student-friendly vein conceived as part of my "distance learning" commitment.[3] Ironically, though, if only for myself as contributor, the pedagogic focus of this series (with an excerpt from my contribution reprinted as Phase IX) serves at this point to relive—and certainly to relieve as well—the classroom snafu of my discovered false analysis regarding Powers' text. For it was only in teaching the novel in a creative writing course that I realized a "minor" change in the published edition since the pre-publication "reading copy" that I once thought myself so lucky to be gifted with. This is the way it went (came crashing) down. On the brink of calling student attention to a moment of prose density and overlap, I realized that the wording, uh, wasn't there in our copy. If reading George Eliot aloud to undergraduates had once brought me to hearing new things (as detailed in that homage to Geoffrey Hartman reprinted in Phase II / 4), here, rather, I was blindsided by the eyes-on undergraduate recognition that I was instead hearing things that were simply not there to see. To say that my flummoxed recoil from a prepared classroom "set-piece" got tactically redirected into a very different kind of "teachable moment" is not to minimize the scholarly shock of this dispiriting discovery. I'll come back to this after excerpting my latest print discussion of the novel in that *Literature and the Digital* handbook, where I had the welcome chance to get the passage right. For all the vexation at my realized previous over-reading—in particular, of a syllabic overlap that wasn't in fact there—the chance to return to the book had happier fallout in the end than just the opportunity to smooth over this mistakenly exaggerated fault line in textual inference. For it was only then, in writing again on Powers' novel—as if in a grand justification of Riffaterre's method, in my long-standing faith it its utility—that I discovered (as italicized in the second paragraph below) the unsaid clichéd matrix of this entire episode. This is the kind of second thought one revels in—rather than the screw-up one shrivels over (confessed evidence still pending, because in such matters context is everything):

> Two decades after Powers' exercise in code-driven, word-riven ekphrasis in the virtual inscapes of *Plowing the Dark*, his 2021 *Bewilderment* goes so far as to imagine a sub-optic simulacrum approaching, in "emotional telepathy," the condition of electronic immortality via preserved affect. Pitched even further forward into sf (sci-fi) technofuturism, the novel tracks its astrobiologist hero's struggle to appease the grieving of his son over the accidental death of the boy's mother. When alive, she was part of an experiment in the brain-scanning of affect's own pulsations, and the fMRI science has evolved since to the point where a mental transcript of his mother's most euphoric moments can be uploaded as mood elevator to the cerebral hardware of her son. When the boy later dies in another bitter accident, the father becomes in turn the experimental subject for a double transfusion of vanished affect as nested brain "print": impalpable imprint, not implant—a "read out"—to be internalized only as decoded, technologically deciphered. What results is a conflation of the two previous high-tech novels in the adjacent electronic realms of AI as VR: here the cognitive approximation of virtual moods.
>
> The gradual restoration of feeling in the transmit from mother to and through son—a feeling first theirs together, then in turn the bereft narrator's under renewed fMRI input—begins by an assonant phrasal chord change of "magnetic" prose "resonance" in a stylistic rather than psychic echo chamber: "I lie in the *tube* and *tune* myself to a print" of

the son's cortical circuitry. The process is known as DecNef ("decoded neural feedback"), with that abbreviation's vaguely necrological vibe in this case of a posthumous delivery system whereby the dead boy is already channeling his deceased mother. In its phrasing, "What they felt, then, I now feel," *then* is both retrospective and consequential: a recovered temporal "then" (cause) under the force of a mediating technological "therefore" (effect). Like a lap-dissolve in an implicitly comma-spliced grammar: "they" thought, therefore I am—am the repository of their continuance, their feelings again not so much for as *in* me. It is, finally, as if the novel's detailed tech miracle of affective transfer were generated by suppressing the clichéd formulation of its own goal (with the anchoring term in question never actually used to evoke the electromagnetic circuits involved). Enacted rather than named is the fantasy that the living and the dead could be *on the same wavelength*. Technical magic figures and inflects the textual: the moods of the dead renewed, dead metaphors literalized.

In just this way, on the novel's last page, the boy's fired synapses instigate the narrator's own: "The thought occurs to him—and I have it." Direct thought transference, yes, an internal "telepathy" again, but with an overtone of a eureka moment: "[Ah] I have it." I get it!—this a reference to the son's wonder at their time together amid the failed stewardship, but persistent beauty, of planet earth: "*Can you believe where we just were?*" As much as with Proust's lantern, DecNef goes out of its way to figure the story's own consumption, its own internalization, as print text. The novel, after all, has been transmitted to us by literary narrative's everyday version of thought transference, with a sorcery all its own. In the phenomenology of reading's ordinary mental ventriloquism, critic Georges Poulet stresses that in reading "I am thinking the thoughts of another"; am, in the grammatical sense of a speaking I, "the subject of thoughts other than my own." In the science fantasy of *Bewilderment*, the worded thoughts of a lost other are *had* (the father's verb in "I have it") as if they were his (subsumed into first-person plural in "where *we* just were") in their very decoding and articulation. As much as with DecNef decipherment, then, in reading Powers' fiction, absent others can live on in me, their thoughts reactivated. It is only the electronic sophistication of fMRI (*functional* Magnetic Resonance Imaging) that has allowed this *purposeful* tracking of the cortical blood flow—as if it were the very life-blood of consciousness. That fMRI abbreviation is an acronym, we'll soon find, with more than ordinary "resonance" even amid the oblique quirks of Powers' cultivated technospeak.

So forward, in conclusion, to another such example in Powers. [...] Regarding the lettering of fMRI (functional MRI) as a refrain in *Bewilderment*, the fsf (functional sci-fi) point is the same, with or without the resulting syllabic afterimage. But its techno-wizardry can only seem more eerily infused and distributed across the acronym's many appearances when its letters are found ghosted as syllabic vocables. For it is then that the term's insinuated inference may indeed "resonate magnetically" (*fMRI* science aside) in the swift enacted transience (f/m/r=effemare) of all things ephemeral. Looming further there in the many iterations of this scientific shorthand, or at least lurking, is a lexical auto-complete (incorporating the shorthand / of "imaging") that resembles not so much an Anglicized technospeak plural like "antenn*ae*," long *e*, as the long *i* plural of a term like "dramatis person*ae*" (fitly enough, given the residual force of the deceased fictional characters involved). Trailing off from the acronym, then, as it flips to yet another phonemic rebus, is the long psychic rather than just phonetic / of extended identity in this novel of "brain prints" and their affective post-mortem upload. [...] In reference to a sci-fi apparatus extrapolated well beyond the far reaches of ultrasound, and in yet another convergence of lexical and electron codes in Powers, the alphabetic vox(c)el here elicits the human raw material of a transcriptive system other than its own. Even the machine's repeated numb acronym, in other words, cannot altogether repress an ulterior syllabic sounding of the very evanescence that its operation—as reading's own emblem or parable—is meant to transcend. [...]

In a recent interview with Ezra Klein on his *New York Times* podcast, Powers guessed that it wouldn't take most readers of *Bewilderment* long to figure out that decoded neurofeedback (DecNef), in its conduit of emotion, is operating as a metaphor for reading. For reading's affect, that is: alternating in relay between narrator and empathetic reader in a circuitry so essentially phonetic that Powers has written eloquently about the iPad dictation of his novels, through voice-recognition software, as an effort to bring the writing closer to the silent enunciation of its reader. Set that down as another computerized case, though generalized and demystified, of affective imprint as reading's blueprint.

The book by Powers strikes me as concluding with one of the most invested allegories of reading since George Eliot's quasi-gothic parable of thought-transference in *Daniel Deronda* (1876), or its related hypnotic intensification in Bram Stoker's *Dracula* (1897). In Powers, the reader is more technologically "end(ear)ed" yet. But my once signal evidence for this out-of-body metempsychosis—and its verbal "resonance"—needed eventual and explicit retraction by your humble(d) commentator. For as I wrote it up for *The Metanarrative Hall of Mirrors*, a pivotal phrasing wasn't as much a funhouse mirror as I had reason to believe. Elated in my advance copy by what seemed to me a definitive slyness in Power's frequent auditory skids, and not double-checking with the published hardback when it appeared during the copyediting of my own proofs, I found myself responding (found out only too late, that is) to what turned out to be an opening-sentence "error" on the book's last page—at the head and climactic onset, no less, of a new and final narrative unit. The sentence in question precedes the phenomenal transfer I do quote in the second paragraph of the handbook excerpt above: "What they felt, then, I now feel." This is because the son's affect has been electromagnetically transferred to the father, and that of his wife as well, already internalized by the boy's: "My wife, too, still inside him"—a nested effect like a reverse pregnancy.

But the whole chapter had begun just before—and this way (I thought): "And then one day my son is in there, inside my head ...." That first preposition was eventually deleted, though, as if mistakenly introduced by back-sliding association with the intended and retained "inside." Alas (says the critic), what remains—the boy's energy simply being "there," rather than "in there"—doesn't trigger the Necker-like flicker effect, like some faint mode of reciprocal fade-out, of the equally true (and all but phonemically indistinguishable) "is in there" / "isn't there." Before the novelist's or the copy editor's final proofread, what seemed to me proven on the pulse of that wavering enunciation—call it, in microcinematic terms, a kind of vanishing audiovisual superimposition—was the presence-within-absence of electrocortical longevity. As is the case with the technologically disembodied medium of the son himself, so I thought with the prose: now you hear it, now you don't. For the eager critic, as with the transferable "brain imprint" at stake in the plot, the extra print preposition was all too readily transmissible under interpretation. But let the inveterate student of "transegmental drift" (from as early as 1990's *Reading Voices*) insist that the principle survives the "rethought" (rather than phonetically self-adjusting) textual instance.

And another, broader axiom about reading persists as well. In my rushed eagerness to track Powers' invention down to the moment, I naturally should do some penance, of the present sort, for reading in advance from the "unauthorized" (interesting word choice) version, the so-called pre-publication "reading copy" (interesting again), but I like to think now that I was "making something" (another teasing idiom, constructivist at base) of what the novelist *did write*—and then took back. As I revise here, so did he too once, intent on smoothing out, perhaps, the slight awkwardness (pleonasm?) of "was in there [, inside]" (rather than simply "was there" [, inside]). And doing so without regretting (or maybe even registering) what there was to lose in metaphysical ambiguity, in psychic synchronicity rather than prose rhythm. That is, we are not in the realm of *errata* so much as revision, reaudition. The novelist's withdrawal (from a penultimate draft) or reclamation (from a possible editor's slip) needn't cancel my first take just because there's no *stet* to insist on. What certainly survives revision—especially in these pages of look-again remarks and second listens—gets to the very nature of finality in writing, elusive, even delusional, with every reading a re-vision. Emblemized here, quite to my admitted surprise at the time, a subtheme of *Attention Spans* is in fact the sense of suspended animation in the work of words: the way writing lives on in us, for us, even one's own writing, is still up to us to make renewed sense of. As evident in other moments not needing last-minute edits, the contrapuntal rhythm of Powers' narration often filters down to the actively poly*phonic* at the level of syllables and their phonemic latches. And for the further and final illustration of such effects, in an earlier and more canonical instance (Proust), I'll beg the indulgence of one more insert from this handbook essay—after I've done scant justice (only actual listening could suffice) to the microphone resonance under discussion in my next and latest book.

20 / ***Streisand: The Mirror of Difference*** (Wayne State University Press, 2023). Arranged like a concert set list, with overture, intermission, and three main acts (early club and TV dates; her nineteen films; and a return to live concerts), Stewart's book puts under inspection (and intensive audition) the entire arc of Streisand's unprecedented career. Concentrating on her self-styled role as an "actress-who-sings," his analysis stresses the way her genius finds its fullest measure in screen song, first in Emmy-winning TV specials, next in Hollywood blockbusters from *Funny Girl* (1968, dir. William Wyler) to *Funny Lady* (1975, dir. Herbert Ross). Then emerging from her decision to direct her own "musical concepts" in *A Star Is Born* (1976, dir. Frank Pierson), with its first commercial use of Dolby Stereo, the book follows her onward to the writing as well as directing of her own starring (and singing) role in *Yentl* (1983). Stewart concentrates not just on the cultural difference she made as the first openly Jewish superstar and mainstream female director but on the internal differentials of a vocal gift that has its own, cinematographic contours. Stewart's special brand of "close listening" is supported at many points by an exacting and expansive scope of musicological analysis from Roland Barthes through Glenn Gould to the latest YouTube video-essay analyses of the Streisand range and delivery. The emphasis throughout, distilling much of his own previous work as well as the star's distinction, is on voice as text.

20 / The Legible Voice

Streisand: The Mirror of Difference (2023)

About Barbra Streisand, at least for once, I can be brief. Everything depends on the remarkable availability of performances on YouTube, with access not only to her earliest TV appearances but to several new orchestrally stripped "a capella" versions of her most famous song numbers, foregrounding her isolated vocals as never before—and rendering them, in my sense, legible in whole new ways. But then her "line readings" always cut through no matter how luxuriant a score to find lexical nuance in enunciation itself. In her work's long-playing soundtrack to half a century of American cultural life, part of an epoch's varying background themes, it's always felt wrong to find the still-material evidence of her now-streaming sound, first on vinyl, then cassette, then CD, filed lazily in the "Easy Listening" bin. Hers is a gorgeously *demanding* voice, in any genre, in every recorded performance: seldom free for long of some ferocious vocal surprise—and never more interesting than when one can watch for anatomical signs of its production on camera. With nothing easy or slackly relaxing about the vocal metadrama of this "actress-who-sings," her delivery elicits a "close listening" that, when I came, on editorial request, to write about it at book length, disclosed more connection with my earlier phonetic as well as cinematographic analysis and teaching than I had otherwise realized.

But that aside for a moment, the origin of this project says it all. When I was asked out of the blue, based on the slim evidence of a 1976 *Sight and Sound* review of *A Star Is Born* (1976, dir. Frank Pierson), whether I would be interested in doing a book on Streisand for the Queer Screens series at Wayne State University Press, I explained that my very real interest in this was only qualified, and I myself therefore probably disqualified, by the fact that any treatment of mine wouldn't in any sense be a "gay studies" approach. "That's fine," said the series editor, David Gerstner, who had me with the next line: "Talent that extreme is queer enough for us." The amplitude of this maxed-out talent became a natural keynote of the volume, amid inevitable passing remarks on queer fandom, cross-dressed feminist thematics, and an occasionally salient homoerotic subtext in her film work. But always the voice first. In that regard I am readily inclined to assert a scholarly continuity, even in this form of pop audition, with the phonetic ambiguities of *Reading Voices* (1990; see Phase II / 3)—as well as with the technical specificities of my four previous film books (in such matters, here again, as freeze-frames, dissolves, shot/reverse shots, and the like). But further, beyond that assertion, and maybe more to the point here in this collection, it might be no surprise that I am also willing to admit the unfiltered strain of sheer aesthetic enthusiasm that has run through my writing from the first Dickens book forward—and that has no choice but to show up again here in a rather undiluted concentration.

> For her first appearance on *The Ed Sullivan Show*, in November of 1962, less than three months before the release of her first album, Streisand began by showcasing just over three minutes of what amounted, mounted, to a compressed five-act play followed by a downbeat ironic finale. There could be no clearer instance of her acting and singing in dialogue with each other, in virtual duet, than this more than ordinarily operatic delivery of a song whose narrative phases are all part of a single post-romantic denouement. In her rendering of "My Coloring Book" (Kander and Ebb, written before their big Broadway hits), Streisand's nervously mercurial intensity of shifting expressions, in fixed medium-closeup, seem in themselves to enact the very lament over ephemerality at stake in this lovelorn ballad. According to the full lyrics of the verse lead-in, as she later recorded it, the figurative "crayon" tones (and musical tonalities) by which the listener is enjoined to "color me"—unfolded on their own without verse preamble in the TV version—range across a full gamut of *picturable* deprivation. They do so by tabulating every probable emotion—except self-pity—in an optic dance of avoidance with the direct eyeline gaze of the camera (a rule violated only briefly,

pointedly, at the early line "these are the eyes"). Regret spreads across the rhyming dissonance of emotional desertion from "gr*ay*" (those same eyes having "watched him" as he "went aw*ay*") through a heart "bl*ue*" (discovering him no longer "tr*ue*") to the "some*how*" of loss with arms colored "empty *now*" (Streisand's own arms opened out in vacancy at this grievance, extending past the bottom of the TV frame). The details to be "colored" by audience projection extend next from worn beads turned "gr*een*" with jealousy (now that an unnamed "she" so cruelly "came betw*een*") to the imponderable chromatics of an unrhymed abstract "lonely." All this, amid the fleeting winces and held-back tears of betrayal, works itself through—in what will become a typifying Streisand fashion—with sufficient reserves of banked fire to sear away any trace of female abjection. After this fivefold litany of heartbreak, the song bears down on the last impossible coloring of absence per se when the phrasing of a man once depended "up/*on*"—after the lyric's own dependent syllabic drop—is put into slightly skewed rhyme with the need, in the recursive refrain, to "color him *gahwnnnn*." And right there, beyond the bracing facial dramatics, right there in the ironic continuum and slow attenuation of that poignantly held (as if clung to) last note—call it in cinematic terms, in its thematized diminuendo, a phonic reverse-zoom—we have another early sign of what would soon become a recognized Streisand specialty: the gradually relaxed yet steadily clarified tenacity of her purest exit notes.

When my sense of her career as three-act set list arrives at its pinnacle in Act II—with her hard-won debut as director, as well as writer and star, of *Yentl*—my dialed-up analysis of the modulations in miked singing also makes direct connection, after all, with the "queer screens" of same-sex desire and its closeted deflections, repeatedly enhanced not just by the mostly comedic performances but by the tact of Streisand's exacting camerawork. In a film that Steven Spielberg was widely quoted to call—no doubt thinking of an earlier actor taking his first turn behind the camera—the most accomplished directorial debut since *Citizen Kane*, the singer has found a new way to enact her gift in a weave of over-dubbed (or call it under-voiced) interior monologue and its vent in expressive song. (Widely quoted was Spielberg, but not alas by me until now, I realized, looking back at *Streisand*—and so another onus of regret for your author and another tiny bonus for this Reader's readers.)

The plot premise: eager Polish girl in 1904 (Yentl), masquerading as a boy (Anshel) so as to study Talmud, falls in love with one of her Yeshiva classmates (Avigdor, played by Mandy Patinkin), who cajoles her into marrying his fiancée (Hadass, played by Amy Irving) once her parents have rejected him, just (for Avigdor) to keep Hadass as near as possible. But more palpable interchanges of desire have characterized the student's friendship long before:

This erotic dimension of intellectual intimacy is briefly defused by the initial comic scene of their shared hostel bed, yet is not forgotten by the plot in driving toward recognition—certainly not after the many quick-cut glimpses of Avigdor's touch-buddy roistering with Anshel, his affectionate jabs and hugs, which have regularly served, beyond near-miss exposure in the disguise comedy, to cast a tentative sexual shadow, or glow, over their student bonding.

When sex with Hadass has been particularly on his mind, he's all the more likely to deflect the physicality of his desire (while still unconsciously to direct it) toward his innocent friend Anshel. Giddy over the prospect of the "wedding night" when still engaged, his rough-house tousling forces a jealous complaint from Yentl: "Why are you always grabbing me?"—an objection whose premise he immediately denies. Instead of being defused en route, in a boys-will-be-boys mode, the queering of such insular Yeshiva norms goes far to explaining, not what it is that finally prevents Avigdor, once the shock is over, from accepting Yentl as an insistently strong woman still seeking access to a man's world of learning—a conjugal dead-end dictated by cultural stereotype—not that, but something else. We begin to understand, once his guard is down, what ignites his volcanic rage at the discovery of Yentl's identity in the first place. He immediately fulminates against her "demon"-like violation of the Talmud, not his personal betrayal by her con job. But the outrage is indeed personal, physical. The latter he comes to relax into, flattered by its motive: her admitted passionate love for him. Until then, however, there seems something filthy and fiendish in female desire outside of its passive place in sex—and by inference something fearful as well, no less, in a warm male response to its masculine disguise.

It may be easy on first viewing to write this stance off as orthodoxy in uptight recoil: the stance, but not its convulsive fury—which Patinkin understands so well he inclines to overdo it. In the rehearsal tape for this confrontation, from the DVD, we see Streisand in the throes of double consciousness, playing her part under the painful lash of his contempt while also, askew to their confrontation, redirecting with her left hand one of the two camera operators needed to compass the emotional vortex of this intrepid wheeling shot, even while urging Patinkin to tone down the volume of his outrage. Her complicated technical idea amounts to having the polarized couple circling each other—an emotional abyss yawning between and beneath them—rather than having them face off in anything like a straightforward intercut debate. Emotion is indeed spiraling out of control. Even the idiom of Avigdor's incensed rage and panic reverts to the protective vernacular of a bitter but still almost half-unconscious paradox, spluttered out in the midst of his screaming frenzy: "Why didn't you tell me (you weren't a man)? "C'mon, answer me like a man." Even with such an idiomatic cliché cruelly rearing its head, he seems trapped between nostalgia and bitter irony, still addressing the vanished Anshel. But when he begins to accept both her truth and her motives—Yentl's now, the transgressive woman's—his only language of recognition reverts to the celebration of pure sensual desire reprised from the much earlier "No Wonder" montage. It was there that Yentl was so readily able, if still ironically, to plug into Avigdor's facile acquiescence in Hadass' deferential modesty and manicured charms. This time it isn't a woman recognizing the obvious appeal of another woman, but Avigdor himself recognizing what he should have seen through to in the eager camaraderie of his prolonged homosocial bonding. Twice repeated for emphasis, even in its ellipses, as the flip side of Hadass' realized charms: "No wonder. Oh my god, no wonder. I wanted to look at you, to touch you." To vary the full earlier lyric: no wonder he loved him. "I thought there was something wrong with me." Yentl to the immediate rescue of homosexual shame: "No, it was me." Even in exonerating him, at this point she is still declaring herself, Yentl rather than Anshel, as the source of the blameful deceit—and in the process excusing his conservative self from erotic guilt, a charge reduced to a mere lapse of heterosexual perceptiveness.

From which lapse, he doesn't immediately recover. Bafflement persists—until her ultimate romantic (as well as gender) confession. Why did she continue the escalating complexities of the deception? Why preserve the masquerade amid the literally geometric complications of triangulated desire? Why not flee, rather than risk pain and exposure? Yentl's final wrenching declaration—"Because I loved you!"—only serves to disarm and "unman" each of them, in relief and exhaustion at once, as they collapse to their knees and into each other's shoulders, their faces for a long few seconds hidden from the overhead camera. What follows when they look back at each other, and upon the truth, is an exchange that Streisand carefully designed (we learn from the DVD about this cross-cutting) so as to flatter him with backlighting while training the stark "hot light"—riveting enough in a different way, of course—on herself. Eventually the camera shifts ninety degrees for a close-up on their faces moving in on a kiss: with lips touching, but not quite opening yet, for just as long as they did in Yentl's resisted kiss with Hadass in the preceding episode. With the camera building toward this *interruptus* of a tempting but arrested passion, as reciprocally approached from each side of the hypercharged two-shot, the orchestral score has been notably mounting as well—only to shut down on the instant with Avigdor's abrupt blurting out of the exorcizing name "Hadass." Marked there is the death of some fluidity of feeling that melody—passing in and out of song until now, and back and forth from monologue to emoted lyric—is meant to essentialize. After the two syllables of "Hadass," the silence is, in terms of drama and genre alike, deafening.

And there's no discounting the homoerotic pressure on this seemingly legalistic second thought in a recall of the wronged woman. Voiced out loud, in that single female name, is not so much an alternate yearning, distancing him from an embrace of Yentl, as it is, so he is quick to explain, a concern over the former's own false marriage, for which he rightly feels responsible—and about which Yentl assures him a contrite explanatory note from her to the rabbis will easily annul. But the erotic spell is broken, and precisely by such social anxieties, such patriarchal legalisms, such conservative reins on desire. And, of course, by the tacit relief they can be expected to bring. Even a moment before, on the cusp of discovery and revision, we sense that the kiss would have been too much for him, this open erotic embrace of the boy who was(n't): too backward-glancing, too much the indulgence of a nostalgic and deviant fantasy. Unequivocal hetero-doxa must intercede—as well as compulsory patrilineage in the choosing of the fitly subservient bride. In the hero's backing instinctively away from a marginally acknowledged queer desire, Hadass proves the perfect retreat. [...]

With Streisand explaining earlier on the DVD how being "from the theater" inclines her to as few edits as possible in a given scene, letting the actors bridge their own transitions, as it were, the most striking exception to this, after the shot/countershot of her bared womanhood, follows again now. After the orbiting camerawork of Avigdor's ensuing ferocity, sex and gender are costars in the reversible impasse of this last shot exchange, biology and emotional teleology. After the circling frenzy of the sexual revelation, that is, the overlapping gender thematic of this climactic episode, peaked at its truncated kiss, subsides into the settled confrontation of opposing "views"—and cinematic viewpoints. This transpires, with all hope of compromise expiring with it, across no less than eight crosscuts as the camera progressively dollies in by turns on each of them, she in the window seat, he across the room, his back to the door. It is here, finally, that Yentl holds firm, with a little insistent shrug, on the "more" she unaccountably wants—with the camera then closing in on his sad but definitive shaking of his head in fade out. Departing from the single takes Streisand quite effectively favors, what she has devised in this case is a masterly capture of difference in the deliberately broken rhythm of montage. A two-shot no longer possible, the closer the camera comes to each of them separately, the farther apart they feel, isolated against each other.

Beyond "The Same Anymore"

So we're back where we started, if not quite, with the original nuptial expectations restored. And so, on Yentl's part, space is made again—a gap opened, a void awaiting infused promise—for yet another and final "solo." The castrating force of role reversal—the man in love with a boy but not the woman s/he would become, the woman more in love with learning than with a man who can't tolerate it—leaves only one way forward. And with a valedictory moment to confirm it: Yentl still bent on her own destiny beyond the sexual selections of orthodoxy, Avigdor literally taking the horse-cart reins of his return to Hadass. In their parting dialogue we get the film's last and most plangent same-sex gesture: "I'll miss you," a doe-eyed Avigdor says, more than convincingly, into the continuing face of her disguise. Miss not the woman he never had, but the friend he doted on and cavorted with. In this final separation, that is, he rubs Yentl's cheek, wryly allowing how her "beard will probably never come in now." This lighthearted quip delivers a heavy dose of homoerotic irony. Here, vanishingly, for one last touch, is the smooth-cheeked boy he has loved, stroked in restraint while the woman's lips have been left unkissed, deflected to a hug instead. His "Goodbye Anshel" is, for this reason among others, corrected at once: "Yentl," she gently admonishes. And he accedes. Goodbye to both, to male pal and to ideal (female) partner, freed as he has been to caress one last time not just the remarkable woman he's giving up but the intriguing young man of his lingering fantasy.

With a last chaste embrace, this detachment from Avigdor in the name of Yentl's own self-determination is now soliloquized, and in deliberate reversal of her congratulatory hug from him back at the Yeshiva, by the leading refrain from that "One of those Moments" anthem. What she'll "remember" all her "life" is the parting of their ways and lives. This emphasis on affect already memorialized, just by saying (or singing) so, thrusts all romantic feeling into the bracketed, the always unactionable, past: a node of closure in going forward. Life must still be lived, must be made, if possible, further memorable. And the next reprise of the film's first lyric, asking as it did where the limit on desire is "written," is at once folded into the film's unforgettable climactic aria (of local severance and forward-looking self-asseveration) that begins as if further back than we've ever been privy to. "It all began," we hear at the start of "A Piece of Sky"—initiating a kind of retrospective loop, catching up the psychogenesis of her disruptive desire even before we encountered her obstreperous energy in the early mirror scene: all began, that is, when she noticed that her domestic horizons were limited by a "window" vantage on only its one eponymous slice or sector of the outer world. Window frame versus mirror. The urge that things should not "be the same anymore," should split from themselves in renewal, is just what has been figured in the many mirrors of difference the film has framed, mounted, and zeroed in upon, dodging their technical capture of the reflected camera whose projected screen image they at the same time emblemize.

Even before returning briefly, below, to the heightened vocal scenography at the climax of *Yentl* (and thus saving, as Streisand does, the best for last), there's enough audited and theorized sound play in my account of "echo neurons"—in the somatic effect of Streisand's lyric production—for this latest book to have been called *Reading Voice*. No surprise, perhaps, after as long a time spent in listening hard to a singer's enunciation over the years as in the hard reading of writing and screen imaging, that the habits would finally intersect. Parallel lines do sometimes veer from disciplinary norms into convergence. And with new discoveries still waiting down the line.

In parenthesizing myself one more time here, I go back to missed vocal evidence not in the spirit of *mea culpa* this time, but just of a palpable "oh my." For missing until now what is provided by this technologically restored detail was universal, couldn't be helped, not my aural oversight alone. Not until its sixty-year-delayed release in November 2022 were listeners able to compare one in particular of the original Bon Soir nightclub tracks—intended as Streisand's live debut album, but only now digitally redone in the studio to improve sound quality—with the onetime vinyl evidence of "Cry Me a River" on *The Barbra Streisand Album* (1963). And thus, amid the technical enhancements (the crystalline vocals left untampered with) on the recovered nightclub set, to note by contrast a typifying moment of voice as text in Streisand's continually rethought delivery, maximizing yet again an enacted force of wording beneath the obvious sense of lyric. In a far more obvious contrast to the low-wick jazz-torch version by Julie London in the mid-1950s, sultry but muted, Streisand's furious treatment of this number (in more than one early TV spot as well) redoubles the song's vindictive refrain—repeating verbatim the central lines about remembering all too well her jilting by an "untrue" and now repentant partner who "told me love was too plebian, / told me you were through with me." But at the song's ironic peripety: "Now you say you're sorry." Nothing doing, it's your turn to "cry me a river"—as if modeled by the flood of comeuppance unleashed by Streisand's delivery. Yet only in the digitally cleansed 2022 Bon Soir version, not in the guest-appearance kinescopes on YouTube, is the sound pellucid enough to register fully what, by contrast, Streisand had gone on to do with the lyric in the studio—at exactly the point where the tacit "but" of "Now you say you love me ..." arrives, in reprise, at the original lyric's delayed and now prolonged and explosive "*And* now." In the throaty contempt of its reiterated romantic dismissal, the snarl in "plebian" achieves at last the broad cross-word rhyme withheld the first time around in the lyric. For now, and all the more so in the studio version, the third syllabic stroke of "plebi*an*" has been hammered out so that its pending rhyme more obviously bridges the enjambed and rapidly amplified "through with *me / AND* now you say ...." As if for vocal stamina in the live version, the marked taken breath at this caesura throws into relief what the studio treatment more shrewdly achieves—the immediacy of emotive backlash in that searing legato span across a clausal break.

I'm hereby entering for the record not my repentant second thoughts this time, but rather the singer's own considered ones in the months between club stage and recording booth. The syllabic shove of that swelling phonic glide offers a literally pronounced, a viscerally compelling, ligature in the rounding—and pounding—out of the song's dramatic irony: a smiting audial overlap of performed erotic reversal. Awaiting, in the five notes of the song's last three words, only the final rasp of tolling overrun from "*ri*ver" to "(r)*ov*er" before the detonation of the scorned "you." In a mood of elation rather than retaliation in the Bon Soir set, hear a comparable phonetic decision when, in "I'll Tell the Man in the Street," after the crisp, clipped *t* rhyme at "everyone I m*eet*"—and again all the more *pronounced*, so to speak, in the studio version—the *t* is instead almost swallowed as the syllabic colloquial glide of "sweethearts" swells in rhyme to the five-second stretch of cross-word echo at "compleeeee(t) (h)earts."

What better example, though there were many like it available in time for publication, of the tightly framed "terrain" of the Streisand sound I had set out to track. A lifelong opera buff, to whom I had sent an author's copy of *Streisand*, opened first to the index, he wrote back, hoping to find that I had registered Glenn Gould's rapturous comparison of her interpretive talent to that of Elisabeth Schwarzkopf's in Gould's otherwise lukewarm review of 1973's *Classical Barbra*. My friend was glad to find I had, and then was sent back in turn, he wrote, to his copy of British musicologist John Steane's *The Grand Tradition: Seventy Years of Singing on Record, 1900–1970*, which I hadn't cited, suggesting that Steane's view of the German soprano would have jibed nicely with Gould's comparative emphasis on Streisand's "infinite diversity and timbral resource." Whether or not Steane may have come to regret publishing just a little too soon, wishing he had Gould's enthusiasm for ES (rather than BS) to footnote, I myself certainly wished I had sent my friend a draft of the chapter in time for including what his email quoted as this perfect distillation of the two singers' shared vocal *focus* from note to note: "What one has in Schwarzkopf is a high degree of awareness—of colours and styles, and of the existence of *choice*. [... Her] performances are reliably greater in yield, in point-by-point enlightenment, than almost anybody else's."[4] My regret at missing this characterization—regarding the considered "choice" behind the choicest of notes—would be far keener if I didn't think the comparative case had in fact been made, again and again, in "point-by-point" listening.

A case made even before the opportunity of going back to 1962 for that audited span of notes above (in post-publication footnote)—another beveling, if you will, of Streisand's phonic mirror: "plebian" in blistering slant rhyme with "me And." And beside such *readings of voicings* in the Streisand book, there are other strands of attention tying back to earlier work of mine—as well as more recent (Phase IX). Apart from the subtle echoic differentials of her phrasing, not only does a proliferating motif of reflected image return in the last of the Streisand films I discuss in my mirror-subtitled book, her 1996 *The Mirror Has Two Faces*, but it appears again in the form of a crucial symbolic prop in the second of her Emmy-winning concerts, y2k's *Timeless*. Yet what really brings the present study (of regathered reflections) into focus as the second of my "mirror" books in as many years (see Phase VIII / 19) is precisely the "reflex action" induced not just aurally, as registered by close listening, but optically. As with its equivalent in lyric line readings, this jolt to cinematographic "objectivity"—or call it panoptic neutrality—occurs when the eyeline gaze of the singing body is abruptly deployed (it feels almost in each case like a weaponized look) at both the vocal turning point of *A Star Is Born* and in the last shot (and twenty-second note) of *Yentl*, the heroine at the stern of an America-bound steamer, looking back while plowing forward, her piercing glance and high note distanced without diminution by reverse zoom at the final rhyme of "A Piece of Sky": "watch me flyyyhiiiigh."

In this case vibrating to the at-last released "I," regendered, of a potentially shattering vocal force, the screen's fragile fourth wall, like the page's descriptive interface elsewhere (its own flatscreen phenomenological surface facing the reader), submits to another metanarrative version of the direct address that preoccupied me over three decades before in *Dear Reader* (1996; see Phase II / 4). Once again, then, and as a necessary axiom of this anthology, there is no emphasis on a critic's career nostalgia—but rather, more to the point, on a professionally banked fund of abiding technical and rhetorical interests across media that may continue to yield results with each new pass (however many years intervene). Only in this sense of return and generative refraction is there any productive (pedagogical) effort at noting "the way we were," personally and/or collectively. So a post-book addendum (herewith Phase IX) on what used to be translated *Remembrance of Things Past*—rather than any search for lost time on my part—can, I hope, be profitably entertained.

Notes

1 Richard Powers, *The Overstory* (New York: W. W. Norton, 2018).
2 Richard Powers, *Bewilderment* (New York: W. W. Norton, 2021).
3 Garrett Stewart, "Literature's Audioptic Platform," in *Cambridge Companion to Literature and the Digital*, ed. Adam Hammond (Cambridge: Cambridge University Press, forthcoming 2024).
4 J. B. Steane, *The Grand Tradition: Seventy Years of Signing on Record* (Portland: Amadeus Press, 1993), 349–50.

IX.

AUDIOPTICS

THE PRESUMED LICENSE TO ADD one more short extract from a printed piece, and then a summarizing endpiece on book covers from the previous tracts (see Phase X), shouldn't seem odd in so freewheeling a Reader (book and lector alike). Since I don't have at hand, unlike some critics, an obvious miscellany of storied pieces, better, the editor and I agreed, to try for some kind of intermittent story: a history of interests pretty much unresisted in the widely varying directions in which they were inclined to lead—even while overlapping time and again in the slipstream of provocations and analytic encounters. Trajectory, not historical landmarks. Not privileging one monograph over another for its supposed centrality (or the perceived popularity of its subjects), the interest might lie instead in the rehearsed domino-effect of exploration, one project toppling upon completion into the next, however previously unnoted in regard to any obvious topical adjacency. I have, therefore, come to view what I have plucked out from these twenty monographs—in their rolling score of analytic wagers, with all the single-essay side bets in between—as the plot synopsis of an unfolding tale that could never have been foretold, certainly not from one decade to the next. So, I'll ante up (rather than up the ante) with a final excerpt offered more in a distillation of antecedent interests than as late-breaking news—and from that same handbook contribution that gave me the chance to set the record straight just now, in Phase VIII / 19, on the last chapter of *Bewilderment*.

< *Literature's Audioptic Platform* >

The typographic chevrons there are deliberately ambiguous, using the familiar less-than icon to point *back*, instead, at long-standing interests so obviously summarized in this new piece—while allowing the other brace or arrowhead to stand either for closing things off or for looking forward. Who knows? Certainly, Proust isn't roped in here as either *sine qua non* or *ne plus ultra*. The motive for including these analytic paragraphs, as a kind of excerpt finale, or perhaps encore, is a far cry from the fusty sense that any critics of narrative or style worth their salt should pepper their vitae with some things—at least something—on Proust. (And in fact certain of the French novelist's metatextual passages on the reading act had already helped launch *Dear Reader* as far back as 1996.) The purpose here is instead to give full weight to the portmanteau coinage ("audioptic") of my handbook contribution. In anticipating the sequential logic of this article, it was as if I were following a trail of breadcrumbs leading back, alongside published footprints, from my work on cinema theory—in part via metamedial instances in Victorian heritage film—to actual Victorian fiction, including its subvocal poetics. At which point the actual drafting of the essay had its way of reversing direction. It now begins with metaphors of magic lantern slides in George Eliot and Henry James—optical figures for various psychic states of collision, overlap, and transience—before following on from the dawn of cinema to a famous anachronistic lantern ekphrasis in Proust:[1]

> After such diverse figurative uses of the phantasmagoric "dissolving view"—as a Victorian metaphor for a surreal emotional blur, for temporal palimpsest, and for optic telepathy—Proust, on the other side of cinema's invention, goes so far as to include an actual lantern apparatus, in a nostalgic narrative context, before dissolving it, too, into a metaphor for reading. [...]
>
> Early in *Swann's Way*, Marcel recalls how his mother, when reading George Sand aloud, "breathed into this very common prose a sort of continuous emotional life." [...] The episode is meant to be generalized, for even silent reading entails "sentences which seem written for [her] voice." In performed wording, the *phrasing* is ultimately one's own. It is just this voicing rather visual script of his mother's book that "directed the sentence that was ending toward the one that was to begin" [...] as clocked here, in mimetic cadence, by Proust's characteristic linking commas: "sometimes hurrying, sometimes slowing down the pace of the syllables so as to bring them, though their quantities were different, into one uniform rhythm." On either side of this excursus on the flux of recitation in *Swann's Way*, as if to frame its centrality, are passages that also concern syllabic pacing in diverse yet complementary ways: first when, early on, a particular story is read aloud in Marcel's bedroom to the accompaniment of a magic lantern display, and later through alphabetic distortions eyed across the engraved marble of his beloved Combray church.

IMAGEdTEXT: Proust's Warp of Words

To the church first, for its own division of labor between the waverings of thrown light and those of malleable text—each on the way back to a primal scene of lantern projection that their separately registered details, verbal and ocular, serve to unpack in their combined tableau of "sculpted stone and stained glass." It is only when recalling how the famous lantern slides, rippling across Marcel's draped bedroom windows, were timed to the reading aloud of a narrative prompt text—only then that we are likely to spot the bond between the shifting colored projections of the church windows and the distorted letter forms carved into inlaid and time-worn floor stones and "read" by Marcel as nonverbal images in themselves. Again word and image come into an uneasy, or at least unfixed, relation. The tinted windows have been frayed frail by the atmospheric exposure, the incised stone whittled down by human tread. Together, if by a circuitous route, these two features, as disfeaturings, return us to the textures of projection and distortion already differently developed in the magic lantern passage. Light flickers unpredictably through the chapel glass, dousing stone with color while at the same time, in their plane of its gridded imagery, equivocating mimesis itself. A snowy mountain pictured in one composite stained panel appears "frosted onto the glass itself" by some assaulting winter. Its "snowflakes," though seemingly "lit by some aurora," result instead from the flecks of erosion in the pitted glazing, "so old that here and there one saw their silvery age sparkle with the dust of the centuries and show, shimmering and worn down to the thread, the weft of their soft tapestry of glass." As planes of visual representation, these windows simulate the assaults of real weather; as artifacts, their translucent "lozenge-shaped panes" are themselves visibly weathered.

So, too, with the surface of the church's entryway floor, which, having endured the tread of centuries, has become "uneven and deeply hollowed at the edges." Lived time has served to "bend the stone and carve it with furrows." Same with the floor-embedded "tombstones" of the abbots that "formed for the choir a sort of spiritual pavement"—a tempting model for the Proustian text in its linguistic *platform*. The stressed stone—"no longer inert and hard matter"—comes to offer, as we read on, a diagram of textual mutation per se. For "time had softened" the inset memorials and "made them flow like honey beyond the bounds of their own square shapes, which, in one place, they had overrun in a flaxen billow." It takes a moment to recognize (through the young Marcel's eyes) what is going on, what has gone on. The rippling run-over of marble shapes is traced further by the cumulative Proustian grammar and the mixed-metaphoric flow of the graven script—so that the once chiseled inscriptions are seen "carrying off on their drift a flowering Gothic capital letter": an eerie textual generativity from the stony grave. We must read as closely as Marcel does the abraded language before him. Once carved in marble, the letters "had reabsorbed themselves, further contracting the elliptical Latin inscriptions, introducing a further caprice in the arrangement of those abridged characters, bringing close together two letters of a word of which the other had been disproportionately distended." Alluded to there is the marmoreal economy of tombstone protocols—with such (unexampled) short-cuts as *vix* or *ann* (for *vixit*, he lived, or *annus*) or such phrasal condensates as the acronym DMS (*Dis Manibus*, to the spirits of the departed). Latin's original shorthand compressions are further travestied in the scrunched letter forms that rivet the young boy's (and eventual writer's) gaze.

Philology seems recapitulated by marble topography. For in the form of exactly the Latin practice that first introduced word breaks into Western script, affording comprehension without mandatory vocalization, here letters lose signification in contingent mergers, cross-threaded into the new floral twists of phantom ligatures and strictly graphic diphthongs, including that fluctuant viscous "honey" of their cresting "flaxen billows." With this emphasis on verbal spacing in cryptic (both senses) abbreviations and swellings alike, we may conjure the fungibility of alphabetic writing even when, as it were, set in stone. The variable rhythm and fused continuities of the Proustian text, in the uptake by present reading, are emblematized— in this bending and blending of letters—as the plasticity, immediate rather than immemorial, of the typeset words, including all its vocalic "overruns," "drifts," "ellipses," "distensions," and "abridgments" (a virtual Proust-thesaurus).

This, we'll now see, is how even the establishing lantern scene early in the novel—in its play between storybook text and unstable lamplit illustration—has in effect paved the way for the distortions of the church's inlaid Latin floorspace. For beyond the mutable luminescence of the stained-glass windows, carved out there as a grounding textual condition is the intangible friability of inscription in the pacing and "caprice" of the reading moment. By junctural analogy, this is the word-to-picture ratio that I've "pronounced" IMAGEdTEXT: the foundational play, in short, between pictured graphic wording and worded pictures.

Son et lumière: Textual Imagineering

Proust's reflexive modernism depends in part on isolating the affect of remembrance from the words that struggle to summon it, only to render the bond more indissoluble in the long run between recovered mental image and the fashioned poetics of recall. And when the remembered scene is in fact that of an image system linked to verbal text, the case takes on an almost laboratory exactitude. Not ten pages into *Swann's Way*, the ripples and dips of lantern projection across a corrugated cloth surface have been synced with—and made

IX. Audioptics 275

figurative for—an inset and mostly uncited narrative text that seems to propel them. In this way, the distorting "fissures" of the optical surface foreshadow the "furrows" of desecrated—and resectored— stone lettering. Anticipating the church's shimmer of stained glass light as well, the lantern's thrown play of color is noted specifically to be operating "after the fashion of the first architects and master glaziers of the Gothic age." The analogy ("after the fashion of") becomes immediately more explicit. The beams of the apparatus "replace the opacity of the walls with impalpable iridescences, supernatural multicolored apparitions, where legends were depicted as in a wavering, momentary stained-glass window." One of these "legends" is submitted in particular to Proust's secondary novelistic depiction: "Moving at the jerky pace of his horse, and filled with a hideous design"—a design moral in this sense, rather than visual— the villainous knight Golo, on his supernatural mount, would "advance jolting toward the castle of poor Genevieve de Brabant." All goes (forward) according to script, captured by this passage's naïve metalepsis—from the narrator's childhood perspective—of a visualized character taking instruction from his own text: "Golo would stop for a moment to listen sadly to the patter read out loud by my great-aunt." From some accompanying (unspecified) commercial booklet—something like the equivalent of cinematic intertitles— these narrative signals are words that the painted knight "would seem to understand perfectly." The result is that he is watched "modifying his posture, with a meekness that did not exclude a certain majesty, to conform to the directions of the text." Instructions take the form of spatial "directions"—with the vulnerable Genevieve's castle steadily in view: a goal to be approached on horseback at whatever frame rate the "glass ovals" were being "slipped between the grooves of the lantern." But always the aunt's read words set the story's materialized pace.

   In the inferred ocular archaeology of this episode, proto-cinematic analogies are hardly far-fetched. They have already been established a few pages before, where in the mental palimpsest (James' "superposed" fade) of half sleep, an awakening Marcel has his usual hard time bringing into focus which of his several past or present bedrooms is presently dawning on him. He can't sort out such temporal overlaps "any better than we isolate, when we see a horse run, the successive positions shown to us by a kinetoscope." In contrast to the increments of chronophotography that historically underlie this allusion to Edison's battery-operated peephole animation, within two pages that photographed horse has reverted to a painted chivalric slide. It has taken this form in order to evince the more wholly unreal and malleable visualizations of the reading eye, whose phonetic slipstream is itself figured as an oral delivery system. Obeying the great-aunt's vocalized wording of the simplified legend, Golo's "slow ride" on his advancing steed was one that "nothing could stop." It was ungrounded in its vector—and thus, even if "the lantern was moved," his progress could pucker, tuck, and buckle across any surface, planar or creased. Combray's figurative "tapestry of glass" is here anticipated in composite form by draped cloth and overlain chromatic waver: "I could make out Golo's horse continuing to advance over the window curtains, swelling out with their folds, descending into their fissures": all gauzy ruffle to the childhood gaze. And all still under orders from the order of the read text.

And beyond textual pace, wording accrues its own chromatics as well. "The castle and the moor were yellow." But "I had not had to wait to see them to find out their color." For in the great-aunt's oral "patter" of the brochure, "well before the glasses of the frame did so, the *bronze sonority* of the name Brabant had shown it to me clearly" (emphasis added). This synesthesia is given by Proust as "la sonorité mordorée du nom de Brabant"—*mordorée* for golden-brown, russet, bronze. The cognate, *bronze*, is available in French as well, but would have fallen flatter on the ear in adjectival position after the noun. The established previous translation by C. K. Scott Moncrieff gives the sonorous punch phrase first, and with something of an over-literal thump, so that "before the slides made their appearance the *old-gold* sonorous name of Brabant had given me an unmistakable clue." With Proust's assonance only pallidly approximated in the two long *o*'s of that hyphenated epithet, nothing of course can top the additional metric and nasalized pick-up from "son" by "du nom de" in the original "la *son*orité *mordorée du nom de* Brabant"—a phrase every bit as undulant as those curtain folds. Yet Lydia Davis' intrepid recent version has its own quasi-Proustian texture, if not quite metrical ring, its overlapped sonority burnished by the rub of elision itself: *Brahn~sahn* (bronze son ...) in anticipation of the golden-toned *Brah/bahnt*. If this sibilant "drift" can be heard to anticipate, at the narrowest compass, the sped-up syllabic continuities of the mother's later reading voice as well the time-smudged meld of Latin characters in those Combray inscriptions, then its phonemic "elision" and "abridgment" may seem all the more apt.

And there is a longer view to take of this episode—or say a longer hearing. Whether or not the contemporary intertitles of silent cinema were on Proust's mind in the wedding of text and projected image, the backdated medial twist speaks for itself. With the dutiful knight taking patiently literal *dictation* from the lantern's narrative manual (in vocal transmission), all imaged motion is matched in lockstep with literary process. Think by comparison of a stymied hero turning to the camera in some metafilmic screen comedy and asking what his next line of dialogue should be. The Proustian scene emerges as a protracted case of reading degree zero (sounded lettering and its produced image) in allegorical overdrive.

That "longer view"—entailing an associated "longer hearing"—posited at the start of the last paragraph is of course coterminous with the scope of this Reader. For punctuating the excerpts throughout is an analytic stance toward literature's "audioptic platform"—and operating in all its textualist connections, *trans*medium, with painting and sculpture as well as film and music. The result is a decidedly elongated overview that can in fact be *visually* summarized in closing. Hence the ensuing afterpiece on the book-jacketed graphics of visual explication. Quite apart from this retrospective inspection of icons (devoted to reading as topic and as practice), certainly the word-image nexus in Proust's emblematic episode of visualized inscription is a fit note on which to close the literary swath of this book-length review: a review not least of a monographic paper trail that often had in mind the visualization of its arguments in the inferences of dust-jacket presentation, let alone via included frame grabs or frontispieces when possible. I've spoken more than once about the decision to go with piecemeal excerpts rather than just a few whole chapters blocked out: opting as I do for stepping-stones rather than pretended cornerstones. As it happens, the lovingly fussed-over cover designs of my books can help, in just a moment, to step off that footpath in short order, succinctly marking each hop, skip, and jump between topics by way of a swift final summary.

With due indulgence, however, another summative moment is irresistible first—as it serves to fuse what must seem the farthest flung of my interests: narrative prose and conceptualist plastic art. It does so in a breakthrough conjunction, not just of the two aesthetic fields, but, Proust still eminently in mind, of the whole audio/visual dualism that everywhere perks up my attention to the workings of the literary medium. But commonalities are broader yet, it is worth stressing again. One of the enduring tendencies or bents in my analytic approach, becoming clearer than ever to me as I drafted these annotations, has to do with how natural it was to move from literary to film studies in the first place—and on two counts of intuitive connection.

Natural, because my interest in the grammar of prose fiction, let alone of metered verse, made each mode of writing, as well as its reading, seem a markedly "time-based" operation; and by way of a subset of, or side-field, to this temporal obsession, music is perhaps even more devoted to and shaped by the cadence of its time-based measures. My attention to the time-based nature of prose was the case even before I pursued more closely the modular commonalities of photogram and "phonogram," not to mention reading's mere snapshot on canvas, which even then had its own odd continuity with my narrative work (thus, in sequence, something like the leaps taken from *Novel Violence* [2009] to *Bookwork* [2011] to *The Deed of Reading* [2015]). But well before that, prose grammar in narrative led me instinctively to the syntax of the shot, as in *Between Film and Screen* (1999) and *Framed Time* (2007). Natural, too, this expanded purview, because a shift of attention moving from the structured build of either serial medium to temporal fixities in the so-called plastic arts was a move smoothed by the syllabic plasticity, as such, that I always saw—or rather heard—in alphabetic language, and often by close analogy not just with the fluctuations of screen camerawork but with the constituent flickering of the film strip. Or put it this way: where Barthes strove to subsume a diversity of rival arts under the signifying intensity of Text, I tended to investigate each aesthetic occasion as activating, in the form of text, the artful malleability of its own medial platform.

This tendency of mine, however devoted, has had its frequent lapses. Among the many moments of blinkered attention I discovered, and knew too well I would, in reviewing my books—even in literary passages I remembered working hardest and most rewardingly over—a good number have already been tabulated in these pages. In this kind of missed opportunity, historical timing has sometimes been to blame, not just yours truly. Inevitably, many films and museum artifacts have been discovered by me, or released to the world, only long after they might have figured productively among the image texts of one book or the other—just as there have been passages of prose and poetry that have come my way too late to confirm my literary intuitions in print. No serious annoyance there, but an observation fit for sharing—since it's part of our shared condition. There's no *definitive* catching up to be done regarding the ongoing genius of any medium, but there can be poignant moments of *occasional* claims, reclamations, and reconstituted auditions of forgotten, belated, or newly emergent intertexts (such as have been attempted between these covers). So that in singling out two conceptual sculptures here at the last, in the deep but unstated complementarity of their gallery pairing, I do so not because they eluded me in previous books, which I would indeed otherwise regret, but rather for the way they can help to conclude the "audioptic" arc of review in this one.

In her rich and challenging 2022 career retrospective at the Tate Britain during the summer I was drafting this commentary, Cornelia Parker (b. 1956) displayed her polymath invention nowhere more powerfully than in a pair of metamedial works from the mid-1990s: "sculptures" given their context among two-dimensional works involving in themselves an unusually high degree of conceptualist "research," its borrowings, and its transmutations. In this same gallery with the wall-hung 3D works that locked-in my attention were photographs taken by the artist on infrared film with a camera once belonging to Rudolf Hess, camp commandant at Auschwitz, and lent to Parker under special dispensation by the Imperial War Museum. Through this disgraced lens, and with such anomalous and often forensic film stock, even Parker's neutral photographs of cloud formations were turned sinister. Representing a shift from still to moving images before displacing the latter into wall art as well, in this same room there were complex Rorschach blots made from the chemical dissolution of confiscated pornographic tapes shredded by British customs officers, whose weird somatic forms in hung frames invited erotic projection in themselves (certainly in light of the paratextual explication). But on another wall was that duet of 3D "negative objects" under shallow vitrines that particularly arrested me: first of all—before anticipating their use here and finally—because of their lamented absence from my *Transmedium* dossier.

These works are "negatives" not in the generative photographic sense at all. They are instead more radically indexical: trace objects unmixed with the iconic in the way a photograph always is (when, for instance, picturing clouds, however filmed, which had to have been there "before" the camera and are now *here* in the image). Parker's "negatives"—as material deposits, what one might call inverted and extruded molds—install only the raw proof of record, now of lettering, now of studio sound. Together, then, in my tendentious terms, they hang there as complementary sculptural phonotexts generated by two kinds of engraving. Without explicitly "tracing" (except by physical evidence) either graphology or phonography back by direct allusion to the stylus—the sharp uninked pen-like tool used at the origin of writing to scrape letters into wax tablets—these adjacent display cases are nevertheless palpably linked across an implicit archaeology of imprint and its variant technologies. The result is a composite "sculptural" dyad as stringently "demediated" as many of the sculpted bookworks (2011, Phase IV / 9) I had discussed even before *Transmedium* (2017), but here with unusually drastic traces of the absent messaging actually getting *materialized* in the process. In the one case (both senses), which is to say in the one vertical vitrine—as if the sculpture were textwork on a museum wall, which of course it is—the assemblage titled *Negative of Words* displays the metallic "leavings" of an engraver's stylus spaced out in glimmering puffs of bunched silver threads, the otherwise invisible matter sacrificed (by exclusion) to meaning on a metal surface; recalling, too, how silver-oxide photography amounts to washing away (or subtracting) "silver" to reveal the particular content of the negative—what is exposed to light and what gets "fixed." It may occur to us further that this is not unlike the white surface beneath inked forms on the scribed page, as invisible as if they were cut away by the pen— and by contrast with whose neutral field, alone, does lettering emerge. Next to it, in *Negative of Sound*, the same subtraction is enshrined. Together, to a transmedial literary eye, the paired display might be called *Negatexts*. In the latter sonic negation, neither wax debris nor metal shavings are the proof of inscription. Instead, displayed in comparable clusters, glossy black now rather than glistening silver, are the definitive spun-off slivers left behind by the grooving out of sound: the delicate vinyl residue from the "cutting" of records, her samples retrieved from audio engineers at Abbey Road Studios. These vinyl leavings are an unidentified aggregate, generic, abstract in their materiality, a concept—not a relic, as they would have been if identified, say, as "outtakes" from The Beatles' *Sgt. Pepper's Lonely Hearts Club Band* (1967). Still, for this author they recall the moment of process within performance in Streisand's

Funny Lady (1975) when, in foregrounded closeup, we see the technician's brush sweeping off the vinyl debris from the original pressing of "More Than You Know"—with the singer (as Fanny Brice) in the background at the mic, working out the lyric as its tracks are being laid down.

In Parker's twinned display, black plastic over against silver metal, two tangible negatives make a conceptual positive. Few works could speak to each other, transmedium, more eloquently or comprehensively. Nor do more, again, to sum up an abiding graphonic stress in my own investigations across media. Together with the cancelled (overwritten) substrate of letteral form spun out in silver negations, those jet-black slicings and shreddings of the recording needle (to clear a path for playback, vocal and otherwise) collaborate in a unified textual concept. Not just in the scoring of their own separate planar supports, they turn the idea of the other medium inside out as well: churning up constituent "differential" negatives in the storage-retrieval circuit of instrumental trace, whether of phonographic records or of embossed worded surfaces. What is removed from view to make lettering appear (as much for inked overlay as for these metallic gougings) is framed for view along with the black waxen strands (more like frozen ink at a glance) that seem to figure a stylus-induced sound trace.

So not just on the wall of the Tate, but here on these last pages of my own "career retrospective," Parker's "found" but refashioned research objects mount a diptych emblem of writing as the proverbial trace of an absence in a double sense. For this is an absence of voiced sound per se, alphabetically silent or otherwise, that remains in each case "evocalized" not in and by those disposable filaments of impressed silver or shellac any more than in and by inked filigree on a page, but only in figured association with the tangible index of an expressive technical intention in whose immediate wake these materialities have been deposited. As two faces of the same foundational negation, these artifacts therefore pair into a parable. Even if all "audioptic" experience in art, whether nominally visual or audible, is best conceived as in fact residual, it is still the case that reading closely—in following out the tracks left behind—can get us more nearly in the groove.

Okay (he takes to the keyboard a couple of days later to realize), it just happened again: another time-delay broadcast curiosity, and once more entirely accidental, with no thought to bleep out anything unwanted in revision. Just inadvertently slow on the uptake yet again. Or call it another loop in the learning curve, doubling back to influences so internalized that they have become instinctual. Yes, in homage to Parker's work, I had drafted this eleventh-hour allegory of my phonotextual preoccupations without realizing, even after all these years, the familiar interpretive model. The thought simply came to me since that the tacit common denominator between Parker's two "negatives" emerged from a commonplace idiom (my usage "in the groove") grown positive over time since its mid-Victorian slang origin—and no doubt in part by association with turntables rather than trenches or ruts, from whose "grooves" sounds find emission.

Did I say "simply came to me"? That's one way, hardly sufficient, of putting it. Better, let the playback loop of such delayed methodological recognition offer a further meta-allegory of perpetual rereading: spotlighting here again, that is, the structuring power inherent in exactly the semiotic "matrix" that I keep having my students learn from the writing of Michael Riffaterre (1924–2006). This thought—or form—is the not just impinging but *generative* dimension of the unsaid—as illustrated most recently by the avoided dead metaphor "on the same wavelength," also spotted by me after the fact, in Richard Powers' *Bewilderment* (2021; see Phase VIII / 19). Chagrin can be kept to an instructive minimum, though, since it is the whole point of the semiotic method in Riffaterre that the sponsoring truism, as "repressed" source for the text's chance of original manifestation, only emerges to consciousness, if at all, *ex post facto*: final upshot of a dialectical encounter with the work in question—even if it be one's own.

Riffaterre: the only major academic luminary under whose influence I have valuably (I hope) fallen—across all my literary, film, and fine art interests, from René Girard through Christopher Ricks to Stanley Cavell and Fredric Jameson, Christian Metz to Friedrich Kittler, Michael Fried to T. J. Clark— whom I never had the high treat of meeting, and in happy cases even getting to know a bit. But who knew there might actually be certain delicious but wholly impersonal "favors" returned in the fair play of academic turnabout? Yes, my latest lapse in recognition springs a memory that I had no plans to replay here, one bound back into my work on the phonotext in a quite unexpected way. For, if pressed, I'd have to admit that among the most treasured professional compliments I ever received, entirely second hand, was hearing from someone—a colleague of Riffaterre's at Columbia or a scholar visiting for a lecture, I can't remember now, so indelible was the tiny anecdote itself—that my friendly acquaintance had run into the famous professor rushing across the Columbia quad one afternoon, off to class with apologies for no time to talk, carrying a copy—to *class* of all places—of *Reading Voices*. How "groovy" is that?

Note

1   Marcel Proust, *Swann's Way*, trans. Lydia Davis (London: Penguin, 2003), originally published as *Du côté de chez Swann* (Paris: Grasset, 1913).

X.

COVERAGE

Book covers have always been for me, once I could exercise some control over them, the unlocked and free-swinging doors to my topics, even my more specific arguments: not just advertisements but first proposals as well as portals, setting the tone at a glance. Whether or not followed by a frontispiece, my effort, however fully I could exert it with designers and marketers, was always to make the academic book jacket or cover serve to front the whole mode of interpretation: an advance abstract in visual rather than verbal form. Call it transmediation degree zero. Author and monograph buyer not least, everyone likes a fetching, in the root sense, book jacket: an open invite to reading. But I've never known anyone more "into it" than I (save perhaps the editor of this book). And not just as a coded way "into" the discussion—the first approach to its approach—but as a first scene of reading on its own visual and graphic terms.

I would often mock-up some tentative fantasy design for a book cover halfway through the process of writing: offering a carrot to the many sticks (and sticking points) of foreseen revisions, but also as a way of keeping the gist in schematic focus. This habitual if intermittent investment in each new cover was newly borne in on me when drafting this commentary. Culling certain representative excerpts from my teacherly agenda on the page was never, in this process, a matter of just flipping through digitally filed pages. I had no pdf proofs or Word documents for most of the books, even those benefiting from the post-Selectric epoch of word processing. So the actual volumes had to be taken down from the shelf again, on the way to the scanner, and ranged to help me reinhabit their trajectory. It was at this point that I couldn't help but review, for the first time ever, the sequence of covers that had, one after the other, and sometimes one in view of the other, announced what had become of my writerly lesson plans as they solidified into book-length demonstrations.

The covers didn't, as I say, just package these various pages for delivery; they attempted what might be thought of as optical adages to organize their book's main emphases. In the intermedia spirit that increasingly came to motivate my investment in their design, they now struck me in review—which is why I review them here—as a kind of summary narrative in themselves: the frames of a twenty-panel graphic novel as academic *Bildungsroman*, or for the more antiquarian sensibility, an at-a-glance "story" as found in *Saint Francis and the Episodes of His Life* in the Bardi Chapel of Santa Croce in Florence. As I looked again, I remembered every little battle fought to get them right, every last-minute image found to secure the effect I was after, every logistical decision of scale and juxtaposition in the fonts I tried to weigh in on. Most of all it came back to me that the more input I had in the selection of both image and typeface, the closer I came to making these layouts reach out as instigations to reading in their own initial right. So let me skim their discourse in summary as a kind of pictorial timeline—an academic life of the mind in pictures.

As a complement to what follows, readers would benefit from access to the cover visuals across my twenty books. Ideally, of course, the evidence would be stacked upon a reader's desk, or laid out chronologically. With resolution and color vibrancy even more assured, a quick online search along the lines of "author name/book title" should do the trick—and soon a sufficient portfolio is quickly at hand. You'll then be able to "follow along" the half-century "stack" of illustrated investigations.

The point isn't just the obvious one. It isn't that a picture may be worth a thousand words, or that you can actually tell a book by its cover. More than this, the lapsed designer and architect in me haunted the author in wanting the jackets or paperback covers to be not just attractive (attracting, marketable) but graphically telling—not just eye-catching but caught up in the main point of the argument. With these goals in mind, it took me a while to catch on about how resolutely *hands-on* an author needed to be to achieve anything like this in the impersonality of a press pipeline. I was told in the mid-1970s, for instance, somewhat facetiously (I hope) by a Harvard Press designer, disclosing a trade secret well kept otherwise, that there are three preferred visual motifs for book covers, statistically determined to bolster sales: nudes, babies, and eyes. I know: seemed just as bizarre to me at the time. In any case, I got eyes for my first book, *Dickens and the Trials of Imagination* (1974): a highlighted band of illumination across the penetrating gaze of a familiar portrait of the middle-aged Dickens in a period-specific dark sepia. For the low-keyed academic norm of the period, it wasn't bad. But it felt somehow generic, *pro forma*—a form not quite befitting the professional offerings attempted therein. Despite the shiny finish, it was lackluster.

From then on, I wanted something more formally proactive. I tried becoming involved earlier in the publication gauntlet, as soon as referees had spoken, boards had voted, and a contract had been countersigned. It was, though, often difficult to get directly into connection with the in-house designer. Still avoiding babies and nudes and eyes to boot, my next Harvard book was in Victorian mourning purple, figuring not the newborn but the suicided young Chatterton, from the famous Henry Wallis painting—though not so much reframed as mounted on the pedestals of an ornate mausoleum. *Death Sentences* (1984) was easy enough to "thematize" in this way, though alas with no sentences, no words, to highlight the textual operations in question. For the clearly invisible oscillatory ripple effects of the phonotext in my next book (*Reading Voices*, 1990), the designer at the University of California Press, encouraged to keep drift and mutability in mind, devised a kind of pre-pixel geometric pattern (limited to tiny circles, squares, and triangles that not only morphed chromatically throughout the grid but also gathered differently colored shadows). The ingredients of this molecular field were seen cascading top to bottom, and back up again, from green-on-blue to blue-on-green through all but indiscernible gradients. Mapped on the very logic of *Reading Voices*: a visualized oscilloscope of "graphonic" energy, I liked to think. This was nonalphabetic and entirely abstract but somehow exactly right. Complementing this was the idea I had first suggested to the press: that the five capped letters of "VOICES" would be stretched to the span of the seven in "READING" and placed just below that gerund at the same centered width, so that its "graphonic" force, thus expanded, would seem to breathe with its own emphasis as verb. For *Dear Reader*, instead, as far from abstract as possible, I found in Brussels Antoine Wiertz's naked *Romance Reader* of 1853 (the first of my nudes, at last): her body in abject textual prostration before the mirror of readerly self-extension, fed novels from a horned devil at bedside. This was chief among the images in that volume that, after my combing European and American museums for other painted readers, led me, two books later, for *The Look of Reading* (2006), to a cover reproduction of *Philosopher Reading in a High Room* from the school of Rembrandt, the reader's shaded person dwarfed by the figurative illumination looming above him through the lineated glow from a giant mullioned window: line and light together. Again, the argument at a glance: more an image to be read in metaphor (letting the light in) than the picture of any reading matter on some visible page.

In between these books on depicted reading across media, for my first film book, *Between Film and Screen* (1999), in its emphasis on the photogram strip, I submitted to the press the high-definition digital image of backlit celluloid images from processed film rolls: color outtakes from the experimental work of nonnarrative film artist Leighton Pierce. These amounted, as if on a drying rack, or pinned-up and hanging, to strip after strip of chromatic frames with mostly indiscernible images: the raw matter of eventual projection in light, color, and shadow. In my return, over half a decade later, and after many more semesters of film teaching, to a second study of the cinematic image for *Framed Time* (2007), that book's adjusted emphasis on the postfilmic basis of digital compositing and breakdown urged a very different cover. I worked with the designer on pixelating the image of the ten-hour proletarian time clock in Fritz Lang's *Metropolis* (1927), as if it were not just caught in the breakup of a digital screening but simultaneously—paradoxically, anachronistically, metahistorically—trapped also between transparent rectangles by the obtrusive hurdle of an abyssal black frameline. Like so many of the films discussed within that book, this single image was staged to conjure up the digital hegemony in (the here recursive) light of the plastic medium it had eclipsed. For the continuance of this crossmedial "narratography" into a next book on its literary register, *Novel Violence* (2009), I worked again with the same University of Chicago Press designer, the gifted Michael Brehm. This cover featured an image, from the periodical version of Thomas Hardy's *Tess of the D'Urbervilles*, illustrating the accidental death of the heroine's family horse, the bloody and disconsolate scene circled in reverberant concentric rings that evoked the ripple effect of this tragic episode and (to my mind at least, its phrasings alike—as sending out the shock waves of their own kind of linguistic violence). On another visit, though, one can easily glean the dark arc of the horizon (in the cover's lower third) with the central, circular image hovering above—as if obstructing a sun backlighting the remainder of the frame. The book's title and subtitle read in turn as if a stencil cut-away made legible by an infill of unseen illumination.

Next, the aptly bibliocentric cover of *Bookwork* (2011) centered its title across two walls of flatly stacked books (approximately 10,000 strong) flanking a narrow central corridor: an image of Slovak artist Matej Krén's punningly named *Passage*, where the walls of books are extended on both sides, upwards and down, by the strategic placement of mirrors that multiply their stacks in infinite regress. Determined entirely by the format of the artist's installation as a private transit zone between the bound weight of textual accretion impending from either side, still the symmetrical framing of the photograph had a way of calling up as well a deep textual gulley bordered, in thousandfold fractal pattern, by composite verso and recto planes in the cumulative book of culture figured by this assemblage. If the "hallway" is a book of books, we "passage"-takers are its contents, navigating—or simply being—the matter or medium between left and right. Atlas-like, we shoulder this density of texts while contemplating our own depth as legible entities.

In a return to film for my next book, *Closed Circuits* (2015), the argument's emphasis on the embedded optics of on-screen surveillance imaging encouraged disjoint frame grabs from CCTV footage and a font resembling a digital clockface. As if the argument itself were as yet inchoate, the separate images had not yet montaged into a forensic storyline in the way implied by the book's subtitle, *Screening Narrative Surveillance*. In conceiving this design, I had wanted the page numbers to advance like a digital time code, from 00.00.01 through 00.02.59, an idea the designer cottoned to, though there was some (I forget what) technical problem with taking this approach. Returning to literary study for *The Deed of Reading* (2015), I asked an artist prominently featured in *Bookwork*, Brian Dettmer, whether I could use a photograph of one of his X-Acto blade book "minings," where layers of a codex are variably excised for a *deep reading*. To my delight, he offered instead to carve up *my own* page proofs for rephotographing as a *trompe-l'oeil* cover sculpture, carving down as he did to the last words of the text: "language is as language does." Along with this complex effect, the book designer surprised me by so fully understanding the idea of the linkage in my conceptually unpunctuated subtitle—a four-word noun phrase as well as a roster of topics separated by asterisks (*Literature * Writing * Language * Philosophy*)—that the words appeared hovering on the cover in a clear-enough descending sequence yet in indeterminate orbit around each other. It was only on the title page that the constellation found its "dots connected" by literalized lines of interrelation, aptly "linking" the terms in an open-weave network rather than a grammatical series, a logical ordering, or a presumed hierarchy. The point of these gathered but multidirectional disciplinary orientations was a point thus graphed from the start.

For *Transmedium* (2017), with those first supposedly salesworthy eyes behind me on the front of the early Dickens book, and still no babies, I got another nude. This was the acoustically inflected digital image, noisy and blurred, in the latest audiovisual experiments of the late intermedia artist Hans Breder: a naked female body, from Breder's 1970s video work, now passed through audio interference from a recorded musical performance by the artist and refiltered through computerized video. Incidentally conflating my own separate interests in time-based imaging and serial acoustics, here is transmedial thinking performed in distillation on a pixelated body traced by the material interference of mechanical audition (albeit with the effect that the pudendum hovers like a right-facing, slightly pitched-upward cursor arrow). More than three decades after the missed chance for picturing the words of some "death sentences" back in 1984, I finally got actual script up front for the cover of *The Value of Style in Fiction* (2018), where one reads, in Edgar Allan Poe's clear handwriting, his interpolated preference for the assonant and ominous "Murders in the Rue Morgue" over the visibly crossed out "Rue Trianon." Style in highly serviceable action.

Coming round by association to the digitally tampered *Metropolis* image of *Framed Time*, 2020's *Cinemachines* featured, simply by enlarged frame grab this time, an on-camera metacinematic breakdown of the postfilmic image in the remote hologram projection—under extreme pixel duress—of the hero's mistress, Joi (Ana de Armas) in *Blade Runner 2049* (2017, dir. Denis Villeneuve), where shattered safety glass doubles for the splintered surface of her digital materialization. By contrast, two books before this, in *The One, Other, and Only Dickens* (2018), there was a photographic rather than a digital breakup: a deliberately split-framed Victorian image of Dickens again, graphically flagging the internal distinction implied by my title—between narrator and stylistic enunciator. Here was a three-way collage of Dickens daguerreotyped in the stabilizing act of reading—very much in continuity with the painter's models of an earlier canvas tradition, and thus a kind of close cousin to the covers of *Dear Reader* and *The Look of Reading* alike. But this triadic refaceting of a single authorial photograph, capturing the three-stage metrics of my title (with solo O-words displayed in caps above each sector of the image: ONE/OTHER/ONLY, while "the" and "and" are rendered in faint script), was then answered with an afterpiece that brought into diptych conjunction a positive image of the Victorian master with its photographic negative. That final juxtaposition was meant to capture unmistakably those two sides of his genius stressed in the book (the One and Only versus the insurgent stylistic Other): his narrative drive and its countervailing phonetic traction.

Any number of circles keep closing in this way across distant (and certainly distinct) book projects. With its continuing emphasis on language as shaping force, *The Ways of the Word* (2021) returned to Slovak artist Matej Krén (b. 1958), whose "Passage" was featured in *Bookwork*, for the photorealist oil painting by the artist of the inner space formed by his hollow column of another 10,000 closed and carefully piled books assembled in a Prague public library—the large-format painting called *Cone* being named for the receding perspective offered by the inward curvature of stacked volumes. Words, bound in books, again make way for visualizations other than their own pages. And all this was fitly and regressively displayed on the cover by the secondary presence of an open book-within-the-book—its *verso* featuring the title as a vertical tower of letters nesting deep into the "book's" gutter, while the subtitle sits atop the *recto* as if usurping the privilege of main attraction; thus "episodes in verbal attention" cues readers to the need for looking twice, and only then do we turn the book (or cant our heads) to get the punchline—along a single axis—that these tricks and techniques are, in fact, "the ways of the word."

The reflexivity of my interests has encouraged me to find ever more complex and graphically suggestive ways of getting it pictured, as in that mise-en-abyme figuration of the nested structures of reading. Close on the heels of *The Ways of the Word*'s intricately thematic cover, and this time against a composite blue-gray photograph of a fabricated hall of beveled reflections, *The Metanarrative Hall of Mirrors* interleaved its title with the subtitle—*Reflex Action in Fiction and Film*, in a smaller, pale-yellow font—to capture the tightly meshed imbrication of media attention and its entailed response. The recessional perspective of mirrors-that-face-mirrors (familiar from funhouse and science museum to say nothing of the occasional bathroom) intimates the depth on offer when interweaving moving images with moving moments of literature. "Reflex action" thus invokes the *involuntary* powers of film and fiction in their impact upon us as well as courts the further senses of reflexivity (such as folding back, turning over, and otherwise overlapping).

What could do justice to another book with *mirror* in its title, if decisively singular this time rather than plural—even if placed in the subtitle? With the press dodging copyright restrictions and billing complications, and so with no frame grabs permissible for the many mirror shots in the actress' film career, the cover of *Streisand: The Mirror of Difference* was the hardest to come by. Only located at the last minute in the Billy Rose Theater Archives of the New York Public Library, an uncredited photograph from the mid-1960s—showing three varying profiles of the recording star in superimposition—is doubled on the cover below the title band, downsized and *mirror-reversed*, to suggest, all told, the variably faceted scale of the star's layered persona (in triplicate, like the most recent Dickens above, though here as if in a shuttle of film stills in some slow-motion movie). Also evoked by this differential imaging are the reverbs of the singer's vocal force in the somatic echo chamber of audition. If that cover was the biggest challenge in the face of over-familiar public domain images, it now all but speaks for itself in the overt multifaceting of the star persona.

Not so—the gift of the self-explanatory—with the most arcane of my covers, namely, for *Book, Text, Medium* (2020). The logic of this vivid image is unapproachable except by extensive authorial (as originally curatorial) gloss. What fronts *Book, Text, Medium* was directly prompted by the book's subtitle, *Cross-Sectional Reading for a Digital Age*—so that the obsolescence of the text-bearing codex is brought almost to the point of travestied legibility in this gallery *bibliobjet*. Yet again, what goes around comes around, as my interests circled back to the conceptualist artist's book—here conceptual with a vengeance. As it happened, too, this image of an *outré* open book benefited from a happy accident of series format. The downward triangular wedge of monochrome background in the Cambridge Twenty-First Century Literature and Culture series made a kind of second bookwork out of the already dizzy conceptual spiral, in its own spiral binder, of Mika Tajima's Whitney-exhibited vitrine-encased codex called *Negative Entropy*. The stabbing apex of the format's upside-down triangle—almost by optical illusion—turns the high-definition image of Tajima's open book, laid out flat in the bottom half of the cover, *recto* and *verso*, instead into an isometric version of itself in a foreshortened perspectival hinge. It is as if its text (or say pages) were slanted ajar, held open, by the hand of an actual "reader"—though with nothing there to be deciphered: just the image of encrypted lines and their inferential media lineage.

None of this is easy to depict in a traditional book like the one you're almost through reading. For this spiral bound "book" at the Whitney, such as it was, answered to the actual weavings by Tajima on display next to it, and did so in the most oblique fashion. Here, paratextual description was the *sine qua non* of the installation's abyssal irony. For what was open to us in the spiral binder were (wait for it) the full-color spectrographic "read-outs"—in color-coded striations—of the mechanical noises made by the whirring engines of a New York University computer hub: the sound in part, one might say, of electronic messaging without the messages. And given the conceptual helix, as it were, of this technological spiral, the gallery-glossed complications of Tajima's media-archaeological "research art" (or let's use again my conflated term "mediarchaeology" for its self-instanced principle) do gradually emerge. We are invited to note how the spun-out linear patterning of the open color-streaked pages evokes—by metamedial irony—the evolution of the same electronics that has in more conventional forms eclipsed the ordinary codex platform. For in proximity, and connection, with the pastel threads of woven wall works hung next to the open book is, ironically, the Jacquard loom punch-card bound in its open spiral form along with the variegated and boldly colored spectrogram print outs. By inference from that bland cardboard template, conjuring the legendary source of early binary computation in the sprocketed on/off mode of factory implementation, we are thus carried far from the spread pages open before us. By the discourse of the installation work all told, rather than the book anchoring it, we seem asked to think in historical palimpsest about the deep history of the strictly digitized book, even perhaps about the weave of language, or the helix of its entanglements, but in connection with the cross-medial recording of ambient noise that has no availability—no voicing— in alphabetic audition. If I'm usually eager for covers meant to speak volumes, this one, in every aspect including its *trompe-l'oeil* cleft of perspective, required instead a good part of an included chapter to parse.

After this optically evocative archaeological *abyme* for *Book, Text, Medium*, equivocating its three terms at once, the following cover, for *Cinesthesia* (2020), was not just self-explanatory but uniquely functional. This was the literalized "entry way," in effect, to my lone e-text publication, with its emphasis on the art film as curated museum object. There I was taken entirely by surprise with a technical inspiration at the publisher's end. I had designed and pitched my own e-text "cover" possibility: the composite image of an ornate gold frame surrounding the scratchy countdown leader of a just-launched film strip, those two inner frames etching out the "START/FILM" sequence. That image was demoted to frontispiece when the gifted digital designer found a way to realize the metaphoric gallery tour of my strictly figurative table of contents as an actual interactive itinerary from one subsidiary museum space to another— "Digital Gallery," "Retinal Lab," "Painting Annex," and so forth. The reader of this uniquely "spatialized" *volume* could now move from one hyperlinked clickable "gallery" to another in direct access to the chapters as well as to individual images projected on or from its walls. Indulge me, Dear Reader, in this last strictly autobiographical fillip. As if compensating for my abandoned architectural dreams, I now could boast the navigable chambers of a built space—however virtual, or virtually realized—based on the text's discursive floorplan, not to mention being able to flourish my own transmedial artifact in a hypertext mode.

Performative in its different way in your hands, even before any pages are spread open for reading, the present cover to David LaRocca's sixteenth book, *Attention Spans*, is again an enactment—though in a surprising artisanal process as *oblique* to standard practice, in either photography or painting, as the splayed spokes of its geometric image. The artwork's compositional dynamic is redeployed here to catch in its own rhythm another titular double play (hear *Reading Voices*): a Necker flip between clause and plural noun whose doubleness is meant, in the case of the present title, to evoke a concentration that compasses its own broad spread of interests. This cropped image from a cyanotype imprint by John Opera, "Radial Composition (Yellow)," typifying an artist's practice on which David LaRocca has more than once written, fans out to the span of its occupied scope—and, for our emblematic purposes, radiates out in turn to the viewer (reader). Further guiding the images, with no real vanishing point in sight, along the emphatic black pathways of their convergent density, what the eye is drawn to and drawn in by becomes another figure/ground reversal true to many of the verbal as well as ocular inversions studied in my cross-medial "opera." Functioning in this way, the visual whittling down of the image's own golden background into tapered arrows of destination points back into the figured scene of invited readerly focus. That's the way Opera's abstract image can be made to concretize, in this new deployment as cover allegory, the reading act itself to which, on its own visual terms, it submits.[1]

In this folder X of one itinerant scholar's "Inventory," the confession of a designer *manqué* has not, of course, been the larger point of these summarizing and interpretive paragraphs. Lining the covers up here, in review, has meant to highlight, each in sequence, if not in strict chronological order, their deliberated designs *on* a specified attention—if seen in their full continuum only after the fact (an order, or logic, all its own). If the twenty textual excerpts themselves (Phases I through VIII), and that extra one on Proust (IX)—when served up now as what one might call a baker's score—have been conceived in exposition like a fast-forward film strip, that is only one optic model. You are also invited to think of the run-through of the covers (in Phase X), as with the excerpts themselves, in the mode of a protocinematic flip-book—or even, again, a zoetrope continuum, spluttering out individual image frames into some kind of oscillating conceptual sequence. In any case, and however successful in their dedicated separate efforts, it's time for the covers—and so the monographs whose arguments they packaged and promoted, well dusted off now—to be put back on the shelf in their role as tomes (that etymology again: cuts, layers, segments) in a twenty-volume deed of reading. It is a shelf whose institutional library equivalent, however widely spaced out over separate disciplinary call numbers, is available to inquisitive students at will: readers coming anew, one generation after another, to cherish the cross-medial deed of interpretation—that intimate working with art's various works—as both a task and a privilege.

Notes

1   As David LaRocca writes:
    Observed at a more granular level—upon closer inspection—the nap of linen canvas is discernable, and yet "Radial Composition (Yellow)" (2015) is, after all, a photograph, albeit a photograph with texture. But then, a photograph of *what*? John Opera's medial practice invites us to answer "of itself"—in so far as the finished cyanotype presents an inscription of light's passage and effects onto photo-receptive emulsion. Processes are different for each body of Opera's work: for the family of instances of which "Radial Composition" is a member, the "photographer" applies the light-sensitive emulsion to ungessoed canvas, then exposes the same surface using UV lights modified to his own design; the black bands of the image are, in fact, the legacy traces of variously timed bulb exposures.

The canvas is then rinsed with water. When the canvas is dry, a transparent acrylic color tint—in this case, the distinctive warm yellow of the cover, as if with the complementary suggestion of sun-like rays making their own direct (rather than negative) mark—is applied, after which the finished canvas is stretched onto a frame.

When we zoom in on the cropped image, we appreciate the photographic materiality of the artwork (viz., that it *is* photographic in nature), and when we zoom out, there is the figuration to consider, namely, that these geometric (or in other cases organic) shapes appear distinctively *abstract*, which is to say, not "photographic" in the sense we customarily use the word. As a third movement (after the zoom in and out, at some middle distance), Opera's photo-canvases give us the hint we have long needed that lens-based photographs are themselves abstractions, a necessary c(l)ue since we have been serially distracted by insisting on calling them "evidence," or otherwise faithfully engrossed in their apparent capacities to provide "windows" onto past worlds ("change mummified" and the realist and revelationist traditions such fixity refracted and further occasioned). In a word, Opera's work calls us to attention.

His bespoke craft—a canny blend of materials from high and low tech, courting a marriage of the modern and medieval (lasers and light sensors along with raw fabric and paint pigment)—spurs us to inquire after the *kinds* of impressions we perceive (these radiating bands, these fanning arrows), including the darker hues that result from the interference of overlapping exposures. What also results is an optical illusion befitting the qualities of human concentration and the viability of Opera's ontological experiments. This happens when training one's eyes below the subtitle, and noticing how the dark area begins to involuntarily expand and contract, pulsing as it moves (making visible a heartbeat in the optic nerve), announcing a supervenient performative energy—an interactivity between text and context, index and consciousness.

See David LaRocca, "Object Lessons: What Cyanotypes Teach Us About Digital Media," in *Photography's Materialities: Transatlantic Photographic Practices over the Long Nineteenth Century*, ed. Geoff Bender and Rasmus R. Simonsen (Leuven: Leuven University Press, 2021), 207–34; and "A Photograph as Evidence of Itself: Representation, Reflexivity, and Tautology in Light-Based Art," *Social Research*, vol. 89, no. 4 (Winter 2022): 915–45. See also "CHICAGO | The Observers: John Opera; January 6–February 25, 2023 and "LISBON | Blue Dream: John Opera; January 20–May 20, 2023," Document Space, Document Gallery, Chicago, documentspace.com; and "Equivalent Simulation: A Conversation with John Opera," *Afterimage: The Journal of Media Arts and Cultural Criticism*, vol. 42, no. 6 (2015): 16–21.

A DIALOGUE ON CRITICAL CONVERSATION

Garrett Stewart and David LaRocca

DAVID LAROCCA: As the last of your TexTcerpts brings us to this propitious opportunity for conversation, we have independently discovered a shared repercussion of reading *Attention Spans*. I describe some of my impressions of the volume in the Introduction—where the felt impact "amount[s] to a cinematic enframing of temporally situated passages of prose." The experience is not just cognitive (though it's heady enough) but somehow almost somatic. The layered time registers—present-day you, past you, and all the "others," including the one and only, in between—create a distinctly vertiginous effect, one that amplifies the energies of the page (*whenever* it was written). The old becomes new again. The new feels situated in the otherwise remote, if hardly antiquated—the distant drawn near for another close-up. As hoped, as expected, *Attentions Spans* is so much more than a customary Reader; it's a masterclass in reading and rereading, a writerly text with readerly potency—with the abiding moral for all readers that one is never done reading, that writing is a mode of reading, and, by extension, that in so far as one persists in reading one is never finished writing.

GARRETT STEWART: Gotta confess, at this end too, in reading over the earliest drafts of my interlineations in these TexTcerpts, that I'd rarely felt so confident of being on the right track in anything I was writing. The layering, like you say, has almost a filmic feel, cross-fade to flashback, iris out to a secondary superimposition. The palimpsest kept even me a little on edge each time I reread. As someone who has been diagnosed recently with late-onset vertigo (it could hardly be later, I quipped to my doctor, but at least it's a mild and very intermittent case), this is a much more enjoyable dizziness. Which I've been pleased to hear from you is contagious.

DL: While it can be tempting to see *Attention Spans* as "the next book" in your ongoing library of titles, gaining its own number in the sequence (#twenty-one?), our independent—and our shared—experience of reading the book suggests otherwise. That it is, in fact, special—somehow set out from the rest, while containing some portion of all the prior. I'm put in mind of your mention of a *summa* ("[t]he results are always more a reboot than a *summa*"), but I would want to quibble with that a bit, resisting how quickly you downplay it. All of the preexisting work—twenty books and a half-century to create them—weigh on every sentence and also elevate the formidable corpus. Keeping with the cinematic frame, we know of the "Director's Cut" and the return to the editing booth—famously, a *redux*. Your method here is itself a reformulation: you have selected text from the originals, call them "cuts," and you're also offering "director's commentary" as you go. Given the *comprehensiveness* of your retrospective—all twenty prior books are loaded into the editing bay simultaneously—how can we not be overwhelmed with a sense of the summative?

GS: One reason it was possible for me to say a minute ago that our deliberated format had launched me on what seemed unequivocally the "right track" is, I realize, because the line of development is essentially a circling back, or spiraling round, on its own momentum—and could hardly be feared to go very far astray. That's the only way I can sit still for the generous metaphor in your first question, about these pages as a "masterclass": only if I myself am still taking it, or say only in the same figurative sense, in its digest of investigations, that all my publications feel suspended in an ongoing conversation with other voices, always in a revise-and-resubmit mode, testing for pedagogic application rather than assent. What's interesting, in this nesting of perspectives, is the very fact of you(r) reading me reading myself again in the process of rereading, reestimating, the passages that once grabbed me, that made me want to read harder in the first place. These things, to quote George Eliot, are a parable. The very form of this edited venture rehearses the gestation under review. It's like the biological principle of ontogeny recapitulating phylogeny, so that this aborning editorial organism builds up its cellular layers like the professional installments of the career it digests and reflects on.

DL: Installments, indeed—actually a quite familiar, almost iconic, round number. By pairing up underrepresented alphabetic categories, even the *World Book Encyclopedia*, along with several others, contrives to come in at only twenty volumes. The question can't be ignored. How so productive? Is there a secret to the persistence of your commitment?

GS: Some would say an open secret: always more of the same. I'll happily accept instead those terms of yours, both of them, the sense of a (1) sustained (2) investment, but it isn't really stick-to-it-ive in any familiar sense. Which is really the answer you're after. There's always been an impatience to figure things out: somewhere between tenacity and antsiness. And restlessness has its own momentum.

DL: So how do you know when you have a new topic, or when, should we say, it has you?

GS: Let's put it, given my aural vulnerabilities, that I often fall victim to the quirky vector of a phonetic anagram: to peruse is to pursue. Being vulnerable becomes the condition for the viable. Halfway through a research project and its in-class tryouts, and certainly well into its (with luck) subsequent publication ordeals and torpors, another topic tends to catch my eye or ear. No surprise, hardened cynics might say (as I hinted just now): they're all secretly the same kind of thing. I'd cop to that in one sense, since decidedly different phenomena or objects in one medium after another keep posing to me questions that lead—by quite distinct evidence, I'd of course insist—to something of the same *level* of apprehension. Same questions (rather than answers) about different processes, probing to an always (in advance) indeterminate—though hardly surface—level about the origin and evolution of their medial makeup by way of my mark-up. This includes everything from etymology to algorithms, pulverized and resculpted cellulose pages to repainted photo-strip negatives, vinyl shavings (my last example in Phase IX) to the phonetic undersong of vocal enunciation in a pop singer's effortless mimetic glides. That doesn't make me some freak of nature right from the start: an *instinctive* media theorist. It only means that what has always fascinated me in cultural production is its material *sine qua non*.

DL: Yes, I see how that restless questioning explains, if anything quite could, the productivity, but what about, so to speak, the conduct of the prose, which for many of your readers has a felt conductivity. Thinking of my work with Stanley Cavell, I will forever cherish our discussions—especially his candid reflections—on the distinctness and distinctiveness of his style: its difficulties and risks, its pleasures and rewards, its varied effects on readers. In a comparable vein of direct address to you, with a similar sense of felt trust between us, I won't be shy here either in asking after such attributes of your prose style—as it was for Cavell, so for you, but differently, we encounter the rigor of diction, the logic of syntax, the evocation of ideas by means of an identifiable, rhythmically attuned voice. We all, at least for the most part, write what we think, and, though perhaps to a lesser extent, write the way we think. But what do you think about the way you write?

GS: Far be it from you to be shy on this head, since you've suffered from it. You remember the fulminating if vague resistance (abstraction, disciplinary jargon, overelaboration, what have you)—and attempted veto—by one of your anthology referees to a piece of mine in one of your collections. Your chastised contributor had been there before, many times. It always stings twice, since it means that the ideas, carefully manifested in just this or that way, aren't coming through either, however the writing may rankle.

DL: But do you really think of your style as so straightforwardly functionalist?

GS: Yes, or at least partly, but of course it depends on what one entertains as the function. So not very often "straightforward" at that. I'm interested in puzzling out complexities in their own key, which means a meld of description and interpretation—often in the same sentence. Paraphrase tends to enact analysis, whether the issue is a novelist's syntactic inversion torquing expectation or a lap-dissolve momentarily miscuing the viewer's sense of transition. Where applicable, I want my sentences to catch the sense of surprise in an encountered provocation.

DL: Do you see that as a continuous motive across all your books, now that you've looked back on all of them so dutifully for this volume?

GS: You know, I do now, more than ever. Along with intermittent embarrassments over an unbridled young writer—a sentiment inevitably involved in reviewing the earliest of my books, with my prose's rather-too-gradual search for concision rather than spacious evocation—what most surprised me was how, if fitfully, this purposeful complexity was there from early on. Hardly in graduate school, where, underread as a onetime architecture major, I made my way through courses with little to say amid all the requisite written words. The sheer saying was all I had to show for myself as I searched for something to talk about. Years later I remember making even Geoffrey Hartman laugh in public when, introducing his Truman Capote Award (as mentioned in "Inventory as Itinerary"), I recalled that in my first graded work in his class, I clutched at the hope, for a brief moment, that the comment "mannered and self-indulgent" might, coming from him, be a compliment. Once I found some topics, though, I tried making sure that the manner, if not entirely curtailed, was growing into a means, the indulgence transformed to more carefully judged and self-tested results. But one point I ought to admit. Formerly just treading water in early graduate courses, I do confess that later, in the so-called "deep dive" of published analysis, and with more linguistics and rhetoric in tow, and gradually image theory, I saw no reason, now and again, not to let a given sentence perform the nervous thrill of discovery in the act of coming up for air.

DL: I think I speak for many of your readers in saying that those are the moments that really get the job done. For all the variety of your topics, that's why I stressed this volume as the tracking, over time, of an inevitable "mastery." This was not meant to sound honorific, still less tone-deaf to the contemporary caution over the word and its history of power asymmetries, but rather to put the matter, fittingly, in the kind of etymological context—a master*ing*, progressing, bettering—that so often interests you in the genealogical undertones and graphical foliations of wording and imaging.

GS: Okay, a gradually and provisionally mastered toolkit, but still brought to the task of classroom efficacy and continual self-repair. In Heidegger's sense: a good deal of accumulated equipment *at* hand, on hand, a lexicon of procedural coinages included, that must still prove itself in being brought *to* hand.

DL: Which is what you seem to be doing—and I'd call it "proof" positive—when you cite yourself not to revisit but to refine a printed passage, so that this palimpsest of twice-edited pages amounts to an original commentary redoubled, if not squared: what I meant by the emergence of a whole new Stewart book. Or, in another fitting figure, an edifice of many rooms and levels to say nothing of garrets—not a memory palace per se, but rather a Hotel Stewart from Barbra's *What's Up Doc?*? (1972, dir. Peter Bogdanovich)—with the double question marks addressing you in twofold fashion. (You remember, I'm sure, how I sent you a while back, when one foresaw your twentieth book on the horizon, a frame grab of Streisand as Judy on the window ledge of the hotel room she was ransacking, looking down on the San Francisco street scene and the prominent *other* hotel marquee, at a safe distance from her chaos, Hotel Stewart—long since, in fact, defunct.)

GS: How could I forget? And, I'll give you that too: twenty-first, gladly. Since I'm in both senses still "shy" of emeritus status, nervous about withdrawal symptoms in the event, I still can make institutional use of the occasional vitae line. Given the considerable retrospective labors—both of renewed love and of occasional alienated affection—that this anthology has turned out to entail for me, there has certainly been no breathing room for another book in between to invalidate the proposed tally. And so far it looks like book twenty-one would be one of my very favorites, in part because it incorporates, right here, the actual dialogue the others only imply. And not least because it would be unassailable on the score of the criticism it has already incorporated and neutralized. Can't you just hear the frustrated reviewer? "It's a little much the way Stewart's superimposed glosses, nakedly refusing to gloss-over any pitfalls or missed richness, forestalls, by brazenly modeling them, the very rebukes he might deserve." Seriously, though, it's the abyssal quality of auto-inspection that your own tertiary reframing and refocusing has made so interesting to me in this recessional layering. Like the famous Hitchcock vertigo-effect, it sometimes feels to me as if I were inhabiting another Stewart's (James') POV, as I simultaneously zoom in and track back in recoil from earlier writing, while you're reframing it all like the director under his VistaVision lens. Did someone say dizzy?

DL: Couldn't be more appropriate to hear you thinking of it this way, given how your own work migrates so often from prose fiction to film, and back again—with other arts, of course, as way stations, as you've called them, along that reversible path.

GS: True, I always do think cinematically about this collaboration, and of course you do too, as your opening metaphors make clear in launching this exchange. I was particularly taken with your early email remarks about one of the many pleasant surprises in the close match of our instincts for one design feature or another, including a pertinent conceptual turn of the volume. How did you put it exactly? Right, I found it: "So much uncanniness! Can sometimes feel like we're sharing the same port in the matrix." This is hardly just the great minds sync alike syndrome. Not merely, as you did, picking up on a famous case in the sci-fi screen genre about whose recurrent metafilmic clues I've written in five different books at least, your vote of—what?—mutual confidence had an extra resonance for me. For it recalled a (the?) signature term in the writing of Michael Riffaterre, with his sense of the "matrix" as the repressed source code of literary technology, silently hard-wired into its subtexts, about which I have written in even more books—and excerpted at least half a dozen times between these covers. But it was also your droll allusion to the whole idea of uncanny thought transference, from the unsaid of writing to the intuition of reading, that I find so hauntingly evoked (literally postmortem, as discussed) in the most recent Richard Powers novel, *Bewilderment* (2021). If you and I were characters collaborating in a sci-fi film about academic publishing in the near future, our dialogue, that novel suggests, would be conducted not by Google.docx but by fMRI brain prints. Which would only be another parable, again as in Powers, for close reading as a kind of telepathy. Unless it were more than a parable—instead a scientific fact about the fate of reading under computerization. Things are happening fast in that line, a point we should return to. In the meantime, radiographic narratography—too late to put that in the glossary?

DL: Never. You keep inventing them, and I'll keep making deposits. But of course they don't come out of the blue. So let's come back to your sense of the "conversations" in which your work is always engaged—as so obviously in your typically extensive endnotes.

GS: Ah, those endnotes. I'd better come back to them too. But first the books in their role, in something other than the popular sense of popularity, as "conversation pieces." In general, I suppose I feel about those published volumes, though in a somewhat more satisfied fashion, the way I did at the time about my many public lectures over the years, here and there on four continents: that they are less critical performances, the monographs, than venues of dissemination. But more settled, because after "taking questions" about their arguments, whether in-progress from live audiences and friends or later from referee readers, I've at least had—and here in this annotated "recollection" yet again, thanks to you—the lag-time needed for getting the answers closer to straight. That's part of what those endnotes have been meant for, of course. I've always thought one of my most useful lessons for graduate students has been how to handle either the "discursive footnote," where journals still permit it, or its equivalent citational reference upstairs in the text. Nothing to my mind is shoddier, or at least sloppier, in academic writing, and more frustrating for its own close reader, than the skimpy or oblique cross-reference, no matter how deferential. I mean the sideways glance, whether askance or not, at works that precede yours without your saying just how—or indicating the ways in which you are adding to the exchange. At best, it leaves the reader unable to appreciate what may well be original in your paragraph; at worst, it seems to be burying debts.

DL: Where acknowledgment becomes a means for bypassing engagement or commentary, and citation made in this spirit is a form of legerdemain—implying intimacy where none has been articulated? If so, we are left to wonder how we got to this place as some function of both professionalization (and editorial practices, market forces, etc.) as well as the instincts and habits of authors. If the arrangement is reversed, however, and we don't see authorial quiescence as a form of tricksterism, then are we dealing with a problem of authority—that is, scholars who don't feel possessed of the *right* to contend with their sources, however much they may be indebted to them? In your own exemplification of endnote composition—a modeling no doubt made palpable to your generations of students—it sounds like you encourage them to think of these footnoted conversations as miniature essays in themselves, as indeed yours often are.

GS: That's right, though with maximum word counts in mind, naturally. Or if the note needs to be herded into the main body of the text, it becomes a kind of parenthetical microcosm (by recap or anticipation) of the broader argument. But such honest reference miniaturizes the operation of close reading more directly yet. Here I come back to a distinction I set out (with) in *The Deed of Reading*: between the ethic of attention per se and the ethics—the moral or political issues—it may or may not go on to locate as a topic for discussion. In this respect, an articulated attention to predecessor critics is as important as any close reading of the literary or film text under review or debate.

DL: By way of disclosing what will be obvious to readers of *Attention Spans*: length constraints have counseled the stripping away of the original apparatus from the excerpted pages above, which are there mainly as a methodological sampler—so that further *conversing with* will then require a gathering of their sources.

GS: That's right, we're not operating by way of the standard Reader format—with its reproduction of original texts *in toto*—but instead with the *reader* as present, in my case, before his own previously published prose, contending with it anew. Which is why it's been worth stressing that crucial dimension of the critical apparatus which is here kept on hold in the interests of pace and overview.

DL: As a student of Charlie Kaufman's *oeuvre*, I'm aware of the meta ironies that allow an author to write an "unauthorized autobiography."[1] If that syntagma stirred a chuckle, we're in the right place, namely, to make explicit the fact that many, if not most, "readers"—anthologies of a writer's selected exemplars—are curated, assembled, and annotated *with no input from the appointed author*. Those players are, ahem, either in the great beyond or are, if still among us, alienated from the means of production. Their names are boldly painted across the cover (trading, doubtless, on their reputations and their allures), while they never saw a galley much less a proof. Herewith, then, a rare sort of specimen …

GS: Let me say it for you: the *authorized* reader.

DL: Very generous of you. And what a wallop that punchline carries. When I was just emerging into literacy, nurtured fittingly (DeLillo-style) by television (circa *Reading Rainbow* [1983–2006]), the diminutive literary critics-cum-playground semioticians would often sign-off on their book reports with a wry "And you don't have to take *my* word for it." Passing the buck or bypassing their televised imprimatur, they shifted the burden to us. How graceful of them. Now I can sit in their company and say the same for *Attention Spans*.

GS: I suppose this is another way of emphasizing how I didn't want to license such a project unless I myself stood to learn from it, making it less after all authoritative than exploratory.

DL: I do hope readers of *Attention Spans* will appreciate how, or why, it does something your prior twenty books did not, could not. Moreover, how its difference from them makes its methodological achievements pertinent to all of them. Picking up from just above, I see the distinction that you're shoring up between an ethic of attention and the ethics of theme or form. But with such shores in mind, I'm wondering about bridges, or maybe tunnels, or perhaps the scale of calibration that helps us ferry *between*. Can you say more about how you find such an approach to what we might call the extratextual dimension of a work's premises or impact—how exactly it can be accessed and addressed by close reading?

GS: Maybe "exactly" isn't the word. Let's say that such access, even if indirect, is noted more "precisely" than otherwise, more exactingly as a textual function. I remember here an oft-quoted remark by Christopher Ricks, as if by way of a job description, and deliberately low-balling it: that "a critic is someone good at noticing things." And more recently, another brilliant and prolific Cambridge don, Steven Connor, has gotten into trouble, as he explains in his new book *Styles of Seriousness* (2023), for resisting the drift toward political importuning in critical rhetoric, seeing, as the critic's task, the assignment simply to be "interesting" rather than "relevant." I would say that the inherent *relevance* of criticism itself is its notice of things *uniquely* interesting, pertinent at whatever scale. Unique to their medium or their moment, historical, political, whatever, but to the latter, often enough, only as filtered through the discernible turns of linguistic or visual mediation.

DL: So "relevance" for you tends to be scaled up too fast from aesthetic form to the public forum?

GS: That's right. I mean that's what's wrong, part of it. But don't get me started again—I'm sure you didn't mean to—on diagnosing another of my allergies, given the many paragraphs spent medicating it in recent books. In fact, it's the medical rhetoric of the "symptom" that's partly at issue in this. For the problem of political relevance has its curious obverse. There's little drearier in my view, in recent critical trends and their catch phrases, than the rebellion against so-called paranoid reading (the Marxist or feminist or postcolonial instinct to find class or gender or racial assumptions sometimes potently latent in a text, even hidden, and therefore worth smoking out from the evidence of its, yes, textual "symptoms"). The way such procedures have become at times numbingly predictable is hardly as disheartening as the rush to rule out their utility in principle. Somehow, from the midst of a widespread politicization of literary study under the banner of just that relevance quotient we've been discussing, this attention to the "political unconscious" (Jameson) of a text can still be branded as a mode of critique that in itself needs fixing by the touted "reparative" approach. This includes its recent cause célèbre: so-called surface reading, whatever that might really look like in practice. It's as if we've come to an interpretive impasse where, reverting to an old poetic adage, we're told that a text should not mean, just be. What's the real suggestion in this? Better than a so-called "hermeneutics of suspicion," no interpretation at all? But what is a surface without its depth? Sounds like an unexamined interface to me. Sign of the times? Then that too should be deciphered.

DL: Odd, I agree, that in an era of what we might call fetishized relevance, explicitly political criticism would be chastised in this quasi-populist way. There does seem something contradictory going on here. A quest for relevance without the suspect hierarchies of rigor?

GS: In the yearning for an activist criticism, it often seems that students of literature or film have given up on a skill set in solidifying a mindset. And it appears to me more and more benighted as our political landscape darkens. Think the Supreme Court—if only *it* would! Stripped of its skeptical precision, close reading is at its most reductive, ludicrous, and indefensible in those "originalist" decisions that take the signified as a thing not historically contingent. Surface reading gone mad. A "well-regulated militia" is just what it says, whatever it may mean. On the other hand, critical legal studies fall under a broad curricular ban, I suppose, because such studies aren't "reparative" enough? Far be it from "suspicion" to apply itself in diagnosing the symptomatics of landed white male privilege in our Constitutive text of texts! And if the very lapsed Irish Catholic in Garrett Fitzgerald Stewart may be forgiven for putting it this way to a man of your surname, the act of reading suspiciously against the received doxa of a predominantly Catholic court, in their *ex cathedra* textual practice, would almost feel like staging the private hermeneutics of schismatic Protest all over again.

DL: No exculpation needed. And I'm quite glad I "got you started" there. Do I perhaps hear in that last declaration a kind of soapbox you'd once have been eager to mount? Is this one of the critical themes you might have looked forward to tackling when you were nominated for the Second Vice President of the Modern Language Association a few years back—and would have succeeded to the presidential post the next year? Did you wish to have the ear of a quasi-captive subscription audience in the 2017–18 pages of *PMLA*? I mean, at least you'd be doing unabashed commentary. Look by contrast at how even the direct and opinionated newspaper "editorial" has been swapped out for the attenuated "guest essay"—so as what?, not to cause alarm among sensitive (different sense of sensitive here) audiences. The *guest*, after all, must be welcomed, tolerated even. Would this climate of sly trades and paltry euphemisms have been something you anticipated pushing back against?

GS: Anticipated yes, as part of the trouble education was, is, up against, but "looked forward to"? The longer I thought about it, even at the time, no. Temperamentally, not statistically, that election was a narrow escape for me, if hardly a near miss. An inveterate close reader is not given to "thinking big" or offering "big ideas," as the voters must have known. A "modern language association" sounds like just the kind of place where I would, often did, find conversation, but I'm relieved not to have been ultimately charged with setting the terms of its public outreach. I was honored to "stand," but I wouldn't have been eager to phrase the organizational stances required. I'm more of a disciplinary than an institutional animal. I like writing, but position papers wouldn't have been easy, let alone presidential addresses or columns, to say nothing of Israeli boycott negotiations and other such reckonings. Or worse still, finding the tone, let alone advice, for confronting in print the gruesome demographics of academic joblessness. It's a timidity in me, undoubtedly. The battles I like fighting, here and there in an essay or monograph, are the ones I can at least hope to win.

DL: On the score of the academic job market, such as it is (for how does one have a market with no buyers, and all the wares discounted?), how difficult do you find it to keep the pedagogical faith, if that's what to call it? As your last remark makes clear, you do see the profession as drastically embattled, for all your continued investment in its aims—aims, I should say, that appear to be a welcome holdover from (and a holding fast to) values and virtues from previous generations. If institutions are deaf to such tuitions, what hope—and what stratagems—for open ears among the disciplines, such as they are; among the disciples, such as they represent the disciplines?

GS: No doubt about it, the battlefront, just the problem of what to *do* about it. Times are hard, vistas bleak, prospects denuded. On this point, no one's in denial. The ivy is dying of drought on the competitive façades of even the so-called League, while the fantasized ivory has long ago been worn away on neglected and crumbling towers everywhere. And in the profound and ever-mounting resistance to expertise among the electorate, both underfunded state and undervalued private schools are losing their edge in schooling the state. Hard to say whether close reading, as a textual logicianship, should be prized more as a renewed bid for the value of expertise or just as a tool for debunking the empty rhetoric of its dismissals.

DL: Let's say both, but still no one's hiring. That employment desert into which the groves of academe have shriveled is often in the back of my mind as I encounter the undimmed verve of your analysis and, especially in these pages, the spans of your imagined "metasyllabus," as you call it, of its career-long "lesson plans." One can easily appreciate the viability of your intensive reading, mental stretch though it may be for undergraduates, but how do you sustain morale at the graduate level and beyond? Or in your terms, how do you contrive to keep the "pleasure principle" intact in such a cheerless, churlish environment, amid all the fiscal bloodletting?

GS: There is no contrivance. If you love it, you love it. Fact is, over the years, many of my best students who have chosen other careers, or had no choice but to abandon Plan A, have harbored a devotion to reading, or at least a renewed and renewing excitement in it, that is emotionally sustaining for them (and when I hear of it, for me as well). The well-intentioned abbreviation "Alt Ac" is a shorthand, in short, that shouldn't be allowed to shortchange the surest "alternative" to academic teaching in the world of liberal education: the residual zone of avocational pleasure in reading—the discriminating reading, that is, of books, movies, museum works, and music too.

But I can anticipate an obvious rejoinder here. This may sound too bland, too much like "quiet quitting." I hope not. No towel is being thrown in, although I have no scheme for fashioning it into a tourniquet. While I worry with the rest of us about the future of our profession, my concern is equally with the practices it has already tended to abandon—and how otherwise they might be sustained. One understands the instant wide interest generated by John Guillory's *Professing Criticism* (2023), written in full view of literature's declining cultural centrality. But where he embeds critical practice in a learned sociology of professionalism over its long *durée*, I am more immediately concerned with the instinct of close noticing rather than the mutating terms of its credentialing proficiency: more with analytic reading as a habit of mind than as the mantle of a discipline, still less as the vesture of a profession.[2] Despite evaporating *job* openings for the literary Ph.D. of any stripe, the *work* of attention remains, on campus and off—and retains its pedagogical edge, whether openly demoted in publishing cachet, simply neglected, fitfully and intuitively engaged, or theoretically renewed under one banner of the other, neo or not. On campus in particular, until there is no instruction left to fund, there is still such work to be done—spurred precisely by the illuminating pleasures of its steadily bettered expertise.

DL: You keep stressing pleasure, by which I assume you mean intellectual gratification as well as amusement, and you'll get no argument from me on that score. Either score, that is. Moreover, the emphasis, along with your influences, has me thinking of Roland Barthes' *The Pleasure of the Text* (*Le plaisir du texte*, 1973)—a title and a project connoting pleasure (*plaisir*) and *jouissance* (bliss, even erotically so). But, anticipating skeptics, isn't there something more (excuse the term) "relevant" yet, in terms of individual as well as social benefit, that might be said for cultivating the "attention span" involved in your work—and in reading it? I suppose I might come at the question via another quasi-medical idiom. Harkening back to ancient philosophical traditions (viz., rhetorical training, spiritual exercises, regarding philosophy as a perpetual contemplation of finitude), isn't there some potential for a kind cognitive therapy involved in the way your writing puts students through their paces, something like a workout in concentration, a focus-building regimen amid all the info-flack and slackened heedfulness of the deepfake and post-truth era? Speaking by analogy, consider how cinematic works that travel under the titles transcendental, slow, meditative, essay, contemplative and the like may be said (at least by me) to create a space and time in which to think.[3] Such films provide conditions for the possibility of introspection, though a newbie or accidental viewer may want a few notes on how to appreciate such endogenous potential. I'm sure I'm not alone in finding in your library of books a similar such space and time for reorienting reading—that is, looking *and* listening—of a special sort. Given the many (historically designated) disciplines you traverse (sometimes at once), a reader is seldom very far from other territories. Consequently, a Stewart reader enters not a discipline or field so much as a milieu, again, not unlike (to my sensibilities) a cinema of attention.

GS: "Relevance," that loaded watchword again, yes. With your appealing cinematic analogy, I call to mind how the Frankfurt school theorists (Walter Benjamin, Theodor Adorno, most explicitly Siegfried Krakauer in connection with the kinetics of cinema) spoke of modernity as a kind of distraction factory. If prescient as well as just trenchant, they might have seen the electronic datasphere coming, including the recent cottage industry of push-back trade books on how to restore focus amid the electronic flux.

DL: And fitting that such a factory has given way to a sector known as the "attention economy," which is to say that *distraction* is the enemy of entrepreneurial gambits. Imagine an economy based on attention (!) with trillions of dollars and the fate of civilization at stake. Still, when won, attention to *what* exactly? Not the durable career of a Hollywood star, groomed and gallivanting to our delight for decades, but some momentary video clip, ephemeral podcast, or terse tweet. Clickbait delivers only more bait. The "influencer" as archetype of quick judgments commodified in the service of an internet of attractions.

GS: Supposedly bucking this tide, among the trade books meant to empower concentration there isn't yet, last I looked, the formulaic title *Attention for Dummies*. It really can't be schooled from scratch. In any case, why not add *Attention Spans* (he says) to this potential best-seller list? But do be sure that you and Bloomsbury play up the pleasure factor for which it advocates, both in the cover description and in every aspect of its marketing. Actually, *scintillation* might be the best word for the zing derived from any such analytic focus, for that fine word tends, in common usage, to bring stimulus and response together in the affect of a textual effect. A scintillating film, a scintillating night at the movies; a scintillating book, a scintillating read.

DL: Barbra's scintillating sound. But even excitation or bedazzlement may require some patience. And everything lately conspires against concentration and reflection, not least that monstrous speed-reading technology you write about in Phase VI / 15, with its curious unmentioned bridge back to Phase VI / 14, given that its computerized word-placement seeks to gut vowel sounds the way shorthand did for Dickens.

GS: Ah, there we go again: wish I had made that connection. Even short of such uniquely "deafening" technology, literary attunement seems under siege everywhere one looks (and would try to listen). And there's even more here than meets the eye—or, worse, little that doesn't do more than meet it. For there's a long-term aural shortfall in the early-level teaching of English in America since the 1990s, much disparaged in the news as I write: promulgated under the "Balanced Literacy" movement—which minimizes the centrality of phonics and encourages learners to find other cues, of context and probability, to guess at words from the likes of opening letters and length, rather than to sound their actual structure (hence meaning) by sounding them out. Literary pedagogy in later education is thus hampered by an underlying learning debility in the last few generations. No wonder so many of my students, including doctoral candidates, respond to my sense of the "other Dickens," or to comparable effects in George Eliot or Virginia Woolf or Toni Morrison, with "I just don't read literature that way." Yet one cherishes those moments when the most focused students do sometimes tune in to what one might call the radioactive drama of syllabic fission—and its interpretive *frisson*—or at least can see a way to make it part of their perception of the text when pointed out to them. But the moments are fewer with each enrollment cycle.

DL: Technology is again a culprit, no doubt, part of the problem rather than some apt (app?) solution. The epoch of "texting" can only have served to neutralize further the listening eye of reading.

GS: Right, an important new chapter in this story of eroding verbal alertness. To put it reductively, it was decidedly easier to teach the concept of "a text," above and beyond writing, when students didn't think they already knew what it meant. Remember when clumsy writing used to be lamented as "all thumbs"; now two-fisted first-digit composition is an expertise. But in an almost continuous SMS regimen, texting is likely to numb one to the *message of the text* in anything like Barthes' sense. When, after reviewing the evolution of silent reading, my latest prose hero, Richard Powers, talks about talking his fiction into voice-recognition software in order to close the gap between composition and subvocal reading,[4] this is a far cry from voice-messaging, with its dated audiotape logo or skeuomorph resembling nothing so much as spectacles turned upside down. No close reading summoned there. Prosthetics and aesthetics don't always keep the kind of close company achieved in Powers' case. (May I digress?—if it's not too late to ask. After saying that about Powers, and before giving you time to respond, my latest course syllabus had rolled over that same week from Colson Whitehead's parody of the portmanteau "Frankenstein word" in "nomenclature branding," *Apex Hides the Hurt* [2006], to Powers' novel *Generosity: An Enhancement* [2009], where I had forgotten that, just a few pages in, his writing-teacher hero passes a downtown Chicago electronics store [boasting "*1000+ mobile, wearable, portable, sportable electronic devices*"] called [almost unpronounceably] "Prosthetechs." I suppose what we might call mere "sight readers," with no ear, could catch the pun without hearing the extra joke about the tongue-twisting glitch in the barbarism of this high-tech pitch.)

DL: So, given the atrophies often resulting from overexercised thumbs, isn't this where the necessary *teaching* of reading can help put on the brakes, slow down long enough to appreciate the actual "construction zone" of strong writing?

GS: Concentration therapy, yes, no question. I mean no question but the ones such reading is so good at searching out answers for. And of course I mean by literary attention something much more wide ranging than phonic acuity. I'm recalling a studied flexible skill that was once in fact marketable in its own right (see again, above: the job market). When it was the former mainstay of a university literary curriculum, such reading used to be a kind of "selling point," not just a talking point, in debates about the cultural capital of "liberal education." Stepping back in time from the current Supreme Court and its unenviable clerks, many law schools, as you know, in the days when they were thriving, used to favor English (and Philosophy) undergraduates not just for their writing but for their reading skills. Interrogation; cross-examination; analysis. They knew the spill-over value of literary criticism and its own special process of "discovery"—in exposition if not deposition. One could say that "Alt Ac" was really in business before the term was even minted.

DL: Yes, "critical thinking," "analytical reasoning," and "close reading," including the more ancient traits of the trivium (logic, grammar, rhetoric), certainly used to be badges of honor, even something of a credential. That is, if we have memories long enough to recall that the *prospect* of law school was often used as a legitimating force—a smokescreen?—for undergraduates trying to underwrite their commitment to the study of English and/or Philosophy.

GS: And now undergraduates will often bypass the "backup" possibility of legal training altogether, starting on day one in computer science. There's no reason even to bother with the humanities at all. Enrollment in English plummets with each passing year without a signal of recovery, the swelling creative writing option being, I suspect, mostly a stopgap. Despite having little sense of what would instigate a renaissance, by pulling again on the thread that such liberal arts training was, in fact, good for the good life, there were also historical reasons for the esteem. Given how much of institutional pedagogy in literature derives, even in disavowal, from New Criticism, it's important to remember that the great rhetorical contribution there was "irony"—a readable means for the saying of one thing while meaning another. Reading was detection, not just explication: interpretation, too disinterested maybe at times, but textually—which is to say intellectually—invested. If irony focused the binocular vision of close reading in its institutional heyday, since then its inherent doubleness has mutated through one ingrate repudiation after another of its supposed formalist claustrophobia: structuralism's emphasis on the "structuring absence" of the text; deconstruction's dwelling on the strictly deceptive "presencing" of the signifier; ideological critique attuned to the unspoken political bias of formal structures themselves, from archetypes through plot formats to cultural idioms. All compelling moves (whether forward or not). But what has been gradually, if not steadily, lost sight of is not just, in William Empson's deathless phrase, "play in the engineering sense": the space-making power of strategic ambiguity (rather than its forlorn cousin undecidability)—lost amid numerous gains, to be sure. But too readily surrendered as well, in the solemnities of "relevance," is playfulness in the other sense, the ludic moves of reading as game. So, I hold out for the pleasure principle yet again, and not least as a lure to students: dramatizing the fun of "comprehension" in its own double sense, as they learn to "wrap their minds around" a given visual or verbal challenge—and not just as a time-consuming puzzle, but as a permanent fixture of their ongoing lives (where the deeper puzzlements of existence await). Eventually, one hopes, further thoughts occur on the way to the voting box, around a cultural conundrum or political blind spot, in communion with friends, parents, and children. So it must sound like I'm submitting for a second time, which I'm actually eager to do, to your proposition: dedicated reading as focus therapy—an escape from the many *forms* of distraction while an antidote to their often noxious *contents*.

DL: I wonder if that question of distraction is part of why you've been drawn so often, like so few of your literary colleagues (that is, even when they do write about movies), to the digital blizzards of VFX in your recent cinema books,[5] from what you call "surveillancinema" to metafilmic sci-fi? I'm guessing you're so deliberately alert to such postfilmic optics for the way they refigure cognitive (more than just extraterrestrial) threats in the modern computer-saturated (and, on screen, so blatantly computerized) world?

GS: Exactly. Couldn't have put it better. Wish, somewhere, I had said it just that way.

DL: So I'm wondering, in turn, short of tutoring a citizenry in close attention, how this might connect for you, or not, back on campus, with the fate of the humanities, including the "digital humanities," to say nothing of humanity at large.

GS: I actually could say something first about humanity. And the Anthropocene itself. Our ancestors used to "read the sky" for omens, including prophesied fatalities. Now we read the atmosphere for signs of its own death. This sense of "reading" is meant more metonymically than just metaphorically, given that reading in this context entails attention to scientifically informed articles and reports, historical records, statistical surveys, as well as political screeds—the whole discourse of disaster, both how dire things are and how many of us are in denial. I don't mean either to aggrandize or, still less, to attenuate the mission of literary close reading in saying so, just to suggest again what we might call its "portable value." You don't need to apply for a doctorate in ecocriticism to leave your undergraduate college as a concerned—and concentrated and *capable*—reader of the writing on this ominous and weather-beaten wall. But, in regard to *literary* reading and its local weather forecasts, I remain unconvinced that the global positioning systems of computer-aided "distant reading" chart the most "relevant" patterns. I'll take Jameson's "cognitive mapping" any day.[6]

DL: I would have been happy to hear you say that, even if I didn't agree, since it reminds me that I wanted to ask you about just that: what you call in your grad course's "Methodological Timeline" the "digital turn" (see "Inventory as Itinerary"). Or not just; it's actually that very turn of phrase I wanted to query as well. Am I right to sense scare quotes around it in your allusion to such going terms, often coming and soon going, especially as the twists and "turns" escalate? Often seems to me the *turn* is more like a euphemism for *trend*. In the spirit of your own etymological readings, it's fitting to note that "trend" itself derives from "rotate." More "spin" than substance?

GS: Sometimes, alas. Let's say at least that the term "turn" is itself in the etymological sense a trope. And what's least appealing about these "departures" (often with no destination in mind) is the way they often constitute just a turning *away*, a calculated forgetting. And in the sense of sheer "rotation," as particularly in the buzz around "neoformalism" a few years back, the efforts seem for the most part to be reinventing the wheel.

DL: In all this trending and turning, I note the *acceleration* of such "turns" in recent years (as captured in your methodological timeline by the compression of intellectual fashions as time rolls on). The spirited cadence of such trends puts the trend-holder, as it were, on notice, while the new method assumes an eclipsing dominance. In fact, I've wondered if you'd consider adding a new turn—maybe the *final* turn?—to your timeline, namely, the "AI turn."

GS: I'm considering it right now, thanks to your question, and am dubious at many levels—in and beyond the classroom. But whether AI is a new "method" of (re)search or the end of all methodology: that's what's so head-turning about its rapid advent. Turning (and one might say cutting) several corners at once, certainly, is AI [artificial intelligence] actually, in the etymological sense, the post-human "revolution" attributed to it? Who can be sure yet, on any disciplinary timeline, where its unique "time-saving devices" might fall?

DL: If we are tracking trends, then, those that amount to something and those that fade away (for having been turned down or tuned out), what about DH [digital humanities], or in other words the bruited "digital turn"?

GS: Too soon to say, I suspect, but to ride the metaphor, that particular turn does seem—dare I say de-termined?—to keep the cart before the horse, turning the reins of reading over from facts on the ground to "big data." The sudden juggernaut of AI can seem like the return in triumph of DH's prodigal offspring.

DL: Short of that imagined and ominous lineage, I'm curious whether you think, in its unusually well-funded incarnation, that DH's exponential claim on curricular attention has begun to taper off?

GS: Looks like it to me—and certainly its job postings (perpetually a stark way of reading the sky, and our fates). Its name has always been a vaunted oxymoron, there to make us rethink the whole idea of humanist thought versus scientific expertise. In its literary application, as you might imagine, the hotspots of its data grids leave me cold. Its emphasis on quanta rather than qualia in "text processing," on scan rather than scrutiny, not least in its exacerbated form of "corpus stylistics" rather than actual reading, is certainly what my own teaching is meant not to repudiate but, putting it mildly, to complement.

DL: You *are* putting it mildly—too mildly? When I'm confronted with DH "initiatives" (another watchword—and watch out for it) that promise "literary text mining for meaning," "the novel as data set," geolocation extraction, genre detection, and the like, I struggle to see how the humanities has survived (in any recognizable or appealing form) the pronounced embrace of computational methods. Despite your *attention* to VFX and CGI and "the digital," your work has struck me as a model for how the humanities retains its methods—and its composure—when coming up against the tsunami of trends heading in the other direction. In such measures of "application"—when the latest, (con)testable technologies are placed under the eyes, and thus before the ears, of a literate embrace—I look to you, time and again, for bulwarks not bull work.

GS: "Composure"? You should see me on a bad day. Odd thing, that humanities is one of the few plurals smaller than its singular. Cities take up more square miles in total than any one of them. But humanity, when under study, is functionally subdivided by its plural—as if the better to bolster it on as many flanks as possible. Humanity certainly needs help, geopolitical, geological—and logical. And media study (literature included) does have something to offer. To read is to think beyond yourself. To read critically is to resist the lures of bad thinking—as well as to apprehend the complexities of good, whether the thinking transpires in words or pictures.

DL: Sounds like we've again moved beyond therapies of attention to its muscular yields.

GS: Hope so.

DL: Simone Weil once wrote that "the development of the faculty of attention forms the real object and almost the sole interest of studies."[7] Her approach—to what she called "school studies"—demanded the cultivation of an "apprenticeship in attention," even as attention itself was, in her conception, a near synonym for the act of prayer. The "education of the young," therefore, "is always conducted under the banner of hope."[8] As you think out loud here (voicing your impressions), can we connect our very latest concerns with the most antique—which is to say: what of education in the dawning era of artificial intelligence, algorithmic computational "thinking," "writing," and the like? What does learning mean for students when the dominant phantom is "machine learning?" And what is art—as a craft, as a mode especially linked to *human* creation, to do with AI art? If education—textual analysis, literary craft, the creation of art—has in some measure been a *refuge* from technological energies of the past few centuries, what happens when AI claims these jobs too?

To give a sense of where we stand, so that we may have to couple our hope with panic, consider the way chatbots, such as ChatGPT, offer predictive composition. AI can write op-eds and autofiction, historical novels and correspondence (and by the day adds new competencies to its resume).[9] Recently a Shakespeare scholar encountered a passage of prose and felt confident that William (or one of his contenders for authorship) did, in fact, write it. The scholar was, to our collective chagrin, defeated because, in fact, an AI "composed" the prose. If there's a grim forecast in the "writing" of such (new/"new") passages, perhaps we can pick up what it would mean to *read* such work—to criticize it? For one thing, there'd be a lot of it to contend with! But then, what does having a thousand times more "Shakespeare" or Shakespeare-like variants (that do not seem *at all* like imitations, ersatz contraband, or "artificial") do for those who wish to offer criticism of it? With such emerging masses of "content" (a word so many are wont to enlist as a symbol of creative work), there'd certainly be some job security. But then, perhaps ChatGPT and its kin can simply write the criticism too—why not? So then, in this expansive and expanding schema—in which AI "writes" Shakespeare, or writes "Shakespeare," and offers criticism of it—who would read the criticism, or want to? Talk about a receding perspective! Feels like I'm missing something fundamental in how this shakes out—and that acute at-a-loss-ness, I'm afraid, appears to intensify as I consider the creation—and the fate—of your books and your writing/reading methods in them. The latest terror seems to (en)code the latest error.

GS: Ah, yes, and far be it from me to claim the obvious nonsense—in fortification of my own preserve—that AI could never in its tin-eared mechanics generate the eye-ear (optico-acoustic) coordination necessary to generate your nice "transegmental drift" in the phonetic slide from terror t'error. It could no doubt generate in microseconds every conceivable such cross-word combination. Here I thought we were probably winding down in our dialogue, and you've gone mega. From R2-D2 among sci-fi film buffs to GPT-3 (Generative Pre-trained Transformer 3 to me, now that I check): quite a specialized application of NLP [natural language processing] and an LLM [large language model], with its bottomless algorithmic pit of "deep learning." Ah, brave new world that has such "sentient" non-creatures in it. One of the wonders of art rather than science, however, is that all this was scrupulously predicted almost three decades ago, and in all its unnerving existential nuance, by Richard Powers' 1995 novel *Galatea 2.2*, where a computer is apprenticed by force-fed textual input, and then further self-trained, to become a literary critic. But now, I readily grant, art is on the line. And first of all originality—with at least one immediate pedagogic tremor, for all its conceivable aftershocks. Note the shared term "prompt" for AI input and undergraduate paper assignments alike. Either one, digitally facilitated, might now spew forth a mechanically impeccable set of insights. Even recalling that plagiarism derives from the Greek for kidnapping, abducting the (brain) child of another, one still has other worries—the ones you're pointing to, of course—about a whole new generation asleep at the wheel while the very idea of originality, critical as well as artistic, is stolen away from cultural aspiration.

DL: AI is developing at such exponential rates that we'll all be Rip Van Winkles soon, caught napping while inherited notions are kidnapped, perhaps permanently. Plagiarism is crucial to our discussion of AI text-generation, for what are these LLMs doing but cribbing? Yet, in our affront—a fear of obsolescence mixed with an envy about increasingly refined offerings—we may be distracted by a reflexive AI/human binary that shouldn't hold. Think back to Ralph Waldo Emerson's "Quotation and Originality" in which he finds himself, like all readers and writers across history, necessarily indebted to forbears:

> [I]n a large sense, one would say there is no pure originality. All minds quote. Old and new make the warp and woof of every moment. There is no thread that is not a twist of these two

strands. By necessity, by proclivity, and by delight, we all quote. We quote not only books and proverbs, but arts, sciences, religion, customs, and laws; nay, we quote temples and houses, tables and chairs by imitation.[10]

In this Emersonian mood, then, we humans are already plagiarists—no matter how clever and original we may seem (or *think* we are). Does an unacknowledged anthropomorphism block us from appreciating how LLMs are achieving precisely what Emerson described back in 1859? Indeed, here I am quoting Emerson, bringing his nineteenth-century lines into conversation with twenty-first-century AI, and then I read him anticipate the move with canny eloquence: "The highest statement of new philosophy complacently caps itself with some prophetic maxim from the oldest learning." The *mise-en-abyme* of the moment makes itself known.

GS: You put the final ironic nail in the coffin of originality by reminding us that the classroom fears about plagiarism via bot are only an epiphenomenon of bot plagiarism itself. Philosophy like Emerson's is certainly welcome at such moments, where it appears that even science doesn't know how to formulate the pertinent questions, let alone offer predictive answers. I read another article than the one you mentioned, by another former Shakespeare scholar, as it happens, in which one of its most eloquent capping paragraphs, subtly speculative and crisply turned in its still rather colorless way, was admitted after the fact to be promptly spun out by ChatGPT, all but instantaneously, after the crafted first sentence as "prompt." That whole last paragraph of mine might be an auto-complete stab at conversation triggered by my first sentence's irony about fantasized computer limitations. In such a case, all that "deep learning" would intentionally fail to dredge up—in any simulation of my discourse—would be, I learned from this same article, some deliberate anachronism falling outside the pre-computed bandwidth of my contemporary academic vocabulary, should I have for instance been inclined, ironically enough, to greet the latest advances in algorithmic prose with either a "trepidatious soul" or "the heebie-jeebies." My computer alter ego, thinking better of it, would have had me wax "cautious" or "wary" or "deeply discomfited" instead. And even the programmers have no idea how such uncanny operations are really happening, let alone where they might lead. But if there is nothing to do about all this, what to *think* about it? That's clearly your big question, and, though unanswerable, it's absolutely right to leave it hanging in the air here, rather than being swept aside. It would seem to me a droolingly stupid complacency to lay back in undimmed celebration, computer fabrication notwithstanding, at the prospect of still more literary "artifacts" worth parsing, maybe even the "true" finish to Dickens' *The Mystery of Edwin Drood* (1870). But it would be just as unwise, just as benighted, to go defeatist too soon, to opt out, blinkers on, from escalating developments in the offing. What can I, really anyone, say? Seems more than a tad pallid to put it this way, but until we really know what's going on, and what's coming, and no one seems to, the best we can do, in the face of a digitized post-humanity, is answer the "deep learning" of AI with our own information gathering, on higher alert all the time, while wielding elsewhere, until otherwise obsolesced, our own equally vigilant deep reading.

DL: It's unnerving, deeply so, to think we're not far from a chatbot variant inclusive of—or dedicated to—your twenty books (and counting), call it the "Garrett Stewart Prose Simulator" (GS-p.s.®). The Stewart-infused LLM will have to handle a prompt demanding highly "self"-conscious poise in the face of existential criticism. Any (human) Stewart reader will be on the lookout for familiar filaments: dismantling grammatical and etymological integuments to reveal the hidden luminosities of language, reshaping rhythm and style with syntactical dexterity, installing points of literary reference (Powers, then Dickens), deploying neologisms from the official GS-p.s. terminological toolkit to heightened effect, even shifting tones as needed (calmly accepting a dire scenario, graciously spinning it to summon a positive precipitate and proactive stance in the face of daunting odds), among other traits. (I was tempted to write "inimitable" [traits], but I guess that word can be permanently retired.) Posterity can comfort itself knowing that with GS-p.s., its simulations always postdating any printed text, lambent Stewart criticism will "live on" in a convincing fashion—fresh dispatches arriving upon command—the postscript eternal.

GS: Dickens' comic phobia about the spread of a misnomered "reading" as performative act comes to mind here, from your Introduction. The One and Only, to say nothing of the once Inimitable, would be rotating in his grave at "a robot's 'reading' of my style." Maybe another way to brace for all this "unnatural" language processing, if not to find it exactly bracing in the usual sense, is to assume that—until a press like Bloomsbury decides to have AI intercede at the editorial stage to smooth out and juice up submitted prose, and to auto-tune the blurbs accordingly—until then, as long as critical reading stays a deliberately little distance *behind* the curve, we'll still be analyzing AI, rather than, in any but a generalized search-engine sense, AI reading us. What better use of our analytic energies, even if they don't carry the force of resistant strategies, whatever those might look like? And as long as they don't congeal into sheer retrenchments. As education stares, or at least peeks, into such an imponderable technological chasm, and though the chiasm of abbreviations might suggest otherwise, we at the University of Iowa have no better a game plan for the AI/IA match-up, let alone any more of a sporting chance, than any other school. But that's not where sleep seems to me most pertinently lost. It's harder and harder to teach the sting of Dickens' social satire, for instance, when his world-historical way with words increasingly leaves students speechless, not with awe but with a kind of comprehension almost mechanical (though hardly electronic) in its own right.

DL: And along with Dickensian satire, we could draw in Jonathan Swift, who more than a century before Emerson, in 1726, imagined The Engine at the Academy of Projectors in Lagado. Compared with our standard-issue "search engine," Swift's vision is more akin to today's LLMs and their capacity to produce output via algorithmic functions. Swift's professor, addressing his pupils, speaks of "improving speculative knowledge" by "mechanical operations," the results of which the world would soon find useful: "Every one knew how laborious the usual method is of attaining to arts and sciences; whereas, by his contrivance, the most ignorant person, at a reasonable charge, and with a little bodily labour, might write books in philosophy, poetry, politics, laws, mathematics, and theology, without the least assistance from genius or study."[11] Three hundred years later, Swift's vision of computational finesse at the mercy of the masses appears ready to dispense with the satire. Since we know "how laborious *the usual method* is of attaining to arts and sciences," call it human-generated, perhaps we'll be tempted—or simply forced, coerced by multinational tech firms—to employ the AI "in a project for improving speculative knowledge" on our behalf, for its own gains (along with the corporate interests that run The Engine). We in the humanities, still dedicated to humanism, may count this as among the most salient moments of "misaligned" AI.

GS: Short of Swift's Academy, there's still our own to be concerned about. I don't want to tire anyone, or mislead them, by proposing that a gift for spotting and naming a syntactic trope or a homophonic pun or an ironic match-cut is some kind of "life skill." But this level of schooled attention does have cross-over value—a transdisciplinary "application"—and can even be construed as the deep foundation of a vital civics lesson as well as what used to be described as a "personal philosophy," or philosophy of life. Wince if you want, but what hope for humans and humanities if people no longer recognize the stakes of such enterprises as "life changing"—if the task of reading is deemed unprofitable (most overtly, of course, in the economic sense, but also in the development and management of one's character)? Certainly for me it's never been, in class, only a disciplinary show-and-tell. From the start, I wanted to share with students my highly focused fascination as a kind of consciousness-raising across media, across cultural forms, and thus across social discourse.

DL: So the "civics" dimension in aesthetic instruction also tracks as a civilizing one?

GS: Partly, of course, but that's not all. The more flexible and adventurous the registers of closeness, the more artifacts to which that scale of investigation applies—the more enabling the calisthenic regimen we've been talking about becomes. Yet anything like a civilizing function must take the pulse of its own changing culture.

DL: Exactly. And we seem to be approaching a kind of impasse in the expectations of creativity. As cultural artifacts multiply, the need—and the instinct—to repeat, recycle, reflect, refract, and recur increases. Despite many fascinating achievements, the proliferation of meta-works also exposes a certain unlooked-for poverty, decay, or decadence in the culture. Being derivative is the *modus operandi*; trading on existing intellectual property is the main business model. Now generative AI is supercharging an already aggressive and pervasive process. Where we have been at the mercy of artists finding ways to couple, nest, or otherwise reference and reflect on preexisting work, the meta curve is now hyperbolically steep. Call it Meta 2.0, or mega-meta. À la Galatea 2.2, whatever art or data or information we have entered into the mainframe will become source material for future source code: "How are you getting on with your attempt to automate literary criticism?"[12] Every prompt will stand to flatten human creation such that all data points lie in wait to be mobilized, eschewing media type, genre, origin, and everything else.[13] That is, unless AI becomes a genre, or the super-genre that absorbs all others. Generative AI is a clandestine plagiarism operation, the LLMs appropriating the breadth and depth of human creative expression, from low to high; then auto-cannibalism will set in as the LLMs feed on themselves, ouroboros-style. Question is: will the repetition and replication deliver weaker, diluted iterations each time, *de-generations* as it were (like an old-fashioned mimeograph machine) or will refinements come to light (where the output from Henry-GPT-James is, even for the dedicated James reader, "as Jamesian" as the author himself might have managed)? If strategies of human attention are weakened, however, if discerning the difference between human-created and AI-generated is a forgone priority, or simply infeasible, then AI output of "recycled" intellectual property may simply be deemed sufficient—good enough simulacra for aesthetic gratification (and priced right too: free or nearly so).[14] Approaching peak simulation feels akin to the heightened high of artificial sweetener: a massive, calorie-free hit with not nearly as much labor. Having done their work creating civilization for ten millennia, the future of art and literacy for humans—novel writing, image making, sound design, theory, criticism, etc.—would lie principally in imagining new prompts.[15]

GS: At this level of cross-media generalization, you tap another vein—and touch another sensitive nerve—in my belated post-publication encounters, quite apart from AI. Let me take up that aspect of your diagnosis first: the flattening effect of a metastasized meta. It's the kind of tardy extra discovery that I might have inserted in the Inventory, but it seems to bear more broadly here on your critique of a kind of nugatory baroque in the excesses of electronic image culture. In January of 2023, after a final draft of the "Inventory as Itinerary" had been completed, I came upon a telling convergence of book art and digital remediation in a Richard Prince retrospective at the Louisiana Museum of Modern Art outside of Copenhagen. The work by Prince that had interested me previously has, I learned, found an almost inevitable upgrade in more recent electronic ironies included in that show, ones that illustrate your point exactly. By this famous American appropriationist from the "Picture Generation"—committed to the found image merely re-presented by photo enlargement, as with his wall-sized Marlborough Men or biker girls cropped overscale from magazine pages—there were more explicit codex extrapolations on display in the repainted pulp fiction book covers that had come into the ken of *Bookwork* (2011). As if in a natural evolution from these objects of material media, Prince gravitates lately away from book covers to the formerly named Facebook and its Instagram imagery. Rather than repainting or rephotographing the seductive female images on his feed, as he did with his nurse novel paperback romances, now he unabashedly recirculates these posted portraits via our latest mode of electronic remediation—the screenshot—extending the found image (in contrast to his previous cropping of lifted photos) by a line or two of his own oblique comments appended to the column of "likes," his often irrelevant byline thus amounting to the artist's electronic signature. The overall image—and the imaged woman within it—has thus undergone no alteration except a print enlargement, at various scales, some greater than life-size, from its original screenshot capture. A century's experiment can seem bookended (no pun intended) when modernism's canonical ready-made has been replaced by the instantaneous techno-remake. The effect is simply to picture media culture back to itself with what amounts to a quirky extra caption. I bring up here this almost zero-degree instance of a transmedium irony in connection with AI because it calls out, to my mind, a kind of structuring opposition in our pervasive electronic culture: the potentially viral image, often a documentary selfie, over against the merely virtual one—the latter entirely made up, the former barely made over in Prince's recirculation. Two halves, it seems to me, of the tendencies you last sketched out: both examples of the meta in distress.

DL: I'm certainly with you there: something like the difference between appropriation and ontological approximation.

GS: Yes, or call it the gap between the all-but-found—the given in a minimal tweak—and the algorithmically fabricated. In any case, dwelling on this has helped me to see that the prospect of AI producing a new Hemingway novel—from all the electronic archive "knows" about, and can automatically recirculate from, Hemingway's style—would be, however successful, its own kind of appropriation and remix. And so part of the de-origination aesthetic you allude to.

DL: As part of our prospective catalogue of territorial handovers to AI—novel writing, literary criticism, image making, music composition, etc.—we are, will increasingly be, forced to adjudicate human instances from AI-generated. The deepfake (of whatever flavor or variety) will become the ghastly, ghostly bogeyman of the present-day and promised post-human age; in these early stages, being tricked by AI has become a form of entertainment, but soon enough—when the stakes and standards are elevated to the level of authorship, one's livelihood, democracy as we've known it, the rule of law, etc.—the laughing will fade to a faint cry. The death of the author takes on new life.[16] Some creative humans may descry in such circumstance a chance for a kind of immortality (novels proliferating postmortem), and yet others can worry about their remaining days on earth and whether *discernment* between human and AI will be possible. Take as one of many paths to pursue the further, harrowing or not (yet), the virtuality of new AI audiobook narration, which is reaching the point, so press releases and some beta-testing suggest, where it can avoid the "uncanny valley" of phonorobotic intonation on the way to achieving the high plateau of cogent elocution itself.

GS: Though so far, far from it—at least from the samples I've heard. But yes, the fact is that computers are indeed writing and reciting for us everywhere we turn, even if that doesn't mean they can actually read.

That last is the point I make in my most recent essay, in response to his own thinking along these lines, in my "Afterword" to John Cayley's rigorous and inventive address to "artificial language" in *Image Generation*.[17] Computation sorts n-grams; humans have the experience of grammatical decoding. Computers can write "like" us, one might claim, only because they can't really read—only sort with astronomic speed. That puts my anxieties slightly to the side of the mainstream press and the new rush of on-campus directives about bot plagiarism. It may be that even online university press cover sheets for manuscript submission, let alone honor-code undergraduate protocols, will soon include an "I am not a robot" check box, complete with a photo-recognition panel. But one remembers that this Captcha function (for Completely Automated Public Turing test to tell Computers and Humans Apart)—with its "catchy" overtone (close reading of little consolation here, though, in brand decoding) of gotcha-if-you-caption-the-pictures wrong—operates not just as latch key to keep you from the site until your fleshly authenticity is verified, but is actually an ongoing training program for AI image recognition.[18] To make the imagined campus turn-in-essay site functional, it would certainly be safer (if more difficult for many students) to ask which images included cursive handwriting than which quotes were by Shakespeare.

DL: Your black comedy not only underscores a further swath of the obsolete in handmade literary activity but reminds us how little we can be confident of in regard to what's next. The way AI is constantly "improving" itself—by virtue of our input, our responsiveness, our "correction"—intimates the next phase of a Cavellian (moral) perfectionism, an onward movement of refinement by degrees. Yet this incremental march to mastery (including imitation of human exemplars) makes contact with one of the prevailing moral virtues of post-modernity, that misbegotten mark of success and self-worth: "productivity." Where humans have been managed into ever-increasing "efficiency" through "life hacks," human output cannot match the speed—and soon the "expertise"—of AI. Maybe the comic asymmetry, with AI churning out reems of "content" by the minute, will send us all to our gardens (and solitary sessions of fiction reading) with clear consciences. Voltaire and Rousseau would be pleased. Meanwhile, thinking of our more perilous position vis-à-vis our computational overlords (in which we incrementally hand over our power to AI), are we losing—encouraged to lose—our grip on the fact or function of "authenticity" in writing, a need to contextualize the author or better, the author's work, replaced by the security-network lingo of "authentication"? Has provenance become an antiquated value? Yet you were speaking of an anxiety not quite mainstream in these matters.

GS: Yes, a poignant danger seems to me, at least on the academic front, less what is deceptive in such workaday electronic verbiage than the so far paltry lament for what is lost to the power of language by such pallid nerveless simulation. Cold comfort, again, that close reading might come to a ready forensic rescue in detecting the radically drab and nonliterary. Or back to the spirit of your mentioning artificial narration in the audiobook domain: how long will it be till we have forgotten the difference—or more likely, ignored it—between vocal text generation and the "real" reading that comes from inner enunciation?

DL: No telling, but I do find that it's all operating headlong, across media, on the same slippery slope.

GS: And more so every year, even every month. In resistance to this post-humanist horizon, what can one really say? Or what can one do, on its literary front, but keep saying: saying something this side of programmed? Since we began this dialogue in late 2022, the humanist dam has certainly burst, opening the floodgates of technomancy and its "creative" simulacra—and we can scarcely expect (speaking sylleptically one last time) to catch either up or our swamped breath. Last year the computer learned to write either like Jane Austen or Paul Auster, your pleasure. And, yes, with the new audiobook technology, the apparatus is wired to read either author out loud, or any other you choose, as if it were actually a human voice box. This is all diametrically at odds with Richard Powers composing his novels on an iPad so that their phonetic pulse would comport more nearly with the somatic production of the reader in *silent* receipt. We're miles from that these days—as regards both production and reception. A virtual Richard Powers novel, say *Galatea 3.3*, could now be algorithmically programmed for strictly digital enunciation. And then of course, in a longer vista—since we can't afford to put anything past the technological future—we have eventual brain implants to contemplate, short-circuiting both outer speech and inner voice.

DL: I wish I could say "Don't exaggerate"—but in fact there's no such thing lately, given the pace of these technological prosthetics. The AI continuum is really operating on the same tilted trajectory across all media systems; sounds like you'd agree.

GS: Right, and no "digital humanist" needs to grease the wheels—or has seemed immediately inclined to regret the deficits. Commercial technology charts its own path. And we're focusing on it here because that path cuts across everything that I've written about over the years. Where Printing on Demand compromised one traditional manifestation of the codex, Literature on Demand is, to say the least, the portended death knell of *belles lettres*. And soon we'll have Films on Demand in other than the routine online sense: not just the theatre-depleting, home-screen experience, but films made to order. Imagine hyper-stylist Stanley Kubrick's posthumous direction of a new feature episode of *Mission Impossible* with a more than preternaturally unaging (a digitally eternal) Tom Cruise. I'm not making this up—or just barely. Wholesale stylistic appropriation for digitally generated screen narrative isn't with or upon us just yet, but early in 2023, well along into our exchange on these matters, the *New York Times* reported on images from a version of the film *Tron* made by visionary director Alejandro Jodorowsky (famous for his failed attempt to get *Dune* made in the mid-1970s).[19] Illustrated under the title "This Film Does not Exist," these were apparent frame captures (or production stills) of credibly costumed characters in a cogent set, though generated entirely by an AI input in search engine cross-indexing between the existing *Tron* films (1982, 2002) and Jodorowsky's archived storyboards. Again, a kind of sampling in a vacuum: the metafilmic in the absence of an actual film.

DL: That would certainly count for the final evisceration of the mode: auto-reference with no autonomous status; reflexivity in a void. Take the television serial, *The Capture* (2019–), which posits a next-gen text for developing the next phase of your long-standing uptake of "surveillancinema," the ever-expanding reach of the "technopticon," and the logic of "closed circuits" (see "Terms of Use"). Among many striking attributes, the show connects CCTV to artificial intelligence, thereby creating conditions for you to extend your conceptual, thematic, and technology critiques—while calling forth an "apparatus reading" of a new vintage. The first season proffers a near-future (present-day?) world in which "correction" of CCTV promises to "turn intelligence into evidence"; season two dramatizes the uses of facial recognition and the emplacement of AI avatars ("digital assets"). In this world, our near-term world, artificial intelligence authors clandestine intelligence by manufacturing medial truths to legally support undocumented, unsurveilled experience. "Planting evidence" 2.0. The human debate is who *authorizes* this application of AI. Traditionally, that is, until five minutes ago, information "leaks" were more damaging the more true the information; but now intelligence becomes simulated, made-to-order information. Our predicament is turned inside out: rather than truth conforming to cinematic evidence, synthetic evidence determines the truth that shapes a cultivated reality. AI engineers describe output errors as "hallucinations"—e.g., when an AI gets some fact wrong, or invents invalid information—but here in *The Capture* the (fake or designed or intentionally summoned) hallucinations are the point. If, like courtroom juries, we're prone to believe what we see (and hear)—perhaps especially credulous because we've been trained to have faith in the veracity of CCTV—what does this televisual takedown of the correspondence value of the closed circuit portend?[20] Are we in need of a new portmanteau to "capture" the spirit of this new specter?

GS: In the jurisprudential terms of that series, what about *verifiction*? We can leave the word unglossaried, but I'm glad you brought up that fiercely timely series. Certainly the looming threat of AI sweeps across all the media that have interested me in my writing, not just in artificial language processing but in artificial imaging. We've come a long way, for sure, from the film released just as I was finishing up work on the conflational ironies of "surveillancinema" for *Closed Circuits*: namely the singularly titled British thriller *Closed Circuit* (2013, dir. John Crowley). Ironizing the ubiquity of surveillance cameras in London at the time, with the film's dull tagline "They See Your Every Move," the plot turns on a deliberately decommissioned CCTV monitor in a prison cell, eliding proof of a murder scene. A decade later, and far advanced along this same line of evidentiary anxiety, that tautly shot British serial, *The Capture*, is so named for optic-leading-to-legal *seizure*, with its updated tagline "Seeing is Deceiving." As you say, the series extrapolates from present electronic conditions—and phobias—to imagine a combination of time-stamped surveillance and AI-generated deepfakes that are figuratively "stitched" together by one of the earliest of cinematic shot changes, the explicitly named "wipe"—though facilitated here (on-camera) by a passing truck or bus obscuring the switch from document to face-matched fabrication. The covert effort is to "catch" in the act, as admissible evidence of terrorist plotting, events merely presumed rather than actually filmed: little motion-picture fictions. But according to its counterterrorism mastermind, in collusion with the CIA, this is not some nefarious deceit but "truth re-enacted" in the absence of record, an optic performativity. Known as Correction, yes, in repair of missing evidence, with its overtone of "correctional" facilitation, the whole electronic nightmare marks its distance from the onetime operation of indexical celluloid, not just with a joking allusion to Steven Spielberg as suspected culprit in the duped footage, but by a macabre turn through which—in the torture chamber of an electronically simulated interrogation—a suspect "loses his digits" one by one. The digital is otherwise lost here by AI scrubbing, whereby criminal bodies are removed from CCTV traces of the elevators or revolving doors of their homicidal access, their agency explicitly "ghosted." After the plot's early crisis of confiscated and "redacted" evidence, the "reality TV" of surveillance files, in the form of their ultimate postfilmic subterfuge, is thus found compromised by a real-time version of computer-generated imagery. According to the American arch-villain, with enough data-banked 3D animations generated from face-recognition software, eventually the "untouched" and undetectable AI images will emerge in the form of a "sheer, unbridled imagination"—a process hard for the viewer not to associate, in medial terms, and beyond any "motion capture," with the pure fabrication of computerized VFX. And the ultimate timely twist in the first season is that CIA oversight is willing to let leak just enough evidence of this top-secret program that it will become the stuff of deep state/deepfake conspiracy theory rather than full-scale political exposé.

DL: I'm gratified by the way your own response to this series gives us a chance to notice and appreciate how the origins of cinema and its much-vaunted "language" (wipes, cuts, eye-line matching, montages, multiple perspectives, parallel editing, and an illusionism that Georges Méliès would have recognized and applauded) interact with up-to-the-second nanoscale circuits capable of digital sound/image generation. We can see such phenomena as operating along a continuum—a spectrum of experiments—or, perhaps in this dawning era of AI consumption of all recorded history: the collapse of the technology into a state of unity awaiting the aforementioned "sheer, unbridled imagination." *Whose* (or with AI looking askance, *what's*) imagination that will be becomes an emergent question as "prompts" direct the machine to fulfill its potential. "Making movies" in the years ahead will involve different talents and wherewithal: as with the faux-*Tron* film stills invoked above, full-length feature-film Frankensteins made-to-order are in the offing, no?

GS: Full movies, yes, feel ripe for this spontaneous algorithmic generation: motorized digital images in place of nonexistent recorded stills. We might get Orson Welles as an "on-camera" Kurtz in *Heart of Darkness*—in the finally realized script of his intended dual role—narrated by a baritone simulation of himself as Marlow in AI voice-over. All it takes is for such audiobook technology to achieve that level of mimetic (rather than just syntactic) conviction. We could have Toni Morrison posthumously reading not her own novels only, but those of Zora Neale Hurston. As things stand so far, and never for long, there are only simulated frame grabs in the AI playbook of unmade movies, but even at that the possibilities are endless for uncast or unfinished projects. Not just imaginary ones, like a sequel to *The Awful Truth* (1937) with Cary Grant and Irene Dunne (together again!) in *Truth and Consequences*. A critic interested in auteur style could discuss—with a new level of abandon in the matter of fair use—how an auto-aged Greta Garbo would have been shot in the role of a European queen either in Luchino Visconti's *Ludwig* (1973), which she is rumored to have declined, or his unfunded Proust film, for which he again approached her. Or we could have plausible screen captures of Barbra Streisand in Ingmar Bergman's operetta *The Merry Window*, a project that withered on the vine after extensive consultation between director and star. Let living artists make their own mistakes; computers can always rectify.

DL: That's why, for one thing, I'm so pleased, as I know you are as well, to have that image from John Opera on our cover; and readers can turn to "Coverage" (Phase X) for further thoughts from each of us on the work. In this cyanotype, Opera's artful coupling of realms—the light-based mark-making familiar from photography and the painterly stroke associated with canvas art—delivers an amalgam fit to contest this era (error?) of generative artificial intelligence. No prompts were fed into DALL-E, Midjourney, or Stable Diffusion. Rather, while photo-sensitive surface awaited its inscribing light, Opera was poised above the canvas, the human hand taking dictation from human habits and haptic innovations all the while heeding the laws of physics set down in time immemorial. And if the resulting linen substrate of the image may seem to soften or blur its "resolution" (and in the process our own convictions about the representational attributes of what we see), this latent evocation of undernourished pixel count would only be part of Opera's image-historical self-consciousness—a veritable annunciation of the auto-index.

GS: And precisely without that vacuum of human craft, that lack of artifactual making, we've been discussing in terms of strictly algorithmic ontologies. Opera's work of material shaping is what makes the image a work, and as such worth "reading."

DL: Our keynote term again, always welcome. Yet the accelerating unknown of our technological future does lately seem to be casting an especially long shadow over one's literary and media professions, among others job descriptions. In regard to paper or online reading, as lector and reader alike, we are endlessly deliberating over what gets exercised—or what should be made lithe and limber. Being so text-focused, as we are, concerned with the *generation* of sentences and the books that contain them, I appreciate anew your repeated invocation of *students*. That is, readers. And their present and future predicament. As we approach the end of our conversation and the end of the book—at the fiftieth anniversary of the appearance of your first book, 1974/2024—there is a natural desire to bring things up to the minute, if only for a minute (and if only allowing that topical reflections might, at last, be hostage to fortune). How jarring, for instance, was it for me when just a couple months after the long-gestating *Metacinema* was published (2021), Facebook suddenly changed its name to Meta? And for you, when your *Metanarrative Hall of Mirrors* appeared the following year from Bloomsbury?

GS: Same here, that odd unwelcome timing. And, for me, the unwanted association was complicated by the suspicion that Facebook's rebranding was not just corporate house-cleaning but downright euphemistic, evoking the impersonal abstractions of metadata to excuse precisely its individuated privacy issues.

DL: A good deal to be on guard for, to be sure, in all these "creative disruptions." Even as we strive for *Attention Spans* to offer a fresh—and refreshing—comment, we are still very much in the mix of the methodological timeline you share with students, still without bearings, without a sense of where things are headed. You mention there's a virtue in being *behind* the curve, and so there's a risk of being ahead of it (and missing its eventual direction). And yet belatedness can seem bad for business.

    Here we are, then, caught up in another computational craze. Ten minutes ago, crypto and NFTs [non-fungible tokens] were the tech *du jour*, now various LLM chatbots loom. Fun, I suppose, to comment on fads—whether or not they turn out to be world transformative (for good or ill, or a bit of both). Still, we meet technology when we meet it; however things shape up in the long run, you appear uniquely positioned to be able to say something that remains vital and pertinent for the long(er) term about how we read and how we write—what the two facets mean for *thinking* full stop.

GS: Its buzz so much in the air lately, and on the airwaves, you rightly indulge the lingo of "creative disruption" in connection with AI, but the worry is of course destruction, the entire overthrow of creativity by generativity. We're not there yet, but everyone, or almost everyone, sees the risk in outsourcing too much mental labor to technology. And where is this more likely to be felt than in institutions of so-called higher learning? English departments, having turned increasingly from discriminating reading to creative writing just when computers can do the latter faster and more grammatically, have traded what was left of their vanishing social capital with the public for tuition revenue—and no one, however casually happy, is really thriving as they might. What sustains me is not what maintains the system in fiscal solvency: it's instead the rare student who, and not least in this "post-truth" era of public politics, catches the fever of precision and revels in the pleasures of a robust literary appreciation never blind to critique, never flabbily passive in reception. Think of it this way in light of campus gym culture: if robopunditry can generate diatribe left and right, and indiscriminately jab at just those alternate poles of the political spectrum, only individual thinking can be relied on—with collegiate close reading one of its best early workouts in pursuit of a finer-toned stamina.

DL: While we've been discussing GPT-3, its successor GPT-4 has recently been released (with versions 5, 6, 7, and beyond feeling predetermined); aside from any specific incarnations, though, the *category* of generative AI is here and appears to only increase in prevalence, disruption, and threat (and, in the above, destruction). Within the brief time segment between iterations, we've witnessed a wide range of public reflection on the extent to which these LLMs and related technologies will disfigure the landscape and overturn expectations about what kind of output is possible from AI (along with all the other advancing and bespoke AI-enabled tools—for text generation, image creation, audio fabrication, and so on). The pundits are lining up on the usual spectrum: from panic to laidback indifference to despair. For one user, ChatGPT is, in fact, not a tool, but a toy—and a technology that will create *more* not less work for humans; for another user, it spells the end of (human) writing as we know it.[21] Still another says chatbots will eradicate human "knowledge jobs" (thus making less "work" for them, after all) as well as manufacture and amplify disinformation.[22] The age of AInxiety is upon us.

GS: Now there's one for your own glossary down the road. And like all good portmanteaus, the first thought fans out all but inevitably into the second. Certainly the age has dawned fast, bursting upon us like your last three syllables.

DL: In *Attention Spans*, then, we are meeting the emergence of generative AI at this nervous early stage of its development— roughly in the window between GPT-3 and GPT-4, so a figurative fraction of a second in the asymptotic ascent of the technology. As we involuntarily enter the slipstream, a range of responses to the predicament cascades—where AI presents a "false promise" (Noam Chomsky), manifests "a moment of immense peril" (Gary Marcus), means saying "goodbye to the future" (Walter Kirn), contributes to "lights out" for humans (Sam Altman, CEO of OpenAI, creator of ChatGPT) or may embody "one of the most transformative innovations in human history" (Tyler Cowen).[23] So, take your pick, and maybe choose more than one. We seem destined to end up in the unforeseeable future somewhere between generative AI fundamentally reshaping our world or offering us a "glorified toaster."[24] There's a vision of AI writing and reading "better" than humans, more precariously, writing *for* humans—and there's the view that it is and will remain "a bloated, pointless mess."[25] Good times.

Yet, in so far as we're here together on this occasion—reading your books and the books you've read (and reread) over the course of a lifetime—what sorts of things come to mind about the emergent, expanding reality of living with LLMs as accomplice to, or inheritor of, your readerly, literary life? Still more, what about readers coming to your work—first, wanting to understand it better; and secondly, wanting more of it (from "you," as it were—after *you*)? With respect to the future of writing, have we gone from Great Textpectations to Textpocalypse?[26]

GS: Maybe going, but not yet gone. For one thing to bear in mind is that the modifier of "large language models" [LLMs] refers to the models, not the resulting linguistic instances, which are often undernourished, puny, and bare boned, even when grammatically able. Or call it fuzzy, even when "accurate." I suppose it's fitting that a visual metaphor comes to mind for the ambiguous sourcing of even a verbal depiction, given what we've said already about AI-generated optic evidence. But most of the nonfictional (but fabricated) sentences dredged from the data mines, the ones I've read, seem slightly out of focus in emergence from their sourceless density of probabilistic options. As if prose could itself be pixelated in a kind of low-resolution intent.

DL: The phenomenon of not knowing what we're looking at—real, fake, human-created, AI-generated—does seem to manifest a "big blur."[27] The ocular occlusion, the soft-focus features, spur me to think anew about the nature of the surface of prose (already engaged above), and with the surface of screens—arriving with questions pertaining to the relative clarity or availability of authorship, the willingness of a text to be interpreted or its resistance to being read. Perhaps we haven't appreciated until now the extent to which reading begins and sustains itself because of a felt trust with the author or artist; though we've watched animations (from 2D cartoons to 3D digi-confections, from CGI world-building fantasies to other graphic deceptions, such as digitally "de-aging" the surface of actors' skin), and though we've read fictions and detected unreliable narrators (hoaxes even!), we've always known these fabulations were made by humans. Now, and increasingly, not so much. Is there something, then in the nature of priority (first this, then that) or pedigree that calls us to reconsider (the above name-checked) "surface reading" in the AI age?[28] Are we not launched mightily upon a new phase of paranoid reading—looking for "symptoms" again, what could "give away" the AI progenitor or alternatively "prove" the human creator? Perhaps this unsettling fate takes the Cavellian condition of "living our skepticism" one degree too far. We stand in need of your countermeasures to surface reading: the penetrating, slow, close, deep, reflexive Stewart stylistics of interpretation.

GS: More likely, there'll be the occasional conference paper on the racial or ethnic bias of the large language database and perhaps a second wind for DH, just where previously thought not digital enough by scientists nor scholarly enough by humanists. Perhaps it can get new leverage by turning its search engines on data drivers themselves, as is already happening with bot-detection apps.

DL: In the meantime, I grew curious about testing the bots with input queries, rather than "outing" them, wondering how their "style" would characterize yours. ChatGPT improved on its "machine learning" in a second try, several months after my first prompt, but the best it came up with seemed a plagiarized pastiche of incidental reviewers' phrasings: adding up to even less than the sum of their lifted and lackluster parts. Below is its rousing summation of your style:

> Stewart's writing is characterized by a keen attention to detail, as he carefully examines the language, structure, and form of the texts he analyzes. At the same time, his work often emphasizes the broader cultural, historical, and philosophical contexts that shape literary production and reception. His prose is frequently marked by a playful and inventive use of language, as he employs puns, wordplay, and other rhetorical devices to explore the multiple meanings and resonances of his subject matter.

GS: With such results, maybe I need to go briefly autobiographical one last time.

DL: Please do—and I hope in the spirit I've gleaned from Cavell, namely, that we should be on the lookout for moments when, as he put it to me, the auto/biographical will "rise to the level of philosophical significance."[29]

GS: One of his many irresistible thoughts, and though I can't promise philosophy, I can extrapolate from my biography. While dismounting any methodological high horse in return to the stable of my hobbyhorses, let me commit again to the phrase "word *play*," its "give" and tensility, as a term that best captures the essence, in given instances, of literary writing: writing as the constitutive play of words. Same with screen play (two words) as a name (names) for the shuttling mirage of image. Right from the first, dictated in part by just this version of a "comparatist" instinct, my overarching classroom stress was—and remains—neither specialist nor period bound. In the late-1960s milieu, teaching was in fact always for me, and before I launched the term, tacitly "transmedium"—more than just recognizably "interdisciplinary" in the coming institutional sense. Long before that curricular groundswell, I taught Dickensian syntactic "montage" (after Soviet director Sergei Eisenstein's famous claims for it) so that my students could better notice its equivalent narrative leverage in American films they were seeing and talking about, from the literally rapid-fire gun-blast cuts in Arthur Penn's *Bonnie and Clyde* (1967) to the supernaturally panoptic fixed frames of Stanley Kubrick's *2001: A Space Odyssey* (1968) to the stoner float of Vilmos Sigmund's camerawork for Robert Altman's *McCabe and Mrs. Miller* (1971) and *The Long Goodbye* (1973). I taught Romantic poets in part so that students might better hear the subtler turns of rock album lyrics that, in the technical term, "hooked" them—as for instance how the eponymous noun phrase "night moves" in the propulsive erotic drive of Bob Seger's hit (can barely believe I remember this!) switches from a *plural noun* for discovered erotic acts to a strictly verbal *force*, as if carried on the release of language's own libido, in the exclamatory refrain "how the night moves!" If the compass of this teaching agenda, pop artifacts included, sounds like it was its own modest harbinger of cultural studies, not so. Its textual insistence was in fact quite the opposite—and remained unamenable over time to the broader generalizations of the latter.

DL: That really is a distinction at the heart of your work, isn't it?: between the top-down and often distantly political agendas of cultural studies, in all its subsidiary "turns," and the bottom-up stress of your immersive approach.

GS: Yes, and as I look back on the spreading developments of the former in both literature and film, even art history, the difference is ultimately between the social deductive (from contextual assumption to textual demonstration) and the medial inductive (from verbal or visual urgency, or disturbance, to its tracked pertinence). And there is nothing hermetic about a hermeneutic instinct that starts from the ground up. If my interests as a young teacher were largely formal and celebratory, the aesthete in me—centaured with the apprenticing media theorist—has evolved since, with so many of the rest of us, into the distraught American voter in a compromised democracy, the worried local and planetary citizen. But with no lessened sense that a relentless close focus, in reading or viewing, is the basis of purposeful discernment. We're back with focus therapy, I realize. Indeed I now teach movies to undergraduates in part so that students will be better Web "browsers" in their own right, processing rather than just consuming the implied text of an image; teach them novels so that the other arts will have an enhanced chance of getting their "stories" through to them; teach the wiles of rhetoric so that, in their ubiquitous screen reading (is scrolling reading?), students might be better equipped to negotiate the terminological false promise of "social media."

DL: If the bibliophile is now a curmudgeon, then exploding the terrain of "literacy"—what it means to be literate, to have a capacity for the grain of text (to become *letter*ate, to be a passionate, critical consumer of prose and pixel), and indeed, more expansively, for the *literary* as mode of relation to experience—seems a savvy move, professional and intellectual. Job security of another sort: extended "relevance." And in the (cringe-inducing) *lingua franca du jour*: remaining "relatable."

GS: Yes, and this necessary moving on from once received values to new validation certainly doesn't have to mean letting go. There's no missing the fact that the bulk of undergraduates are now born in the twenty-first century. Printed matter as much as cinema (you know, that ninety-minute-or-so affair that so preoccupied folks in public during the twentieth century)—those are largely bygone, part of *history*. But history, literary and film included, is of course what has always most needed teaching. And maybe especially now, with the technological future so dazing and hazy. In its spooky miracle, AI is a predicament that brooks no predictions about its limits—as you and I well know who keep being blindsided by new developments even as we try to sustain this exchange on a certain recognized footing. Most recently, it might as well have been yesterday rather than last week, I had occasion to recall your mentioning the treasured feedback you had once received from Werner Herzog on a film documentary of yours. This came to mind when I stumbled upon an "infinite conversation" reported (and sampled) on the *Scientific American* website, where voice-simulated Herzog and Slavoj Žižek debate, in ecological and political terms, and in signature German and Slovenian accents matched roughly to their contrasting rhetorical styles, everything natural under the sun—including in passing, as it happens, the outdistancing of human nature by technology.[30] All this in an AI-simulated back-and-forth that could spin out forever—as I'm beginning to fear our own interchange will if we're not careful.

DL: Maybe we should arrange for an AI audiobook of *Attention Spans* as both exemplification and resistance, with so-called voice actors replaced by less than pitch-perfect simulacra. But don't worry, I think we can soon round off this bot-free chat after just a further few questions that I'm curious to hear your thoughts on. To wit, if we (who is the *we* now?) are in recovery mode, trying to do our part before our part is done, what sort of use should we be applying ourselves to? Or more specifically, as a "teaching aid," to oversimplify matters, how best should one approach *Attention Spans*? Given that our "dialogue" here is about to give you the "last word" in this collection—except, of course for the glossaried words you've marvelously fashioned over the years to complete those many "conversations" that are then logged and sorted in the bibliography—what do you want to say to *your readers* before you sign off on this reframing of volume twenty-one? My impression is that readers—all readers—need help lately, good advice, points of reference, things to read, things to do to help them become better readers, and so on. Sounds like you'd readily agree with me that there's little or no hyperbole in thinking that we're confronted by serial and simultaneous emergencies, and at different scales (in both senses): metabolic, sociopolitical, planetary. What about education? Is panic warranted? A decline of reading or a shift in what is read and why? A different sense of what it is important to read? Not an emergency then but a transformation of values? If there is an educational crisis, what should we be worried about as we respond to it? Words addressed to the present and future of what we mean by the liberal arts, otherwise, yes, the "humanities"? For me, as I know for you, from your books alone, such arts commence, live, and thrive under the aegis and grace of reading.

GS: Even beyond warming to the richly paired nouns of your inspiriting (as well as inspired) last phrase, I'd of course entirely agree. If I may be permitted a last little bout of close reading on exit, it might help serve to wrap, if not sum, things up. In that phrase of yours, "aegis and grace of reading," one notes (dotes on) the audiovisual syncopation, Greek against Latin, across a silent graphemic match (almost a sly anagram) entirely muted by phonemic enunciation (the *a* and *g* of *aeg* only wed to "*g*(r)*a*(c)*e*" by optic tease, so that they are fused as a doublet somewhere almost beneath consciousness under the threefold drive and final "ive" rhyme of the verbs). You should be the last person to nip in the bud this celebration of your own spurt of phrasal bravura, so you'll allow me to add that your rewarding turn takes its place in the long list of such unearthed pairings in my work, known in classical rhetoric by the term hendiadys: the figure of twinning, the lexical two-fer (and thus twin in its own way to my favored syllepsis), most memorably in the A and B of C mode that Empson found in Shakespeare, as in *Hamlet*'s "the book and volume of my brain." Delivered in your phrasing under the very sponsorship of its own advocacy, the mimetic capaciousness imputed to "reading" divides the normative logic of either "graceful auspices" or "auspicious grace" into a more prismatic faceting of attributes. You may not have had all this consciously in mind by which to delight me, along with the rest of our readers, in this send-off, but phrasing of this caliber—and internal calibration, however spontaneous—taps directly into the inexhaustible "book and volume" of the literary archive, otherwise the *breadth and play* of its snappiest turns. Or, why not, performs the very *amplitude and span of attention* due to it. No computer could dream up that phrasing for you.

DL: Oh, good, I wasn't sure you'd catch all that. Seriously, though, the energy of that riff brings another question, or worse a doubt, to the surface. The longer we talk, just as the more I reviewed your excerpts (which confirm your sense of what is important, worth dwelling upon), or let me say the more interested a party I become (book after book after book), the more I worry about the legacy of all this intensity. (Admittedly, such an ongoing concern motivated the invitation to *Attention Spans* even as it makes itself more saliently known at a rarefied moment such as this—when I can ask you point blank what doesn't at all feel like a moot point.)

GS: I appreciate your concern, your worry, about the heritage of such attention. To the extent that it's shared more widely in the hallowed if progressively hollowed-out halls of the academy, we'll be okay. For a while longer, at least. But such passionate interest—along with a vaunted analytic "intensity"—is far from guaranteed, that's for sure. Best to say that all bets are off. As my "Inventory as Itinerary" has looked back *en abyme* at the strata of my writings in their role as cross-medial readings, it's been hard not to sense another and different abyss pending, where, AI aside, anything like the serious reading of even serious writing will have lost its cultural purchase altogether. As you know well, who worked so closely with him, the incomparable Stanley Cavell had, and has, his immediate followers. Other household names as well, less dear to my heart. All I myself can hope for, looking back here on my own devotions to page and screen, is that something simply *comparable*—neither derivative nor particularly indebted—might still follow. But as I introduced the phases of my work in that travelog-as-itinerary, and as I've taken up your continually encouraging questions in this dialogue, hopes keep catching in the throat between pep talk and dyspepsia, every tempted spurt of rah-rah for coming students clogged by the specter of last hurrah. One more for the team, sure, but too much in the form of an elegy for its nearly depleted ranks.

DL: I sense that, certainly, and realize that all you have are the students you can immediately reach, in the here and now, but in the future … an increasing blur. This volume is conceived, of course, in the hopes of extending that reach and the viability of its felt impact.

GS: And how could it hurt? But candor requires me to admit that few of the students in my latest style course for "advanced" English and Creative Writing majors really got it, into it, something out of it, while the rest seemed to pay the heed they might to a foreign language requirement (intelligible, perhaps, during the classroom hour, but forgotten by the time they reach the campus café). This is not the luck of the draw, for them or me. It's demographic. For so many students, graduate students too, who wouldn't enjoy the anagram any more than the activity, any so-called attention *span* for close reading, may already have suffered an irreparable *snap*. The cord of continuity across generations is nearly severed in these verbal matters. I register this often enough when even talented doctoral candidates talk mechanically about having to go back in their essay or chapter draft—a process tabled until now—and "close read" the passage in question. That use of the adjective "close" as adverb in this shorthand verb phrase is a formulation I'm particularly allergic to—suggesting as it does, in its terminological alienation, that the dutiful process, whatever it might really involve, would be somehow its own justification, whether or not anything interesting came to light. This distance from the feel of words isn't just a cultural shift, of course, but in (large) part a technological one—broader than the burgeoning literary smarts of AI and its skill at instantaneous "signature effects." Such a transformation in the whole instinct for reading is part of what I wanted to stress (in Phase VI / 15) when revisiting a book whose subtitle might well undergird, and again a bit on the defensive, this whole subsequent volume as well: *Cross-Sectional Reading for a Digital Age*. As noted in rounding off Phase VI there, what Friedrich Kittler's universal mediatization of the cognitive subject chipped away at in the post-Enlightenment axioms of humanist pedagogy has come true in cyber prosthetics (or, Powers again, "prosthetechs"). And this has its trickle-down—and drain-away—effect in what we might call live-action reading.

    Teaching sentence form at the undergraduate level, the joys of lexical complexity and its interpretation, sometimes feels like teaching *lieder* or recitative as prototype to students enrolled in some class on contemporary cross-fertilizations called "Page Rap: Literature Hip-Popped." That's why ending the phases of this Inventory with the book on Streisand has, more than mere chronology, a metacritical rightness to it. I think of her in connection with good friends in the academy still going strong (in their resolutely intensive *literary* criticism) against tides of verbal attrition, like Sharon Cameron and Susan Wolfson. And who knows what I might have wished I had known in advance of my *Streisand* book, or at least by the time of *Attention Spans*, after the pending academic conference at the University of Frankfurt ("Critical Barbra") to be held just about when this present volume is scheduled to appear. The point I can make now isn't just that Streisand's vocal production—as with digital special effects and book sculpture as well as with Toni Morrison's euphony— is readable by the likes of me. As shared with the craft of acting, the point is that Streisand represents, all too datedly, I'm afraid, the mostly lapsed art of "line reading" itself in popular song, the lost talent of close singing, of *interpretation*. Could we vary the meme of publicity backfire and call this level of attention "the Streisand effect"? That's of course a rhetorical question—but, more to the point, yet another case of something I wish I had said in that last book itself, using the "textualist" acuity of Streisand's phrasing as model for the close listening she deserves. Another friend, after reading Wesley Morris' celebratory *New York Times* review of that remastered 1962 *Live at the Bon Soir* album I briefly analyze in the Inventory's P.S. to my book (see Phase VIII / 20), quipped in an email—when quoting Morris' accolade about "phrasing that could turn a song into a literary event"—"Hey, someone should write a book about that observation. WAIT: someone has."[31] Not really; more accurate to say, in regard to Streisand's treatment of the received "song literature," that my book—all the clearer to me now—is about the immediate "event" of interpretation per se, her own close readings delivered over to the responsive ear.

DL: I'd readily accept that: a kind of curtain call for hermeneutics at the level of mass appeal. But where does all this leave us—or more directly, where or how would you like to conclude matters for the time being? How do you imagine your continued teaching in literature and creative writing, live or in print, to be what it always has been for you—part of a broader media study—given the recent convulsive advances in the entire media landscape we've been discussing?

GS: Going back to that last inspiring formulation of yours (hope squirming eternal), let *me* ask a last question, or more than one.

What exactly do we want to count as reading's true "aegis"? By the "grace" of whose protection does it thrive? Through whose offices or auspices is it validated? Always a go-to for me, as you know, Barthes put it famously, in his grand writerly book on the readerly, S/Z (1970)—as if in a spin on "a little knowledge is a dangerous thing." He insisted that although a little formalism takes you away from history—focused, this suggests, on a strictly aesthetic archive rather than on the world of social action—enough formalism brings you back: back, in part, of course, via the history of forms. One could vary that maxim for the present crisis of cultural literacy. A little close reading may take you away from significance into the coils of signification, but enough close reading burrows back to the full messaging of the medium, always historically conditioned. So that if reading removes you a bit from the world, it becomes in the end a means of reacclimating to that world, reclaiming it, with more accuracy of impression. The premium is on nuance, subtlety. That's really what I meant by suggesting that aesthetic interpretation is its own kind of civilizing force: whether debunking the stoked social phobias of a Hollywood action thriller, unpacking the gender baggage of a European art film, prying loose the canonical intertext of a popular novel, measuring sector by sector the cultural inference of a painted portrait's graphic background, hearing the aspirational inflections in the contoured sound play of a metadramatic singing voice. Nuance, subtlety: an ideally transferrable skill set. When has a political leader lately been too nuanced or subtle for our own good?

DL: You've got me there. Yet again, then, reading as a civics lesson.

GS: Ultimately, yes: a commutable (and communicable) mode of vigilance. You asked if "crisis" wasn't a word for what we're in. Where *wouldn't* one look to confirm this? So, in one last twist of etymology, it's nothing less than critical, if I may, to remember the shared derivation, from the Greek, of crisis and the criticism that rises to combat it. Maybe I should simply leave it this way about the therapeutic as well as (italics mine) *hermeneutic* value of medial scrutiny. Given my doubts about the aggregate ethic of digital humanities within the ethics of the infosphere, it would be good to think that close reading, too, should count as "knowledge work." And for some students, certainly, it does. I spoke of the increasing "few" so inclined, but their fitness is real—and can be coached to a regimen. So, after reaching back to my first teaching, let me go even farther back again, and go yet more privately autobiographical, in "speaking for myself at least" about the overcome frustrations of aesthetic mystery. Yet this may be the most important—and generalizable—thing to say of all in looking back on our volume. And in an ironic loophole for the professional impasse resulting from a dwindled premium on immersive literary attention, I'm talking about something that may actually for many graduate students—given earlier tutored instincts—survive its frequent exclusion from the flattened-out sanctified relevancies of their broad-stroke, monochromatic thesis prose. Surely many novice readers must also feel as I keenly did—in my first collisions with major literature and film: that there are wonders lurking palpable in a "text" (only later so-called) that one aches to have translated into one's own articulate comprehension—in the "wish I could express" mode: itches that need scratching, though in places hard to reach with words. The more recent public-transport surveillance mantra, "If you see something, say something," isn't as easy in reading—or film viewing, or museum going—if you don't have the vocabulary. To want it, and work for it, can be a long-term challenge—and gratification—complete (though never over) with its own self-fueling momentum. That's in fact what is modeled by the trial-and-error (and try-again) nature of the "metasyllabus" stepped through here as a self-pedagogical "itinerary" in the sequence of my writing as well as teaching. And just as with the best classroom moments—flagged by the title of this dialogue—the tries are guided by a critical conversation with other writers who have found ways, and words, for such intensities of perception. Once past my private hump of underprepared intimidation in graduate school, I have ever since kept finding, for myself and my students alike, that the more one can say about something—a novel, a film, a gallery installation—the more one may see in the next such encounter. Closing in doesn't just open up but aids in moving forward. What it finds ways to indicate about what it discovers trains a command of expressive attention waiting always for new use. To vary the programmer's jargon, then, and whether or not aimed in any direct way against electronic overreach, such knowledge works. And keeps working for you.

Notes

1 David LaRocca, "Unauthorized Autobiography: Truth and Fact in *Confessions of a Dangerous Mind*," in *The Philosophy of Charlie Kaufman*, ed. David LaRocca (Lexington: University Press of Kentucky, 2011), 89–108.
2 John Guillory, *Professing Criticism: Essays on the Organization of Literary Study* (Chicago: University of Chicago Press, 2023).
3 See, for example, "Contemplating the Sounds of Contemplative Cinema: Stanley Cavell and Kelly Reichardt," in *Movies with Stanley Cavell in Mind*, ed. David LaRocca (New York: Bloomsbury, 2021), 274–318.

4 Richard Powers, "How to Speak a Book," *New York Times Book Review*, January 7, 2007.
5 See *Cinemachines: An Essay on Media and Method* (2020), *Cinesthesia: Museum Cinema and the Curated Screen* (2020), and *The Metanarrative Hall of Mirrors: Reflex Action in Fiction and Film* (2022). An even more recent film book, *Streisand: The Mirror of Difference* (2023), accordingly doesn't address VFX.
6 Fredric Jameson gives his fullest definition of this concept in *Postmodernism, or the Logic of Late Capitalism* (Durham: Duke University Press, 1991), 51–2, although the epistemic parameters it sketches in regard to social forms of knowing have been previously tested out, on prose fiction, as a quadratic grid of character options under ideological constraint in *The Political Unconscious* (Ithaca: Cornell University Press, 1981) through Jameson's frequent deployment there of the "semiotic square" borrowed from the narratology of A. J. Greimas.
7 Simone Weil, "Reflections on the Right Use of School Studies with a View to the Love of God," in *Waiting for God*, trans. Emma Craufurd (New York: Harper & Row, 1951), 105. Knowingly or not, Mary Oliver echoes Weil's sentiment in her final book of prose, *Upstream: Selected Essays* (New York: Penguin, 2016): "Attention is the beginning of devotion" (8).
8 Mario von der Ruhr, *Simone Weil: An Apprenticeship in Attention* (New York: Continuum, 2006), 37.
9 Francesca Paris and Larry Buchanan, "35 Ways Real People are Using A.I. Right Now," *The New York Times*, April 14, 2023, nytimes.com.
10 Ralph Waldo Emerson, "Quotation and Originality" (1859), *The Complete Works of Ralph Waldo Emerson*, Concord Edition (Boston: Houghton, Mifflin & Co., 1904), volume 8, 178–9.
11 Jonathan Swift, *Gulliver's Travels* (London: Benjamin Motte, 1726), pt. III, ch. 5.
12 Richard Powers, *Galatea 2.2* (New York: HarperCollins, 1995), 67.
13 See remarks on the end of genre in David LaRocca, "From Lectiocentrism to Gramophonology: Listening to Cinema and Writing Sound Criticism," in *The Geschlecht Complex: Addressing Untranslatable Aspects of Gender, Genre, and Ontology*, ed. Oscar Jansson and David LaRocca (New York: Bloomsbury, 2022), 201–67.
14 Joe Coscarelli, "An A.I. Hit of Fake 'Drake' and 'The Weeknd' Rattles the Music World," *The New York Times*, April 19, 2023, nytimes.com.
15 Charlie Warzel, "The Most Important Job Skill of This Century," *The Atlantic*, February 8, 2023, theatlantic.com.
16 See Stephen Marche's novella, *Death of an Author* (New York: Pushkin Industries, 2023), "written" via authorial inputs and published under the name Aidan Marchine, his AI pseudonym. Elizabeth A. Harris, "Peering Into the Future of Novels, With Trained Machines Ready," *The New York Times*, April 20, 2023, nytimes.
17 Garrett Stewart, "Afterword," in John Cayley, *Image Generation: A Reader* (Denver: Counterpath, 2023), 153–62.
18 Keith Collins, "How ChatGPT Could Embed a 'Watermark' in the Text It Generates," *The New York Times*, February 17, 2023, nytimes.com.
19 Frank Pavich, "This Film Does Not Exist," *The New York Times*, "Opinion," January 13, 2023.

20 Tiffany Hsu and Steven Lee Myers, "Can We No Longer Believe Anything We See?," *The New York Times*, April 8, 2023, nytimes.com.
21 Ian Bogost, "ChatGPT is Dumber Than You Think," December 7, 2022 and "ChatGPT is About to Dump More Work on Everyone," February 2, 2023; Stephen Marche, "The College Essay is Dead," December 6, 2022; and Daniel Herman, "The End of High-School English," December 9, 2022, all in *The Atlantic*, theatlantic.com. Maureen Dowd, "A.I.: Actually Insipid Until It's Actively Insiduous," *The New York Times*, January 28, 2023, nytimes.com.
22 Lydia DePillis and Steve Lohr, "Tinkering With ChatGPT, Workers Wonder: Will This Take My Job?," March 28, 2023; Tiffany Hsu and Stuart A. Thompson, "Disinformation Researchers Raise Alarms About A.I. Chatbots," *The New York Times*, February 8, 2023, both in *The New York Times*, nytimes.com. Ben Chrisinger, "It's Not Just Our Students—ChatGPT Is Coming for Faculty Writing Too," *The Chronicle of Higher Education*, February 22, 2023, chronicle.com.
23 Noam Chomsky, "The False Promise of ChatGPT," *The New York Times*, March 8, 2023, nytimes.com; Walter Kirn, "Goodbye to the Future," *Compact*, February 8, 2023, compactmag.com; Gary Marcus, "Why Are We Letting the AI Crisis Just Happen?," *The Atlantic*, March 13, 2023, theatlantic.com; Sarah Jackson, "OpenAI Executives Say Releasing ChatGPT for Public Use Was a Last Resort after Running into Multiple Hurdles — and They're Shocked by Its Popularity," *Insider*, January 25, 2023, businessinsider.com; Tyler Cowen, "Bank Runs, Crypto Scams, and World-Transforming AI," *Honestly*, March 21, 2023.
24 Jacob Stern, "GPT-4 Might Just be a Bloated, Pointless Mess," *The Atlantic*, March 6, 2023, theatlantic.com.
25 Chris Moran, "ChatGPT Is Making Up *Guardian* Articles," *The Guardian*, April 6, 2023, theguardian.com.
26 Matthew Kirschenbaum, "Prepare for the Textpocalypse," *The Atlantic*, March 8, 2023, theatlantic.com.
27 Stephen Marche, "Welcome to the Big Blur," *The Atlantic*, March 14, 2023, theatlantic.com.
28 Stephen Best and Sharon Marcus, "Surface Reading: An Introduction," *Representations*, vol. 108 (Fall 2009): 1–21.
29 See David LaRocca, "Must We Say What We Learned? Parsing the Personal and the Philosophical" (1–48) and "Autophilosophy" (275–320), in *Inheriting Stanley Cavell: Memories, Dreams, Reflections*, ed. David LaRocca (New York: Bloomsbury, 2020), esp. 11, 301, 312.
30 Giacomo Miceli, "What an Endless Conversation with Werner Herzog Can Teach Us About AI," *Scientific American*, January 17, 2023, scientificamerican.com.
31 Wesley Morris, "Barbra Streisand on Her Pristine Early Recordings: 'That Girl Can Sing,'" *The New York Times*, November 4, 2022, nytimes.com.

Terms of Use
Coinages Cashed Out—A Selective Glossary

Locations in which the terms first appear, or importantly recur, are noted following the forward slash

aftertext: the reverberant phrasal or visual wake of reflexive media recognition in the reading of page or screen / *The Metanarrative Hall of Mirrors.*

antiphonemics: the antiphonal quality of certain phrases in seeming to release their pertinent doubles—as with Shakespeare's mutability Sonnet 15, in which "everything that grows / holds in" its perfection only for an hour—and thus from whose mimetically swift transition "grows old" looms large as its own fleeting phonemic enjambment; inspired by, but in contrast to, Christopher Ricks' concept of the "anti-pun" (a "solicited misconstruction" that haunts a line inoperably) / *Reading Voices.*

apparatus reading: an adjustment of the psychoanalytic deconstruction of screen viewing (often allied to feminist critiques of the male gaze) known as "apparatus theory," where the collusion of camerawork and editing "sutures" the viewer into a position of false intimacy and disavowed complicity in the credible generation of screen space. Stewart stresses instead those less passive means by which the work of the apparatus can be made deliberately legible by certain directors, hence readable in its narrative function / *Cinemachines.*

audioptic: as with **graphonic** below, the latest portmanteau overlap in homage to the sound(ed) sense of literary language / "Literature's Audioptic Platform" (apportioned here as Phase IX).

bibliobjet: the sculptural codex form that has surrendered all bibliographic utility to its material objecthood (as the French elision suggests)—even as it tacitly generates formal "figures of speech" for its own lost field of reading that become in themselves textually "legible" / *Bookwork.*

bookhood: the page-bound imaginary of textual consumption that survives the digital transformation of e-reading as a cultural archetype / *Book, Text, Medium.*

cimnemonics: an aptly tortuous portmanteau for moments when some psychic break into the narrative past or future gets figured in connection with celluloid or digital mediation—and thus connects with Deleuze's distinction between the "actual" and the "virtual," the latter still within the precincts of the "real"—as in the rapid progressive time warps, by digital morphing, of teen into adult protagonists in Pedro Almodóvar's *Bad Education / Framed Time.*

cinécriture: borrowed from French film theory to indicate the discursive inscription of image flow as narrative "writing" / *Between Film and Screen.*

cine::graph: a term for the hybrid rendering of the celluloid photogram chain (or later pixel array) in either reprinted still photography or as a repainted optic field—with the term's typography characterized by the double-colon approach to transmedial subheads in figuring a reversible turnstile between implied medial supports / *Transmedium*.

cinemachines: a foundational portmanteau marking the inextricable mesh between apparatus and apparition in the institution of cinema, a term pluralized in Stewart's usage since it is meant to compass everything from hand-cranked optics in the late Victorian period through big-screen celluloid projection down to streaming digital. It is with this in mind that one senses, for instance, the deliberate throwback lap-dissolve of those digitally vanished alien spacecraft in the sci-fi film *Arrival* / *Cinemachines*; *The Metanarrative Hall of Mirrors*.

cinematographic sentence: See below **Fframe-advance prose**.

cinesthesia: the revisionary cine-esthetics that brings moving-image art into the curated gallery context, as if with a fusion of perspectives evoked by the hybrid sensorium named by its homophonic double synesthesia / *Cinesthesia*.

closed circuits: borrowed from the acronym CCTV to identify surveillance video and applied by association (explicit in film after film) with a narrative system in which a deciphered *mise-en-abyme*—specifically a screen-within-the-screen—is situated to replay or query the spectator's potentially voyeuristic relation to the film as a whole even as it admits to the film's awareness of itself as a film (of films) / *Closed Circuits*. See also **surveillancinema** and **technopticon**.

comedial: the laughably exaggerated access to technologies of screen process in what philosopher Henri Bergson saw as comedy's essential mechanization of the human body / *Cinemachines*.

conceptualism 2.0: the latest phase of Conceptual art that either mobilizes computer imaging directly or investigates the vestigial zones of its outmoded predecessors from the vantage of a post-analog era / *Transmedium*.

conscription: the co-production of textual affect between script and readerly contribution, whether invoked by direct address (interpolated) or acted out (extrapolated from) in an internal reading scene / *Dear Reader*. See below **interpolation**.

cultural stylistics: an account of compositional device in whatever medium—verbal, visual, musical, and so on—registering the way formal design is sensitized to, rather than transcendent of, context. In the analysis of post-allegorical art, cultural stylistics would stand to the local disposition of a secular genre (its graphic articulations in painting, its phrasal enunciations in the novel) the way iconology stands to iconography in more traditional modes of pictorial analysis: detecting the ideology of recognized patterns on a site-specific basis within the discursive field of a given social moment / *The Look of Reading*.

demediation: the disappearance of legible text from the pigment-stroked surfaces of most open books in scene painting that becomes all the more salient in the effaced or inaccessible page surfaces of those conceptualist **bibliobjets**—rather than conventional artists' books—whose gallery appearance materializes the physical mass without the cultural function of the traditional codex, objectifying raw material over print matter / *Bookwork*.

digital intertext: designating, within certain contemporary thriller plots and their special effects, a tacit cross-reference from paranormal phenomena to their technological "naturalization" by computer electronics—as when the fantasy of first-person time travel (*Donnie Darko* [2001, dir. Richard Kelly], etc.) may seem to be a cover story for a youth culture of interactive video addiction / *Framed*

Time, a version of the **technique\text/context** paradigm later articulated in *The Metanarrative Hall of Mirrors*.

digitime: an elided coinage for the effects of a time-based narrative medium when given over to digital generation, with "off-frame" space no longer pressing in on a single celluloid module to edge it forward into the next by way of visualized transition. *See also* **temportation** as one result of this abjured seriality of time consciousness at the medium-inflected level of screen narrative / *Framed Time*.

dysjuncture: the disturbance in phonetic juncture that topples one syllable into the next (or back to the last) with some surplus lexical fallout, as when Wordsworth's sense of a primal "radiance," now "forever taken from my sight," seems elevated to a collective human lament by the homophonic absorption of the personal modifier into the shadow wording—and transient **epiphony**—"from eye sight" / *Reading Voices*.

echology: a system of internal checks and balances based on syllabic or lexical recurrence, as applied in reference to the systemic "ecology" of Richard Powers' novel *The Overstory* (2018) / *The Metanarrative Hall of Mirrors*.

echo neurons: by analogy with the mirror neurons of psychobiology, activated in response to the effect of others, these are the affective triggers by which the "topography" of sound in vocal performances (Barbra Streisand's as case in point)—understood not just according to Roland Barthes' "grain of the voice" but as an expansive visualized (almost cinematized) "terrain" in its own right—has its immediate somatic register in the listening body. One result: a "topographic" reading of the voice as text and sonic *texture* / *Streisand*.

epiphony (*sic*.): a moment of textual revelation sprung from the phonetic enunciation of a word or phrase not necessarily epiphanic in any other sense, as in many of the homophonic puns Stewart finds in literary texts from all periods—for instance, nearest at hand alphabetically, the **echology** whereby, in the forest-preservation drive of Richard Powers' novel *The Overstory*, "bar code" on tree-pulped cardboard boxes resonates in ironic contrast to "bark ode"; or when Whitman, in claiming a cosmic balance between life and death, writes of the "urge and urge and urge of the world" as if it were at one with its "urgent urgent dirge" / *Book, Text, Medium*; *The Metanarrative Hall of Mirrors*.

epitome: in Stewart's special narratographic sense, the figural moment in the classic literary death scene (ironized as euphemism in Marlow's "He died as he lived" regarding Kurtz's end in Conrad's *Heart of Darkness* [1899]) in which, with language at the limit of representation, it can only trope on what precedes oblivion, "transposing" duration into finality—often by summing up the former in some final figure of speech. This metaphoric compression of a preceding lifeline, in the third term of Stewart's template, regularly entails a "displacement" of extinguished subject onto an alter ego, double, or surrogate. The literary functions of this knotted structural triad (**transposition**, **epitome**, and **displacement**) find their narrative force in just this convergence of similitude, summary, and substitution / *Death Sentences*.

evocalization: a term insisting on the way images *evoked* in literature are implicitly accomplished through vocal adumbration from the midst of silent alphabetic processing / *Reading Voices*; *The Deed of Reading*.

Fframe-advance prose: by analogy with the double sense of "frame" in celluloid cinema—the image cell on the strip and, simultaneous with it at a different scale, the rectangular field of the moving image in projection—the F/f model applies as well to the gap between syllabic matter and syntactic momentum in the kinesis of the "cinematographic sentence," as when at the end of D. H. Lawrence's *The Rainbow* (1915), long before the Ken Russell film's special effect, the titular "arch"-itecture of hope layers its chromatic striations via the overlaps of a twofold comma-spliced grammar, the rough verbal equivalent of serial cinematic cross-fades: "Steadily the colour gathered, mysteriously, from nowhere, it took presence upon itself, there was a faint, vast rainbow" / Cinematographic prose as one of *The Ways of the Word*.

flicker effect: borrowed from the oscillatory intermittence of the celluloid track, as smoothed out over industry time with technological efforts at "flicker fusion," a parallel term to describe certain phonetic quaverings—namely, waverings—in the evocalization of prose and poetry / *Between Film and Screen* in its links back to *Reading Voices*.

graphonics: the texture of phonetic enunciation inseparable at one level from the processing of alphabetic graphemes—and often lifted to another level by literary phrasing; first introduced with examples from English poetry that included Coleridge's meta-lyrical "Eolian Harp" (1796), celebrating as it does an animism "Which meets all motion"—including that of verse sequence—"and becomes its soul." Such a synesthetic transfusion is glossed by the next line's chiastic apposition "A light in sound, a sound-like power in light" that in its own right levitates with a momentary phonic dominance over the graphic if we hear the soul punningly (cf. **epiphonically**) "alight" in the plucked wind-harp strings of verse's own syllabic cadences / *Reading Voices*.

hyporealism: in contrast to the now-preferred term hyp*er*realism for the photorealist image on board or canvas, this transmedial (and etymological) "under"-lay involves artifacts whose superficial photographic accuracy is composited in fact, on closer inspection, by an undergridding, and less an undergirding than an undermining, of, for instance, woodblock striations simulating video scan lines on television (Christiane Baumgartner) or thousands of thumbnail Google images assimilated ironically to the looks of a low-definition photo reprint—as with a notorious Abu Ghraib prison photo micro-composited by Juan Fontecuberta with images of Bush, Rumsfield, Cheney, and other perpetrators, sites, and effects of the war on terror / *Transmedium*.

immersive (vs. surface) **reading**: designated in the face of neoformalist reductionism as the kind of penetrative attention that doesn't, as in a travestied symptomatic reading, peel away surface for ideological depths but instead maneuvers in and through and beyond any sense of surface—an approach (implicit in all Stewart's literary studies) that gets tested in a comic key, after its first official formulation, on a character in *Bleak House* (1852) who "tends"—across assonance and syllepsis as well as by way of a badgered temperament—"toward meekness and obesity," his habitual manner leaving him prey to the unspoken, never surfaced, truth of his acerbic wife as the **transegmental** "Mrs. S/*n*agsby" / *The One, Other, and Only Dickens*.

interpolation (vs. **extrapolation**): the often paired modes inclusion and induction that divide up the reflexive field in the narrative work of **conscription** / *Dear Reader*.

lexigraph: the "wordwork" of visual art that emerges from the eclipse of figure painting—in examples from lettrism to what is now often categorized as asemic writing—that in a long view of representation can be seen to derive from the classic scene of open-book reading minus the reading body / *The Look of Reading*.

matrix: borrowed from its frequent literary and cinematic deployment in Stewart's analyses for the canvas scene of reading, as a name there for an embryonic rectangle (the open page) that forms—or the generative form that shapes—the ensuing composition; a term specifically indebted to its use in the literary semiotics of Michael Riffaterre, where it indicates some core idea (often an unspoken idiom or "repressed" cultural or literary cliché) whose poetic manifestation depends on the indirection of its figurative variants (as subtexts) across the duration of a literary text / *The Look of Reading*.

mediarchaeology: one aptly compacted word for the historical depth of developmental sediment made immanent at certain impacted moments in a single image, whereby, unlike the two-word version of typical film studies, a local node of the medium enacts its own prehistory, as with the digital "aging" of Victorian photographs in Terence Davies' *A Quiet Passion* (2016) / *Cinemachines*.

metaphonetics: one of the many (more familiar) meta terms (metafilmic, metacinematic, metanarrative, with their overlapping etymology in "along with" and "beyond" and "behind") that refer to language's reflexive self-identification in process; for a special case when phonemic play gets thematized by a kind of recognized metatextual enunciation, see the double phonetic twist in Stewart's punning epigraph from Richard Powers: "a man's speech should exceed his lapse, else what's a meta for?" / *The Metanarrative Hall of Mirrors*.

microplot: a localized verbal or visual format in which some broader inflection or tension of story is rehearsed, replayed, or condensed into phrasing's (or filming's) own constitutive action, grammatical or cinematographic, with a resulting stylistic force inherent to the medium. When in the sepulchral atmospheric opening of Conrad's *Heart of Darkness*, for instance, the titular moral dusk thickening over the Thames "farther back still seemed condensed into a mournful gloom," the undecidable double grammar of that spatial and temporal adverb "still" (farther back yet/even yet) serves to condense into a progressive murk the once and future half-light of this narrative's horizons / *Novel Violence*.

narrative "quarantine": a structural device in Dickens' first novel, *Pickwick Papers*, arranged to inoculate the spirited picaresque comedy of its main plot by siphoning off morbid states of mind, bracketing these in the confines of framed tales that, in subtler form, would repeatedly serve Dickens' metanarrative purposes in later novels / *Dickens and the Trials of the Imagination*.

narratogram: the smallest unit of marked effect in a given medium, filmic or lexical, that is capable of taking a narrative charge—in loose analogy with the photogram on the film strip / *Framed Time*.

narratography: a quasi-stylistic subset of narratology (the "science" of storytelling form) focused on the actual linguistic or filmic inscription of plot in diction and syntax, shot and cut, rather than on narrative's broader cognitive parameters in any medium. It is thus *a mode of reading*, not inscription—modeled on the suffix of cartography rather than calligraphy—that tracks the effect of storytelling momentum, its ironies, peripeties, reversals, and foreclosures, at the level of the **microplot** / *Framed Time; Novel Violence*.

optical allusion: in and beyond special-effects cinema, the moment of on-screen visualization whose execution calls up in one way or another the optical conditions of its own narrative manifestation / *Framed Time*.

phonotext: those inscribed phonic (if not fully sonic) cues emitted by the script of written text that narrow the gap between decipherment itself and imagined audition / *Reading Voices. See above* **graphonic**.

photogrammatology: on the model of Derridean grammatology, the differential register of sequence (optic rather than alphabetic, photogram in contrast to "phonogram") that denaturalizes, by the shifts of seriality per se, any true continuum of screen view—as comparable to the processing of functional alternatives in the gramma of phonemic sequence, excluding all vocal priority (in the deconstructive emphasis) from the network of pertinent opposition that makes for linguistic signification / *Between Film and Screen*.

platformatics: an inference of second-wave conceptual book art that, under the sign of the codex as "internal machine," emphasizes the substrate of the page's discursive surface as an engineered medial platform more than a hinged object, as in the codex binding of sonnets ("little songs") with an embedded microphone to sing them out / *Book, Text, Medium*.

prose friction: the traction and drag that is part of the inertial momentum of narrative writing, as when, across all its lesser syllabic scrapes and recurrences, Poe's bluntly redundant and lexically throbbing "mighty *great* and terrible ringing sound" in *The Fall of the House of Usher* is soon followed by the "*grating* of the iron hinges of her prison" / *Novel Violence*.

reflex action: that localized function of novel reading and film viewing in which the momentary metatextual recognition of medial determinants can be distinguished from encompassing metanarrative formats, so that recognizing in Richard Powers' *Plowing the Dark* (2000) a sudden alphabetic pictogram in the assonant mention of "the old scroll's closed O" has its own scribal involution (and optic manifestation) apart from its potential resonant place in a novel of scriptive (algorithmic) virtual reality / *Dear Reader; The Metanarrative Hall of Mirrors*.

reverse ekphrasis: in an inversion of *ut pictura poesis*, where words aspire to image the world through ekphrastic evocation (so-called word-painting), Stewart identifies in the canvas "scene of reading" the opposite attempt to capture in brush-worked fixity the time-based experience of textual consumption and internalization, doing so through the peripheral inferences of setting and composition, as when reading in a tree-shaded, intermittently sun-dappled hammock projects into setting at once the weightlessness and the shimmer and the very leaves of engrossed reading / *The Look of Reading*.

secondary vocality: building on Walter Ong's (1912–2003) famous supplement to his transhistorical divide between orality and literacy, whereby post-print technologies such as phonography and sound film provide "secondary orality," Stewart stresses the inbuilt vocality of silent reading itself in its **graphonic** basis / *The Deed of Reading*.

semioptics: Stewart's conflation of semiotics and optics to address that aspect of visual studies probing the artificial or synthetic nature of basic ocular processing in representational art, where seeing becomes a "decoding" of discrete graphic signals rather than a naturalized act of recognition / *The Look of Reading*.

soundscape: a function, in literary "audition," not of pen-scraped transcriptions of heard things but of **subvocalization**, a matter of phonic rather than sonic **voice** / *Reading Voices*.

special AffX: playing on the screen industry's abbreviation vfx for "visual special effects," especially in the latest digitized action cinema of cgi (computer-generated imagery), the equally phonetic play on "affect" rather than "effect" points to the way these typically thematized manifestations of the screen's projective mechanism can be registered against the drive of plot at moments of reflexive medial impact, as when the shattered safety glass of the getaway car in *Blade Runner 2049* (2017, dir. Denis Villeneuve) doubles (triples?), in optical overlay, at once for the pixel disintegration of the panicked electronic heroine's own remote holographic projection and for its mere "simulated" breakup by narrative computerization / *Cinemachines*.

subvocalization: the inevitable though inhibited engagement of speech muscles in the silent motionless enunciation of a text—indeed, even in silent thought / *Reading Voices*; *The Look of Reading*.

surveillancinema: that condition of the motion picture apparatus whose narrative framing, at both visual and thematic levels, often secures a link between the kind of optic oversight associated with the likes of cctv imaging and—beyond the restricted optics of private voyeurism—with the equally unseen seeing of omniscient camerawork at large / *Closed Circuits*. See also **closed circuits**; **technopticon**.

syllepsis: favored in Stewart's usage, though equivalent to zeugma, in part for the way its etymological "taking together" exposes a logically forced parallel within the split syntax of its typically comic disjunction (from Dickens' first novel, for instance: "fell into the barrow, and fast asleep, simultaneously"; "went home in a flood of tears and a sedan-chair"). This syntactic trope is frequently pursued in Stewart's work as a metanarrative as well as metalinguistic forked path, intrinsic to literary structure in its exemplary play between literal and figurative understanding / *The Deed of Reading*; *The One, Other, and Only Dickens*.

technique\text/context: a basic template for the "beveled" nature of reflex action in the reading moment, of film as well as fiction. This paradigm, among other iterations, is varied for literature to prose\plot/premise and more broadly, across media, to style\plot/theme, where in all cases some ripple at the center of attention can slant recognition either back to structuring functions or outward to conceptual inference. See, many times over, the infinite regress of Citizen Kane in his hall of mirrors at Xanadu, which, when reverting from this "text" of ironic fragmentation to the cinematographic "technique" of avoided camera reflection, reflects outward as well on the broader thematic and sociological "context": private as well as public figure as sheer image, even to himself / *The Metanarrative Hall of Mirrors*.

technopticon: computerized variant of Foucault's panopticon (a centralized apparatus of surveillant oversight and behavioral norming based on Jeremy Bentham's prison architecture)—and thus closer to Deleuze's society of "control." Exemplified variously from George Orwell's "telescreens" in *1984* (1949) to the cctv computer-hub manhunt of *The Bourne Legacy* (2012) / *Closed Circuits*. See above **surveillancinema**.

temportation: aside from time travel more generally, the term in *Framed Time* for the impossible moment when temporality and portability, time and spatial motion, are seen to collapse into each other, whether in the flight from a traumatic memory trace or its revisitation and erasure / *Framed Time*. See above **digitime**.

thematerialization: the textured and narratively inflected process whereby a medium (screen image among others) is made materially manifest as a function of thematic development, as for instance a celluloid superimposition of separate human closeups as trope for the likes of split motive or discrepant time frames / *Between Film and Screen*.

timespace: implosion of the Deleuzian categories of "movement-image" and "time-image" in a paradoxical pacing-out of time's recovered subjective zones / *Framed Time*. See above **temportation**.

transegmental drift: a self-modeling terminological example of that breaching—from syllable to syllable—of an established lexical segmentation that springs (here with tran/s/egment) a verbal double-take in the process. From poetry to prose, examples (by way of phonetic alter egos) range from the first instance in verse from *Reading Voices* (Tennyson's "silent-speaking words," about posthumously read letters, regrouped around the sibilant juncture as the equally paradoxical "silence-speaking words") to Toni Morrison's narrator (cited in *The Deed of Reading*) sounding out "slavery" from her final defiant oxymoron "Slave. Free." / *Reading Voices*; *The Deed of Reading*.

transmedium: not a genre of art production so much as a mode of its perception; less a noun than an "adverb" in its taking up, that is, the when, where, and how of perception in works that operate *transmedium* (with an emphasis on the etymological "across" rather than "beyond" or "over" familiar from other usages). The artifacts in question manifest a more or less explicit fusion (*trans*fusion) of medial components or orientations—including those that keep pigment and automatic indexicality in simultaneous play (photorealism); that laminate word shapes and images in composite text art; or that capture live-stream film frames digitally jammed in a glitch aesthetic, the last in recent work by Éric Rondepierre / *Transmedium*.

voice: what enters text not from the timbre of authorial speech but from the fiber of phonetic writing—and is then elicited in reading by **secondary vocality** / *Reading Voices*; *The Deed of Reading*.

TIMELINES
A TOPOGRAPHICAL BIBLIOGRAPHY

Apprentice Stylistics

Virginia Tufte, and Garrett Stewart, *Grammar as Style: Exercises in Creativity* (New York: Holt, Rinehart & Winston, 1971).

The Prose of Victorian Fiction

Garrett Stewart, "The 'Golden Bower' of *Our Mutual Friend*," *ELH*, vol. 40, no. 1 (1973), 105–30.

1 / Garrett Stewart, *Dickens and the Trials of Imagination* (Cambridge: Harvard University Press, 1974).

Garrett Stewart, "Teaching Prose Fiction: Some 'Instructive' Styles," *College English*, vol. 37, no. 4 (1975), 383–401.

Garrett Stewart, "Lawrence, 'Being,' and the Allotropic Style," *Novel*, vol. 9, no. 3 (1976), 217–42.

Garrett Stewart, "The New Mortality of *Bleak House*," *ELH*, vol. 45, no. 3 (1978), 443–87.

Garrett Stewart, "Forster's Epistemology of Dying," *Missouri Review* (Spring 1979), 103–21.

Garrett Stewart, "Lying as Dying in *Heart of Darkness*," *PMLA*, vol. 95, no. 3 (May 1980), 319–30.

Garrett Stewart, "The Narrator in *Heart of Darkness*: A Reply to John V. Hagopian," *PMLA*, vol. 96, no. 2 (March 1981), 272–3.

Garrett Stewart, "The Secret Life of Death in Dickens," *Dickens Studies Annual*, vol. 11 (1983), 177–207.

Garrett Stewart, "Signing Off: Dickens and Thackeray, Woolf and Beckett," in *Philosophical Approaches to Literature*, ed. William Cain (Lewisburg, PA: Bucknell University Press, 1984), 117–40.

Garrett Stewart, "'Beckoning Death': *Daniel Deronda* and the Plotting of a Reading," in *Sexuality and Death in Victorian Literature*, ed. Gina Barreca (New York: Macmillan, 1989), 69–109.

Garrett Stewart, "'Count Me In': *Dracula*, Hypnotic Participation, and the Late-Victorian Gothic of Reading," *Lit*, vol. 5 (Fall 1994), 1–18.

Garrett Stewart, "A Valediction for Bidding Mourning: Death and the Narratee in Brontë's *Villette*," in *Death and Representation*, ed. Elisabeth Bronfen and Sarah Webster Goodwin (Baltimore: Johns Hopkins University Press, 1994), 51–79.

4 / Garrett Stewart, *Dear Reader: The Conscripted Audience in Nineteenth-Century British Fiction* (Baltimore: Johns Hopkins University Press, 1996).

Garrett Stewart, "Tess's Implicated Reader," in *Tess of the d'Urbervilles: Case Studies in Contemporary Criticism*, ed. by John Paul Riquelme (Boston: Bedford Books, 1998), 537-51.
Garrett Stewart, "Dickens and Language," in *The Cambridge Companion to Charles Dickens*, ed. John O. Jordan (Cambridge: Cambridge University Press, 2001), 136-51.
Garrett Stewart, "The Ethical Tempo of Narrative Syntax: Sylleptic Recognitions in *Our Mutual Friend*," *Partial Answers*, vol. 8, no. 1 (2010), 119-45.
Garrett Stewart, "Syllepsis Redux and the Rhetoric of Double Agency," *Partial Answers*, vol. 10, no. 1 (2012), 93-120.
Garrett Stewart, "Diction," in the *Oxford Handbook of Victorian Poetry*, ed. Matthew Bevis (New York: Oxford University Press, 2013), 93-111.
Garrett Stewart, "Lived Death: Dickens's Rogue Glyphs," in *Dickens's Style*, ed. Daniel Tyler (Cambridge: Cambridge University Press, 2013), 231-52.
Garrett Stewart, "On the Brontëesque," *Victorian Review*, vol. 42, no. 2 (Fall 2016), 234-41.
14 / Garrett Stewart, *The One, Other, and Only Dickens* (Ithaca, NY: Cornell University Press, 2018).
Garrett Stewart, "The Late Great Dickens: Style Distilled," in *On Style in Victorian Fiction*, ed. Daniel Tyler (Cambridge: Cambridge University Press, 2021), 227-43.

Moving Pictures/Celluloid Imaging

Garrett Stewart, "The Long Goodbye from Chinatown," *Film Quarterly*, vol. 28, no. 2 (1975), 25-32.
Garrett Stewart, "Exhumed Identity: Antonioni's Passenger to Nowhere," *Sight and Sound*, vol. 45, no. 1 (Winter 1975-6), 36-40.
Garrett Stewart, "Modern Hard Times: Chaplin and the Cinema of Self-Reflection," *Critical Inquiry*, vol. 3, no. 2 (1976), 295-314.
Garrett Stewart, "The Woman in the Moon," *Sight and Sound*, vol. 47, no. 2 (1977), 77-85.
Garrett Stewart, "Close Encounters of the Fourth Kind," *Sight and Sound*, vol. 48, no. 2 (1978), 167-74.
Garrett Stewart, "Keaton Through the Looking Glass," *Georgia Review*, vol. 33, no. 2 (Summer 1979), 348-67.
Garrett Stewart, "Death Watch," *Film Quarterly*, vol. 37, no. 1 (Fall 1983), 16-22.
Garrett Stewart, "Thresholds of the Visible: The Death Scene of Film," *Mosaic*, vol. 16, no. 1/2 (1983), 33-54; reprinted in *Film/Literature*, ed. George E. Toles (Winnipeg: University of Manitoba, 1983), 35-54.
Garrett Stewart, "The 'Videology' of Science Fiction," in *Shadows of the Magic Lamp: Fantasy and Science Fiction in Film*, ed. George Slusser and Eric S. Rabkin (Carbondale: Southern Illinois University Press, 1985), 159-207.
Garrett Stewart, "Singer Sung: Voice as Avowal in Streisand's *Yentl*," *Mosaic*, vol. 18, no. 4 (Winter 1986), 135-58.
Garrett Stewart, "Photo-gravure: Death, Photography, and Film Narrative," *Wide Angle*, vol. 9, no. 1 (1987), 11-31.
Garrett Stewart, "Negative Imprint: Film, Photogram, and the Apocalyptic Moment," *Genre*, vol. 29, no. 1-2 (1996), 193-241.

Garrett Stewart, "'This Vertiginous Film': Signifying Death in *Citizen Kane*," in *Perspectives on Citizen Kane*, ed. Ronald Gottesman (New York: G. K. Hall, 1996), 430-48.
Garrett Stewart, "*Cinecriture*: Modernism's Flicker Effect," *New Literary History*, vol. 29, no. 4 (1998), 727-68.
Garrett Stewart, "The Photographic Ontology of Science Fiction Film," *iris*, vol. 25 (Spring 1998), 1-33.
5 / Garrett Stewart, *Between Film and Screen: Modernism's Photo Synthesis* (Chicago: University of Chicago Press, 1999).
Garrett Stewart, "Body Snatching: Sci Fi's Photographic Trace," in *Alien Zone II: The Spaces of Science Fiction Film*, ed. Annette Kuhn (London: Verso, 1999), 226-48.
Garrett Stewart, "Kubrick's *Odyssey* as Filmic Epiphany," in *Moments of Moment: Aspects of the Literary Epiphany*, ed. Wim Tigges (Amsterdam: Rodopi, 1999), 401-19.
Garrett Stewart, "Crediting the Liminal: Text, Paratext, Metatext," in *Limina/Film's Thresholds*, ed. Victoria Innocenti and Valentina Re (Udine, Italy: Forum, 2004), 51-76.
Garrett Stewart, "Vitagraphic Time," in "Self-Projection and Autobiography in Film," ed. Linda Haverty Rugg, special issue of *Biography*, vol. 29, no. 1 (Winter 2006), 159-92.
Garrett Stewart, and Nataša Ďurovičová, "Amnesias of Murder: *Mother*," *Film Quarterly*, vol. 64, no. 2 (2010), 64-8.
Garrett Stewart, "Pre-War Trauma: Haneke's *The White Ribbon*," *Film Quarterly*, vol. 63, no. 4 (2010), 40-7.
Garrett Stewart, "Curtain up on Victorian Cinema or The Critical Theater of the Animatograph," *BRANCH: Britain, Representation and Nineteenth-Century History*, ed. Dino Franco Felluga (2011), https://tinyurl.com/y3ouey80.
Garrett Stewart, "Haneke's Endgame," *Film Quarterly*, vol. 67, no. 1 (2013), 14-21.
Garrett Stewart, "'Assertions in Technique': Tracking the Medial Thread in Cavell's Filmic Ontology," in *The Thought of Stanley Cavell and Cinema: Turning Anew to the Ontology of Film a Half-Century after* The World Viewed, ed. by David LaRocca (New York: Bloomsbury, 2020), 23-40.

Screen Adaptations

Garrett Stewart, "Coppola's Conrad: The Repetitions of Complicity," *Critical Inquiry*, vol. 7, no. 2 (Spring 1981), 455-74.
Garrett Stewart, "Film's Victorian Retrofit," *Victorian Studies*, vol. 38, no. 2 (1995), 153-98.
Garrett Stewart, "Citizen Adam: The Latest James Ivory and the Late Henry James," *Henry James Review*, vol. 23, no. 1 (2002), 1-24.
Garrett Stewart, "Literature and Film, not Literature on Film," in *Teaching Film*, ed. Lucy Fischer and Patrice Petro (New York: Modern Language Association, 2012), 243-59.

Subvocal Poetics

Garrett Stewart, "*Lamia* and the Language of Metamorphosis," *Studies in Romanticism*, vol. 15, no. 1 (1976), 3-41.

Garrett Stewart, "Catching the Stylistic D/rift: Sound Defects in Woolf's *The Waves*," *ELH*, vol. 54, no. 2 (Summer 1987), 421–61.

Garrett Stewart, "*Lit et Rature*: An Earsighted View," *LIT: Literature, Interpretation, Theory*, vol. 1, no. 1/2 (Fall 1989), 1–18.

3 / Garrett Stewart, *Reading Voices: Literature and the Phonotext* (Berkeley: University of California Press, 1990).

Garrett Stewart, "Just of Snow," *Robert Frost Review*, vol. 3 (1993), 61–2.

Garrett Stewart, "Modernism's Sonic Waiver: Literary Writing and the Filmic Difference," in *Sound States: Innovative Poetics and Acoustical Technologies*, ed. Adalaide Morris (Chapel Hill: University of North Carolina Press, 1997), 237–73.

Garrett Stewart, "Keats and Language," in *The Cambridge Companion to Keats*, ed. Susan J. Wolfson (Cambridge: Cambridge University Press, 2001), 135–51.

Garrett Stewart, "Phonemanography: Romantic to Victorian," in "Soundings of Things Done," ed. Susan J. Wolfson, special issue of *Romantic Circles Praxis Series* (Spring 2008).

Garrett Stewart, "Hamlet's 'Serious Hearing': 'Sound' vs. 'Use' of 'Voice,'" in *Shakespeare Up Close: Reading Early Modern Texts*, ed. Russ McDonald, Nicholas D. Nace, and Travis D. Williams (London: Arden Shakespeare, 2012), 257–63.

Garrett Stewart, "On Geoffrey Hartman," in "About Geoffrey Hartman: Materials for the Study of an Intellectual Influence," ed. Frances Ferguson and Kevis Goodman, special issue of *Philological Quarterly*, vol. 93, no. 2 (2014), 225–7.

Garrett Stewart, "Echo Neurons, Secondary, Vocality, and the Lex-Seam," in *The Act of Reading*, ed. Nathan Jones and Sam Skinner (London: Torque #2 Publications, 2015), 37–72.

Garrett Stewart, "'Secondary Vocality' and the Sound Defect," in *Sound Effects: The Object Voice in Fiction*, ed. Jorge Sacido-Romero and Sylvia Mieszkowski, *DQR Studies in Literature*, 59 (Leiden: Brill/Rodopi, 2016), 32–57.

Garrett Stewart, "Dredging the Illegible: Photogram, Phoneme, Ph … Ontology," *Amodern*, no. 6.

Narrative Theory as Media Study

Garrett Stewart, "Leaving History: Dickens, Gance, Blanchot," *Yale Journal of Criticism*, vol. 2, no. 2 (Spring 1989), 145–82.

Garrett Stewart, "The Foreign Offices of British Fiction," *Modern Language Quarterly*, vol. 61, no. 1 (2000), 181–206.

Garrett Stewart, "Dickens, Eisenstein, Film," in *Dickens on Screen*, ed. John Glavin (Cambridge: Cambridge University Press, 2004), 123–44.

8 / Garrett Stewart, *Novel Violence: A Narratography of Victorian Fiction* (Chicago: University of Chicago Press, 2009).

Garrett Stewart, "Screenarration: The Plane and Place of the Image," in *The Cambridge Companion to Narrative Theory*, ed. Matthew Garrett (Cambridge: Cambridge University Press, 2018), 183–200.

Garrett Stewart, "Open-Circuit Narrative: Programmed Reading in Richard Powers," in "On Form," ed. Andrew Taylor, special issue of *Novel: A Forum on Fiction*, vol. 55, no. 3 (2023), 547–65.

Post-Filmic Cinema

Garrett Stewart, "Frame/d Time: Toward a Photogrammar of the Fantastic," in *Stillness and Time: Photography and the Moving Image*, ed. David Green and Joanna Lowry (Brighton: Photoworks/Photoforum, 2006), 127–50.

7 / Garrett Stewart, *Framed Time: Toward a Postfilmic Cinema* (Chicago: University of Chicago Press, 2007).

Garrett Stewart, "Digital Fatigue: Imaging War in Recent American Film," *Film Quarterly*, vol. 64, no. 2 (June 2009), 45–55.

Garrett Stewart, "Cimnemonics vs. Digitime," in *Afterimages of Gilles Deleuze's Film Philosophy*, ed. D. N. Rodowick (Minneapolis: University of Minnesota Press, 2010), 327–50.

Garrett Stewart, "Screen Memory in *Waltz with Bashir*," *Film Quarterly*, vol. 63, no. 3 (Spring 2010), 58–62.

Garrett Stewart, "Counterfactual, Potential, Virtual: Toward a Philosophical Cinematics," in *Cinema and Agamben: Ethics, Biopolitics and the Moving Image*, ed. Henrik Gustafsson and Asbjorn Gronstad (New York: Bloomsbury, 2014), 161–91.

Garrett Stewart, "Fourth Dimensions, Seventh Senses: The Work of Mind-Gaming in the Age of Electronic Reproduction," in *Hollywood Puzzle Films*, ed. Warren Buckland (Oxford: Blackwell, 2014), 165–84.

Garrett Stewart, "War Pictures: Digital Surveillance from Foreign Theater to Homeland Security Front," in *The Philosophy of War Films*, ed. David LaRocca (Lexington: University Press of Kentucky, 2014), 107–32.

Garrett Stewart, "Surveillance Cinema," *Film Quarterly*, vol. 69, no. 1 (2015), 106–8.

10 / Garrett Stewart, *Closed Circuits: Screening Narrative Surveillance* (Chicago: University of Chicago Press, 2015).

Garrett Stewart, "Digital Mayhem, Optical Decimation: The Technopoetics of Special Effects," *Journal of Popular Film and Television*, vol. 45, no. 1 (2017), 4–15.

16 / Garrett Stewart, *Cinemachines: An Essay on Media and Method* (Chicago: University of Chicago Press, 2020).

Garrett Stewart, "A Metacinematic Spectrum: Technique through Text to Context," in *Metacinema: The Form and Content of Filmic Reference and Reflexivity*, ed. David LaRocca (Oxford: Oxford University Press, 2021), 63–83.

Literary History and Language

2 / Garrett Stewart, *Death Sentences: Styles of Dying in British Fiction* (Cambridge: Harvard University Press, 1984).

Garrett Stewart, "Introduction: The Science of British Literature 1819/1851/1882–94," *PMLA*, vol. 117, no. 3 (2002), 428–32.

Garrett Stewart, "Metallusion: The New, the Renewed, and the Novel," Review essay of Christopher Ricks, *Allusion to the Poets*. *Modern Language Quarterly*, vol. 65, no. 4 (December 2004), 583–604.

Garrett Stewart, "The Avoidance of Stanley Cavell," in *Contending with Stanley Cavell*, ed. Russell Goodman (Oxford: Oxford University Press, 2005), 140–56.

Garrett Stewart, "Self-Relayance: Emerson to Poe," in *Stanley Cavell, Literature, and Film*, ed. Andrew Taylor and Áine Kelly (New York: Routledge, 2013), 57–79.

11 / Garrett Stewart, *The Deed of Reading: Literature * Writing * Language * Philosophy* (Ithaca, NY: Cornell University Press, 2015).
13 / Garrett Stewart, *The Value of Style in Fiction* (Cambridge: Cambridge University Press, 2018).
Garrett Stewart, "Prose," in the *Oxford Research Encyclopedia of Literature*, ed. John Frow (Oxford: Oxford University Press, 2018).
Garrett Stewart, "Actual Reading," in *Further Reading*, ed. Matthew Rubery and Leah Price (Oxford: Oxford University Press, 2020), 112–23.
Garrett Stewart, "Organic Reformations in Richard Powers's *The Overstory*," in "On the Novel," ed. Michael Wood, special issue of *Daedalus*, vol. 150, no. 1 (Winter 2021), 160–77.
18 / Garrett Stewart, *The Ways of the Word: Episodes in Verbal Attention* (Ithaca, NY: Cornell University Press, 2021).

Pictured Reading

Garrett Stewart, "Reading Figures: The Legible Image of Victorian Textuality," in *Victorian Literature and the Visual Imagination*, ed. Carol Christ and John Jordan (Berkeley: University of California Press, 1995), 345–70.
Garrett Stewart, "Painted Reading, Narrative Regress," *Narrative*, vol. 11, no. 2 (2003), 125–76.
Garrett Stewart, "The Mind's Sigh: Pictured Reading in Nineteenth-Century Painting," *Victorian Studies*, vol. 46, no. 2 (2004), 217–30.
6 / Garrett Stewart, *The Look of Reading: Book, Painting, Text* (Chicago: University of Chicago Press, 2006).
Garrett Stewart, "'Written in the Painting': Word Pictures from Italy," in *Imagining Italy: Victorian Writers and Travellers*, ed. Catherine Waters, Michael Hollington, and John Jordan (Newcastle upon Tyne: Cambridge Scholars Publishing, 2010), 216–42.

Book Objects

Garrett Stewart, "Lector/Spector: Borges and the *Bibliobjet*," *Variaciones Borges*, no. 24 (2007), 173–96.
Garrett Stewart, "Rakuzin's Books, Case by Case," in *The Book of Art* (Tel Aviv: Bineth Gallery, 2008), 21–35.
Garrett Stewart, "Belles Lettres and the *Bibliobjet*: from the Artful to the Unreadable Book," in *Back to the Future Book*, vol. 1, *The Past Issue*, ed. Laurenz Brunner and Tan Walchli (Bern: Federal Office of Swiss Culture, 2008), 116–36.
Garrett Stewart, "Bookwork as Demediation," *Critical Inquiry*, vol. 36, no. 3 (Spring 2010), 410–57.
Garrett Stewart, "Book Quirks," *Critical Inquiry*, vol. 37, no. 2 (2011), 355–63.
9 / Garrett Stewart, *Bookwork: Medium to Object to Concept to Art* (Chicago: University of Chicago Press, 2011).
Garrett Stewart, "The Deed of Reading: Toni Morrison and the Sculpted Book," *ELH*, vol. 80, no. 2 (2013), 427–53.

Garrett Stewart, "Between Print Matter and Page Matter: The Codex Platform as Medial Support," in *Media | Matter: The Materiality of Media/Matter as Medium*, ed. Bernd Herzogenrath (New York: Bloomsbury, 2015), 47–68.

Garrett Stewart, "Visualizing Books, Virtualizing Readers," in *The History of the Book: Yearbook of English Studies*, ed. Sandro Jung and Stephen Colclough (London: Modern Humanities Research Association, 2015), 262–79.

15 / Garrett Stewart, *Book, Text, Medium: Cross-Sectional Reading for a Digital Age* (Cambridge: Cambridge University Press, 2020). [Cross-file under "Literary History and Language"]

Transmedial Perspectives

Garrett Stewart, "Transmedium," *Iowa Review*, vol. 44, no. 3 (Winter 2014/15), 106–21.

12 / Garrett Stewart, *Transmedium: Conceptualism 2.0 and the New Object Art* (Chicago: University of Chicago Press, 2017).

17 / Garrett Stewart, *Cinesthesia: Museum Cinema and the Curated Screen* (Montréal: caboose, 2020), distributed as Kindle text by Indiana University Press.

19 / Garrett Stewart, *The Metanarrative Hall of Mirrors: Reflex Action in Fiction and Film* (New York: Bloomsbury, 2022).

Garrett Stewart, "Verbal Fframe Advance: Toward a Cinematographic Sentence," *NLH* vol. 53, no. 1 (2022), 139–60.

Garrett Stewart, "Literature's Audioptic Platform," in *Cambridge Companion to Literature and the Digital*, ed. Adam Hammond (Cambridge: Cambridge University Press, forthcoming 2024).

Close Listening

Garrett Stewart, "Novelist as 'Sound Thief': The Audiobooks of John le Carré," in *Audiobooks, Literature, and Sound Studies*, ed. Matthew Rubery (New York: Routledge, 2011), 109–26.

Garrett Stewart, "Sound Thinking: Looped Time, Duped Track," in the *Oxford Handbook of Sound and Image in Digital Media*, ed. Carol Vernallis, Amy Herzog, and John Richardson (Oxford: Oxford University Press, 2013), 465–82.

Garrett Stewart, "Prose Sense and its Soundings," in *Sound and Literature*, ed. Anna Snaith (Cambridge: Cambridge University Press, 2020), 234–51.

Garrett Stewart, "Afterword," in John Cayley, *Image Generation: A Reader* (Denver: Counterpath, 2023), 153–62.

20 / Garrett Stewart, *Streisand: The Mirror of Difference* (Detroit: Wayne State University Press, 2023).

ACKNOWLEDGMENTS

GRATEFUL ACKNOWLEDGMENT is here offered to the following publishers for their generous permission to reproduce portions of Garrett Stewart's writing in this volume: the University of Chicago Press, Harvard University Press, Cornell University Press, Cambridge University Press, the Johns Hopkins University Press, University of California Press, Wayne State University Press, Bloomsbury, and caboose. (See below, "List of Publications," for publication details. See also in this volume, "Timelines: A Topographical Bibliography" where entries 1 / through 20 / are featured.) Such thanks to these presses are first of all due, that is, for allowing these excerpts from Stewart's writing life to appear alongside each other in this novel form and forum. While, it's true, some of the copyrights had reverted to Stewart, or were his all along, it's nevertheless a pleasure to have the institutional support and well-wishes of the publishers, one and all, who first sent this work of ongoing importance into public circulation.

More proximately, it's my great good fortune to have another occasion to thank Editorial Director Haaris Naqvi, one of Bloomsbury's genuine visionaries, for helping to make *Attention Spans* materialize. Editorial Assistant Hali Han has been a conscientious accomplice from the proposal stage through production. For late-stage saves, Mandy Collison and Annie Burkhart. John Opera graciously granted permission to reproduce "Radial Composition (Yellow)" (2015). The design team, with Eleanor Rose at the helm once again and Opera's image at the ready, created a cover that I'm very happy for readers to judge the book by, since it offers a symbolic gesture of the activity of attention that awaits within: a point of focus followed by a burst of radiating pathways.

For their invigorating encouragements and informed admonitions, both given in measures that mattered for charting the course of this collection and in fulfilling it, I'm sincerely indebted to the press' anonymous referees. As the volume's first readers-in-concept, I hope the book in hand has achieved what they admired in its prospectus.

A remarkable and rewarding season was spent working on the book in Cortona entirely because of the imagination and generosity of Diana Allan. Her hospitality afforded a sacred environment in which to think, read, write, and edit: access to an antique realm that effortlessly conjures a sense of the depth of time—elaborated time spans—and thus continuous reminders and moments of immersive contact with the present predicament of attenuated attention spans. Thanks further to Frances LaRocca for a welcoming nest at the Ridge house in Lewiston. And *mahalo* to Lorna K. Hershinow for precious, serial episodes of respite in Kāneʻohe.

Speaking of gratifying epochs, for the past two decades K. L. Evans has transformed my sense of the possibilities and potencies of consecutive thought. Knowing how cherished this book, this collaboration, has been for me as a galvanic intellectual adventure, she has been a helpmeet of distinguished proportions. For these and many other salutary modes of loving support, I'm grateful to her anew and as ever. For lovingly teasing me about my ingenuous enthusiasm for this project and my collaborator ("Dad, you don't have to keep saying, 'my friend, Garrett,' you can just say 'Garrett.' We know who you're talking about."), I have two brilliant daughters to thank, Ruby and Star. (When the elder of the two recently cited Garrett's close reading of Virginia Woolf's *To the Lighthouse* in a college essay, drawn from *The Value of Prose in Fiction*, "the thud of mortal cause in the same syntactic breath as bereft effect," it lifted her prose—and my spirits—to new heights.)

Garrett Stewart's contributions to this book are evident in both curatorial extract and incisive commentary, an authorial and authorizing double performance made with customary verve by our *consigliere* of structure, sign, syntax, and syllable. Bringing these lines alive as live wires of current to be energized by, occasionally shocked by, and perpetually drawn from for yet further endeavors in an electrifying education—they are charged with the heat and luminosity Terry Castle once described as befitting his "work of ardent imagination, unimpeachable scholarship, and flaring, often pyrotechnic, brilliance." Equipped with a tireless capacity to create and then refine his felicitous offerings, Garrett's is a propulsive force to behold—and now its precipitates can be held by readers as they are heralded by me. Stewart, ever stalwart in his own interpretive commitments, was just as steadfast in his support of my vision for this project and efforts to articulate it. In matters of sustained attention—granted, blended, beautifully concentrated—his was an imaginative investment without which this volume would have remained, for me, a private phantasm. The intellectual gratification at every stage of development—from first sketch to final proof—has been immense. And as a writer and pedagogue devoted to the intimate overlap of grammar and illumination, of style and sense, Garrett, in his generous counsel, will continue to inspire and enrich my efforts—even as I spend the coming years continuing to savor the many full works represented by excerpts featured in *Attention Spans*.

And so, to Garrett, finally because foremost, I offer abiding gratitude for accepting the expansive, unlooked for labor of this volume; sharing genuine and inexhaustible cheer throughout the book's development; entrusting a life's worth of prose to my care; helping me feel a measure of capability in the face of the daunting task I'd somehow set for myself (while the referees' caution and elevated expectations hovered perilously at the margins); gifting an apprenticeship in attention; granting a profound tutorial in virtuosic close reading; affording behind-the-scenes access to the ways of making paradigm-shifting syntax, innovative diction, and radical nomenclature coinages; modeling (like no other) the craft of molding distinctive sentences (like no other) that register, time and again, euphoric yields from textual and mediated encounters; and all the while—in my case, for a decade and more prior, across a span of time that encompasses the appearance of his last eleven books—sustaining a correspondence worthy of the letterpress: fittingly, some of those lines have been integrated between these covers. All to say, to boldly underline, just how much I've been the beneficiary of Garrett's inimitable brand of inventiveness and magnanimity—and thus uplift. Any age is a good age for having one's sincerity rewarded with benefaction, one's intellectual efforts recognized for their potential (and coached in the direction of achievement)—and in these respects, his talents are endless and peerless. I'll remain moved by his trust and his confidence, forever hold dear our exhilarating epistolary conversations, and happily count his readerly voice as an intimate subvocal literary companion to my own. May the foregoing and similarly propitious effects be felt by this book's readers.

List of Permissions

The University of Chicago Press

5 / *Between Film and Screen: Modernism's Photo Synthesis* (Chicago: University of Chicago Press, 1999).

6 / *The Look of Reading: Book, Painting, Text* (Chicago: University of Chicago Press, 2006).

7 / *Framed Time: Toward a Postfilmic Cinema* (Chicago: University of Chicago Press, 2007).

8 / *Novel Violence: A Narratography of Victorian Fiction* (Chicago: University of Chicago Press, 2009).

9 / *Bookwork: Medium to Object to Concept to Art* (Chicago: University of Chicago Press, 2011).

10 / *Closed Circuits: Screening Narrative Surveillance* (Chicago: University of Chicago Press, 2015).

12 / *Transmedium: Conceptualism 2.0 and the New Object Art* (University of Chicago Press, 2017).

16 / *Cinemachines: An Essay on Media and Method* (Chicago: University of Chicago Press, 2020).

Harvard University Press

1 / *Dickens and the Trials of Imagination* (Cambridge: Harvard University Press, 1974).

2 / *Death Sentences: Styles of Dying in British Fiction* (Cambridge: Harvard University Press, 1984).

Cornell University Press

11 / *The Deed of Reading: Literature * Writing * Language * Philosophy* (Ithaca: Cornell University Press, 2015). Used by permission of the publisher.

14 / *The One, Other, and Only Dickens* (Ithaca: Cornell University Press, 2018). Used by permission of the publisher.

18 / *The Ways of the Word: Episodes in Verbal Attention* (Ithaca: Cornell University Press, 2022). Used by permission of the publisher.

Cambridge University Press

13 / *The Value of Style in Fiction* (Cambridge: Cambridge University Press, 2018).

15 / *Book, Text, Medium: Cross-Sectional Reading for a Digital Age* (Cambridge: Cambridge University Press, 2020).

The Johns Hopkins University Press

4 / *Dear Reader: The Conscripted Audience in Nineteenth-Century British Fiction* (Baltimore: Johns Hopkins University Press, 1996).

University of California Press

3 / *Reading Voices: Literature and the Phonotext* (Berkeley: University of California Press, 1990).

Wayne State University Press

20 / *Streisand: The Mirror of Difference* (Detroit: Wayne State University Press, 2023).

Bloomsbury

19 / *The Metanarrative Hall of Mirrors: Reflex Action in Fiction and Film* (New York: Bloomsbury, 2022).

caboose

17 / *Cinesthesia: Museum Cinema and the Curated Screen* (Montréal: caboose, 2020), e-text.

CONTRIBUTORS

Garrett Stewart has taught fiction, film, and textual theory at the University of Iowa since 1993, where he is the James O. Freedman Professor of Letters. Besides his previous long-term positions at Boston University and the University of California at Santa Barbara, he has had visiting appointment at Stanford University, Princeton University, the University of Fribourg (Switzerland), the University of London (Queen Mary), and the University of Konstanz. Pursuing always a methodology of close-grained verbal or visual analysis—in books on language in Dickens (1974), the death scene in British fiction (1984), the phonetic undertow of literary writing from Shakespeare to Woolf (1990), and the "Dear Reader" address of Victorian novels (1996)—Stewart was led by that last topic to a subsequent study of the scene of reading in painting, from saints with books in illuminated manuscripts through Rembrandt to Picasso and Francis Bacon. In approaches to the moving rather than the still image, his 1999 investigation into the "photogrammar" of traditional cinema was brought up to date in 2007 by a sequel volume on the new digital conditions of screen narrative, *Framed Time: Toward a Postfilmic Cinema*. In 2009, *Novel Violence: A Narratography of Victorian Fiction*, awarded the Perkins Prize from the International Society for the Study of Narrative, named in its subtitle the method of this and the previous film book, searching out the "microplots" of narrative development in the inflections of technique, audiovisual or linguistic. Since then, concentrating on the conceptual violence done *to* rather than *in* books, *Bookwork: Medium to Object to Concept to Art* (2011) follows up on the two-dimensional image of reading with a close look at the ironies of illegibility in conceptual book sculpture, whether in found, altered, or fabricated volumes, engaging again with the digital epoch on another front: its rapid transformation of the reading experience. Stewart's work on cinema continued in regular reviewing for *Film Quarterly*, and he was elected in 2010 to the American Academy of Arts and Sciences. His dozen monographs since then, including an interactive e-book on moving-image art in museum display, have continued to probe the medial infrastructure of film and literature, ranging from an account of "surveillancinema" to his latest cross-over study, *The Metanarrative Hall of Mirrors: Reflex Action in Fiction and Film* (2022) and *Streisand: The Mirror of Difference* (2023).

David LaRocca studied philosophy, film, rhetoric, and religion at the State University of New York at Buffalo; University of California, Berkeley; Vanderbilt University; and Harvard University. He is the author or contributing editor of more than a dozen books, including *Emerson's English Traits and the Natural History of Metaphor* (2013), *The Philosophy of Charlie Kaufman* (2011), *Movies with Stanley Cavell in Mind* (2021), and *Metacinema* (2021), and the author of over a hundred articles, chapters, and reviews published in, among other places, *Afterimage, Cinema, Epoché, Estetica, Film and Philosophy, Liminalities, Religions, Transactions, Post Script, The Senses and Society, Social Research, The Midwest Quarterly, Journalism, Media and Cultural Studies, The Journal of Aesthetic Education*, and *The Journal of Aesthetics and Art Criticism*. Currently Associate Editor at the journal *Philosophical Investigations* and on the Advisory Board at *Conversations: The Journal of Cavellian Studies*, he has held visiting research or teaching positions at Binghamton University, Cornell University, the State University of New York College at Cortland, Harvard University, Ithaca College, the School of Visual Arts, and Vanderbilt University. He served as research assistant to Stanley Cavell and Giuliana Bruno, apprenticed with painter Philip Burke and photographer Alessandro Subrizi, made documentary films with William Jersey and Robert Elfstrom, participated in the School of Criticism and Theory as part of a seminar led by Emily Apter, and workshopped with Abbas Kiarostami, Edward Tufte, and Werner Herzog. As a documentary filmmaker, he produced and edited six features in *The Intellectual Portrait Series*, directed *Brunello Cucinelli: A New Philosophy of Clothes* (2013), and codirected the award-winning *New York Photographer: Jill Freedman in the City* (2018). A recipient of the Ralph Waldo Emerson Society Distinguished Achievement Award (an honor previously conferred on Stanley Cavell), he received a teaching commendation from Harvard Extension School and a teaching innovation grant from the College at Cortland, State University of New York. Formerly a Writer-in-Residence at the New York Public Library, he contributed to a National Endowment for the Humanities Institute and conducted research as Harvard University's Sinclair Kennedy Traveling Fellow in the United Kingdom. DavidLaRocca@Post.Harvard.Edu, www.DavidLaRocca.org